The Second-Person
Standpoint

The Second-Person Standpoint

*Morality, Respect,
and Accountability*

Stephen Darwall

Harvard University Press

Cambridge, Massachusetts

London, England

2006

64592200

112772598

Library of Congress Cataloging-in-Publication Data

Darwall, Stephen L., 1946–
The second-person standpoint : morality, respect, and
accountability / Stephen Darwall.
p. cm.
Includes bibliographical references (p.   ) and index.
ISBN-13: 978-0-674-02274-4 (alk. paper)
ISBN-10: 0-674-02274-2 (alk. paper)
1. Ethics. 2. Authority. 3. Responsibility.
4. Respect for persons. I. Title.
BJ1012.D333   2006
171'7—dc22   2006041229

For Julian and Will

Contents

Preface

I have, I imagine, been thinking about the topic of this book for a long time without realizing it. Since the age of three, I have had an eye condition (called a "strabismus") that makes it impossible for me to direct both of my eyes to the same object at the same time. This hasn't affected my vision much. The most noticeable effect has been one that Hume refers to in the *Treatise* in considering the curious metaethical position that causing false belief is the source of moral wrong.[1] If this were true, Hume says, then "those who are squint-sighted" would be immoral, since we often "imagine they salute or are talking to one person, while they address themselves to another" (Hume 1978: 462n). That's been my problem: I've had difficulty getting people to recognize that I'm trying to recognize them.[2] And I suppose that that has led me to wonder what exactly is involved in reciprocal recognition, to think about its pervasiveness in human experience, and, more recently and self-consciously, to think through its significance for moral theory.[3]

It is a familiar fact that something we take for granted actually involves a complex sensibility we don't fully appreciate. Most people don't realize, for example, that they accept elaborate norms of conversation (governing conversational distance, for instance) until they reflect on cases where these are egregiously violated. The same is true with a whole host of

1. Hume mistakenly attributes this position to William Wollaston.
2. But maybe I'm not the only one. See note 41 of Chapter 6.
3. That's not the only thing that led me to focus on these issues. Having a mother who was afflicted with schizophrenia and whose last years with the family before institutionalization (in the 1950s) were spent in a prison of silence was certainly another. And other factors have played significant roles also.

phenomena involving "the second-person standpoint." We have an implicit commitment to norms of respect and "second-personal authority" (the authority to address claims, demands, and expectations) that it can take reflection on cases where these are transgressed to appreciate.

More to the point here, I have come to believe that the second-person standpoint has a fundamental importance for moral theory and that it is impossible fully to understand many central moral ideas without it. In this book, I argue that moral obligation and responsibility (accountability), respect for and the dignity of persons, and the distinctive freedom of moral agents are all irreducibly second-personal. And I attempt to present, moreover, an argument that can vindicate the authority of moral obligation and these other ideas, again, from the second-person perspective.

Here I must beg the reader's patience. Although I hope the phenomena I will be pointing to in this book are familiar enough, I will be analyzing them in unfamiliar ways with abstract terms like "second-personal reason" and "second-personal competence." And many of my claims will be ambitious; some, no doubt, will be overly so. You may find your patience wearing thin. If so, there may, however, be a remedy. If your reaction takes the form of irritation or annoyance, it may flower into a Strawsonian reactive attitude of some kind, maybe something approaching resentment at my hubris or the waste of your time. If this happens, try stepping back and examining this thought or feeling; you may find the ideas of second-personal reason and authority lurking within. Of course, if your reaction is boredom or simply lack of interest, this remedy won't work.

In thinking through the ideas I develop in this book, I have incurred many debts to many people, almost too many to try decently to name even all whose help I distinctly remember. I have gotten enormously helpful reactions when presenting versions of these ideas in various forums and venues over the last several years. I am extremely grateful to numerous philosophy departments, societies, and individuals who invited me to present them. It was especially valuable to be able to work through early drafts of the manuscript in two graduate seminars, one at Ohio University in 2003 and the other at the University of Michigan in 2005. And I have benefited from innumerable interactions of other kinds. In addition to many other people, I am indebted to Kate Abramson, Donald Ainslie, Elizabeth Anderson, Brian Apicella, Nomy Arpaly, Carla Bagnoli,

Marcia Baron, Jack Bender, Alyssa Bernstein, Lorraine Besser-Jones, Simon Blackburn, Michael Bratman, Aaron Bronfman, John Broome, Vivienne Brown, Allen Buchanan, Sarah Buss, Vanessa Carbonell, Jules Coleman, David Copp, Randall Curren, Jonathan Dancy, Justin D'Arms, Julian Darwall, Will Darwall, Steven Daskal, Remy Debes, Richard Dees, John Deigh, Robin Dillon, Chris Dodsworth, Jamie Dreier, Andrew Eshelman, Nir Eyal, William Fitzpatrick, Samuel Fleischacker, Robert Frank, Harry Frankfurt, Robyn Gaier, David Garvin, Gerald Gaus, Allan Gibbard, Peter Graham, Robert Gressis, Charles Griswold, Michael Hardimon, Christie Hartley, Sally Haslanger, Daniel Hausman, Susan Hawthorne, Barbara Herman, Pamela Hieronymi, Thomas E. Hill Jr., Ted Hinchman, Paul Hoffman, Tom Hurka, Paul Hurley, Nadeem Hussain, P. J. Ivanhoe, Daniel Jacobson, Agnieszka Jaworska, Marie Jayasekera, Robert Johnson, Rachana Kamtekar, Rob Kar, Daniel Keen, Christine Korsgaard, Michelle Kosch, Richard Kraut, John Ku, Arthur Kuflik, Rahul Kumar, Joel Kupperman, Rae Langton, Mark LeBar, David Levy, Ira Lindsay, Erica Lucast, Eric Mack, Tito Magri, Douglas MacLean, Michelle Mason, Joe Mendola, Martha Nussbaum, Howard Nye, Derek Parfit, James Petrik, Philip Pettit, Sara Postasi, Jerry Postema, Luke Potter, Ryan Preston, Wlodek Rabinowicz, Peter Railton, Joseph Raz, Andrews Reath, Connie Rosati, Jacob Ross, Emma Rothschild, Geoff Sayre-McCord, T. M. Scanlon, Brian Schaefer, Tamar Schapiro, Eric Schliesser, Franklin Scott, Mark Schroeder, Nishi Shah, Nancy Sherman, Walter Sinnott-Armstrong, Anthony Skelton, Matthew Smith, Michael Smith, Jim Staihar, Jason Stanley, Michael Stocker, Sigrun Svavarsdottir, Julie Tannenbaum, Valerie Tiberius, Kevin Toh, Mark van Roojen, David Velleman, Peter Vranas, Kendall Walton, Gary Watson, Eric Weber, Marshall Weinberg, Andrea Westlund, Susan Wolf, David Wong, Allen Wood, Gabriel Zamosc-Regueros, Kate Zawidzki, Lei Zhong, and Arthur Zucker.

I have also received substantial institutional support without which this book would have been impossible. A National Endowment for the Humanities Fellowship in 1998–99 supported work on a different project, but one that got me thinking about the ideas I develop here. The James B. and Grace J. Nelson Endowment in the Department of Philosophy at The University of Michigan enabled me to take a year of research leave in 2002–3, during which I wrote the first draft of the book. And I am completing the manuscript now with sabbatical support from The University of Michigan.

Some parts of the book draw on previously published material. Part of Chapter 5 is based on "Autonomy in Modern Natural Law," in *New Essays on the History of Autonomy,* ed. Larry Krasnoff and Natalie Brender (Cambridge: Cambridge University Press, 2003) and appears with the permission of Cambridge University Press. Chapter 6 draws from "Respect and the Second-Person Standpoint," *Proceedings and Addresses of the American Philosophical Association* 78 (2004): 43–60; it appears with the permission of the American Philosophical Association. And some material from Chapter 10 builds on "Fichte and the Second-Person Standpoint," *International Yearbook for German Idealism* 3 (2005): 91–113; it appears with the permission of Walter de Gruyter, Inc.

I am thankful also for the help that I have gotten from Harvard University Press and its staff and readers. Lindsay Waters has been a source of encouragement and wisdom. And the two readers for the Press provided many very useful suggestions.

As always, I am most grateful to my colleagues, students and faculty in the Department of Philosophy at The University of Michigan, especially Elizabeth Anderson, Allan Gibbard, Peter Railton, and, during the time I wrote this book, David Velleman, all of whom make Ann Arbor an ideal place to do moral philosophy.

Finally, I dedicate this book to my sons, Julian and Will Darwall. Nothing has supported me more in writing it than the encouragement and appreciation they have shown when we have talked about its ideas. I am in their debt in this and in many other ways.

The Second-Person
Standpoint

— PART I —

— 1 —

The Main Ideas I

People are self-originating sources of claims.
—JOHN RAWLS, "KANTIAN CONSTRUCTIVISM IN
MORAL THEORY"

Call *the second-person standpoint* the perspective you and I take up when
we make and acknowledge claims on one another's conduct and will.[1]
This might be explicit, in speech, as with the performatives J. L. Austin
botanized—demanding, reproaching, apologizing, and so on—or only
implicit, in thought, as with Strawsonian reactive feelings like resentment
and guilt (Austin 1975; Strawson 1968).[2] But whether explicit and
voiced—"You talkin' to me?"—or only implicit and felt, as in a resentful
sulk, the I-you-me structure of reciprocal address runs throughout
thought and speech from the second-person point of view.

Austin taught us that speech acts addressed to others have "felicity
conditions" that must be met for them to come off properly or, indeed,
at all (Austin 1975). For an utterance to count as a command, for example, certain conventional authority relations must be in the background, and this must be common knowledge between speaker and addressee. Austin was not concerned with ethics, however. The questions
he cared about were social and linguistic: What conditions must be satisfied for speech acts to succeed in conventional terms? It is enough for
an utterance to amount to a command in this sense that the speaker has
relevant authority *de facto;* she need not have it *de jure.*

Our questions, however, are normative. A command is a form of ad-

1. My terminology derives, of course, from the grammatical second person. It thus
differs from, although it is not totally unrelated to, the use in Davidson 2001. More closely
related is the genus of addressed thought and speech. But there are forms of addressed
thought that do not seem to involve claim making.

2. Austinian performatives will be discussed in Chapter 3 and reactive feelings and
attitudes in Chapter 4.

dress that purports to give a person a distinctive kind of *(normative) reason* for acting, one I call a *second-personal reason*.[3] What makes a reason second-personal is that it is grounded in *(de jure)* authority relations that an addresser takes to hold between him and his addressee. Unlike practical reasons of other sorts, therefore, second-personal reasons must be able to be addressed within these relations.[4] And, as I show, second-personal reasons are distinctive also in the kind of claim they make on the will.

Austinian felicity conditions are what must hold for a speech act to count as an act of some conventionally defined kind, say, a command, or for it not to be what Austin calls an "abuse," that is, a genuine act of that kind that nonetheless violates some convention for that kind of act, say, an insincere promise (Austin 1975: 16).[5] We, however, are interested in what we might call "normative felicity conditions": what must be true for second-personal reasons actually to exist and be successfully given through second-personal address.

When someone attempts to give another a second-personal reason, she purports to stand in a relevant authority relation to her addressee. I shall say that her address *presupposes* this authority. By this, I just mean that her having the authority is a necessary condition of the validity of the reason she purports to address and is thus a normative felicity condition of successfully giving her addressee the reason. *Qua* attempting to give her addressee the reason, therefore, she must assume this authority, as

3. Throughout, except where context makes clear, I will be referring to *normative reasons* rather than *motivating reasons,* that is, to reasons *to* do something, rather than whatever reasons someone actually acts on or any motivational state that explains one's act causally or teleologically. And I will follow ordinary usage, according to which "give someone a reason" is a "success" phrase: X gives Y a reason to do A only if there is a normative reason for X to do A.

4. I will frequently use "address a second-personal reason" as short for "purports to give an addressee a (second-personal) reason by addressing a demand or claim." Strictly, it is the claim or demand that is addressed. As I shall use the phrases, "addresses a claim or demand" and, consequently, "addresses a second-personal reason" are not success phrases. Although if X addresses a claim or demand to Y, X assumes or presupposes the authority to make the claim or demand of Y, X may lack this authority. In this case, although X purports to give Y a reason rooted in his claim (and so, in my terms, "addresses the reason"), no normative reason is actually given. I am grateful to Mark Schroeder for pressing me to clarify these points.

5. See the discussion of Austin in Chapter 3. I am indebted here to Kevin Toh for clarifying the discussion.

she must assume the satisfaction of any normative felicity conditions of giving the reason.

In addition to the specific presuppositions carried by different specific forms of address, a major claim of this book is that second-personal address has certain presuppositions built into it in general. To enter intelligibly into the second-person stance and make claims on and demands of one another at all, I argue, you and I must presuppose that we share a common second-personal authority, competence, and responsibility simply as free and rational agents.

Second-Personal Reasons

To get the flavor of the kind of point I am trying to make, compare two different ways in which you might try to give someone a reason to stop causing you pain, say, to remove his foot from on top of yours.

One would be to get him to feel sympathetic concern for you in your plight, thereby leading him to want you to be free of pain.[6] Were he to have this desire, he would see your being in pain as a bad thing, a state of the world that there is reason for him (or, indeed, for anyone who is able) to change. And he would most naturally see his desire that you be pain-free not as the source of this reason, but as a form of access to a reason that is there anyway.[7] In desiring that you be free of pain, he would see this possible state of affairs as a better way for the world to be, as a possible outcome or state that, as Moore put it, "ought to exist for its own sake" (Moore 1993: 34).[8]

Structurally, the situation would be entirely analogous to a purely epistemic case, for example, one in which you give him reasons to believe that you are in fact in pain. Were he to credit the way things seem from

6. Hume supposes we are standardly led through sympathy to take account of the welfare of others: "Would any man, who is walking along, tread as willingly on another's gouty toes, whom he has no quarrel with, as on the hard flint and pavement?" "Let us suppose such a person ever so selfish; let private interest have ingrossed ever so much his attention; yet in instances, where that is not concerned, he must unavoidably feel *some* propensity to the good of mankind, and make it an object of choice, if every thing else be equal" (Hume 1985: 225).

7. On this point, see Bond 1983; Dancy 2000; Darwall 1983; Hampton 1998; Pettit and Smith 1990; Quinn 1991; and Scanlon 1998: 41–55.

8. He would most likely desire this not just for its own sake, but for your sake as well. On the relevance of this latter, see Darwall 2002b.

the perspective of his desire, he would accept a *state-of-the-world-regarding* and *agent-neutral* reason for removing his foot.[9] The reason would not be essentially for him as the agent causing another person pain. It would exist, most fundamentally, for anyone who is in a position to effect your relief and therefore for him, since he is well placed to do so.[10] Finally, in "giving" him the reason in this way, you wouldn't so much be addressing it to him as getting him to see that it is there anyway, independently of your getting him to see it or even of your ability to do so.[11] There are two points here. First, in pointing to the reason, you would be directing him epistemically rather than practically, albeit on a question of practical reason. *Qua* this form of reason-giving, you would be asking him to agree, as it were, that there is a reason for him to do something

9. Agent-neutral reasons contrast with agent-relative reasons, whose formulation includes an ineliminable reference to the agent for whom they are reasons (like "that it will keep a promise I made," "that it will avoid harm to others [i.e., people other than me]" and so on). Agent-neutral reasons can be stated without such a reference: "that it would prevent some pain from occurring to someone (or some being)." On the distinction between agent-relative (also called "subjective" or "agent-centered") and agent-neutral (also called "objective") reasons, principles, values, and so forth, see Darwall 1986a; McNaughton and Rawling 1991; Nagel 1970, 1986; Parfit 1984; and Scheffler 1982. For a discussion that raises a question about the value of this distinction, see Korsgaard 1996d.

I argue for the claim that sympathetic concern involves there seeming to be agent-neutral reasons to further someone's welfare in Darwall 2002b: 68–72. I do not deny, of course, that someone who already accepted various agent-relative norms might not be moved through empathy and sympathy to feel some special responsibility for relieving the pain. My point is that this would not come through sympathy alone.

Note also that there is an important difference between sympathy and empathy here. I am indebted to Nir Eyal for the following: "A beggar looks at passers-by in the eye, and lets them see his obviously painful wound, which clearly requires treatment. He continues to look at them intently. His conduct may be read as a communication of something like 'Help me! You see I am in pain.' " Cases like this seem to be mixed, in my view, combining appeals to sympathy with implicit (second-personal) claims. To the extent that there is an appeal with a continued second-personal engagement that takes the passer-by into the afflicted person's perspective, what we have is the address of a second-personal claim.

10. Note that superficially agent-relative reasons may be grounded more deeply in agent-neutral considerations and values, and/or vice versa. For example, rule-utilitarianism holds that rules of right conduct include agent-relative principles, such as those defining rights of promise and contract, on grounds of overall agent-neutral value.

11. Just as might be the case if you were trying to get him to see reasons to believe that you were in pain. A grimace might suffice without your having to presume any authority on the question.

rather than asking him to agree to do it. Any claims you might make would thus be on his beliefs about practical reasons and not directly on his will. Second, your being able to give him the reason would not depend in any way on his seeing you as trying to give it to him or as having any competence or authority to do so. Anything you might do to get him to see the reason would serve. It might be most effective, indeed, if he were to see you as so defenseless and vulnerable as to be unable even to reason with him, like a young child.

Alternatively, you might lay a claim or address a purportedly valid demand. You might say something that asserts or implies your authority to claim or demand that he move his foot and that simultaneously expresses this demand. You might demand this as the person whose foot he is stepping on, or as a member of the moral community, whose members understand themselves as demanding that people not step on one another's feet, or as both. Whichever, the reason you would address would be agent-relative rather than agent-neutral.[12] It would concern, most fundamentally, his relations to others (and himself) viewed from his perspective within those relations, in this case, that his keeping his foot on yours causes another person pain, causes inconvenience, and so on. The reason would not be addressed to him as someone who is simply in a position to alter the regrettable state of someone's pain or of someone's causing another pain. If he could stop, say, two others from causing gratuitous pain by the shocking spectacle of keeping his foot firmly planted on yours, this second, claim-based (hence second-personal) reason would not recommend that he do so.[13] It would be addressed to him, rather, as the person causing gratuitous pain to another person, something we normally assume we have the authority to demand that persons not do to one another.[14]

12. See the references in note 9.

13. A test for whether a given reason or principle is agent-relative or agent-neutral is to consider a case where it recommends someone's doing something and augment the case by stipulating that, as it happens, were the person not to perform that action (described in the relevant reason- or principle-sensitive way), it would bring about one other person's doing an action of the very same kind. If the reason is agent-neutral, then it should make no difference whether the agent performs the act without the other person's doing so or forbears the performance, thereby bringing about the other's performance. If it does make a difference, then the reason or principle is agent-relative. "Don't tread on me" and "Don't tread on other persons" do not reduce to "Bring it about that people are not tread upon."

14. Suppose he rejects your request, enjoying being able to keep you under foot. Now

What is important for our purposes is that someone can sensibly accept this second reason for moving his foot, one embodied in your claim or demand, only if he also accepts your authority to demand this of him (second-personally). That is just what it is to accept something as a valid claim or demand.[15] And if he accepts that you can demand that he move his foot, he must also accept that you will have grounds for complaint or some other form of accountability-seeking response if he doesn't. Unlike the first state- or outcome-based reason, this second is second-personal in the sense that, although the first is conceptually independent of the second-personal address involved in making claims and holding persons responsible, the second is not. *A second-personal reason is one whose validity depends on presupposed authority and accountability relations between persons and, therefore, on the possibility of the reason's being addressed person-to-person.* Reasons addressed or presupposed in orders, requests, claims, reproaches, complaints, demands, promises, contracts, givings of consent, commands, and so on are all second-personal in this sense. They simply wouldn't exist but for their role in second-personal address. And their second-personal character explains their agent-relativity. As second-personal reasons always derive from agents' relations to one another, they are invariably fundamentally agent-relative.[16]

It is perhaps obvious that reasons that depend on orders or requests are second-personal in this sense, but I argue that moral obligations and demands are quite generally second-personal also. (This was implicit in my remark above that you might demand that someone stop causing you

---

you have an even weightier claim. For now he is not simply causing you gratuitous pain, he is making you the object of his sadistic pleasure. And however much trouble we can legitimately put people through to ensure they not step on our feet, we can certainly put them through more to prevent their sadistically victimizing us. I am indebted here to discussion with Marshall Weinberg.

15. There are, of course, ways of accepting demands, say out of self-interest in a negotiation, that are different from accepting something as a valid demand.

16. The formulation of the reason may not always be agent-relative, however. Suppose, for example, that the best way of grounding the categorical imperative is, as I shall be suggesting, in an authority persons presuppose when they address one another second-personally. It is at least conceivable that what the categorical imperative itself requires is a principle of conduct that can be specified agent-neutrally. R. M. Hare, for example, believes that the categorical imperative can be seen to entail the sort of universal prescriptivism he favors and that this entails a form of act-utilitarianism (an agent-neutral theory). See Hare 1993.

pain not just as his victim, but also as a member of the moral community.) I claim that to understand moral obligation as related to moral responsibility in the way we normally do, we have to see it as involving demands that are "in force" from the moral point of view, that is, from the (first-person plural) perspective of the moral community.[17] As I clarify presently, however, this does not diminish their second-personal character, since that concerns their "demand addressing" quality.[18]

Of course, there might be agent-relative norms and reasons constraining our conduct toward one another that are not second-personal. We might think of the feet of persons as something like sacred ground that we all have reason to avoid stepping on, without supposing that this has anything to do with anyone's authority to demand this, even God's. Once, however, we have the idea that there exists a reason to forbear stepping on people's feet in the fact that this is something we can or do reasonably demand of one another, or that we are *accountable* for this forbearance, we have the idea of a second-personal reason—a kind of reason that simply wouldn't exist but for the possibility of the second-personal address involved in claiming or demanding.

Since second-personal reasons are always fundamentally agent-relative, the second-person stance is a version of the first-person standpoint (whether singular or plural). It is the perspective one assumes in addressing practical thought or speech to, or acknowledging address from, another (whether as an "I" or as part of a "we") and, in so doing, making or acknowledging a claim or demand on the will. It involves practically directed and directive thought, thought that is addressed to, and that makes a claim on, a free and rational agent. What the second-person stance excludes is the third-person perspective, that is, regarding, for practical purposes, others (and oneself), not in relation to oneself, but as they are (or one is) "objectively" or "agent-neutrally" (including as related to

17. This would be like Hart's interpretation of Bentham's doctrine in *A Fragment of Government* as involving "quasi-commands" rather than the explicit commands of statute law. In such cases, Hart says, the command is taken to be implicit in acts of punishing. I will be saying the analogous thing about moral accountability (Hart 1990: 93–94). This analysis is the same as Strawson's on the demand quality of reactive attitudes, which I discuss under "Strawson's Point" below and in Chapter 4 (Strawson 1968). I am indebted to Rae Langton and others for pressing me on these points and to Rob Kar and Kevin Toh for discussion of Hart's view.

18. For the claim that the moral point of view is "first-person plural," see Postema 1995. It is also a theme of Korsgaard's writings.

the person one is). And it rules out as well first-personal thought that lacks an addressing, second-personal aspect.

Thus, although second-person address is always also first-personal, it is never merely first-personal. One can occupy a first-person perspective, whether singular or plural, without explicitly addressing anyone. And even if all speech (and perhaps thought) involves implicit address of some form, a central theme of this book is that addressing second-personal practical reasons differs from other forms of reason-giving (advice, for example) in the distinctive claim it makes on the will.

Logical and Personal Relations

It may help to understand the idea of a second-personal reason to consider it in light of a criticism that Christine Korsgaard makes of Thomas Nagel's idea that "deontological constraints" are agent-relative.[19] Quoting Nagel's remark that such constraints "permi[t] a victim always to object to those who aim at his harm," Korsgaard replies that "this is absolutely right," but that "the theory that deontological reasons are agent-relative . . . cannot accommodate it" (Nagel 1986: 184; Korsgaard 1996d: 297–298). I argue that moral requirements are connected conceptually to an authority to demand compliance. Korsgaard notes that from the fact that an agent has an agent-relative reason to do something, it does not follow that anyone has a reason to complain if he does not do it. In our terms, no second-personal authority follows. In my view, however, it is not the agent-relativity of the reason that explains the deficit. Indeed, as I have said, second-personal reasons invariably are fundamentally agent-relative in the most familiar sense of having an ineliminable reflexive reference to the agent.[20] The truth is that whether a norm or reason is agent-relative or agent-neutral, unless it is itself second-personal, no reason to object follows directly from the fact that an agent contravenes it; indeed, no reason to object follows whatever the weight or priority of the norm or reason. Someone could acknowledge a norm or reason, whether agent-relative or agent-neutral, of whatever priority or stringency, without yet acknowledging anyone's authority to demand that he comply with it. The

19. They must be agent-relative, Nagel believes, because they hold, for example, that it is wrong to harm someone oneself, even if that is necessary to prevent exactly equivalent harm by someone else. I am indebted here to discussion with Chris Dodsworth.

20. See note 9.

former is, as it were, a matter of the logical form or weight of norms or reasons, whereas the latter concerns their second-personal authority.

Ultimately, Korsgaard wishes to reject the agent-relative/agent-neutral distinction and to argue that all reasons for acting must be capable of being "shared." As she puts the point regarding the reasons involved in "deontological" moral obligations, "they supervene on the relationships of people who interact with one another. They are intersubjective reasons" (Korsgaard 1996d: 298). It is a fundamental point of agreement between this claim of Korsgaard's and the outlook I defend in this book that moral obligations are irreducibly second-personal in this way (although unlike Korsgaard, I fail to see why all reasons for acting must be shareable in this sense).[21] In my view, however, the second-personal aspect of moral obligation cannot be explained by non-second-personal features of their logical form, nor by whether they are public or private in any usual sense.[22] As I hope to make clear, second-personal authority is simply an essential, irreducible aspect of moral obligation.

Whether a reason is second-personal is a matter not of logical relations but of personal relations. Second-personal reasons structure our relatings to one another. And I argue that those connected to moral obligation and the equal dignity of persons are what we are committed to whenever we relate to one another second-personally at all.

A Circle of Irreducibly Second-Personal Concepts

Second-personal reasons are invariably tied to a distinctively second-personal kind of *practical authority:* the authority to make a demand or claim.[23] Making a claim or a demand as valid always presupposes the authority to make it and that the duly authorized claim creates a distinctive reason for compliance (a second-personal reason). Moreover, these notions all also involve the idea of responsibility or accountability. The authority to demand implies not just a reason for the addressee to

21. However, Korsgaard also apparently believes that moral obligations can be grounded in the constraints of first-personal deliberation alone. I argue against this in Chapter 9.

22. In Chapter 9, I discuss Korsgaard's deployment of Wittgenstein's private language argument in Korsgaard 1996e.

23. See Joseph Raz's idea of a "normative power" in Raz 1972. I am indebted to Gary Watson for this reference.

comply, but also his being responsible for doing so.[24] Conversely, accountability implies the authority to hold accountable, which implies the authority to claim or demand, which is the standing to address second-personal reasons. These notions—second-personal authority, valid claim or demand, second-personal reason, and responsibility to—therefore comprise an interdefinable circle; each implies all the rest. Moreover, I contend, there is no way to break into this circle from outside it. Propositions formulated only with normative and evaluative concepts that are not already implicitly second-personal cannot adequately ground propositions formulated with concepts within the circle.

For example, it is important in what follows that practical authority of this irreducibly second-personal kind differs from, and cannot be reduced to, authority of other sorts. Consider epistemic authority, for example. Even if the ways in which we respect epistemic authority are frequently second-personal—giving weight to someone's epistemic claims in discussion about what to believe—epistemic authority is not itself second-personal; it is third-personal. It depends fundamentally on a person's relations to facts and evidence as they are anyway, not on her relations to other rational cognizers. Even in cases of testimony where we take someone's word for something, this second-personal authority can be defeated by deficiencies of epistemic authority of the ordinary third-personal kind. If we have reason to distrust her beliefs or judgment, we also have reason to reject her second-personal epistemic claims. Moreover, it is possible to respect epistemic authority entirely privately without any form of acknowledgment to others as, for instance, when someone acts on a credible stock tip he overhears while serving drinks in the boardroom.

The authority to address second-personal reasons for acting, however, is fundamentally second-personal. When a sergeant orders her platoon to fall in, her charges normally take it that the reason she thereby gives them derives entirely from her authority to address demands to them and their responsibility to comply. This is not a standing, like that of an advisor, that she can acquire simply because of her ability to discern non-second-personal reasons for her troops' conduct. That is the point of Hobbes's famous distinction between "command" and "counsel."[25] The sergeant's

24. Thus, Michael Dummett remarks that the right to command entails that "the *right to reproach* is an automatic consequence of disobedience" (Dummett 1990: 9).

25. "They who less seriously consider the force of words, do sometimes confound law

order addresses a reason that would not exist but for her authority to address it through her command. Similarly, when you demand that someone move his foot from on top of yours, you presuppose an irreducibly second-personal standing to address this second-personal reason.

This does not mean, of course, that a claim to the authority to address either claims or demands in general or of some specific sort will not need justifying, or that someone might not come to have some such standing at least partly by virtue of her knowledge or wisdom. The point remains that the standing itself neither is, nor simply follows from, any form of third-personal or epistemic authority. And I maintain that the only way any such second-personal standing can be justified is within the circle of four interrelated ideas of claim, accountability, second-personal reason, and the species of authority that is related to these. Ultimately, I claim, it must be justifiable from within a second-person standpoint.

There is thus an important difference between the idea of an authoritative or binding norm in the familiar sense of a valid ought that entails genuine normative reasons, on the one hand, and that of an authoritative (second-personal) claim or demand on the other. A central claim of this book, for instance, is that what is called the inviolable value or *dignity* of persons has an irreducibly second-personal element, which includes the authority to demand certain treatment of each other, like not stepping on one another's feet. To be sure, dignity partly involves there being ways one must conduct oneself toward persons and ways one must not, that, as it is sometimes put, persons are beings who may not be treated in certain ways (Kamm 1989, 1992; Nagel 1995). But that is only part of it, since there can be requirements on us that no one has any standing to require of us. We are under a requirement of reason, for example, not

---

with *counsel.* . . . We must fetch the distinction between *counsel* and *law*, from the difference between *counsel* and *command*. Now COUNSEL is a *precept*, in which the reason of my obeying it is taken from *the thing itself* which is advised; but COMMAND is a *precept*, in which the cause of my obedience depends on the *will of the commander*. For it is not properly said, *thus I will* and *thus I command*, except the will stand for a reason. Now when obedience is yielded to the laws, not for the thing itself, but by reason of the adviser's will, the law is not a *counsel*, but a *command*, and is defined thus: LAW *is the command of that person (whether man or court) whose precept contains in it the reason of obedience:* as the precepts of God in regard of men, of magistrates in respect of their subjects, and universally of all the powerful in respect of them who cannot resist, may be termed their laws" (Hobbes 1983: XIV.1; see also Hobbes 1994: XXV). In my view, failure to observe this distinction infects Joseph Raz's account of authority in Raz 1986. See also note 29.

to believe propositions that contradict the logical consequences of known premises. But it is only in certain contexts, say, when you and I are trying to work out what to believe together, that we have any standing to demand that we each reason logically, and even here that authority apparently derives from a moral or quasi-moral aspect: our having undertaken a common aim.[26] Requirements of logical reasoning are, in this way, fundamentally different from those that are grounded in the dignity of persons—and different also from moral requirements more generally. I claim that it is part of the very concept that moral obligations are what those to whom we are morally responsible have the authority to demand that we do. Clearly this is no part whatsoever of the concept of a demand of logic or a requirement of reason.[27]

Our dignity as persons includes, I maintain, an irreducibly second-personal authority to demand respect for this very authority and for the requirements with which it gives us the standing to demand compliance. Dignity is not just a set of requirements with respect to persons; it is also the authority persons have to require compliance with these requirements by holding one another accountable for doing so. Someone might accept the first-order norms that structure the dignity of persons and regulate himself scrupulously by them without accepting anyone's authority to demand that he do so. He might even accept these as mandatory norms in some suitable sense without accepting anyone's claim to his compliance. I claim, however, that he would not yet fully acknowledge the dignity of persons or respect persons for their dignity. These involve an irreducibly second-personal dimension.

There is hence a general difference between there being normative reasons of whatever weight or priority for us to do something—its being what we ought to or must do—and anyone's having any authority to claim or demand that we do it.[28] If, say, God has the authority to demand

26. Of course, these further constraints are frequently in the background, as they are, for example, whenever we do philosophy, say, right now. Because of the relationship you and I are currently in, each of us does have authority to call the other to account for logical errors, a standing that, without some such context, we lack. But however frequently that or some relevantly similar context obtains, the authority comes not just from the requirement of reason, but also from some other presupposed feature of the context.

27. I am indebted to Peter Graham for this way of putting the contrast.

28. Although not, of course, its being what we morally must do (are morally required to do), since this is what members of the moral community have the authority to demand we do.

that we comply with certain norms, his authority to demand this cannot be reduced to any normative reasons that the norms might themselves generate or entail, nor, indeed, to his knowledge of these.[29]

Strawson's Point

We can see the same underlying idea from a different direction by considering P. F. Strawson's influential critique of consequentialist approaches to moral responsibility in "Freedom and Resentment" (1968). Against accounts that seek to justify practices of punishment and moral responsibility by their "efficacy . . . in regulating behaviour in socially desirable ways," Strawson argued that social desirability is not a reason of "the right *sort*" for practices of moral responsibility "as we understand them" (72, 74). When we seek to hold people accountable, what matters is not whether doing so is desirable, either in a particular case or in general, but whether the person's conduct is culpable and we have the authority to bring him to account. *Desirability is a reason of the wrong kind to warrant the attitudes and actions in which holding someone responsible consists in their own terms.*

We can call this *Strawson's Point*. We find essentially the same idea in Dewey. "There is an intrinsic difference," Dewey writes, "in both origin and mode of operation between objects which present themselves as satisfactory to desire and hence good, and objects which come to one as making demands upon his conduct which should be recognized. Neither can be reduced to the other." And lest we think that Dewey might not mean anything essentially second-personal by "demands," Dewey adds in a footnote: "Men who live together inevitably make demands on one another" (1998b: 319).[30] So we might call this Dewey's Point as well.

Strawson's Point illustrates a more general phenomenon that can

29. As I mentioned in note 25, Raz argues (1986) that the species of authority with which we are concerned, for example, political authority, can be grounded in epistemic authority. But as Nomy Arpaly has put it to me, "Just because I know more than you doesn't make me boss." Thomas Jefferson makes a similar point, when he says, "Because Sir Isaac Newton was superior to others in understanding, he was not therefore lord of the person or property of others" (Jefferson 1984: 1202). I am indebted to Charles Griswold for this reference. Raz's view deserves a more careful treatment than I can provide here, which I intend to provide on another occasion.

30. I am indebted to Elizabeth Anderson for this reference.

be dubbed the *wrong kind of reason problem*. For example, there might be pragmatic reasons to believe some proposition, but that doesn't make that proposition credible (Shah 2003). It doesn't justify believing it in terms of reasons and standards that distinctively apply to belief. Similarly, as D'Arms and Jacobson have pointed out, it is a "moralistic fallacy" to conclude from the fact that it would be morally objectionable to be amused by a certain joke that the joke is not funny.[31] The former is a reason of the "wrong kind" to justify the claim that a joke does not warrant amusement in the relevant sense (D'Arms and Jacobson 2000a).

To be a reason of the right kind, a consideration must justify the relevant attitude in its own terms. It must be a fact about or feature of some object, appropriate consideration of which could provide *someone's reason* for a warranted attitude of that kind toward it.[32] It must be something on the basis of which someone could (and appropriately would) come to hold the attitude as a conclusion of a process of considering (deliberating about) whether to do so. In considering whether to believe some proposition *p*, for example, it is simply impossible to conclude one's deliberation in a belief that *p* by reflecting on the desirable consequences of believing *p*. That is a reason of the right kind for desiring to believe that *p*, but not for believing that *p* (as is shown by the fact that one can come to desire to believe *p* by reflecting on the desirable consequences of believing *p*). The *desirable* concerns norms and reasons that are specific

---

31. D'Arms and Jacobson argue that this poses a problem for response-dependent or, as they call them, "neo-sentimentalist" accounts of various evaluative and normative notions, since it shows that, say, the funny can't be understood in terms of amusement's making sense or being warranted by just any reasons. There is a distinction between an emotion or attitude's being "the right way to feel" and its "getting [the relevant value] right." See also D'Arms and Jacobson 2000b. For an excellent discussion of how what they call "fitting-attitude" (or "FA") analyses can deal with the problem of distinguishing reasons of the right from reasons of the wrong kind, see Rabinowicz and Ronnøw-Rasmussen 2004. (See also Olson 2004.) I am indebted to Julian Darwall for discussion of this general issue and to Joe Mendola for a question that helped me to see that Strawson's Point is an instance of it.

32. Rabinowicz and Ronnøw-Rasmussen express essentially the same point by saying reasons of the right kind also appear in the content of the attitude for which they are reasons: the attitude is toward something "on account of" these reasons (2004: 414). As W. D. Falk pointed out, a favoring that is relevant to value is "by way of true comprehension of what [the object] is like" (1986: 117).

to desire, and the *credible* concerns norms and reasons that are specific to belief.

Similarly, the *responsible* and the *culpable* concern norms for the distinctive attitudes and actions that are involved in holding people responsible and blaming them. The desirability—whether moral, social, personal, or otherwise—of holding them responsible, or reasons why that would be desirable, are simply reasons of the wrong kind to warrant doing so in the sense that is relevant to whether they are responsible or blameworthy.[33] The former concerns reasons and norms of desire, and what is thus desirable, even from the moral point of view, is simply a different question from what we are justified in holding someone responsible or blaming them for in the relevant sense.

Strawson dubbed the distinctive attitudes involved in holding people responsible "reactive attitudes," with prominent examples being indignation, resentment, guilt, blame, and so on. And Strawson pointed out what commentators have since stressed, namely, that reactive attitudes implicitly address demands. They invariably involve "an expectation of, and demand for" certain conduct from one another (1968: 85).[34] Reactive attitudes invariably concern what someone can be held to, so they invariably presuppose the authority to hold someone responsible and make demands of him. Moral reactive attitudes therefore presuppose the authority to demand and hold one another responsible for compliance with moral obligations (which just are the standards to which we can warrantedly hold each other as members of the moral community). But they also presuppose that those we hold accountable have that standing also. They address another, Strawson says, in a way that "continu[es] to view him as a member of the moral community; only as one who has offended against its demands" (93). It follows that reactive attitudes are second-personal in our sense, and that ethical notions that are distinctively relevant to these attitudes—the culpable, moral responsibility, and, I argue, moral obligation—all have an irreducibly second-personal aspect that ties them conceptually to second-personal reasons.

33. Compare Prichard's objection to attempts to vindicate morality and moral obligation in terms of self-interest in Prichard 2002.

34. Gary Watson stresses this (1987: 263, 264). Note also R. Jay Wallace: "there is an essential connection between the reactive attitudes and a distinctive form of evaluation . . . that I refer to as holding a person to an expectation (or demand)" (1994: 19). See also Bennett 1980; Scanlon 1998: 272–290.

Rights

Another central ethical concept within the second-personal circle is that of a *right*, most obviously, of a claim right. You might think, for instance, that non-inadvertent stepping on your feet violates a right you have against other persons. If so, then what you think is not just that others should, or even must, take care not to step on your feet. The holding of even mandatory norms does not amount to the existence of a right. As Feinberg stressed, to have a claim right is to have someplace to "stand," if you will permit the metaphor in this context, to claim or demand that to which one has the right. It includes a second-personal authority to resist, complain, remonstrate, and perhaps use coercive measures of other kinds, including, perhaps, to gain compensation if the right is violated.[35] In addition to there being weighty reasons against others stepping on your feet, indeed, in addition to members of the moral community having the standing to demand that people not step on your feet, if you have a right, then you have a standing to make a special demand against people who might step on your feet—you have the authority to resist, claim compensation, and so on.

This is implicit in Hohfeld's famous formulation (1923).[36] According to Hohfeld, someone has a claim right to another person's doing something only if that person has an obligation to her to do that thing.[37] And this consists not simply in its being the case that the other ought or has good and sufficient reasons to do it, even that the reasons for him to do it are exclusionary in Raz's sense of not being appropriately weighed against otherwise competing considerations (1975), but in the claim-holder's authority to demand compliance and, perhaps, compensation for

35. "Having rights, of course, makes claiming possible; but it is claiming that gives rights their special moral significance. This feature of rights is connected in a way with the customary rhetoric about what it is to be a human being. Having rights enables us to 'stand up like men,' to look others in the eye, and to feel in some fundamental way the equal of anyone" (Feinberg 1980: 151). Compare Mill: "To have a right, then, is, I conceive, to have something which society ought to defend me in the possession of" (1998: ch. 5).

36. I am indebted to Mark LeBar for reminding me of Hohfeld's relevance here.

37. Hohfeld sets out the "jural correlatives" between persons as follows: (1) S has a right against T if, and only if, T has a duty to S; (2) S has a power with respect to T if, and only if, T has a liability with respect to S; (3) S has an immunity with respect to T if, and only if, T has a disability with respect to S; and so on (1923: 65–75).

non-compliance.[38] Rights are thus associated conceptually with second-personal reasons. There may of course be non-second-personal reasons for others to do what we also have a right to demand their doing, but the reason that is distinctively associated with the right is second-personal. It simply wouldn't exist but for the possibility of its being addressed in invokings of the right.

Rights of other kinds are second-personal as well, if less obviously. If the person who stepped on your foot were within his rights or morally free to have done so (had a Hohfeldian "liberty"), then neither you nor anyone else would have had any standing to demand otherwise or complain. In his famous "Are There Any Natural Rights," Hart argues, following a venerable tradition running through Fichte and Kant, that the idea of rights is conceptually connected to there being a distinctive justification for restricting freedom.[39] The central element of this conceptual area, Hart writes, is there being "no incongruity, but a special congruity in the use of force or the threat of force to secure what is just or fair or someone's right" (1965: 178). It is important in what follows that the relevant "congruity" cannot be fully captured in non-second-personal terms.[40] This is an aspect of Strawson's Point, and it connects with deeply related ideas of Pufendorf and Fichte that I will set out presently. A justification "of the right sort" for imposing upon another's freedom and directing his will exists only if one has the authority to make a claim on

38. See Thompson 2004. Also, compare here Locke's famous distinction between the right every individual has in the state of nature to punish transgressions of natural rights and victims' rights "to seek reparation." Both are second-personal, and both are held as members of the moral community, but only the latter involves a second-personal address on behalf of the victim (Locke 1988: II, §7–11).

As I've mentioned and shall stress more strongly in the next chapter, someone's being under a moral obligation not to step on your foot also entails a second-personal authority (in this case, of the moral community). What is distinctive in the case of rights is the distinctive authority of the right holder, including to demand compensation, as is implicit in Locke's distinction between the authority to punish (as a member of the moral community) and the authority to demand compensation (as the right-holding victim).

39. Hart notes that he is here broadly following Kant's doctrine in the *Rechtslehre* (Kant 1996c: 230–231). We will consider a further expression of this idea in Fichte's claim that a second-personal stance presupposes a "principle of right" ("I must in all cases recognize the free being outside me as a free being, i.e., I must limit my freedom through the concept of the possibility of his freedom") (2000: 49).

40. I am indebted here to discussion with Tom Hurka.

his will (and if no one, including the person herself, has the authority to complain or demand otherwise). Otherwise, an imposition of will is coercion pure and simple.

Now we are concerned less directly with rights than with *moral obligation*. As Hart himself notes, however, despite the fact that 'moral obligation' can sometimes be used as a "general label" for what "morally we ought to do," the concept has a more properly restricted content that is intimately connected with that of rights (1965: 178).[41] Neither concept can be understood independently of the idea of the (second-personal) authority to claim or demand. Just as a right involves an authority to claim that to which one has a right, so also is moral obligation conceptually tied to what the moral community can demand (and what no one has a right not to do). And what I am morally free to do is what no one can justifiably demand that I not do either as a member of the moral community (no conflicting moral obligation) or as an individual (no conflicting right).

The Presuppositions of Second-Personal Address

Addressing second-personal reasons of any kind, I argue, always carries certain presuppositions concerning the second-personal authority, competence, and responsibility of addresser and addressee alike. I shall be focusing on pure cases of second-personal claiming and reason-giving, abstracting from manipulation, cajoling, or any other form of nonrational influence (alternatively, on actual cases, *qua* second-personal address). In a pure case, an addresser attempts to give an addressee a reason for acting that is grounded in normative relations that, as I argue, he presupposes the addressee can be expected to accept. What is built into this presupposition? Quite a lot.

Fichte's Point

The post-Kantian German idealist Johann Gottlieb Fichte claimed that pure second-personal address always presumes to direct an agent's will through the agent's own self-determining choice. Only in this way, Fichte

---

41. However, Hart sometimes seems to restrict obligations even further to those that are voluntarily assumed or created (1965: 179n). I am indebted here to Rob Kar.

argues, can it simultaneously address and direct her as a free agent. Call this *Fichte's Analysis* of second-personal address. I defend Fichte's Analysis and follow Fichte further in arguing that Fichte's Analysis supports *Fichte's Point*, namely, that any second-personal claim or "summons" *(Aufforderung)* presupposes a common competence, authority, and, therefore, responsibility as free and rational, a mutual second-personality that addresser and addressee share and that is appropriately recognized reciprocally (Fichte 2000). The terms of second-personal address commit both parties to seeing each other as, in Rawls's famous formulation, "self-originating source[s] of valid claims" (1980: 546). Whatever more specific difference-defining authorities they presuppose, each is committed also to assuming that free and rational persons have a dignity or authority in common to address (and be addressed) second-personal reasons.[42] And each must also presuppose their common second-personal *competence,* a capacity to determine themselves by these reasons, which capacity includes motivation that, because the reasons are irreducibly second-personal, cannot be reduced to desires for any outcome.[43]

There is thus, I argue, a form of reciprocal respect that is built into all second-personal reason-giving, even when the authority relations it explicitly presupposes are at odds with the full equality we now believe to characterize the moral point of view. Any pure case of claiming or demanding presupposes the standing necessary to enter into second-personal reasoning at all. Specifically, it presupposes a distinction between legitimate forms of address that, as Fichte puts it, "summon" persons to determine themselves freely by second-personal reasons (however hierarchical), on the one hand, and coercion, that is, impermissible ways of simply causing wanted behavior that "depriv[e the agent] of its ability to act freely," on the other (Fichte 2000: 41).[44] This means that whenever

42. These are, more strictly, presuppositions of their address and acknowledgment, respectively, in the sense mentioned earlier in the chapter. The individuals themselves might not accept or even reject them. I will return to this point presently.

43. Ultimately, I argue, this competence amounts to Kant's "autonomy of the will": "the property of the will by which it is a law to itself independently of any property of the objects of volition" (Kant 1996b: 441). Also, see Gibbard 1990: 68–82, on the psychology of norm-acceptance. We might still call such states desires, but if so, we will need nonetheless to recognize that they are "principle-dependent" rather than "object-dependent" desires. For this distinction, see Rawls 2000: 45–48, 148–152.

44. A similar idea seems at work in the writings of Emmanuel Lévinas about encountering the "other," for example, Lévinas 1969. I am indebted here to Rachana Kamtekar.

second-personal address asserts or presupposes differential authority, it must assume also that this authority is acceptable to its addressee simply as a free and rational agent.

Fichte realized the fundamental significance of his point for the philosophy of right, and so made it part of a "Deduction of the Concept of Right" at the outset of his *Foundations of Natural Right*.[45] If a right, by its very nature, involves the authority to claim or demand, so also, Fichte argues, does second-personal address presuppose both the competence and the authority of addresser and addressee alike freely to determine themselves by second-personal reasons, that is, reasons whose validity itself depends on that very authority and their ability freely to determine themselves by acknowledging it. And this, he argues, commits addresser and acknowledging addressee to accepting a fundamental principle of right: "I must in all cases recognize the free being outside me as a free being, i.e., I must limit my freedom through the concept of the possibility of his freedom" (2000: 49). The very distinction between coercion, that is, attempting to direct someone's will without second-personal reasons he can be expected to accept, on the one hand, and making a directive claim on someone's will backed by second-personal authority, on the other, itself presupposes that addresser and addressee share a common authority as free and rational, which they reciprocally recognize in the address and uptake of an *Aufforderung*.

Fichte connects this insight, also correctly in my view, to a fundamental difference between theoretical and practical reason. Second-personal address both makes possible and simultaneously makes us aware of a species of practical freedom that lacks any analogue in the theoretical realm. I develop and defend this claim, relating it to Kant's notion of autonomy of the will. It turns out, I argue, that Fichte's Point is exactly what is needed to work out properly the central Kantian ideas of the dignity of persons and autonomy of the will.

Pufendorf's Point

A final piece of the puzzle that is needed, along with Fichte's Analysis to establish Fichte's Point, is an idea that Samuel Pufendorf advanced in the

---

For an illuminating discussion of the way in which, according to Lévinas, encountering an other "face to face" involves a second-personal demand for respect, see Putnam 2002.

45. Published in 1796–97, just before Kant's *Rechtlehre*. See Frederick Neuhouser's very helpful introduction to Fichte 2000.

course of defending a theological voluntarist theory of moral law in the seventeenth century. According to Pufendorf, moral obligation's connection to responsibility is explained by the fact that the moral law derives from God's commands. Moral obligations are all ultimately owed to God. But Pufendorf also thought that obligations can arise in this way only if God addresses us as rational agents and if we and he understand this address in a certain way. *Pufendorf's Point* was that genuine obligations can result only from an address that presupposes an addressee's second-personal competence.[46] To intelligibly hold someone responsible, we must assume that she can hold herself responsible in her own reasoning and thought.[47] And to do that, she must be able to take up a second-person standpoint on herself and make and acknowledge demands of herself from that point of view. For God to be able to obligate us by his command, consequently, God (and we) must assume that we can be moved not simply by a fear of sanctions that might coerce compliance, but by "acknowledg[ing] of [ourselves] that the evil, which has been pointed out to the person who deviates from an announced rule, falls upon him justly" (Pufendorf 1934: 91). This is the difference between a kind of coercion, on the one hand, and free self-determination by an internal acceptance of an authoritative demand, on the other. To be obligated by God's command, we must be able to take a second-personal standpoint on ourselves and be motivated by internally addressed demands whose (second-personal) authority we ourselves accept.

Properly appreciating Strawson's, Fichte's, and Pufendorf's Points together will enable us to see why any second-personal address whatsoever presupposes a common second-personal competence, responsibility, and authority that addresser and addressee share as free and rational agents. It is assuming a second-person standpoint that gets us inside the circle of interdefinable second-personal notions and that commits us, moreover, to the equal dignity of free and rational persons. Substantially the same point can be put in Rawlsian terms by saying that it is second-personal address that gets us into the space of "public reason" and the "reasonable" rather than the (merely) individually "rational" (Rawls 1980, 1993). Any such address unavoidably presupposes that its addressee can accept as

46. Pufendorf's Point resonates with Hart's distinction between being obliged (by force or circumstance) and being obligated (1961: 6–8).

47. On the significance of the ability to hold oneself responsible, see Westlund 2003. Cf. Kant's remark that "I can recognize that I am under obligation to others only insofar as I at the same time put myself under obligation" (1996b: 6:417).

reasonable both the claims it addresses and the authority on which these claims are based, and it consequently assumes relations of reciprocal respect and mutual accountability, which are mediated by public reasons and a conception of the reasonable.

It is entirely possible to give people reasons for acting that are not second-personal, however, without assuming any common competence and authority to address reasons to one another. If, say, God can get us to see the risks of hellfire, he will have given us a reason not to sin regardless of any second-personal authority he or we might have or lack. Neither need he presuppose that we can be expected reasonably to accept anything. In other words, whether we are "reasonable" in any sense that is relevant here will simply follow from whether we can see and be moved by the relevant reasons. Similarly, you can get someone to see that you are in pain, that it is a bad thing that you are, and consequently that there is reason for anyone who can to alter this bad state without that raising any issue of your authorities with respect to each other. When, however, we address second-personal reasons, the existence of the reason itself depends upon whether its addressees can reasonably accept the authority relation from which it ostensibly flows. This is a consequence of Fichte's Point. And it is why a contractualist framework like Rawls's or Scanlon's must ultimately tie "what we owe to each other," that is, what we can authoritatively demand from one another, to mutual respect and a test of reasonable agreement (Scanlon 1998). I argue that it is the equal authority we presuppose from the second-person standpoint that most deeply underlies contractualism.

I should make clear that I do not claim in any of this that participants in second-personal interaction invariably do accept or are aware of these presuppositions, or even that the necessary assumptions must be accessible to them.[48] The idea of moral community between free and rational persons is a significant achievement of relatively recent human history, and there is no reason to think that it was even available, say, to an ancient Hittite issuing an order or making a request. Pufendorf himself would no doubt have rejected what I am claiming he is committed to by the distinctions he made. My thesis is that the assumptions I identify are presuppositions of second-personal address in the sense that (second-personal) reasons can be validly addressed only if these assumptions hold.

---

48. I am indebted to Eric Schliesser for pressing me on this point.

They are "normative felicity conditions" of the (pure) address of second-personal reasons in general.

Indeed, the very distinction between a pure case of second-personal reason-giving and nonrational forms of influence—or the abstraction: *qua* second-personal address—is no doubt itself relatively recent. When I say that addressing second-personal reasons carries certain presuppositions, I should be understood as talking about the pure case, which, along with its implicit presuppositions, only comes clearly into view retrospectively (although from this latter perspective, the presuppositions will seem to have always been implicit).[49] My claim is that a common second-personality is a necessary condition of the success of second-personal address in its own terms, that is, for the relevant reasons actually to exist and be given.

As an analogy, consider the familiar thesis that punishment can be fully justified only on an assumption of freedom of the will. There is probably no reason to think that this latter idea, at least in its modern form, was available to the ancient Hittites either, but they surely had punishment of a sort.[50] No doubt their practices differed in various ways from what we would consider punishment as a pure case. But that is just the point. Freedom of the will can plausibly seem a presupposition of punishment in the pure case (in its own terms) as we now distinguish it. And similar things, I argue, are true of the pure address of second-personal reasons in general.

49. This is, of course, a favorite theme of Hegel's in *The Phenomenology of Spirit* (1977).

50. See Neufeld 1951. For an interesting discussion of the development of our contemporary notion of responsibility and associated practices of legal accountability, which argues that courts were initially conceived of as sites of neutral and reasoned adjudication between parties who would otherwise exact or suffer vengeance, see Pound 1922: ch. 4. I am indebted to Randall Curren for this reference and for helpful discussion. See Chapter 4 below for a discussion of the difference between the desire to retaliate or avenge and reactive attitudes as implicitly seeking second-personal recognition or respect.

— 2 —

The Main Ideas II

Moral Obligation's Purported Normativity

The most familiar characterization of moral obligations' purported normative force is in terms of their putatively *categorical* character, their purporting to be what Kant (1996b) called "categorical imperatives." Philippa Foot (1972) points out that this cannot mean just that moral obligations are categorical in form, that they "apply" independently of their relation to the agent's ends. Requirements of etiquette are unconditional in this way also, but nobody thinks that their putative normative force is anything like that of moral requirements. Foot concludes that the Kantian claim must rather be that moral obligations "necessarily give reasons for acting to any man" (309). Frequently this claim is strengthened to what Scheffler calls the "thesis of overridingness": "it can never be rational knowingly to do what morality forbids" (1992).[1] In other words, moral obligations always give agents conclusive reasons for acting that outweigh or take priority over any potentially competing considerations; or, at least, they always purport to do so.

This surely captures part of what is felt to be special about moral requirements, but only part. Compare logical requirements. If a conclusion follows from known premises, then we are under a requirement of reason to infer it that apparently applies to all rational beings also, considerations to the contrary notwithstanding. But there is an important difference between moral obligations and requirements that are imposed by logic. Morality involves a distinctive kind of accountability by its very nature. If I fail to act as I am morally required without adequate excuse, then distinctively second-personal responses like blame and guilt are

1. David Brink calls this the "supremacy thesis" (1997: 255).

thereby warranted.[2] But it is only in certain contexts that responses like these seem appropriate to logical blunders, and even here what seems to be in question is a moral error of some kind (as when I have a special responsibility for reasoning properly).[3] Moreover, although a connection to accountability is part of the very concept of moral obligation, it is obviously no part whatsoever of the idea of a logical requirement.[4]

Mill famously remarked that "we do not call anything wrong, unless we mean to imply that a person ought to be punished in some way or other for doing it; if not by law, by the opinion of his fellow creatures; if not by opinion, by the reproaches of his own conscience." We may think there are strong moral reasons for people to do something and "dislike or despise them for not doing" it; but unless we think "blame" or some other form of "punishment" is warranted, perhaps just the feeling of guilt, we do not think it "a case of moral obligation" (Mill 1998: ch. 5). Many philosophers today broadly concur with these Millian sentiments (Adams 1999: 238; Baier 1966; Brandt 1979: 163–176; Gibbard 1990: 42; Skorupski 1999: 142).[5] Matters of moral obligation are the moral community's "business," as Kurt Baier puts it (1966: 223). When we are morally obligated, we are not morally free to act otherwise; members of the moral community have the authority to hold us responsible if we do. Moral obligations are thus *to* others in a more robust way than those of logic are.[6] Anyone who feels guilty about logical errors would seem to have a "moralized" sense of the logical.

I develop this theme and argue that any account of the distinctive normativity of moral obligation that fails to capture this second-personal element is deficient. What's more, I argue that this second-personal aspect also helps to explain why moral obligations purport to be supremely authoritative in the more familiar sense of being categorical and over-riding.

The root of this latter explanation is the conceptual connection be-

2. Indeed, the very idea of an "excuse" is not internal to the rules of logic; it must be understood in relation to a broader context that includes other norms.

3. I don't mean, of course, that logical errors aren't subject to criticism, or that we don't sometimes use words like "blame," as when a teacher says that he doesn't blame his student for a given error on a first try.

4. Again, I am indebted to Peter Graham for this point.

5. See also Ewing's distinction between two senses of 'ought', one concerning the weight of normative reasons, the other conceptually related to blame (1939: 3). I am indebted to Howard Nye for reminding me of this passage.

6. See Thompson 2004.

tween moral obligation and responsibility, specifically, obligation's tie to warranted blame. Along lines similar to Bernard Williams and others, I argue that blame implies that the blamed agent had reason enough not to do what we blame him for doing in something like the way that Moore held that asserting p implies that one believes that p (Gibbard 1990: 299–300; Moore 1942: 540–543; Shafer-Landau 2003: 181–183; Skorupski 1999: 42–43; Williams 1995: 40–44). Just as it is unintelligible to assert something but deny that one believes it, so also does it make no sense to blame someone for doing something and then add that he had, nonetheless, sufficient reason to do it, all things considered. It is common to blame and other second-personal reactive attitudes through which we hold one another responsible that they presuppose not just that the person shouldn't have done what he did "morally speaking," but that he shouldn't have done it period. A person who in one moment "admits" his guilt, but in the next, asserts that he had, nonetheless, good and sufficient reasons for doing what he did could hardly be said to have accepted responsibility for his action. Or to put the point the other way around, if someone can establish that he had sufficient reason to do what he did, then he will have accounted for himself and shown thereby that blame is unwarranted.

The Scope of Moral Obligation

I should emphasize that nothing in the idea of moral obligation as involving reciprocal accountability rules out its scope or content extending beyond the needs and interests of free and rational individuals considered as such. For all I say in this book, what we are morally responsible for might include, for example, the protection of cultural treasures, wilderness, and/or the welfare of other sentient beings, quite independently of the relation any of these have to the interests of free and rational persons. I take no stand here on whether or not this is so. What I say entails that if we have such moral obligations, then these are among the things we free and rational agents have the authority to demand of one another. Of course, even if we do not, even if, say, harming wilderness or members of other species were not in itself to violate any demand for which we can be held morally accountable, there would still be weighty reasons against such harm. In any case, what I do argue is that moral obligations essentially include demands free and rational individuals have standing to make of one another as such and that we are committed to the standing to make these demands by presuppositions of the second-person standpoint. Whether we are morally accountable for more is obviously an important question, but it is not one I can address here.[7]

Of course, even if moral obligations concerning other species, say, can be accommodated within the kind of framework I am sketching, it may still be objected that there is no place in it for the idea that these obligations are owed to the beings themselves if they lack second-personal competence and so, according to my argument, the authority to demand anything. But the kind of view I develop may have resources for response even here. First, although I am bound to insist that moral obligation, like the concept of a right, cannot be understood independently of authoritative demands, the thought that moral obligations can be owed to beings who lack second-personal competence might be able to be elaborated in terms of trustees' (for example, the moral community's) authority to demand certain treatment on their behalf (perhaps also to claim certain rights, compensation, and so on, for them). Thus, Dr. Seuss's character the Lorax (a free and rational being) declares, "I speak for the trees" (Dr. Seuss 1971). Second, to the extent that we find the thought that we owe obligations to nonrational beings a natural thing to think, it seems likely that we also impute to them a proto- or quasi-second-personality, for example, as when we see an animal's or an infant's cry as a form of complaint. In any case, what I seek to show in this book is that the second-personal competence that makes us subject to moral obligation also gives us an authority to make claims and demands of one another as members of the moral community. Whether the scope or content of moral obligation extends farther is a question I do not here consider.[8]

Vindicating Moral Obligation: The Kantian Project

Whether moral obligations purport to be supremely authoritative is one question, but whether they actually are is another.[9] The project of vin-

---

7. I am indebted to Allen Buchanan for pressing me to clarify the points in this paragraph.

8. I am indebted to Jim Staihar and Howard Nye for discussion of the points in this paragraph.

9. Alternatively, we could say that moral obligations are supremely authoritative by definition, but then the question just becomes whether the specific injunctions we take to

dicating morality's putative authority poses one of moral philosophy's great challenges. A mark of the Kantian tradition has been to take the challenge seriously and attempt to meet it (Darwall 1983; Gewirth 1978; Korsgaard 1996f; Nagel 1970). Kant's own strategy apparently changed significantly from the *Groundwork* to *The Critique of Practical Reason*, however. What held constant throughout was his "Reciprocity Thesis," Kant's conviction that the moral law is equivalent to what he called "autonomy of the will": "the property of the will by which it is a law to itself (independently of any property of the objects of volition)" (Allison 1986; Kant 1996b: 440).

Consider, first, how Kant argues in the *Groundwork*. At the end of *Groundwork*'s section 2, Kant remarks that it is consistent with his arguments to that point that morality is nothing but a "figment of the mind." He believes he has already proven in sections 1 and 2 that morality's fundamental principle is the Categorical Imperative (CI) and that it holds if, and only if, the will has the property of autonomy (the Reciprocity Thesis). But so far he has simply analyzed the "generally accepted" concept of morality. All he has shown, consequently, is that *if*, and only if, there is such a thing as morality is conceived to be, then "the categorical imperative, and with it autonomy of the will, is true and absolutely necessary as an *a priori* principle" (1996b: 445). To vindicate the moral law, however, it is insufficient to establish this biconditional, since it is merely an analytic truth that is consistent with morality's and autonomy's both being mere "figments." He must establish either that autonomy really holds or that the CI does (either will do because of the Reciprocity Thesis). And both, he says, are synthetic *a priori* claims that require the kind of critique of practical reason he sets about providing in section 3.

In *Groundwork* 3, Kant attempts to establish autonomy of the will as an independent premise and to prove the CI on its basis. He claims that autonomy is a necessary presupposition of the practical standpoint—we "cannot act otherwise than *under the idea of freedom*"—and then argues (via the Reciprocity Thesis) that in presupposing autonomy a rational agent is committed to the CI (the moral law) (1996b: 448). Contemporary Kantians, most notably Christine Korsgaard, often pursue some version of this strategy also (Hill 1985; Korsgaard 1996b, 1996e, 1996f).

---

be moral obligations are moral obligations in fact. So far as I can see, nothing hangs on this semantic choice.

I argue that any such attempt must fail. Autonomy of the will, as Kant defines it, is a form of freedom that is distinctively practical and that lacks any analogue in theoretical reasoning. However, the only argument that Kant gives in *Groundwork* 3 (1996b: 448) for the proposition that we must presuppose autonomy in practical reasoning is that we must assume a freedom of reason in forming any judgment, whether practical or theoretical. Kant's idea seems to be that if we see our thinking or judgments in any area as simply directed from without, we will not be able to regard ourselves as reasoning or making rational judgments in that area. No doubt this is true, but it doesn't follow that the reasons on the basis of which we judge are not themselves drawn from features of our judgment's object (and hence, in practical deliberation, from properties of the objects of our desire and volition). When we reason about what to believe, at least about empirical matters, for example, there is a clear sense in which we need to see our thinking as responding to independent objects and states of the world about which we are attempting to form beliefs.[10] Theoretical reasoning evidently involves no form of freedom that is analogous to autonomy of the will, the will's being "a law to itself (independently of any properties of the objects of [desire and] volition)" (Kant 1996b: 440).

But neither, I argue, need autonomy be assumed in just any intelligible practical reasoning. Consider what practical reasoning would be like if it were structurally analogous to rational belief formation about the empirical world. (I am not saying for a moment that this is a plausible picture of practical reasoning, only that it is an intelligible one, and that since autonomy would not be assumed in such reasoning, it cannot, therefore, be an inescapable presupposition of the practical standpoint.) A naïve theoretical reasoner takes her experience as evidence of states of an independent world (the objects of correct beliefs). An analogously "naïve" practical reasoner might take her desires and other forms of "practical experience" like pleasure and pain as forms of epistemic access also, only this time, not to the world as it is, but to how it would be good or bad

10. This point holds whether or not transcendental idealism is true. Even a transcendental idealist will need to draw a distinction between object- or state-responsive thinking (like that involved in ordinary belief formation about states of the world, i.e., the objects of empirical belief) and thinking that isn't. It is significant in this regard that Fichte contrasts practical freedom from any we can have in "representational activity" (2000: 19), as does Kant in the *Critique of Practical Reason* (1996a: 20).

for the world to be, how it should or should not be.[11] To an agent with a desire that *p*, it will seem that the world should be such that *p*, as if *p* would be a good thing, hence, as if there is reason for her to bring *p* about, and similarly for experiences of being pleased or pained that *p*. Naïve practical reasoning on this basis would therefore see reasons for acting as deriving from features of the objects of desire and volition and so would not presuppose autonomy in Kant's sense.

So I argue that Kant's *Groundwork* argument fails, as must, indeed, any argument that attempts to prove that autonomy is an inescapable assumption of any possible practical reasoning.[12] The problem, as I diagnose it, is that it is only deliberation from the second-person standpoint that requires us to assume autonomy of the will.

By the time Kant wrote *Critique of Practical Reason*, he had apparently abandoned the *Groundwork*'s strategy of trying to establish the moral law from a prior premise of autonomy as an inescapable assumption of any practical reasoning. There he holds that we have no independent way of establishing autonomy other than through our consciousness of a particular kind of reason, namely, being bound by the moral law. What Kant calls the "fact of reason" (1996a: 31), the awareness of our freedom through consciousness of being bound by the moral law, itself assumes morality's supremacy and cannot therefore be used to establish it.

I think Kant was right to give up the strategy of the *Groundwork* and to argue that consciousness of autonomy of the will involves an awareness of being bound by and able to act on a reason of a distinctive kind. Perhaps we can now glimpse why I claim that the requisite kind of reason must be second-personal. First, as I mentioned in the last chapter, any second-personal address or acknowledgment commits us to the equal

11. This is not far from the picture Dennis Stampe provides in "The Authority of Desire" (1987).

12. As I argue in Chapter 9, I differ here with writers like Korsgaard and Wood who attempt to provide a sound reconstruction of the Formula of Humanity, autonomy, and related concepts from presuppositions of practical reasoning alone (Korsgaard 1996b, 1996e, 1996f; Wood 1999). As I point out in more detail later, although Korsgaard shows a keen appreciation of the role of reciprocity and mutual accountability for a Kantian framework (Korsgaard 1996a, 1996d: 301), she also believes that autonomy and the Categorical Imperative in its various formulations are transcendental presuppositions of the practical standpoint. I believe this to be mistaken. In my view, there is no way of deriving these ideas outside of the second-person standpoint and within a comprehensive theory of practical reason that is enriched by it.

dignity of persons, conceived as equal second-personal authority, and to the idea that addresser and addressee alike are capable of acting on reasons that are grounded in this authority and so are irreducible to the value of any outcome or state (hence to any property of any object of desire). Second-personal address thus commits us to the idea that agents capable of entering into relations of mutual accountability must have within this capacity (second-personal competence) a second-personal authority that is a source of reasons and norms independently of any features of desired (or desirable) outcomes or states along with the ability to act on these norms and reasons. When we acknowledge the summons of another free and rational agent, we confront, in effect, the "fact of reason." We presuppose the equal dignity of rational beings and our ability to act on a "law" or reason—a second-personal reason grounded in this dignity—that derives not from the value of any state of affairs or outcome that might be the object of a desire, but, ultimately, from what it is to be one free and rational person interacting with others.

Second, consider briefly how the "fact of reason" functions within Kant's own argument in the second *Critique*. Kant asks us to imagine someone whose prince demands that he give false witness against an honorable man on pain of death (1996a: 30). Kant notes that no one can say for sure what he would do in such a situation, but Kant nonetheless insists that anyone in the situation would have to admit that he could refuse the prince's request, since he would judge that he should do so. Because we all already implicitly acknowledge the authority of the moral law, we are forced to conclude that we have the capacity to act on it. We cannot coherently think that it is impossible to do something and still think, from the practical standpoint, that it is something we should do. If we can't do something, then the practical question is what else to do in light of that fact.

Obviously, if acknowledging the authority of moral obligation is what requires us to assume we can act on a law that binds us independently of our desires (including for survival), then we cannot assume autonomy in an argument for the authority of moral obligation. But as I've said, Kant is no longer interested in that strategy. Nonetheless, Kant clearly takes this example as evidence, not just that anyone must admit that he could comply with this moral obligation (in accepting it), but that he can comply with the Categorical Imperative in general, since Kant presents a formulation of the CI ("So act that the maxim of your will could always hold at the same time as a principle in a giving of universal law") just after the passage we have been discussing (1996a: 30).[13] And that, after all, is what would be necessary for him to have established in order to show that we must accept autonomy of the will—that we are bound by a *formal* principle of the will. But why should that be? All we know so far is that we can act on a principle of right we accept, irrespectively of our desires for any outcome. It is consistent with this that, as deontological intuitionists like Richard Price (1974) and W. D. Ross (1930) believed, this is explainable by an independent fact of right rather than by anything like autonomy of the will. Why suppose there must be some formal principle of the will like the CI that stands behind our moral obligations?

Suppose we were to consider, however, not just that anyone in the situation Kant describes ought to reject the prince's demand, but also that he would be morally responsible for doing so. In the second-personal address of holding him responsible, we would have to assume that he had within him a source of motivation to do as he was morally obligated. We cannot intelligibly hold someone to a demand as a moral agent without supposing that he could hold himself to that same demand by acting on the relevant second-personal reasons. And if we think that any rational person in that situation would be thus answerable, we are committed to thinking that what makes a rational person subject to moral obligation must itself include a source of motivation to do as he is morally obligated. The need for this presupposition comes not from supposing there to be normative reasons for someone to do something, regardless of their priority or weight but rather from the distinctively second-personal reasons that are involved in moral obligation. It comes from what Gary Watson calls "constraints of moral address" (1987: 263, 264). It follows, I argue, that the second-personal competence that makes us subject to moral obligation must include a source of the (second-personal) reasons in which moral obligation consists, along with the capacity to act on these reasons. In presupposing this, we effectively presuppose autonomy of the will. The capacity of will that make us apt to be held responsible, second-personal competence, is a "law to itself," since it is the basis of second-personal authority.

13. Which Kant there calls the "Fundamental Law of Pure Practical Reason" (1996a: 30).

A Second-Personal Interpretation of the CI

What then does second-personal competence consist in? Well, it must consist in something like the capacity to make demands of oneself from a second-person standpoint: in being able to choose to do something only if it is consistent with demands one (or anyone) would make of anyone (hence that one would make of oneself) from a standpoint we can share as mutually accountable persons. But that is just a second-personal version of the CI. In fact, the most natural way of interpreting the CI and kindred moral principles like the Golden Rule is second-personally, in terms of demands that one (anyone) would sensibly make of all from the shared standpoint of a member of the moral community. What matters for moral obligation is not what one would like or prefer all people do, but what one would expect of others, what demands one could endorse anyone's being able to hold others to as members of a community of mutually accountable equals. What forces an assumption of autonomy of the will, therefore, is the second-personal aspect of moral obligation, that is, that what is morally obligatory is what we are responsible to one another for doing.

But isn't acting on demands that others can make of one heteronomy rather than autonomy, being governed by them rather than by oneself? Or, to put it another way, how could autonomy consist in a law that comes from nothing outside of the will itself if it is realized in second-personal interaction? The response to this objection is that when one decides to reject the prince's demand because this is what the moral community authoritatively demands, the second-personal perspective of a member of the moral community is as much one's own as it is anyone else's. One demands the conduct of oneself from a point of view one shares as a free and rational person.

A Foundation for Contractualism

An account of the second-person standpoint along the lines that I develop in this book provides the most natural way of motivating the moral theory known as "contractualism." Contractualists sees morality as most fundamentally concerned with "how *persons are to relate to one another*," to quote one insightful commentator (Kumar 1999: 284).[14] Or as Scanlon puts it, "The contractualist ideal ... is meant to characterize" a specific "relation" with others: "mutual recognition" (1998: 162). Moral principles have a distinctive *role* on a contractualist view: they mediate mutual respect.[15] They don't just tell us what actions we should or must perform; they mediate a fundamental interpersonal *relation:* mutual respect between mutually accountable persons.[16] These are all irreducibly second-personal matters.

For Scanlon, the problem of accounting for morality's authority is that of explaining "the *priority* of right and wrong over other values" or accounting for their special "importance" (1998: 148, 149). In the paper in which he originally formulated the position, Scanlon (1982) maintained that the "motivational basis" of contractualist morality is a desire to act in a way that can be justified to others. In *What We Owe to Each Other,* however, Scanlon departs from his prior view and claims that contractualism's basis is the "value" and "appeal" of standing to others in the relation of mutual recognition, both in itself and as an ineliminable aspect of other valuable relations such as friendship (1998: 158–168).

This is obviously an attractive idea, but like Mill's attempt to explain the bindingness of morality in the appeal of "unity with our fellow creatures," to which Scanlon in fact compares it, it is hard to see how it can adequately account for the nonoptional character of moral obligation (Mill 1998: ch. 3). This is another instance of Strawson's Point; such an argument seems to provide a reason of the wrong kind. By contrast, the approach I sketch promises to explain how the standing to make claims and demands on one another as free and rational persons is something to which we are jointly committed whenever we take up the second-person stance more generally rather than simply being an ineliminable aspect of interpersonal relations we find appealing.

A central issue in the debate between consequentialist theories of right and deontological theories such as contractualism has been whether a

14. Compare Korsgaard's remark that, on a Kantian view, "the subject matter of morality is ... how we should relate to one another" (1996d: 275). See also Schapiro 2001 and 2003b.

15. As Rahul Kumar says, they provide a "basis for a shared understanding of the kind of consideration ... persons may legitimately expect of one another, as a matter of mutual respect for one another as persons" (1999: 284).

16. Compare Elizabeth Anderson's (1999) relational theory of equality.

satisfying philosophical rationale can be provided for agent-relative restrictions ("deontological constraints") (Nagel 1986; Scheffler 1982). Consequentialists since Moore have argued that if, for example, betraying or causing harm to others is to be avoided, then that must be because it is a bad thing.[17] And if it is bad, then it is equally bad regardless of the perpetrator. So if, for example, an agent could do something that would amount to her betraying another person but it would also prevent an exactly similar betrayal involving two other people, say because another would-be betrayer would be sufficiently shocked at seeing the first agent's betrayal that she would give up her treacherous plans, then these two outcomes should cancel each other out from the moral point of view. The fact that one betrayal would be by the agent herself should make no intrinsic difference to what there is reason for the agent to do. There will end up being a net gain of one betrayal in the world whatever she does.

It is well known that, in addition to being part of moral common sense, agent-relative constraints can be derived within contractualism or, for that matter, within indirect consequentialist approaches such as rule utilitarianism.[18] The problem has remained of how to give any of these derivations a deeper philosophical rationale that itself confirms rather than undermines the case for agent-relative constraints. The problem with indirect consequentialism, for example, is that even if we think there are (agent-neutral) consequentialist reasons to call actions that violate common sense agent-relative moral constraints "wrong," or to want people (ourselves included) to think them wrong, it is not obvious how a consequentialist can herself sensibly think (simultaneously with accepting the deeper agent-neutralist reasons) that agents really should avoid performing such actions, when doing so would advance the overall agent-neutral value.

If a foundation for contractualism can be found in commitments within the second-person standpoint, this can provide, I believe, the kind

17. For some of the history of this debate and a different proposal about how to justify agent-relative constraints, see Darwall 1986a.

18. See, for example, Kumar 1999. For rule utilitarianism, see Brandt 1979; Hooker 2000; Johnson 1991; Parfit 1984. For a (seemingly) dissenting view, see Brand-Ballard 2004. I say "seemingly" because Brand-Ballard's arguments put pressure on the claim that the agent-relative deontological constraints of the strength of common sense can be derived within contractualism, although not, perhaps, on the claim that agent-relative constraints of some sort might be.

of rationale for agent-relative restrictions that is needed. It would vindicate reasons that are in their nature relational, that concern, not how it would be good for the world to be anyway, or even what kinds of acts are called for by their intrinsic nature, but how we are to relate to one another owing to claims and demands that we cannot avoid assuming we have the authority to address to each other as one free and rational person among others. It would provide the right kind of reason.

— 3 —

The Second-Person Stance and
Second-Personal Reasons

When one says You, the I of the . . . I-You is said, too. Whoever
says You does not have something for his object . . . he stands
in relation. Relation is reciprocity. My You acts on me as I act
on it.

—MARTIN BUBER, *I AND THOU*

The task of this chapter will be to clarify the distinctive form of second-
personal engagement that will be our main concern in this book: the
addressing of second-personal reasons. There are many kinds of interaction, including many involving mutual awareness, that do not involve
the reciprocal recognition that exists when one person gives another a
reason to do something. Even within the set of reason-givings, for our
purposes we sharpen our focus further in two ways. First, many such
interactions also involve nonrational influence—intimidation, seduction,
and so on. We are concerned solely with the pure giving of reasons,
abstracting from nonrational factors (or with interactions *qua* second-
personal address). Second, there are reason-givings where the reasons are
not themselves second-personal. Our focus is on the (second-personal)
address of second-personal reasons.

Something that looks like reciprocal recognition occurs also in nonrational settings. When two dogs lock gazes, for example, and eye each
other with caution, eagerness, or hostility, there is certainly a form of
mutual awareness, even if we don't suppose that dogs have the rich array
of higher-order attitudes that typically accompany mutual human awareness.[1] But awareness of this kind is not yet second-personal in our sense.

---

1. For example, one dog may eye another eagerly and begin to play to induce mimicking
play in the other. But even if we can call such behavior intentional, it wouldn't amount

It need involve no form of address, much less address of the other as a person. Two prize fighters, peering into each other's eyes for clues about the other's movements, are not really addressing each other (so far anyway). Their thought and experience involve a combination of first- and third-person perspectives that do not yet amount to a second-person stance, even when taken together. Each watches the other watching him. Neither relates to the other as a "you" to whom the first is a "you" in return. In Martin Buber's terms, the "I" of each is an "I-It" rather than an "I-You" (1970: 55).

Suppose, however, that one shoots a look of disdain at the other. This still may not be second-personal in any respect; it need not express disdain to the other. A look that shows (or even that seeks to show) disdain may not communicate it or even seek to. (Compare throwing a ball at someone, even throwing a ball at someone who is watching you throw it at her, with throwing a ball to her.) And even when someone communicates disdain, the attitude he communicates is not itself second-personal; it expresses no second-personal reason. Unlike indignation, resentment, and other Strawsonian "reactive attitudes," disdain lodges no claim or demand that essentially includes an RSVP.[2] If a fighter says, "You ain't got nothin'" in response to a direct hit, he may be presupposing authority on the question of his opponents' pugilistic resources, or on the evaluative question of whether the opponent is appropriately disdained as an inferior fighter, or on various epistemic issues related to these, but he assumes thereby no authority to claim or demand anything of his opponent's will or actions.[3]

---

to a second-personally addressed invitation in the sense of this book. For discussion that stimulated this example, I am indebted to Will Darwall.

2. For relevant discussion, see Chapters 4 and 6. Another good example of a reaction that is unlike reactive attitudes in having no second-personal component is disgust (which involves the desire not to engage, but to distance, disgorge, expel, etc.) On disgust, see Miller 1997.

3. This insult does, of course, issue a kind of challenge to his opponent to respond. But the insulter need not claim or demand his opponent's response. There seem to be two separable aspects of such a challenge. One is an implicit claim of fact (and hence a claim on his opponent's beliefs and theoretical reasoning, if that doesn't seem too ludicrous in the context), namely, that he will win and there is nothing that his opponent can do about it (or do about his insult). The second is a challenge to his opponent's honor (in the conventional sense that outsiders or alienated insiders may reject and that can come apart from his moral dignity; on this distinction, see Chapter 6). This latter sense does have a

Imagine now that one boxer says or expresses something to the other that does make such a claim. Suppose it is Muhammad Ali taunting Floyd Patterson in their 1965 heavyweight title fight with the relentlessly demanding question, "What's my name? What's my name?" This now is second-personal in the sense I have in mind. It is a demand to answer with the "You tell me ..." understood. Questions can sensibly be addressed only to beings with the capacity and standing for creditable response.[4] And this question evidently presupposes, not just the normative standing to ask, or even to demand an answer to, questions in general, or even to this question in particular, but also the authority to demand recognition by the name that Ali gave himself. (Patterson, you may recall, insisted on calling Ali "Cassius Clay" even though Ali had changed his name on converting to Islam.) This puts the case squarely within the territory with which we are concerned. Of course, Ali's was not a pure case of second-personal address. His purpose was also evidently instrumental, to dispirit and humiliate Patterson, to toy with and break him. But even here, to the extent that Ali regarded Patterson's merciless beating as deserved, he may have seen what he was doing in second-personal terms. He may have thought he was executing justice, person-to-person, exacting recognition of himself as a person.

Or consider the Vicar of Wakefield's remark that his daughters "had early learnt the lesson of looking presumption out of countenance" (Goldsmith 1901: 52). Is his statement second-personal in our sense, or not? It depends. If "looking presumption out of countenance" means looking at would-be suitors in ways that seek simply to cause discouragement or deflation of hopes for greater familiarity, then nothing second-personal need be going on at all. And even if the looking is a form of address, say to express disdain, then no claim or demand may be expressed, except, again, on the question of what to believe about the daughters' availability and attitude or on how noble or base it would be to presume anything about them. On the other hand, if their looks ad-

---

clear second-personal dimension, but even here there seems no implicit claim or demand on the other's conduct. Finally, consensual participation in the fight does have a second-personal aspect. Each invites his opponent's response (even preemptive) and waives any rights against assault he might ordinarily have (and, in contemporary professional boxing anyway, both apparently waive any rights against insult as well).

4. Of course, an assertion to an opponent that his punches are "nothin'" also presupposes the opponent's competence to understand the remark, and so on.

dress, as it were, the charge of presumptuousness, then they do make a claim or demand on the suitors' will or conduct. They invite, request, or demand that the suitors back off. And, if so, they presuppose the authority to address the suitors in this way, and signify as well, as from the standpoint of the moral community, that the suitors had no authority to address them as they had.[5]

Less dramatic and literary instances of second-personal address abound. Christine Korsgaard gives an example of a student who appears at the office door and asks if one is free to talk (1996e: 141).[6] The student may presume no claim on one's time beyond that involved in considering her request. But she does presuppose that, as well as whatever else one presupposes when addressing a request or a question. She addresses herself to you as an independent person, in this case, as the person to whom she stands in a certain pedagogical relation. And she presupposes that you and she can take all this for granted in common.

5. Consider the difference between a disdainful rolling of the eyes and a look that expresses resentment or indignation ("looking daggers"). The latter clearly addresses its object (with an RSVP) in a way that the former does not. A vivid recent example is the famous "staredown" the Italian ice dancer, Barbara Fusar Poli, gave her partner of twelve years, Maurizio Margaglio, after he dropped her during the completion of their "original dance" in the Ice Dancing competition at the 2006 Winter Olympics in Torino, Italy. According to one account, "When the music stopped, the two stood facing each other for nearly a minute at center ice, Fusar Poli steaming as her eyes burned through Margaglio" (Juliet Macur, "After Staredown, a Détente for an Italian Pair," New York Times, February 21, 2006). Or as the caption under a photograph of the "staredown" in the Internet edition of the San Diego Union-Tribune had it: "Barbara Fusar Poli to partner Maurizio Margaglio: Look me in the eye and tell how you dropped me" (http://www.signonsandiego.com/sports/olympics/20060220-9999-lz1x20falls.html). Suppose, however, that Fusar Poli had disdainfully rolled her eyes after the fall and skated off in disgust. Any expressive address in that case would most likely have been to the cognoscenti off-stage. Things went better the next night, as Macur vividly describes: "They . . . performed cleanly with emotion and resolve, as the crowd hushed. . . . And when their program was done, Fusar Poli fell to her knees. Margaglio, looking stronger, stood over her, his hands on her hips. When she rose, they fell into an embrace. They hugged, and he lifted her and twirled her around. She kissed him on the cheek. He kissed her, again and again. In the end, they finished eighth, but they were talking again. The crowd, now watching the most public kiss-and-make-up at the Olympics, began chanting, 'Italia!' "

6. As I mentioned before, this is only one of several places where, as I shall indicate, Korsgaard shows a keen awareness of second-personal aspects of moral thought and interaction. Where Korsgaard and I may differ is over how fundamental a role the second-person standpoint has in explicating the authority of moral obligation. This will become clearer in Chapters 9 and 10.

There are important differences between these forms of address and ways that one might regard, say, one's pet cat. There can certainly be trappings of second-personality in the latter. One speaks and expresses emotions to and not simply at one's cat. Nonetheless, although we of course discipline them, we don't press claims against or hold our pets accountable in the same way we do with one another. So we need not presuppose nor reciprocally acknowledge that we (and they) have the competence needed to make this appropriate, for example, recognizing that we each have independent perspectives that we can each enter into.[7] Granted, when I look into my cat's eyes, I can't get over the feeling that he is looking also into mine in some personal way or shake the hope that he is seeing me in some way other than "the guy who feeds or pets me." But I find it utterly impossible to sustain the thought that he can imaginatively enter into my point of view or acknowledge me as a being with an independent perspective.[8] But this is precisely what Ali's, the Vicar's daughters', and the student's addresses presuppose.

Empathy and Adam Smith on Exchange

This brings out the centrality of *empathy* to the second-person standpoint. We consider this in greater detail in Chapter 7, but it will be helpful to have some of the main elements before us now. When I see another as a "you," I see her as having the same relation reciprocally to me. I relate to her as relating reciprocally to me. What does this involve? Partly, it involves a rich set of higher-order attitudes: I am aware of her awareness of me, aware of her awareness of my awareness of her, aware of her awareness of my awareness of her awareness of me, and so on.[9] Still, this can't be all there is to second-personal engagement since, as we have

7. It is consistent with this that our treatment of animals would be much better for all concerned if it involved much more mutual responsibility than is usual. On this, see Vicki Hearne's fascinating *Adam's Task: Calling Animals By Name* (1986). I am indebted here to Elizabeth Anderson.

8. Perhaps some indirect evidence is the following. People who undergo stress (in timed mental arithmetic tests and extended immersion of a hand in cold water) exhibit lower pulse rates and systolic and diastolic blood pressure when in the presence of their pets than in the presence of their spouses. Might this be partly due to the fact that we are less likely to feel judged by other animals? See Allen, Blascovich, and Mendes 2001. Of course, I need take no view on whether there are other species capable of taking the second-person standpoint.

9. I have been helped here by Vranas 2001.

seen, mutual awareness that is not second-personal can have a similar structure. All of the awarenesses, at whatever level, might be non-second-personal, and if they are, they will not amount to second-personal awareness, no matter how high we pile them. The key difference is that she and I must be mutually aware of our second-personal *relating*. We must have a second-personal perspective on one another. I must be able to see her as responding (more or less rationally) to my address, which she also regards as an intelligible response or address to her.

This is what brings our respective perspectives into the interaction and requires that we be able to take each other's up. I must be able to see the other's response to my address as more or less rational from her point of view. I must be able to see my address through her eyes. Similarly, for her to make sense of my address, she has to see it as something that makes sense from my perspective. To see this vividly, consider a case where address misfires. "Do you have the time?" one person asks. "I'm sorry," the other replies; "I'm doing something right now." How does the first interpret this reply? She knows without recalling, let us suppose, what she meant: "What time is it?" But to figure out what the other thought she meant, she needs to remember what she said and consider how the other might have interpreted that from his point of view. As she recalls her words—not as if saying them, but from the perspective of her hearer—it occurs to her what her interlocutor must have taken her to mean: "Do you have time now to do something with or for me now (that would take longer than, say, telling the time)?"[10]

Second-personality thus requires empathy or the capacity to put oneself in another's shoes. Imaginative projection into another's standpoint or "simulation," as it is sometimes called, is not the only thing that 'empathy' can refer to.[11] And things get further confused by the fact that writers frequently use 'sympathy' to refer to a variety of phenomena that include

10. Here is an even more striking example. Recently, while running a road race, I saw someone wearing an Air Force Academy sweatshirt who was cheering on the runners. Recalling that I had gone to bed too early the night before to find out the score of a football game I was interested in between the Air Force Academy and Notre Dame, I called out as I ran past: "Who won?" Without missing a beat, he replied: "Notre Dame." Had he not put himself into my perspective, my interlocutor's most natural interpretation would have been: "Who won the race?" (The faster runners had already finished.)

11. For some interesting papers on the relevance of simulation in the philosophy of mind, see Davies and Stone 1995; Goldman 1989, 1992; Gordon 1986, 1992.

simulation as well as other forms of empathy (such as emotional contagion and shared feelings).[12] I prefer to use 'sympathy' for feelings of concern for others that are felt, not entirely as from their point of view, but
as from a third-person perspective of one who cares for them, and to use
'empathy' for feelings that either imaginatively enter into the other's
standpoint or result from his feelings by contagion.[13] Second-personal
interaction requires empathy in the sense of simulation or imaginative
projection into the other's point of view (while, it should be noted, re-
taining a sense of one's own independent perspective).[14]

A number of philosophers have argued that empathy (simulation) is
involved quite generally in attributing mental states to others (Goldman
1989, 1992; Gordon 1986, 1992).[15] There seems to be impressive experimental evidence for this hypothesis. In one experiment, Amos Tversky
presented subjects with the following story:

> Mr. Crane and Mr. Tees were scheduled to leave the airport on different
> flights, at the same time. They traveled from town in the same limou-
> sine, were caught in a traffic jam, and arrived at the airport 30 minutes
> after the scheduled departure time of their flights. Mr. Crane is told
> that his flight left on time. Mr. Tees is told that his was delayed, and
> just left five minutes ago. Who is more upset? (Kahneman and Tversky
> 1982)

If you are like 96 percent of Tversky's subjects, you will say more or less
instantly that Mr. Tees is more upset than Mr. Crane. How did you
decide? Alvin Goldman (1989) argues that it is unlikely that we all possess
common-sense theories that overlap on a generalization that we apply to
the instant case or that we all think consciously about how we ourselves
have felt in the past and infer by analogy. It seems far likelier that you
simply unconsciously projected into Tees' and Crane's respective situations and imaginatively simulated feelings "in their shoes." If this is right,
it will turn out that the ability (of at least one important kind) to attribute

12. Adam Smith (1982b) and David Hume (1978), for example, use 'sympathy' primarily to refer to simulation (or fellow feeling resulting from simulation) and emotional
contagion, respectively.

13. I discuss different forms of empathy and sympathy in Darwall 1998.

14. For the distinctive importance of this last element, along with an insightful discussion of the moral significance of empathy more generally, see Deigh 1995.

15. See also the articles in Kögler and Stueber 2000.

beliefs and feelings to others is intimately bound up with the capacity to engage one another second-personally.

Adam Smith, whose *Theory of Moral Sentiments* is one of the most comprehensive and subtle accounts of empathy's role in human thought and practice, broadly agrees with the simulationist claim. The only way to grasp "what other men feel," Smith says, is by "conceiving what we ourselves should feel in the like situation. . . . Though our brother is upon the rack, as long as we ourselves are at our ease, our senses will never inform us of what he suffers" (1982b: 9). It is no coincidence that Smith combines his insight into empathy's ubiquity with a keen appreciation of profoundly second-personal aspects of certain distinctive moral phenomena—specifically, of justice, mutual accountability, respect, and dignity—as demonstrated at various points later in this book.[16] It is not far wrong, indeed, to think of Smith as one of first philosophers of the "second person," if not the very first.

The *Wealth of Nations*, for example, virtually begins with a discussion of the human capacity for the distinctive form of second-personal interaction that Smith calls "exchange" and its relation to mutual respect.[17] When other animals need help, Smith says, they have no other "means of persuasion but to gain the favour of those whose service [they] require[e]. . . . A puppy fawns upon its dam, and a spaniel endeavours by a thousand attractions to engage the attention of its master" (1976: 25). Currying sympathy and favor requires no capacity for second-personal address or for empathy. These are non-second-personal responses that can be gauged and elicited third-personally. Recall our initial example of getting someone to feel sympathy for you and your pained feet. The other's sympathetic concern need not respond to anything expressed from

16. Especially in Chapter 7. Emma Rothschild has pointed out to me many other examples of the importance of recognition in Smith. The "purpose of all the toil and bustle of this world," Smith writes, is "to be observed, to be attended to, to be taken notice of" (1982b: 50). The dismal lot of the poor man is that he "goes out and comes in unheeded" and is "out of sight of mankind" and "observed and attended to by nobody" (Smith 1976: 795). Rothschild notes that Smith uses the phrase "other people" eighty-four times in the *Theory of Moral Sentiments*. According to the InteLex database of philosophical texts (http://www.nlx.com) it appears forty-three times in *Wealth of Nations*, although no more than five times in, for example, Hume's *Treatise, Enquiries, Dialogues,* and *Essays* combined.

17. For a reading of Smith that stresses this theme, see Fleischacker 2004a, 2004b; Rothschild 2001.

you, much less to any address that invites the other to give you standing in a second-personal relation.[18]

Of course, we humans frequently do rely on one another's sympathy. Often, this is just fine, even desirable. "But man has almost constant occasion for the help of his brethren, and it is in vain for him to expect it from their benevolence only" (Smith 1976: 25). Given the vagaries of human life, we often cannot expect others to care for us in this way. Moreover, attempting to gain others' favor can expose us to risks of subservience. By "servile and fawning attention," we may put ourselves at others' mercy and be vulnerable to their condescension if not domination.[19] Happily, Smith believes, nature has given human beings a more dignified alternative: "the general disposition to truck, barter, and exchange" (25). Free exchange, in Smith's view, involves a second-personal address that presupposes a form of mutual respect.

We are familiar with the Smithian idea that in a society with a well-functioning economy, rich and poor alike meet their needs and wants through formal and informal markets that are sites for mutually advantageous exchanges. "It is not from the benevolence of the butcher, the brewer, or the baker, that we expect our dinner, but from their regard to their own interest" (Smith 1976: 25). But although its operative motive is self-interest, exchange is impossible without a presupposed second-personal normative infrastructure. Why are other animals incapable of exchange? "Nobody," he says, "ever saw a dog make a fair and deliberate exchange of one bone for another with another dog. Nobody ever saw one animal by its gestures and natural cries signify to another, this is mine, that yours; I am willing to give this for that" (25). Smith evidently thinks of exchange as an interaction in which both parties are committed to various normative presuppositions, for example, that the exchange is made by free mutual consent, that neither will simply take what the other has, and so on. Both parties must presume that the other is dealing fairly, not in the sense that what is offered is of fair value (*caveat emptor*—self-

---

18. Again, this is a theme of Darwall 2002b.

19. It is an important point that dominance and submission have something of a second-personal look and feel, but don't presuppose any authority *de jure*. They don't even presuppose authority *de facto*. That would require the address to present itself as having authority *de jure*, whether it actually had it or not, and dominance doesn't require that. It is more like the position of a prize fighter who says, "What you gonna do about it?"

interest and bargaining regulate that), but that each is dealing honestly, that the offered goods will actually be delivered, that each is free to refuse the deal and walk away without coercion, that neither will attempt to reacquire through coercion what he freely trades away, and so on.

Exchange thus involves a reciprocal acknowledgment of norms that govern both parties and presupposes that both parties are mutually accountable, having an equal authority to complain, to resist coercion, and so on. To engage in exchange at all, therefore, one must be capable of the requisite reciprocal recognition, and this requires empathy. To gauge whether the other is bargaining in good faith, each must attempt to determine: whether the other is attempting to determine whether one is bargaining honestly, whether the other is attempting to determine whether one is attempting to determine whether the other is bargaining honestly, and so on. All this requires that both be able to put themselves imaginatively into the other's standpoint and compare the responses that one thinks reasonable from that perspective with the other's actual responses, as one perceives them third-personally.[20] So what is required is not merely empathy, but also, as we shall see, regulation of both parties by claims, demands, and norms that make sense from a second-person standpoint.[21]

20. It is worth pointing out that Smith's historical account of the institution of property and its civil protection is in no tension with thinking that exchange and property presuppose a second-personal infrastructure. Although you and I must presuppose reciprocal standing intelligibly even to negotiate a deal, we still face problems of determinate mutual assurance and expectations that only established formal practices and institutions can solve. In Chapter 8, we consider the fundamental difference between this idea and Hume's contention that just practices of property and promise can arise simply strategically, through mutually advantageous conventions. And in Chapter 7, we consider the second-personal human psychic mechanisms that make such cooperation possible. For Smith's views on the historical development of property institutions, see Smith 1976: 715 and 1982b. I am indebted here to discussion with Charles Griswold.

21. In "Of the External Senses," Smith connects empathy to respect even in our interactions with other animals: "When he lays his hand upon the body either of another man, or of any other animal, though he knows, or at least may know, that they feel the pressure of his hand as much as he feels that of their body: Yet as this feeling is altogether external to him, he frequently gives no attention to it, and at no time takes any further concern in it than he is obliged to do by that fellow–feeling which Nature has, for the wisest purposes, implanted in man, not only towards all other men, but (though no doubt in a much weaker degree) towards all other animals. Having destined him to be the governing animal in this little world, it seems to have been her benevolent intention to inspire him with

Goading versus Guiding

We return to the relation between empathy and second-personal thought and discourse in Chapter 7. We turn now to the difference between rational and non-rational forms of interpersonal influence. As we are defining it, second-personal address is reason-giving in its nature (and is distinguished further by the distinctive kind of reason it seeks to give). To focus properly on second-personal reason-giving, then, we must keep in mind W. D. Falk's distinction between "goading" and "guiding" (1953).[22] Our task is complicated by the fact that even the pure address of second-personal reasons has, as I have already suggested, a directive element that is lacking in pure advice. As I understand it, second-personal address makes a claim on the addressee's will (and not, like advice, only on her beliefs about what there is reason for her to do). It presumes to tell another person, not just what to do in the way advice does, but also, in some way or to some extent, to do it. Nevertheless, it is a central theme of this book (and a reflection of Fichte's and Pufendorf's Points) that such directive claims and demands differ fundamentally from coercion and other goadings. Second-personal address seeks to direct a person through her own free choice and in a way that recognizes her status as a free and rational agent.

It is relatively easy to distinguish between rational and nonrational influence at the extremes. A moral treatise addressed to the public at large that aims dispassionately to convince its readers of the justice of its cause by rational argument is evidently trying to guide rather than goad.[23] A bully whose threatening looks put down challenges clearly goads rather than guides. But there are many cases in between that are not so clear. What about an offer that is unwelcome precisely because both parties know that the offeree will be unable to decline against his better judgment? Even if offers generally guide, this one might reasonably be regarded as goading. The felicity conditions for offers include that the of-

---

some degree of respect, even for the meanest and weakest of his subjects" (1995). I am indebted for this reference to Eric Schliesser.

22. Falk wrote this as a response to emotivist and prescriptivist metaethical theories, which he thought were insufficiently insensitive to the distinction, assimilating guiding too much to goading.

23. This is so even if it addresses second-personal demands. Cf. Kant on the public use of reason in "What Is Enlightenment?" in Kant 1996f: 17–22.

feree is free to decline, in the sense that it is presupposed by both parties that he may and can do so. An offer made because the offeree cannot but accept has the superficial appearance of a guiding but the "deep structure" of a goading.

Suppose, however, that the offer is not unwelcome, but that the offerer attempts to induce acceptance by forms of influence that are only incidentally related to reasons for accepting. Salespeople learn early on, for instance, that insinuating a personal relationship that operates under the radar of mutual awareness is usually a more effective strategy than dwelling on features. Charming, cajoling, humoring, dazzling, and intimidating all aim to persuade nonrationally, rather than (primarily, anyway) to give reasons. That doesn't mean that guiding must consist in simply listing bloodless facts. There are reasons—for example, about what it is like to undergo certain experiences—that we can only appreciate by forms of imaginative engagement that alter our usual ways of seeing things, for example, as by a powerful film or novel, or, as Hume put it, "by an eloquent recital of the case" (1985a: 230).

Coercion by threat is generally thought to goad, but it is worth pausing to consider why this should be so. We must distinguish, first, between "rational" coercion and literal force or intimidation. The latter seek to circumvent or undermine rational processes in a way that rational coercion does not. When someone threatens in, as it were, an unthreatening way, by saying something like, "I feel bound to tell you that if you don't do A, then evils X, Y, and Z will occur," she may correctly suppose that this gives the coerced agent a genuine reason, which the agent may appreciate and act on. So why don't threats guide rather than goad? Obviously, if someone else were simply to inform the agent of the threat, which he honestly believed to be a reason to acquiesce, this would be guiding rather than goading. Why does it become goading when the threat is voiced, even "unthreateningly," by the threatener?

When someone simply informs another of an evil that will befall him if he does something, even if it is the person herself who will cause the evil, the reason given is not distinctively second-personal. It need not be capable of being addressed to exist nor need it be addressed for someone to come to have it. I may arrange for someone to learn of my intention to do X, Y, and Z should he not do A in ways that involve no form of address whatsoever (perhaps I get him to read it in my diary).

Of course, a threat doesn't simply inform. Perhaps the reason why threats goad is that they create a reason in the sense that whether the threat is given or carried out is itself up to the threatener. True enough, but there are many cases where one person creates a reason in giving it to another that do not thereby become goadings rather than guidings. When you order the Eggs Benedict, you give the waiter a reason for bringing it to you that didn't exist prior to your request. But here you are guiding, not goading. The difference is that in this case you and the waiter both accept the background authority relations that give you standing to order and thereby create reasons for him to act in this way. Nothing like this holds with pure threats, although it does, of course, with what are sometimes called "threats" that are backed by mutually accepted law, custom, or morality. If a teacher "threatens" to give a pop quiz unless her students read their assignments more assiduously, and all agree that this is fully within her authority, then she doesn't simply goad her students—she gives them a further reason to study. What she does is not really a threat in the coercing or goading sense; she puts them on notice of a sanction that it is within her authority to apply.

What makes coercion by "rational" threats goading rather than guiding, in my view, is that it purports to create reasons in something like the way that legitimate claims or demands do, that is, second-personally, but without the appropriate normative backing for the threatened "sanctions," which consequently provide only the superficial appearance of an accountability relation. It is as if they attempt to substitute the power involved in a credible threat for the notice of an authorized sanction that would turn their goading into a second-personal guiding. Indeed, it is not unusual for threats or other forms of coercion or manipulation to be accompanied by self-indulging rationalizing fantasies of justified authority. Tyrants and batterers frequently comfort themselves by imagining the righteousness of their cause. Or they may flip back and forth between a self-serving rationalization for their "authority" and threats pure and simple.[24]

Suppose, however, that someone has the authority to apply some sanction. Suppose, to return to our earlier example, that you have the authority to lift, firmly but gently, someone else's foot from on top of yours if he refuses to remove it voluntarily. Suppose you inform him of this, putting him on notice that, if he doesn't move his foot, then you will

24. See the discussion of Stalin in Chapter 6.

move it for him. If you have this authority, then however directive your demand, this threatening notice will not amount to coercion. It would, however, be coercion if you were to threaten to move his foot firmly but gently from, say, your favorite part of the public sidewalk, since you have no authority to demand that he do that. In my view, the very distinction between coercion and notification of, as Pufendorf put it, "an evil" that "falls upon [one] justly" can only be made within the circle of second-personal concepts and, ultimately, from a second-person standpoint (Pufendorf 1934: 91).[25]

Speech Acts and Felicity Conditions

In the next section we briefly consider second-personal theoretical reasoning—the addressing of reasons for belief—in order to prepare the way for some important contrasts that are necessary to understand the distinctive character of second-personal practical reasons. Before that, however, it is useful to have before us more explicitly the Austinian framework for analyzing speech acts that we have implicitly been assuming. This is especially relevant to understanding second-personal practical reasons. Nonetheless, it becomes clear in the next section that it is necessary also if we are to grasp how we can address reasons for belief, as well as practical reasons that are not peculiarly second-personal.

Austin (1975) was concerned with how the conventional character of language makes it possible for people to perform a wide variety of "speech acts" in uttering a sentence—to name a ship, take a spouse, issue a warning, place a bet, and so on. Austin analyzes speech acts along three dimensions: (a) the locutionary (semantic content of the utterance), (b) the illocutionary (what the agent does in uttering a sentence), and (c) the perlocutionary (what further effects uttering a sentence brings about). Thus, an uttering of "There is a lion loose in the area" may simultaneously express a semantic content concerning the presence of *Panthera leo* (locutionary), constitute a warning (illocutionary), and save the lives of those who hear it (perlocutionary).

Illocutionary acts invariably involve an element of address, even if only to an audience at large, as can be brought out by surveying Austin's categories. Austin lists the following kinds: "verdictives" (judicial verdicts and other official findings), "exercitives" (other exercisings of authority,

---

25. See also Nozick 1969.

such as voting or claiming), "commissives" (which commit the speaker, like a promise or contract), "behabitives" (second-personal reactions to actions or events, such as blaming, thanking, or apologizing), and "expositives" (addressed "acts of exposition," such as affirming or denying) (1975: 150–163). Our concern is primarily with the distinctively second-personal reasons that are presupposed, invoked in, or related to *exercitives, behabitives,* and *commissives.*[26] In the next section, however, we focus on the *expositives* that are involved in *theoretical* (non-second-personal) reason-giving.

Austin holds that illocutionary acts of all kinds have "felicity" conditions: what must be true for the agent to succeed in performing an (conventionally defined) illocutionary act of a specific kind—for example, for a speech act to be a warning or an order—or what must be true for the act to have been performed properly (in conventional terms). When conditions of the first sort are unmet, Austin says that the act "misfires"; no act of that specific kind occurs. And when those are satisfied, but conditions of the second sort are not, he says that the illocutionary act is "abused." An act of the relevant kind is performed, but not properly (1975: 18). Again, 'proper' here should be understood in conventional, not in normative, terms. An outsider who finds an applicable convention thoroughly objectionable may nonetheless correctly judge an act proper in these conventional terms. (In this case, although the outsider must agree that the Austinian (conventional) felicity conditions are satisfied, she may deny that the "normative felicity conditions" are—no genuinely normative reason, she thinks, has been thereby addressed.)

> Two especially relevant felicity conditions of the first sort are the following:
>
> A.1. There must exist an accepted conventional procedure having a certain conventional effect, the procedure to include the uttering of certain words by certain persons in certain circumstances.
>
> A.2. The particular persons and circumstances in a given case must be appropriate for the invocation of the particular procedure invoked. (26, 34)

By a conventional procedure, Austin means something that has sufficiently wide *de facto* authority. Suppose that one person attempts to chal-

---

26. Although illocutionary act kinds are defined conventionally, and not normatively, it is nonetheless the case that they normally purport to address genuine normative reasons.

lenge another to a duel with the archaic, "My seconds will call on you." As Austin notes, this would have amounted to a challenge in earlier times, but because most people now reject dueling and its associated codes of procedure and honor, it is possible now to shrug off such an attempt as ridiculous (although, notoriously, not in certain settings) (27). Because the requisite *de facto* authority is absent, the attempted challenge "misfires." When, however, the codes were widely enough accepted, this was not so. When enough people accepted that someone challenged is under an obligation to take it up on pain of dishonor and recognized this form of words, then uttering them was normally sufficient, so long as other conditions held, to issue a challenge and thereby create the obligation to respond, at least so far as the conventions were concerned. You can't get an 'ought' from an 'is', so the thought is not, again, that any genuine obligation *(de jure)* followed from the existence of the challenge. Rather, the idea is that the challenge could itself exist in Austin's *de facto* conventional sense only if enough people accepted that the person challenged was under an obligation *(de facto)* to respond.

In addition, there are other conditions that, though not necessary for the relevant illocutionary act to be performed, are nonetheless necessary for it not to be an "abuse" of the relevant speech act and so be unhappy in another respect. These conditions require that participation in the practice be authentic and sincere in various ways.[27] Austin's examples of abuses include insincere promises, congratulations, and advice (40–47). If I make a promise with no intention of keeping it, then, so long as the other felicity conditions are satisfied, I promise all right, but in doing so I violate norms that my promise itself presupposes. Similarly, if one person challenges another, but does not accept, and has no intention of abiding by, the norms of honor and "respect" that structure the practice of dueling, he challenges "abusively."

Austin's framework can be applied to speech acts in which one person attempts to give another a (normative) reason to do something. There are norms of advice-giving (with non-second-personal reasons), for example, which advisors and advisees implicitly presuppose when they respectively give and receive advice. Even if one does not in fact accept these norms, if one presents oneself as advising, the other is entitled to assume that one does or, at least, that one will conduct oneself as though

27. These are Austin's Γ.1 and Γ.2 (1975: 15).

one did. Moreover, the norms also give the other grounds for censure if they are violated. If it turns out that my "advice" was simply self-serving, you have grounds for complaint. Similarly, when one person attempts to give another a second-personal reason, through an order, claim, request, or whatever, she presupposes that both parties accept norms that ground these reasons and the standing to address them.

Addressing Reasons for Belief

Philip Pettit and Michael Smith (1996) have argued for a version of these claims regarding the mutual giving of reasons for belief and action, in general (see also Bohman 2000).[28] In their view, we invariably take up a "conversational stance" that carries significant assumptions whenever we seriously express our views to one another about what there is reason to believe and do. Pettit and Smith do not discuss the addressing of second-personal reasons as a special case. It is helpful, therefore, to consider their discussion, both for the light it sheds on the role of reciprocal recognition in all serious conversation about what to believe and do and to provide a contrasting background against which to grasp the distinctive connection between reciprocal recognition and second-personal practical reasons.

"Conversation," Pettit and Smith say, "is the means whereby we recognize others and seek recognition from them" (1996: 430). In serious "conversation of an intellectual kind," people "authorize their interlocutors and in turn assume authorization by them" (430, 432). When the issue is what to believe, both parties presume in common that "they are each authorities worth listening to" and that, when they differ, "a review of the evidence commonly available can usually reveal who is in the wrong and thereby establish agreement" (430–431). The point is not that participants in serious common inquiry must believe either that the other party is credible or judicious or even sufficiently intellectually competent to be worth engaging in serious discussion. Rather, discussion in earnest must proceed on the assumption that the other is a competent theoretical reasoner. Otherwise, a genuine discussion with her about what to believe simply doesn't make sense in its own terms.

---

28. A similar view about the second-personal character of assertion lies behind Dummett's views on truth in Dummett 1990. I am indebted here to Rumfitt forthcoming.

Specifically, Pettit and Smith claim that participants who take up the "conversational stance" must each assume: (1) that there are norms that govern what each should believe, (2) that each can recognize these norms, and (3) that each is capable of guiding her beliefs by them (1996: 433). The point, again, is that mutual reason-giving makes sense in its own terms only if this is presupposed. It makes sense to engage in a discussion for the purpose of determining what to believe only if one assumes that the other is a competent reasoner and that she accepts and is guided by norms for belief. Of course, there might be all sorts of extrinsic reasons for entering into a conversation that has the appearance of authentic interactive inquiry that do not require such an assumption. Or one might take "discussion" with another as evidence in some other way (as in, "I always believe the opposite of what he says").

This is a stronger claim than the general Austinian point about speech acts. An advisor must generally assume, for example, that her advisee is sufficiently capable of normative guidance to follow her advice. But this doesn't commit her to assuming that he can give advice himself or take part in a genuinely mutual conversation about what to do. Still, even if not all theoretical and practical reason-giving presupposes the reciprocal authority that serious conversations have as "the price of admission," I argue that addressing distinctively second-personal practical reasons does invariably presuppose a common authority that addresser and addressee have alike as free and rational agents. The holding of this assumption is, I claim, a "normative felicity condition" of any second-personal address whatsoever in the sense that it is a necessary condition of the second-personal reasons actually existing and being given through address.

In this section, however, our purpose is to understand the presuppositions of theoretical reason-giving so that we can then contrast these with those of addressing second-personal reasons. A few words are needed, therefore, about belief. By its very nature, belief is responsible to an independent order of fact, which it aims to represent in a believer-neutral way. Belief is regulated by an independent truth (Shah 2003; Shah and Velleman forthcoming). Unlike, for example, an assumption that p, a belief that p is mistaken when p is false, though an assumed proposition is no less false than a believed one. Of course, what reasons people have to believe things about the world depend in many ways on where they stand in relation to it. But ultimately their reasons must be grounded in something that is independent of their stance, namely, what is the case believer-neutrally. Our beliefs are simply the world (including our place in it) as seen (committedly) from our perspective; what we should believe depends ultimately on the world as it actually is.

This has important consequences for what we must assume when we address reasons for belief to one another. As recent discussions of testimony have brought out, there are cases in which doxastic reasons are at least superficially second-personal (Burge 1993; Coady 1992; Foley 1994; Hinchman 2000; Moran 2005). Someone can give you a reason to believe something not just by pointing to evidence, but also by simply telling you it is so. When you believe something for this reason, you give the person whose testimony you trust a kind of second-personal authority in your own reasoning about what to believe. But this authority is not second-personal all the way down. It ultimately depends upon and is defeasible by epistemic authority. If you come to believe that the person's testimony is absolutely unreliable, you will no longer give him second-personal authority in a serious conversation about what to believe.

Someone can address reasons for belief, therefore, only if we take him to have some epistemic authority, or, at least, only if we don't take him to have none. Even if we unavoidably make such an assumption, in Davidsonian fashion, in interpreting him as minded at all, it is nonetheless the presumed relation to the facts as they are anyway that, as we must assume, earns him the standing to give reasons to us. Were we to believe his utterances to be only randomly related to the way things actually are, he could give us no reasons for belief, if indeed we could interpret him as saying anything at all. As I indicated earlier, this contrasts with the authority to address second-personal practical reasons. Although knowledge and wisdom, even about practical affairs, is sometimes a ground for endowing someone with some kinds of second-personal authority over conduct, it is not what such authority consists in. And there are some kinds of second-personal authority, arguably that of persons as such, that require relatively little epistemic authority.

Addressing Second-Personal Practical Reasons

Pettit and Smith discuss the mutual giving of practical reasons as though it were fully analogous to reciprocal theoretical reasoning. Just as conversants about what to believe mutually recognize norms for belief and their competence to be guided by them, along with the standing both have to address reasons based in these norms, so likewise, Pettit and Smith argue, do individuals involved in a serious conversation about what to do commit themselves to analogous assumptions concerning norms for desire and action, their capacity to guide themselves by these norms, and their standing to give reasons grounded in them.

If practical reason-giving were fully analogous to theoretical reason-giving, then we should expect all authority in the former also to be fundamentally epistemic, albeit about what there is reason to desire and do. Even if the agent's question is what to do rather than what to believe, we would appropriately think that someone is in a position to give a practical reason to another only if she has knowledge or reasonable belief about reasons for the person to act whose existence is, except in arcane cases, quite independent of her giving them to him or even of her capacity to do so. She would thus earn the authority to stand in the reason-giving relation to the other by virtue of her access to something that holds anyway, independently of their relation: the relation-independent facts of what he should do.

This model works well enough for some forms of practical reason-giving, specifically, whenever the reason-giving relation is that of advice.[29] Advisors purport to give reasons to their advisees that hold independently of the advising relation or of their competence to stand in it. This picture is misleading, however, for the distinctively second-personal practical reasons with which we are primarily concerned in this book. Recall our familiar example. Eliciting someone's sympathy by manifesting your evident pain is not exactly advising, but it is like it, and like theoretical reason-giving, in that the reason he comes to see is independent of any standing you might have to give it to him.[30] The reason would hold and could be successfully given even if, perhaps especially if, you were an infant and utterly incapable of advising anyone.

If however, you address a demand that he move his foot, you initiate a reciprocally recognizing relation and presuppose the authority in which you take the reason you address to be grounded. And you implicitly

29. Even in the case of advice about second-personal reasons, although the reasons' existence is not independent of their being able to be addressed in making second-personal claims and demands, it is independent of the advisor's epistemic authority and knowledge.

30. Of course, this case is also unlike advice in not presupposing even epistemic authority.

endow your addressee with the competence to consider and act on your request or demand and also, in this case, recognize his authority to address like reasons back to you in relevantly similar circumstances. Unlike reasons for belief and practical reasons one might give in advice, reasons of this kind are second-personal in their nature.[31] Their very existence depends on being able to be addressed person-to-person. Unlike the reason having to do with the simple badness of your being in pain, the fact that you can and do reasonably demand that he move his foot simply would not obtain but for the common competence and authority to enter into second-personal relations of reciprocal address. The authority you presuppose is second-personal all the way down.

I argue therefore that the authority to address practical reasons can take forms that are quite different from the epistemic authority that is presupposed either by theoretical reason-giving or by other forms of practical reason-giving, like advice, where the reasons are not second-personal.[32] Second-personal reasons of all kinds presuppose an authority to address second-personal reasons that cannot be reduced to or derived from propositions of value or right that do not already presuppose some second-personal standing to claim or demand. In a slogan: You can't get a second-personal demand out of something that doesn't already (at least implicitly) involve second-personal authority. Or, to paraphrase Bernard Williams: "Second-personal authority out, second-personal authority in."[33] This is a fundamental difference between theoretical and practical reason. In theoretical reason-giving, the authority to enter into the reason-giving relation to another person ultimately derives from the putative authority's

31. There are, however, deep connections between the kind of competence and authority we presuppose in collaborative theoretical reasoning and holding people responsible in the moral sphere. Discovery and fact-finding are themselves part of the latter. Someone can answer or account for her conduct only by honestly seeking to discover and acknowledge the truth of what she did. And societies that have strong traditions and institutions of inquiry seem better able to sustain public accountability more generally, and vice versa.

32. On the difference between epistemic authority and practical authority that includes the standing to command or demand, see Wolff 1970: 7.

33. Williams's slogan was "Obligation out, obligation in" (1985: 181). One way of formulating the main thesis of Chapters 3 and 4—that moral obligation must be understood in terms of second-personal reasons—is to say that the formulation in the text is not just a paraphrase of Williams's slogan, but that the point it formulates is the genus of which that formulated by Williams's slogan is a species.

access to facts that hold independently of that relation or the competence to enter into it.[34] Second-personal reasons of the kind we are interested in, by contrast, are relational all the way down. They ultimately derive from normative relations that reciprocally recognizing persons assume to exist between them.

Second-Personal Reasons, Accountability, and Respect

There is another important feature of second-personal reasons that fits them distinctively to accountability. As we have seen, to recognize a second-personal reason is implicitly to acknowledge someone's authority. This means that when second-personal reasons are proffered, issues of *respect* are invariably at stake. If the private fails to heed the sergeant's orders, he doesn't simply act contrary to a reason that sheds favorable light; he violates the order and so disrespects the sergeant and her authority. If your foot-treader fails to respond to your demand, he fails also to meet your legitimate expectation and so disrespects your standing to make the claim and, therefore, you. Even in a case where one has no genuine claim except to make a request or a plea, if someone to whom one addresses the request refuses even to give one a hearing, this too is a kind of disrespect.

Disrespect is, in its nature, a violation of, an offense against, or an affront to a *dignity*, to which the appropriate response is some second-personal attitude or action that seeks (demands) recognition of the dignity from the violator. Whatever grounds the dignity of a person, officer, or institution to address a claim, order, request, and so on, also grounds actions and attitudes by them, or on their behalf, that seek to reestablish reciprocally recognizing respect. "Reactive" attitudes and actions themselves implicitly address second-personal reasons to the violator that presuppose the very authority of which the actions and attitudes seek to reestablish reciprocal recognition.[35] In the next chapter, we consider the ways in which reactive attitudes like blame, reproach, resentment, and

34. It is also possible for someone to have second-personal theoretical authority by virtue of their competence in reasoning, quite independently of the credibility of their premises. But this isn't fundamentally second-personal either. I am indebted here to discussion with Jack Bender and Mark LeBar.

35. In this connection, see Bernard Williams (1995) on the "proleptic" mechanism of blame.

indignation are second-personal. They address violators in a way that, as Strawson puts it, "continu[es] to view him as a member of the moral community; only as one who has offended against its demands" (1968: 93). Reactive attitudes can thus reinforce and reestablish reciprocal respect as an equal member in a mutually accountable community.

— PART II —

— 4 —

Accountability
and the Second Person

In this chapter and the next, I begin to put forward my main arguments for the claim that moral obligation is essentially second-personal. At this point, this is primarily a thesis about the *form* of moral obligation: that moral demands are essentially tied to second-personal accountability. (Ultimately, it includes a claim about moral obligation's *content*: that it at least partly derives from our equal dignity as free and rational persons.) This chapter focuses on the second-personal character of moral accountability. In the next, I discuss the connection between accountability and moral obligation.

In his famous essay, "Freedom and Resentment" (1968), P. F. Strawson argued influentially against consequentialist compatibilist views that hold that determinism poses no threat to practices of moral responsibility since these can be fully justified by their "efficacy . . . in regulating behaviour in socially desirable ways" (72).[1] Punishment is justified by its incentive and deterrence effects, and, although standard excuses can be given a similar rationale, there is no corresponding warrant for excusing an act just because it was caused. Wrongs done in utter ignorance or under extreme duress are appropriately excused, since punishment under those conditions cannot deter. But there is obviously no consequentialist justification for treating determinism as an excuse generally.

Against these approaches, Strawson argued that social desirability cannot provide a justification of "the right *sort*" for practices of moral responsibility "as we understand them" (1968: 74). When we seek to hold

1. Strawson's example of such a view was Nowell-Smith 1948. A classic statement is Schlick 1939.

people accountable, what matters is not whether punishment is prag-matically desirable, either in a particular case or in general, but whether it is deserved and we have the authority to mete it out. Desirability is a reason of the wrong kind to warrant the attitudes and actions in which holding someone responsible consists in their own terms. This is *Strawson's Point*.

As we noted in Chapter 1, Strawson's Point is an instance of the *wrong kind of reason problem*. Pragmatic considerations for belief do not make a proposition credible; moral reasons against being amused do not un-dermine a joke's humor; and considerations of the desirability—whether personal, social, or even moral—of holding someone responsible do not make him blameworthy for what he did.[2] In each case, the right kind of reasons for warranting the relevant attitude in its own terms must derive from distinctive norms for attitudes of that kind: for belief, for amuse-ment, and for the attitudes and actions that are distinctively involved in holding people responsible. It must be a fact about or feature of an object, appropriate consideration of which could provide the basis (someone's reason) for a warranted attitude of that kind toward the object.[3] It is impossible to come to believe some proposition *p* by reflecting on the fact that it would be desirable to believe *p*, (devilishly) impossible to find something unfunny (though possible to have one's sense of humor stilled) by considering the moral offensiveness of finding it so, and impossible also to feel guilty or to resent a wrong by reflecting on the desirability (personal, social, or moral) of having these feelings.

We can see these points by reflecting on the class of responses that Strawson famously termed "reactive attitudes," which he held to be es-sential to human practices of moral responsibility. Strawson distinguishes two kinds—"participant" and "impersonal"—both of which respond to "transactions" between individuals (1968: 74). *Participant* (or *personal*) *reactive attitudes* are those, in the first instance, of individuals in the transactions themselves—the *transagents*—although participant attitudes

2. See Chapter 1, note 31.

3. Rabinowicz and Rønnøw-Rasmussen put essentially the same point by saying reasons of the right kind also appear in the content of the attitude for which they are reasons: the attitude is toward something "on account of" these reasons (Rabinowicz and Rønnøw-Rasmussen 2004: 414). As W. D. Falk pointed out, a favoring that is relevant to value is "by way of true comprehension of what [the object] is like" (1986: 117). See also Derek Parfit's distinction between "object-given" and "state-given" reasons (2001).

can also be had by relevant others "on their behalf" as if from their point of view. Strawson's examples include gratitude, resentment, forgiveness, love, and hurt feelings (72). *Impersonal reactive attitudes* are "impersonal or disinterested or generalized analogues" of these, including moral indignation, disapprobation, and, when the object is oneself, feelings of obligation, guilt, compunction, and remorse (84–85). Impersonal reactive attitudes are felt, not as if from the transagents' standpoints, but as from an impartial standpoint: the moral point of view. For example, resentment is felt as from the perspective of a wronged or injured individual, but indignation is felt as from the standpoint of the moral community.

I claim that reactive attitudes arc always implicitly second-personal and that they therefore invariably carry presuppositions of second-personal address about the competence and authority of the individuals who are their targets, as well as about those who have them.[4] Personal reactive attitudes are felt as if from the second-person standpoint of a relevant transagent, and impersonal reactive attitudes are felt as from the standpoint of members of the moral community. It will follow that reasons that can warrant these attitudes—that can be reasons of the right kind— must be second-personal reasons.

Consider indignation, for example. To feel indignation toward someone is to feel that he is to blame for wrongful conduct and therefore appropriately held accountable for what he has done, even if only by being subject to reactive attitudes from himself and others. Moreover, and this is part of Strawson's Point, indignation differs from its seeming that a sanction would be desirable, or even that some evil's befalling him would make for a more valuable or fitting whole (poetic justice). The feeling of

---

4. Michelle Mason makes what I take to be a similar claim, saying that there is a sense in "which it is true that all the reactive attitudes are in fact moral attitudes: namely, the sense in which it is true that to regard one as within the scope of the particular reactive attitude is to regard one as answerable to an expectation or demand that forms part of a system of expectations, demands and rights the regulation in accordance with which it is necessary for aspiring to moral community with us" (2003: 244). Mason makes a persuasive case that at least a form of contempt should also be understood as a reactive attitude. It is a particularly interesting case, since, as Mason argues, although it presupposes a background demand on its object as a person, it may not seem to address the demand, since its natural expression is a form of withdrawal. I think, however, that contempt of the sort she is discussing must, if it is to be a reactive attitude as she claims, presuppose that the withdrawal is a way of holding its object accountable and not a non-"reactive" response like, say, disgust, or, indeed, like other forms of contempt.

indignation invariably includes a sense of authoritative demand that may be absent from the feeling that something would be desirable or fitting. Consider what beliefs moderate or undermine indignation. If we come to believe that someone does not deserve blame, say, because he could not possibly have known the true character of what he was doing or because he was under extreme duress, then this will reduce or even defeat our indignation toward him. But if we learn that attempting to hold him accountable would be undesirable, say, because it will provoke him further, this will hardly undermine indignation.

Similar points hold for personal reactive attitudes. Resentment, for instance, is felt in response to apparent injustice, as if from the victim's point of view. We resent what we take to be violations against ourselves or those with whom we identify. If you resent someone's treading on your foot or, even more, his rejecting your request or demand that he stop doing so, you feel as if he has violated a valid claim or demand and as if some claim-exacting or responsibility-seeking response by you, or on your behalf, is justified. What you feel is not just (or even) that this response would be justified as an effective or desirable means to desirable relief. And although you might think that some such response would make for a more morally fitting whole, that thought is not itself part of resentment. Resentment seems rather to be warranted simply by the other's conduct and by what you and he can validly, that is, authoritatively, claim and demand of one another. "You can't do that to me," you might think, referring, not to your respective power, but to your authority.

Strawson argues that appreciating the role of reactive attitudes in moral responsibility is of central relevance to the problem of free will. The question of whether, and how, to hold others responsible is one that arises within human relationships (that is, relatings) in which we are disposed, through reactive attitudes, to presume an authority to hold others to expectations that we take to define those relations.[5] In a slogan: The moral sense of 'responsible for' is conceptually tied to 'responsible to' (whether to individuals or to one another as members of the moral community).[6]

5. This is also a theme that Scanlon sounds in Scanlon 1995.

6. More cautiously, as far as the concept of moral responsibility is concerned, it is tied to responsibility to those with the authority to hold morally responsible (the moral community). In the next chapter, I argue that theological voluntarism and Kantian views provide competing conceptions of the moral community, respectively, as God and as all free and rational agents (the realm of ends).

Responsibility distinctively concerns how, in light of what someone has done, she is to be related to, that is, regarded and addressed (including by herself) within the second-personal relationships we stand in as members of the moral community. To keep this point before us, I will usually use the term 'accountable' rather than 'responsible', since there are senses of 'responsible' that differ from the sense that I have in mind. For example, 'responsible' can refer to causal responsibility regardless of moral implications, and there are broader senses even of moral responsibility, for example, what is sometimes called "responsibility as attributability," that differ from the distinctive kind of moral responsibility, "responsibility as accountability," with which we are concerned.[7] My point is that holding someone responsible in this latter sense is ineliminably second-personal.

Strawson contrasts "the attitude (or range of attitudes) of involvement or participation in a human relationship," that is, a second-person stance, on the one hand, with "the objective attitudes (or range of attitudes) to another human being, on the other" (1968: 79). We take an "objective" attitude toward those we see as unfit for "ordinary adult human relationships," such as very young children and those with "deep-rooted psychological abnormality," and regard them as appropriately subject to "treatment" or "management" rather than to reactive attitudes and forms of interpersonal address that involve them (1968: 81).[8] Consequently, the real issue that determinism poses is whether accepting it "could, or should . . . lead us always to look on everyone exclusively in this [objective] way" (81). Strawson famously holds that it could not.

Our interest in this chapter is not so much free will as the nature of moral accountability, specifically, its second-personal character. Nonetheless, it is worth noting the connection between these. If Strawson is right,

7. On the distinction, see Watson 1996. The former sense concerns what we can credit someone with in a way that is relevant to broader forms of evaluation that need not be second-personal at all. For example, warranted pride may depend upon whether I am responsible for something concerning me in this sense, and this need involve no warranted claim or demand. See also, Scanlon 1998: 248f. Scanlon calls the sense I have in mind "substantive responsibility." I am indebted here to discussion with Andrew Eshelman, Lei Zhong, Jim Staihar, and Susan Wolf.

8. Obviously, this raises many issues about matters of degree, responsibility and disability, and respect and treatment of those we are not prepared to hold fully responsible. I cannot begin to deal adequately with these here. For most of these purposes of this chapter, all we need to focus on are clear cases in both categories (i.e., those who are apt for second-personal accountability and those who are not). I return to this issue, again inadequately, at the end of this chapter.

it is only because we view one another in the distinctive second-personal ways we do when we relate to each other that the questions of responsibility (as accountability), freedom of the will, and what might undermine these even arise. The issue of free will gets its grip, therefore, *because we view and address one another (and ourselves) second-personally*. Again: we can be morally responsible (accountable) for what we do in a way that makes free will an issue only because we are morally responsible to one another, that is, because we have the authority to address demands to one another as members of the moral community.[9] It is second-personal address (as in reactive attitudes) that commits us to assuming the freedom of addresser and addressee alike.

Reactive Responses as a Form of Address

In the next four sections, I seek to show that reactive attitudes invariably involve:

(a) a form of (second-personal) address,
(b) which presupposes an other's competence and standing to be thus addressed (second-personal competence and authority) and
(c) which responds to the person's conduct
(d) with respect to persons (at least).[10]

In this section, we are concerned with (a), hence with continuing our consideration of the second-personal character of reactive attitudes themselves. Strawson explicitly says that both personal reactive attitudes and their generalized or vicarious analogues invariably involve "an expectation of, and demand for, the manifestation of a certain degree of goodwill" (1968: 85). Moreover, Strawson's examples can be shown to involve the (at least, implicit) addressing of these demands.[11]

9. Note, again, the caveat in the preceding footnote.
10. See the short discussion of this issue in Chapter 2.
11. However, Strawson excludes shame. He lists "the more complicated phenomenon of shame" as reactive, although he doesn't say why (1968: 86). For the reasons given in the next paragraph, I think this may be a mistake (at least for non-second-personal forms of shame). Nothing hangs on this for my purposes, however. If Strawson is right and I am wrong, then either there are second-personal aspects of shame I am not appreciating, or there are not, in which case my claims in this chapter can be interpreted as about reactive attitudes other than shame. Of course, shame can figure in reactive attitudes and emotions without itself being reactive. We say, "you ought to be ashamed" in a reactive

Consider, for example, the difference between guilt and shame. Guilt is a reactive attitude. To feel guilty is to feel as if one is appropriately blamed (to blame) and held responsible for something one has done.[12] Guilt feels like the appropriate (second-personal) response to blame: an acknowledgment of one's blameworthiness that recognizes both the grounds of blame and, more importantly for us, the authority to level it (even if only "to God"). To feel guilt, consequently, is to feel as if one has the requisite capacity and standing to be addressed as responsible, and this puts it in tension with a purely "objective" view of oneself in Strawson's sense. Finally, guilt's natural expressions are themselves second-personal—confession, apology, making amends, and self-addressed reproach.

Like guilt, shame feels as if one is rightly regarded or seen in a certain way. But here the relevant regard is not second-personal; it is third-personal. One sees oneself as an object of the other's regard or "gaze"—of her disdain, perhaps, or of her just seeing through one's public persona to something one is ashamed to have seen.[13] Sartre famously remarked that "I can be ashamed only as my freedom escapes me in order to become a *given* object" for the other (1957: 260).[14] To feel guilt, by contrast, is to feel oneself authoritatively addressed as free. The "view from

vein, but here we mean not just that were the person to feel shame she would be accurately representing her shameful state, but that experiencing shame is a psychic state that she should undergo or experience because of what she has done. In such contexts, shame is functioning as a sanction. Moreover, there is such a thing as moral shame, namely shame at one's conduct or character. But although moral shame is essentially concerned with persons as objects, it is not reactive in the sense of being characteristically addressed second-personally. I have been helped here by discussion with John Deigh, and by Deigh 1983. See also Mason unpublished.

12. On this point, see Greenspan 1992. For other elements of the contrast between guilt and shame, see Gibbard 1990, ch. 7; Morris 1976; Rawls 1971, secs. 67, 70–75; Williams 1993: 89–90; and Wollheim 1984. For a contrasting view, see Stocker, forthcoming. An especially interesting discussion of guilt can be found in Buber 1965. I am indebted to David Levy for this reference.

13. For a fascinating discussion of shame that stresses the latter element, see Velleman 2001. Another example of a reaction that isn't a reactive attitude is disgust. See Miller 1997.

14. As Paul Hoffman has pointed out to me, at least some kinds of shame (certainly moral shame, and perhaps others) involve a feeling not just of recognizing a third-person regard, say, disdain, but also of struggling against it agentially. Arguably this is involved in the kind of shame Sartre is discussing. The point remains that even shame of this kind responds as if to a third-person view rather a second-person address.

guilt," as we might call it, is incompatible with a purely "objective" view of oneself in Strawson's sense. One feels that one should and could have done what one didn't do and, therefore, feels appropriately blamed for that reason. And whereas guilt's characteristic expression is second-personal, shame inhibits second-personal engagement—one feels like escaping from view.

Shame and guilt both give an imagined other's regard authority. But the authority shame accords is fundamentally epistemic and third-personal. One sees the other as having standing to see one in a certain way (and oneself as correctly thus seen). Guilt, however, recognizes an irreducibly second-personal practical authority of the sort we noted at the outset. It acknowledges the authority to make a demand, that is, to address a second-personal reason for acting.

Consider now the rest of Strawson's examples.[15] His exemplary participant or personal reactive responses are, again, gratitude, resentment, love, forgiveness, and hurt feelings. Resentment and forgiveness are perhaps the easiest cases. Resentment is felt as if in response to a violation of a legitimate claim or expectation, and not simply as directed toward the violator, but as implicitly addressing her. This is what makes resentment "reactive" rather than "objective." It is a form of "holding responsible," an address of the other as a person with the capacity and standing to be addressed in this way and charged. If it turns out, for example, that someone's foot has been forced on top of yours by the shifting of a heavy package on a careening bus on which you both are traveling, knowing that might not change your desire to get his foot off of yours, but it will lessen your resentment or perhaps redirect it to a new object (the driver).

Forgiveness's second-personal character is most easily understood in relation to resentment. To forgive is, roughly, to forbear or withdraw resentment.[16] Forgiveness acknowledges the other's responsibility for wronging one, but refrains from pressing claims or "holding it against" him.[17] Of course, one can forgive or feel forgiveness without communicating it. But forgiveness nevertheless functions within the second-

15. Again, excluding shame.

16. The classic statement of this position is by Bishop Butler. See Butler 1900: sermon numbers VIII and IX. See also Murphy and Hampton 1988.

17. Above we noted that resentment can be felt for injuries to those with whom one identifies. Similarly, it is possible to forgive injuries to those with whom one identifies.

personal space of holding responsible. If there were no such thing as resentment, indignation, and their kin, there would be no such thing as forgiveness.

Gratitude is like forgiveness in being parasitic on legitimate claims or expectations. We are appropriately grateful when people benefit us or act as we wish when we lack any relevant claim or expectation of them. Gratitude is felt, moreover, in response to an action by a responsible agent. It is true that we speak of being grateful for good weather, for example, but this evidently involves the conceit that the weather is a free gift, as if from God.[18] And gratitude's natural expression is also second-personal, a grateful addressing of the benefactor that reciprocally recognizes that he has benefited us beyond what we had any claim to expect. "You shouldn't have done that," we say, but we clearly don't mean to be finding fault. Finally, unaddressed (or, more certainly, unexperienced) feelings of gratitude can themselves be ungrateful.

Strawson's examples of "love" and "hurt feelings" may seem less straightforwardly second-personal. Surely there are forms of love that are not second-personal at all. One can care deeply for nonpersons, and caring for persons need not show itself in even imagined address nor be seen as essentially responsive to their conduct. Most love may not be entirely unconditional, but it needn't be second-personally conditional. Pretty clearly what Strawson has in mind, however, are loving or other friendly relations that are maintained by reciprocally recognizing mutual address. And hurt feelings must be understood within that same framework. Feelings are hurt when people act in ways that seem contrary to expected personal regard, where one takes the other reciprocally to have recognized the expectations or takes it that he should have done so. One need not see oneself as having a claim to the other's regard that would warrant resentment.[19] But one feels as if some issue of rejection and mutual trust has been raised.

18. It may, however, be beneficial to live with this conceit. On this point, see Emmons and McCullough 2003. Is this more evidence of second-personal psychological mechanisms? On this, see Chapter 7.

19. Although this obviously can happen also, as with Medea's response to Jason's leaving her for the Princess of Corinth or, as in the lyrics of Alanis Morissette's "You Oughta Know" (1995): "And I'm here to remind you / Of the mess you left when you went away. / It's not fair to deny me / Of the cross I bear that you gave to me / You, you, you . . .

That leaves us with Strawson's examples of impersonal reactive feelings, both the other-addressed ones—moral indignation and disapprobation— and those that are self-addressed: guilt, compunction, and remorse. Here we can be brief. Moral indignation is a feeling that someone is rightly held responsible for some conduct and is itself part of holding him thus accountable. As Strawson points out, we feel indignation and disapprobation when we feel we can demand, as members of the moral community, that people act in certain ways. Indeed, Strawson says, "the making of the demand *is* the proneness to such attitudes" (1968: 92–93).[20] This is an important point that we need to bear in mind: we address moral demands partly by its being common knowledge that we are prone to impersonal (but still second-personal) "demanding" attitudes and to more explicit ways of holding one another responsible.

These same points hold also with reflexive impersonal reactive attitudes. In these cases, however, the demands are self-addressed, as has been illustrated already by guilt. Compunction and remorse seem relevantly similar, if more muted or qualified. As Jonathan Bennett points out, "self-reactive attitudes" involve a kind of "interpersonal relation . . . between one's present self and some past self" (1980: 44).[21]

Presupposing Second-Personal Competence and Authority

What gives Strawson's discussion of reactive attitudes its special relevance to the issue of free will is that reactive attitudes invariably address demands, and, as Gary Watson notes, there are "constraints on moral address" that must be presupposed as normative felicity conditions of addressing a demand (1987: 263, 264).[22] "To be intelligible," Watson points

oughta know." This also occurs in Bob Dylan's "Desolation Row" (2004: 181–183): "Yes, I received your letter yesterday / (About the time the door knob broke) / When you asked how I was doing / Was that some kind of joke? / . . . / Don't send me no more letters no / Not unless you mail them / From Desolation Row."

20. Compare Hart on Bentham on "quasi-commands" in law. (See Chapter 1, note 17.)

21. I am grateful to Daniel Keen for this reference.

22. Note also, R. Jay Wallace: "My main contention is that there is an essential connection between the reactive attitudes and a distinctive form of evaluation . . . that I refer to as holding a person to an expectation (or demand)" (1994: 19). See also Bennett 1980.

Note should also be taken of similar points in Scanlon (1998: 272–290), since they have a special relevance to our consideration of the way the second-person standpoint can ground a contractualist approach to morality in Chapter 12.

out, "demanding requires understanding on the part of the object of the demand" (264). The point is not that making a demand is unlikely to be effective unless its object has the capacity to understand it. It is rather that reactive attitudes are "forms of communication" that are simply unintelligible in their own terms without the presupposition that their objects can understand what is being said and act on this understanding.[23] The point is an Austinian one about the felicity conditions of a speech or quasi-speech act (transposed, albeit to a normative key). Even if expressing reactive attitudes to those who lack the requisite capacity, like very young children or the insane, causes them to behave desirably, reactive attitudes there "lose their point as forms of moral address" (265). The effectiveness of moral address is a matter of perlocutionary force, whereas addressees' having (and being assumed to have) the capacity to recognize and act on second-personal reasons is, I claim, a felicity condition of its distinctive (normative) illocutionary force. More precisely relevant to our point, it is a normative felicity condition of the relevant second-personal reasons' existing and being successfully given through address.

Again, one need not believe that someone one addresses has the requisite capacity and standing. The point is rather that moral address presupposes these things. Watson is saying that we address others on the assumption that they can understand and be guided by what we are saying. And I am adding that what we presuppose in second-personal address is *second-personal competence*,[24] that those we address can guide themselves by a reciprocal recognition of the second-personal reasons we address and our authority to address them, that they can take a second-personal perspective on themselves and act on reasons they accept from that point of view (by making the relevant demands of themselves).[25]

23. Watson remarks, as we noted above, that the communicative (second-personal) character of reactive attitudes does not mean that they are "usually communicated; very often, in fact, they are not. Rather the most appropriate and direct expression of resentment is to address the other with a complaint and a demand" (1987: 265).

24. The moral competence requisite for (equal) membership in the moral community (second-personal competence) is what Rawls calls a "range property." In this sense, people are not more or less competent members of the moral community, since everyone who is within the range is equally within the range. On this point, see Rawls 1971: 508.

25. There are very interesting issues that I cannot do justice to here concerning autism and related conditions that involve deficits in empathy and hence in second-personal competence. Jeanette Kennett (2002) has argued that people with high functioning autism are

It is important to my main constructive argument that addressing any second-personal reason through a claim or demand invariably presupposes that the addressee can recognize its validity and (freely) act on the reason through this recognition. If you express resentment to someone for not moving his foot from on top of yours, you implicitly demand that he do so. And any second-personal reason you implicitly address presupposes, first, that he can recognize the validity of your demand and, second, that he can move his foot simply by recognizing a conclusive reason for acting deriving from your authoritative demand (whether or not, it is worth noting, you have his sympathy). And if I express indignation as a disinterested bystander, I too must make these assumptions. A putatively authoritative demand whose validity someone cannot possibly recognize and act on is guaranteed to be infelicitous. The point is not, again, that such a demand cannot achieve compliance. It may well, but that is a matter of its perlocutionary force. It is that the address is guaranteed to fail in (normative) illocutionary terms, that is, as an addressing of an authoritative demand or second-personal reason.[26] The second-personal competence of the addressee is a normative felicity condition of second-personal address in general.

Claiming or demanding is not just calling some claim or demand to someone's attention. It is addressing a distinctively second-personal kind of reason to another person that aims to direct his will, but in a way that

---

indeed capable of moral responsibility and that this supports a Kantian rather than a Humean picture of moral agency. It does seem correct that high functioning autism is consistent with highly principled conduct. If I am right, the Categorical Imperative and related moral principles should be understood in fundamentally second-personal terms. Nonetheless, it could still turn out that, even though high functioning autism may be inconsistent with a full appreciation of fundamental moral motivations and the basis for principles of moral obligation, those with this condition might still reliably determine their conduct by these principles and so be able to function as members of the moral community. Of course, I have been emphasizing that being guided by certain norms does not yet acknowledge the second-personal authority that is essential to moral responsibility. But there might be ways of reliably tracking these more properly second-personal aspects also. I am indebted here to Walter Sinnott-Armstrong.

26. At this point, I am not so much arguing for this as claiming it. Part of the argument for the claim, of course, is the claim's role in an overall picture of second-personal address and reasons that I will hope will seem compelling and able to explain significant ethical phenomena. More focused arguments come, however, with the presentation of Fichte's Point in Chapter 10.

recognizes his authority and independent practical reasoning. As Strawson emphasizes, to respond to another's conduct with a reactive attitude is "to view him as a member of the moral community; only as one who offended against its demands" (1968: 93).[27] Reactive attitudes are thus unlike critical attitudes of other forms, disdain, for example, that presuppose no authority on the part of their objects. I believe that the role of second-personal attitudes and the second-person stance in mediating (mutual) accountability in Kantian and contractualist ethical conceptions marks a deep difference with the ethical views (frequently ethics of virtue) of thinkers like Plato, Aristotle, Hume, and Nietzsche (to give four prominent, but quite different, examples), for whom evaluation of conduct and character does not take a fundamentally second-personal form.[28]

We should be clear about the kind of freedom that second-personal address presupposes. Beings may be capable of other varieties of free choice but still lack the distinctively second-personal *moral freedom* we presuppose in reactive attitudes. When we respond reactively to someone who fails to respect a moral demand, we attribute to her the capacity to act on the distinctive kind of reason, second-personal reason, that is connected to the authoritative demand.

Imagine, for example, a being with what the Cambridge Platonist Ralph Cudworth (~1670) called "animal free will."[29] Such a being, Cudworth thought, might have the ability critically to revise its desires, make an assessment of what is likeliest to satisfy informed desires in the long run, and act on this assessment.[30] Cudworth agrees that incentives could be devised so that a being with animal free will could conform its conduct to a law of conduct. But he holds that such beings could not be under genuine moral obligation, that is, be authentically subject to a moral demand, if they are unable to recognize these demands as intrinsically

27. This is also, I believe, the grain of truth in Hegel's famous idea of a "right to punishment" (1991: 126–127); that is, failure to hold someone accountable can be a failure to respect his dignity as a rational person.

28. See Korsgaard 1996a for an excellent discussion of this aspect of the Kantian framework.

29. This appears in his unpublished manuscripts on freedom of the will, held in the British Library. References will be to manuscript number and page number. I discuss these in Darwall 1995a: 109–148.

30. This is roughly the kind of self-determination that Locke defends in the *Essay* (1975). I discuss Locke's conception in relation to his theory of moral obligation in Darwall 1995a: 149–175.

reason-giving (and so lack "moral free will"). To be genuinely morally responsible, and therefore capable of being morally obligated, a being must be capable of holding itself responsible, and it can do that only if it can take a second-personal perspective on itself and recognize and act on authoritative demands. Were beings only to have animal free will, "laws could no otherwise operate or seize upon them than by taking hold of their animal selfish passions . . . and that . . . utterly destroys all morality" (4980, 9).

Reactive attitudes presuppose the capacity to take moral demands as conclusive reasons for acting.[31] And this involves the capacity to hold oneself responsible and, I argue, determine oneself by a second-personal reason, that is, an agent-relative reason whose validity is grounded in presupposed normative relations between persons and that is therefore independent of the value of any outcome or state.[32] Reactive attitudes therefore implicitly presuppose motivational capacities that are irreducible to evaluations (and associated desires) whose objects are outcomes or states (like those implicated in sympathy). At the minimum, they involve the acceptance of (agent-relative) norms of action, which is an essentially action-regarding state of mind that cannot be reduced to a favorable regard for any state of the world or outcome.[33] But it follows further from Strawson's Point that even presupposing just this much is insufficient for second-personal responsibility to be fully intelligible in its own terms. We must also presuppose a distinctively second-personal competence, the ability to take the second-person stance of the moral community on oneself and be motivated by demands that one would sensibly address to anyone from that perspective.

31. Cudworth calls this "moral free will." Compare Kant: "I can recognize that I am under obligation to others only insofar as I at the same time put myself under obligation" (1996d: 417–418).

32. See note 16 of Chapter 1. I note there that it is consistent with the idea of second-personal reason that its formulation is actually agent-neutral. What matters is that the reason derives from something fundamentally agent-relative, namely, the agent's place in a network of relations of authoritative claim and demand. It is consistent with this that the reason itself is agent-neutral. Thus, one might argue from the fundamental proposition that every person has an equal claim to happiness, say, that we can reasonably demand that persons follow the principle of utility, which is agent-neutral. Thus, nothing said so far rules out act-consequentialist theories of right. I am indebted here to discussion with Allan Gibbard and Jim Staihar.

33. See the discussion in Chapter 2 and, especially, in Chapter 7. See also Gibbard 1990 on the mental state of norm acceptance.

Pufendorf's Point amounts to roughly the same thing, as I show at greater length in the next chapter. The pure second-personal address that is involved in moral obligation—as Pufendorf sees it, in God's addressing valid demands to us—requires the assumption that we can hold ourselves responsible through our own acceptance of the requisite authority, rather than just by fear of any sanctions someone with such authority might impose. For actions to be imputable to us as accountable agents, the person to whom we are accountable and we must both assume that we can be moved, not simply by a fear of sanctions that might coerce compliance, but by "acknowledge[ing] of [ourselves] that the evil, which has been pointed out to the person who deviates from an announced rule, falls upon him justly" (Pufendorf 1934: 91). We must be able to blame ourselves as we do in feeling guilt.

A consequence of all this is that we can intelligibly address demands through reactive attitudes only to those we assume able to take the very same attitudes toward themselves. Addressees must be assumed to be able to take a second-person perspective on, and make the same demands of, themselves through acknowledging their validity as in self-reactive attitudes like guilt, and, of course, by appropriately regulating their own practical reasoning. In doing this, they take up the very same point of view that an addresser takes up in holding them responsible. They hold themselves responsible through blaming themselves. In seeing themselves as to blame, they regard themselves as warrantedly blamed from the perspective of a member of the moral community.

In Response to His Conduct (as a Person)

It follows that reactive attitudes respond to an individual's exercise of the very capacities they presuppose: conduct as a person in respecting the demands they address. The object of a reactive attitude is always some individual conceived as free and rational in the sense of one who can recognize, freely accept, and act on the distinctive second-personal reasons the demand addresses. And what the attitude responds to is precisely the individual's exercise of these capacities, how she conducts herself in light of the relevant second-personal reasons. Since these reasons themselves structure second-personal relations, we might say that reactive attitudes respond to how an individual conducts herself *as a second person*. They respond to how she relates to and conducts herself (second-personally) toward those with the authority to make claims and demands of her. Since, as I argue in Chapters 6 and 10, both respect for someone's dignity as a person and, indeed, the dignity itself, are essentially second-personal phenomena, it will follow that *the very concept of person is itself a second-personal concept.*[34]

(At Least Partly) With Respect to Persons

Reactive attitudes thus concern themselves not with a person's overall agency, but specifically with his conduct with respect to claims or demands that other persons have standing to make of him.[35] They respond, that is, not simply to how he regards, or acts regarding, others, but to how he respects others in the sense of recognizing their valid claims and demands along with their authority to make them. They respond to how he conducts himself second-personally.

In this way, reactive attitudes always concern a form of respect that we realize when we relate to someone second-personally and acknowledge a second-personal reason and the authority relations that ground it, whether through the reactive attitudes themselves or by regulating our practical reasoning in the ways they call for. I return to the relation between respect and second-personal reasons in Chapter 6.

(At Least Apparently) Nonmoral Cases

To this point, we have been considering reactive attitudes in distinctively moral contexts. One might think, however, that reactive attitudes, at least personal ones, can figure also in nonmoral cases. If the sergeant's troops refuse to fall in when she orders them to, she is apt to resent this, and although her resentment will presuppose a demand that her charges can recognize and act on, it may seem a distortion to view her authority as moral. Nonetheless, it is clear enough that she must presuppose *de jure*

34. Compare here Locke's idea, discussed in the next chapter, that 'person' is a "forensick term," that is, one essentially connected to imputing legal or moral responsibility (1975: 386).

35. It is consistent with this, again, that some such demands we make of one another as members of the moral community concern how persons are to conduct themselves also toward non-persons, whether infants, the incapacitated, other animals, or even other aspects of the environment, beyond even anything that would be required by demands or claims of individual persons.

authority of some kind. Resentment doesn't represent its object as simply contravening one's will, but as contravening some justified demand. Moreover, if she feels impersonal reactive attitudes like indignation or blame, these will come as from a point of view she shares with them as members of the moral community. In feeling that they are to blame, she must think that they would rightly blame themselves and hold themselves responsible from the same point of view from which she blames them.

Of course, it is possible to think there are justified relations of authority that are not derivable from the mutual accountability of free and rational persons. For most of human history, in fact, it has seemed to most people that any justified order is quite incompatible with the kind of moral equality that many readers of this book, at least, might be willing to take for granted. Pufendorf himself probably thought this. I argue, however, that the address of second-personal reasons of any kind carries presuppositions that, when fully worked clear, commit addresser and addressee alike to their second personal competence and to an equal second-personal authority rooted in that, hence to the equal dignity of persons and to morality as a form of mutual accountability. Here, however, I simply wish to point out that any addressing of demands carries presuppositions of second-personality, just as it does in the moral case.

Consider the demands that a king or emperor makes of his subjects, for example, the Edict of Milan, which the Roman emperors Constantine and Licinius promulgated to stop Christian persecution in the Roman Empire. If Constantine and Licinius resented violations of this demand and blamed violators when they lacked adequate excuse, then in interpreting them as addressing (and so guiding) their subjects by second-personal reasons and not goading them, even by rational coercion, we must see them as having been committed thereby to regarding their subjects as capable of recognizing the edict's *(de jure)* authoritative backing and of guiding themselves by it. The normative felicity conditions of a command that can generate genuine second-personal reasons include the addressees' capacity for such a practically effective recognition. *Qua* second-personal address, the edict presupposed subjects' aptitude for this second-personal relation, specifically, their capacity for a reciprocal recognition and acceptance of their responsibilities to the emperor and, as well, their capacity to discharge their responsibility through this recognition.

I believe that the situation is the same with any reactive attitude, like blame, resentment, or indignation, that addresses a second-personal rea-son. In every such case, the addresser is committed to presuppositions that parallel what Watson calls the "constraints of moral address," namely, that the addressee is capable of the requisite second-personal reciprocal recognition, mediated through his own reactive attitudes and practical reasoning.

Respect, Dignity, and Reactive Sanctions

I have been stressing reactive attitudes' tie to presuppositions of freedom and equality. But aren't reactive attitudes, well, reactionary? Retribution can be difficult to separate from revenge and retaliation. Like Nietzsche, we may feel that attitudes like indignation and resentment are really a cover for cruelty or sado-masochism, a desire to see others or ourselves suffer, to extract a pound of flesh, or worse.[36] Even Mill, who maintains that the idea of moral wrong is essentially related to reactive attitudes, nonetheless claims that these are not intrinsically moral responses. They only become moral when they are appropriately regulated by sympathy and directed toward the public good.[37] Granted, Mill says, we wouldn't have the idea of justice or moral wrong if we didn't have emotions like resentment and the "natural feeling of retaliation or vengeance," but such a "sentiment, in itself, has nothing moral in it"; "what is moral is, the exclusive subordination of it to the social sympathies" (1998: ch. 5).

So why don't reactive attitudes involve the desire to retaliate? Don't "retributive" sentiments invariably bring in hostility and animosity, or at least some desire to balance a harming evil with some proportionate harm? Two ideas seem to be utterly essential to reactive attitudes. The first is that of a claim or demand, and the second is that of the corre-sponding statuses of addresser and addressee: the authority to address the

36. Think of Abu Ghraib and also the Zimbardo prison experiments, in which ordinary undergraduates pretending to be prison guards sadistically abused the "prisoners" (Zim-bardo, Ebbeson, and Maslach: 1977). See also Nietzsche 1994, especially the second essay (" 'Guilt,' 'Bad Conscience,' and the Like"). For a recent critique along somewhat similar lines, see Baier 1993. For a good contrast, however, see an interview of Nigerian human rights activist, Ayesha Imam, by Terry Gross, which discusses the phenomenon of Muslim men attacking Muslim women on the street as "punishment" for gender or sexual asser-tiveness, but within the context of a strong defense of accountability and rights: http://freshair.npr.org/day_fa.jhtml?display=day&todayDate=12/05/2002.

37. In this, I believe, he fails to appreciate Strawson's Point.

demand and the standing to be thus addressed and, consequently, to have to answer to the addresser, to be accountable or responsible to her for acknowledging and discharging the demand. Beyond these two essential elements, however, everything else seems, in principle, up for normative discussion and debate.[38]

It is a familiar idea that a theory of punishment can be retributive in spirit but still reject any thesis of strict proportionality—an eye for an eye, or whatever. Moreover, as Lawrence Stern (1974) has pointed out, examples like Gandhi and King show that it is possible to distinguish between accountability and reactive attitudes, on the one hand, and retaliation and revenge, on the other (see also Watson 1987: 286). Gandhi, King, and, we could add, Mandela certainly addressed demands, expressed attitudes that addressed demands, and explicitly and implicitly held others accountable for respecting them. But they did these in ways that enhanced (or made more visible) their own dignity and that respected that of their addressees precisely because they rejected retaliation.

Moral accountability does not have to be tied to any specific reactive attitude or even, in principle, to specifically human reactive attitudes at all.[39] And even reactive attitudes like resentment and indignation can be distinguished from the desire to retaliate or gain vengeance, as we shall see presently.[40] What is central is simply reciprocal recognition of the

38. It follows from Strawson's Point, however, that this discussion must take place within the second-person standpoint. I argue in Chapter 12 that we should think of the contractualist framework in precisely this way. In that same spirit we might here say that the question of precisely what form practices of mutual accountability should take is itself appropriately addressed as a substantive problem of normative theory within contractualism.

39. For example, if one thinks of blame as necessarily involving the expression of anger or some form of hostility, it need not involve blame in this sense. It must however involve blame in the formal sense of holding culpable.

40. It is interesting in this connection to compare ancient Greek forms of responsibility. Drakon's homicide code mandated exile for someone who killed a fellow Athenian unless the killer was pardoned by all of the males of the victim's immediate family. However, if anyone retaliated against the killer in exile, so long as the killer stayed clear of public spaces on the frontier, such as markets and sacrificial meeting places, then that person was subject to a like sentence as well. Here we see a beginning of a distinction between justified and unjustified retaliation that moves in the direction of moral responsibility as we understand it. The desire to retaliate is here disciplined externally and procedurally, rather than by an internal distinction from resentment whose object is injustice. See Stroud 1979. I am indebted to Randall Curren for this reference and for very helpful discussion.

standing to make certain demands of one another, that is, in the moral case, mutual respect of the equal dignity of free and rational persons. Persons are accountable to each other for respecting their equal dignity, and reactive attitudes demand, and mediate accountability for, this form of respect. Exactly what can be required of individuals who violate these demands is a normative issue that should presumably turn on what sanctions would best realize the ideal of equal respect.[41]

When someone uses your foot as his footrest, this is an injury not just to your foot, but also to your person. It is a failure to respect your standing or dignity as someone who may not be so treated and who has the standing as one among others to hold others to this.[42] Adam Smith observes that we are apt to resent disrespect for our person as much or more than any physical or psychic injury. What most "enrages us against the man who injures or insults us," Smith writes, "is the little account which he seems to make of *us* . . . that absurd self-love, by which he seems to imagine, that other people *may* be sacrificed at any time, to his conveniency" (1982a: 96).[43]

It is consistent with the object of reactive attitudes' invariably being disrespect, of course, that what they seek is still retaliation of some form, to hurt back, to give as good as we have gotten. On reflection, however, that cannot be right, as Smith himself saw. If reactive attitudes were retaliatory, then they would seek to return disrespect for disrespect. But as Strawson pointed out, moral reactive attitudes are themselves a form of respect. They view their targets as, like those who feel them, "member[s] of the moral community," and thus address them on terms of mutual respect (1968: 93). They seek reciprocal recognition of the (equal) dignity that they both claim (of the addresser) and presuppose (of the addressee). Smith writes insightfully that when we resent injuries, what our resentment is "chiefly intent upon, is not so much to make our enemy feel pain in his turn, as . . . to make him sensible, that the person whom he injured did not deserve to be treated in that manner" (1982: 95–96).[44]

41. For example, within a contractualist framework.

42. Again, I defend this conception of dignity in Chapter 10.

43. Cf. Strawson's remark that in "much of our behaviour the benefit or injury resides mainly or entirely in the manifestation of the attitude itself" (1968: 76).

44. In their introduction, Raphael and Macfie point out that Smith wrote, in his "Letter to the Editors of the *Edinburgh Review*" of July 1775, that he could "describe, from his own reading . . . Rousseau's *Discourse on Inequality*" (Smith 1982a: 10).

The implicit aim of reactive attitudes is to make others feel our dignity (and, less obviously, their own).

If this is right, reactive attitudes, and the practices of moral accountability they mediate, actually seek the reverse of what retaliation is after. Whereas to retaliate is to return disrespect for disrespect, holding someone accountable respectfully demands respect for disrespect. Reactive attitudes "continue to view [their object] as a member of the moral community" (Strawson 1968: 93).

Laura Blumenfeld (2002) provides a vivid illustration of this phenomenon in a fascinating description of her attempts to find the man, Omar Khatib, who had shot her father, David Blumenfeld, in order to hold Khatib responsible in some appropriate way.[45] David had visited Jerusalem in 1986 during a period in which Omar and other members of a rebel faction of the PLO made several attacks on tourists in the Old City. David was such a tourist, and he narrowly escaped death when Omar's bullet only grazed his scalp. In her journey, Laura spends several years in Israel trying to get close to Omar, who is still in jail. Presenting herself to Omar's family as a journalist, she gets to know them and begins to correspond with Omar in letters the family smuggles to him in jail. Through these letters, Laura and Omar strike up a relationship without Omar or his family knowing Laura's true identity. Omar remains unrepentant throughout, seeing what he has done not as an attack against another person, but as an impersonal political action. Likewise, Omar's family sees the shooting as "nothing personal," a form of "public relations, a way to get people to look at us."

Blumenfeld finally hits upon a strategy for accountability and the circumstances to pursue it. A psychologist at Hebrew University, Hanoch Yerushalmi, convinces her that "the only substitute for revenge is acknowledgment." "Acknowledgment," he says, "is . . . accepting responsibility. It's when you 'own your own guilt' " (Blumenfeld 2002: 292).

Laura sees her chance the first time she and Omar lay eyes on each other at a legal proceeding to hear Omar's request to be released from prison because of deteriorating health. At a crucial point in the proceedings, Laura stands up and demands to speak. When the perplexed Israeli

45. Blumenfeld's book is titled *Revenge: A Story of Hope*. Like some reviewers of the book, I think Blumenfeld's term "constructive revenge" is actually a misnomer for the mutually respecting, or reciprocally recognizing, accountability that Blumenfeld actually describes (and achieves).

judges ask why, she begins by saying she has gotten to know the Khatib family and that she believes that Omar is sorry for what he has done. She says also that she has spoken to David Blumenfeld and that he agrees that Omar's request should be granted. When the justices challenge her right to speak, she replies to the hushed courtroom that she indeed has a right because she is David Blumenfeld's daughter. Shocked by this development, Omar and his family begin to weep. Blumenfeld writes: "Omar's mother, who did not understand my Hebrew, looked around the room, bewildered and said, 'Why are my children in tears?' " Asked by a judge why she has made this intervention, Laura says that she wanted Omar to know that "we're people. Not 'targets.' We're people with families. And you can't just kill us." Afterward, Omar writes to Laura, apologizing for being "the cause of your and your kind mother's pain." (Laura's mother had also been at the proceeding.) For the first time, he acknowledges the personality of his victim, calling him "David." He also writes to David, expressing his "deep pain and sorrow for what I caused you" (Blumenfeld 2002: 265–267).

Blumenfeld's story confirms Smith's diagnosis. Reactive attitudes seek respect. They seek to engage the other second-personally, and they succeed when the other takes up the address, acknowledges its terms, and thereby respects the dignity of the addresser, both the demand she addresses and her standing to address it.[46] Respect thus enters into reactive attitudes in three distinct places: (1) their *object*, more precisely described, is always some form of apparent disrespect; (2) their *aim* is to demand respect; and (3) their *mode* involves respect for the person to whom they are held—they respectfully demand respect.

Accountability, Freedom, and Noncentral Cases

But this may raise another worry. If reactive attitudes necessarily presuppose that those we seek to hold accountable have the ability to recognize

46. Another poignant example can be found in the Very Reverend James Whyte's remarks at the memorial service for the victims of Pan Am 103 in Lockerbie, Scotland, in December, 1988: "We may be tempted, indeed urged by some, to flex our muscles in response, to show that we are men. To show that we are what?" Quoting now from Whyte's obituary in *The Scotsman* of June 27, 2005 (p. 39): "His calm and balanced reasoning seemed to strike a chord with all in the church and those watching on television. To see more young die, more rescue workers labour in more wreckage, he argued, was a sign, not of virility, but of inhumanity. 'That is what retaliation means,' Whyte concluded. 'I, for one, will have none of it, and I hope you will not either. Justice yes, retaliation no.'"

the validity of the second-personal reasons we address and to act on that recognition, might this not raise the bar too high? What gives us confidence that others actually have this ability, or that we do ourselves?[47]

It is unnecessary to establish independently that we do have moral freedom (second-personal competence) in order to hold one another accountable justifiably. As Kant's "fact of reason" shows, it can be enough that we have no particular reason to think we do not have moral freedom that would defeat the inescapable assumption that we do to which second-personal address commits us. But that doesn't mean that this hypothesis cannot be defeated. After all, the whole point of Strawson's distinction between objective and reactive attitudes is that there are beings we appropriately do view "objectively" precisely because they lack the requisite freedom to intelligibly be held accountable. And there are also cases, as Strawson points out, when people whom we generally are prepared to hold accountable fall into conditions, severe mental illness, for example, during which we appropriately withhold reactive attitudes. There is no reason, indeed, why this cannot also happen in one's own case. In an early stage of schizophrenia say, someone might make moral judgments of herself that have a presupposition of moral freedom that, regrettably, no longer holds.

So even if we are entitled to a defeasible presumption of moral freedom, this can be rebutted by the facts on the ground. And thus a version of the worry reemerges. Even if we exclude the uncontroversially "objective" cases Strawson mentions, including very young children and those suffering from delusional insanity, there seem to be many cases where we wish to hold others accountable though we seem to have very good evidence that they are not free to act on moral reasons in the way our practices of holding someone fully responsible seem to presuppose.

We can hardly deal with this worry with any thoroughness here. In general, I believe that to do so systematically, we would have to think of what I have said so far as applying to a central ideal case (what we might call the case of "full responsibility") and see other cases as departures that must be understood in one way or another by reference to the central second-personal case. In some instances, for example with children, we

---

47. Of course, the normative presuppositions of any specific form of second-personal address can be defeated also. In Chapters 10 and 11, I argue that morality's authority can be vindicated by an appreciation of their role in second-personal address in general and of the distinctive form of practical freedom we have by virtue of our capacity for second-personal relations.

seem simultaneously to move on two tracks in the process of inducting them into full second-personal responsibility, sometimes treating them proleptically as though they were apt for second-personal address as a way of developing moral competence while nonetheless realizing ("objectively") that this is an illusion that must also be recognized.[48]

Something similar may be true where there are deficits that rule out full responsibility, such as people with Alzheimer's disease or Down's syndrome, but where there is no such forward-looking process. Here we may work along two tracks as well, perhaps a fully, at least putatively, second-personal track in relatively limited areas along with continuous negotiation about the limits.[49] And there may be cases, which we will consider further presently, where we seem to hold someone fully responsible even in the face of the conviction that he really couldn't have been expected to determine himself by the demands we make in holding him responsible. Such cases must always create some discomfort, I think, since we treat them as though they were a central second-personal case, perhaps to affirm to ourselves and to one another the demands we make on the person we hold accountable, in the belief that the necessary presuppositions of doing so may very likely not be satisfied.[50]

That all said, I would like to say something briefly about two quite different kinds of cases. One is that of people we attempt to hold accountable for forms of abuse and violence that they attempt to excuse as due to uncontrollable emotion. In these cases, as I see it, we are generally right to suppose that the assumption of freedom is not defeated. The second, which really may pose a challenge to the presupposition is that of an extreme psychopath, perhaps someone like Robert Alton Harris, who was convicted in 1978 of the horrific killing of two teenage boys, whom Gary Watson discusses in just these terms.[51]

Cases of the first kind are well exemplified by varieties of domestic

48. I am indebted here to Schapiro 1999 and 2003a. Also see Dewey 1998a: 343, which reference I owe to Elizabeth Anderson.

49. I have been helped here by discussion with Christie Hartley and by her work on how the disabled should be represented within contractualism (2005).

50. I am indebted to Charles Griswold and Richard Kraut for discussion here.

51. Harris was executed in 1992, the first California execution in twenty-five years. Watson gives many of the details of Harris's life (Watson 1987: 268–271), quoting from Corwin 1982. See also an article by Harris's lawyer in his appeals of the death sentence (Laurence 1997).

violence, road rage, and the like. On analysis, it is often clear enough that the acts of abuse or violence were freely chosen, that the principals could have done otherwise but indulged themselves in thoughts and feelings that rationalized their actions in one way or another. One sign that this is so is when victimizers do not consistently stick to the claim that what they did was an excusable wrong, but lapse also into purported justifications of their actions as deserved or as a kind of "correction" that really was for the good for the victim. In unguarded moments, the emotions and attitudes they express are not grief and regret for what they have done along with disquieting confusion about how they could have acted in this way, but instead project some sense of justification. What seems to be going on here is something like what Kant called "self-conceit," frequently tied to some legitimating ideology, like male sovereignty.[52] It is not that the person is dead to moral categories; rather he distorts them for his own purposes.

The case of psychopaths, however, seems very different. Although at points in his life Robert Harris may have been more like the kind of person just discussed, by the time of his most grisly murders he manifested a coldness and utter imperviousness to moral demands, even in the corrupted form of self-conceit, suggesting that he was inapt for moral address, a moral outlaw who was outside the moral community. Despite this, there may be reasons for holding people like Harris accountable.

As Watson describes it, Harris's coldness resulted from prior willful choices to repudiate the moral community, born partly of a history of being a victim of terrible abuse himself—not exactly a Kantian timeless choice of evil, but more like a series of repudiating choices.[53] It may be that at later points Harris was unable to do other than continue on the "road to hell" he had chosen before.[54] Treating him as accountable now,

52. I discuss Kant on self-conceit in Chapter 6.

53. Watson suggests this at Watson 1987: 271. Meno Myejes's screenplay, *Max* (2002), implies something similar about Hitler. Discussing it, Myejes says, "Hitler, like Osama and Saddam and Milosevic, obliges us by representing an uncomplicated picture of evil. But nobody wakes up one day and slaughters thousands. They make choices, one at a time." He also remarks that his movie "isn't about Hitler's great crimes. The audience knows all about them already. This is about his small sins—his emotional cowardice, his relentless self-pity, his envy, his frustration, the way he collects and nurtures offenses" (Malanowski 2002: 1, 36).

54. Harris's sister was quoted as saying, "He told me he had his chance, he took the road to hell and there's nothing more to say" (Watson: 1987: 270). Even at this point,

however, respectfully repudiates the repudiation. Even if it carries a pre-supposition that is now literally false, it can have an important expressive function for the community nonetheless: upholding the dignity of the person. Moreover, there may simply be no publicly reliable way of distinguishing cases where there is literal incapacity from those where people are still capable of moral redemption, but freely choose not to redeem themselves (perhaps Harris at some earlier point, or even later—who knows?). So even when we are confronted with cases like that of Robert Harris, a presupposition of moral freedom may be a justified form of "practical faith," which we may lack sufficient evidence to defeat.[55]

However, if we come to the view that this presupposition is in fact defeated in particular cases, this need put no significant pressure on the presupposition as it operates in our ordinary practices of accountability.[56] We can still find an appropriate justification for limiting a genuinely non-second-personally-competent psychopath's liberty in self-protection. And the very fact that we will have to think of our justification in other terms, that is, as not genuinely holding the psychopath responsible, will be evidence for the second-personal character of our practices of moral responsibility as they normally function.[57]

---

however, if Harris was still capable of resenting injuries done to him, he was still a participant in the second-person standpoint, only highly selectively. I am grateful to Arthur Ripstein here.

55. The allusion, of course, is to Kant's postulates of the existence of God and immortality of the soul in *The Critique of Practical Reason*.

56. See Robert D. Hare (1993) for a pessimistic view of the possibilities of overlap between psychopathology and emotional mechanisms, like empathy, that are necessary for second-personal competence.

57. I've been helped here by discussion with Vanessa Carbonell.

— 5 —

Moral Obligation
and Accountability

It is a curious feature of the contemporary philosophical scene that, although Strawson's critique has been very influential in debates about
responsibility and free will within moral psychology and the philosophy
of action, its implications for the metaethics of moral obligation as well
as for normative moral theory have been largely ignored. In this chapter,
I argue that there is an intrinsic conceptual connection between moral
obligation and moral responsibility, one Strawson himself implicitly relies
upon. It follows, I argue, that Strawson's influential critique of consequentialist accounts of moral responsibility can be turned into a powerful
criticism of consequentialist theories of moral obligation, most obviously,
of act-consequentialism, but arguably also of indirect consequentialist approaches such as rule-consequentialism.[1] When we reflect on obligation's
intrinsic connection to (second-personal) accountability, we see that sub-
serving an external goal is a reason of the wrong kind to justify moral
obligation no less than it is to warrant claims of moral responsibility. Like
moral responsibility, moral obligation is an irreducibly second-personal
concept. That an action would violate a moral obligation is, I here argue,
a second-personal reason not to do it.

Accountability and the Metaethics of Moral Obligation

One way to see this is to note that Strawson includes a "sense of obligation" as a (reflexive) reactive attitude and that he characterizes the

---

1. Except, again, when these are themselves grounded in the second-personal idea that
all persons have an equal claim. On this point, see note 32 of Chapter 4 and "Contractualism and Rule-Consequentialism" in Chapter 12. I am indebted here, again, to Allan
Gibbard and Jim Staihar.

skepticism he takes pragmatic approaches to responsibility to be responding to as holding that if determinism is true, "then the concepts of
moral obligation and responsibility really have no application" (1968: 86,
71). As Strawson sees it, skepticism about free agency puts pressure on
both moral responsibility and moral obligation. Strawson doesn't say directly why this should be so, but it is clear enough that he takes moral
obligation and responsibility to be intrinsically related conceptually, and
not just as a matter of substantive normative judgment. What we are
morally obligated to do, he seems to be thinking, is what members of the
moral community can appropriately demand that we do, including by
responding with blame or other reactive attitudes if we fail to comply
without adequate excuse.

Perhaps the best-known invocation of this idea is, ironically enough,
by a consequentialist thinker, namely, John Stuart Mill.[2] In the course of
considering in chapter 5 of *Utilitarianism* (1998) how a utilitarian might
account for rights and justice, Mill provides a genealogy of conceptions
of justice and concludes that "the primitive element, in the formation of
the notion of justice, was conformity to law" and that this involves the
idea of warranted sanctions. Mill evidently means this as a conceptual
point. More importantly for our purposes, Mill goes on to apply this
conceptual analysis to "moral obligation in general." And then he famously adds:

> We do not call anything wrong, unless we mean to imply that a person
> ought to be punished in some way or other for doing it; if not by law,
> by the opinion of his fellow-creatures; if not by opinion, by the re-
> proaches of his own conscience. This seems the real turning point of
> the distinction between morality and simple expediency. It is a part of
> the notion of Duty in every one of its forms, that a person may rightfully
> be compelled to fulfill it. Duty is a thing which may be exacted from a
> person, as one exacts a debt. (1998: ch. 5, para. 14)

Mill seems to be on safe ground in saying that our concept of wrongdoing is essentially related to accountability. Even if it is natural to think

2. In Mill 1998: ch. 5. Another landmark is Rawls's argument in "Two Concepts of
Rules" (1955) that practices are frequently constituted by rules that forbid participants to
appeal to any external goals the practice might be thought to achieve. For an excellent
discussion of this point, see Johnson 1985. Also relevant is Hart's famous distinction between the "internal" and "external" perspective within a regime of law or other set of
norms (1961: 55–57).

that a person falls short of full virtue if she does only what can be required of her—is a "minimally decent," rather than a good, Samaritan, in Judith Thomson's (1971) terms—it seems unnatural to suppose that she thereby does wrong. What is wrong is what we can be morally expected not to do, what the moral community assumes the authority to hold us to. We hesitate to impute wrongdoing unless we take ourselves to be in the range of the culpable, that is, unless the action is such that the agent is aptly blamed or the object of some other form of accountability-seeking reactive attitude if she lacks an adequate excuse.[3]

This aspect of the concept of moral wrong has been stressed also by a number of contemporary writers. John Skorupski says that calling an act "morally wrong . . . amounts to blaming the agent" and that the idea of moral wrong can't be understood independently of that of blameworthiness (1999: 29, 142). Allan Gibbard quite explicitly follows Mill's lead in proposing that "what a person does is *morally wrong* if and only if it is rational for him to feel guilty for having done it, and for others to be angry at him for having done it" (1990: 42). And we can find versions of this Millian idea in other writers also (Baier 1966; Brandt 1979; Shafer-Landau 2003). (It is consistent with these views that there remains a distinction between the wrongness of acts and the blameworthiness of agents. Someone may not be to blame for wrongdoing if he has an excuse.)

Perhaps most striking is the role the connection plays in neo-Nietzschean critiques of morality and moral obligation, most prominently by Bernard Williams.[4] Williams's version of the Nietzschean critique that morality is an enslaving ideology, a form of false consciousness that shackles and sickens, runs through conceptual relations he sees between

3. The original meaning of 'impute' is relevant here: "To bring (a fault or the like) into the reckoning against; to lay to the charge of; to attribute or assign as due or owing to" (*Oxford English Dictionary*, online edition). See also Pufendorf on "imputativity" below. As T. M. Scanlon has pointed out to me, however, there may be cases where we take ourselves to have the authority to blame someone and make demands of them even when we don't think they act wrongly, as, for example, when someone does the right thing, but for utterly unconscionable reasons, say, out of a virulent racism.

4. Especially in Williams 1985. For a discussion, see Darwall 1987. See also Williams 1995 and Baier 1993. Nietzsche's diagnosis of morality "in the pejorative sense" is primarily given in Nietzsche 1994. For useful discussion, see Leiter 1995 and 1997.

It is worth noting that, although Williams is a critic of what we might call the "internal" aspects of second-personal accountability of the "morality system," he does embrace the

moral obligation, blame, and reasons for acting.[5] Williams evidently assumes that it is a conceptual truth that violations of moral obligations
are appropriately blamed and that blaming implies the existence of good
and sufficient reasons to do what someone is blamed for not doing. The
idea is not, of course, that normative reasons follow from the fact of
someone's being blamed. Rather, in blaming one implies or presupposes
that there are such reasons. According to Williams (1995), this presupposition is a bit of false consciousness. And what makes it so, according
to him, are his famous *internal reasons thesis*, which asserts that all normative reasons for action must be anchored appropriately in the agent's
own "motivational set" (be "internal reasons"), and his claim that nothing
guarantees any connection between what we take to license blame when
we attempt to hold agents accountable and their own motivations.[6]

It is important to the argument of this book that Williams is actually
right about these conceptual connections between imputing wrong and
blame and between blame and attributing authoritative reasons. Moral
obligation really is conceptually related to standards of minimally decent
conduct that moral agents are accountable for complying with. And the
forms of moral accountability—blame, guilt, indignation, punishment,
and so on—really do imply that agents have reasons (indeed, conclusive
reasons) to do what they are morally obligated and accountable for
doing.[7] Moreover, depending on how we understand the idea of a "motivational set," it may also be possible, consistently with the substantive
normative claims of this book (that equal second-personal authority

---

idea of human rights and the "external" forms necessary to enforce them. But this means,
I believe, that participants in moral practices of enforcement, including all citizens when
they participate in public discourse, are unable to accept reasons of the right kind for the
second-personal demands through which they seek to enforce their rights. Their justification must consist in something like the desirability of using power, not any authority to
use it. In my view, Hume's ideas about justice lead to the same result (see Chapter 8).
Both run afoul of Strawson's Point. I am indebted here to discussion with Simon Blackburn.

5. Williams encourages the association with slavery himself by referring to morality as
the "peculiar institution" in the title of chapter 10 ("Morality, the Peculiar Institution") of
Williams 1985.

6. The former is a version of what I have called "existence internalism" (Darwall 1983:
54–55).

7. Again, this is implied or presupposed in holding people accountable. It is not implied
by the fact that we hold them accountable. We shall consider this point further presently.

grounds second-personal reasons), to hold a version of Williams's internal reasons thesis. However, I argue that reasons for acting are not constrained in any way by an agent's state- or outcome-regarding desires or even by his capacities to form such desires.[8] Any desires that are implicated in action on second-personal reasons, including action on the reasons we imply when we hold persons accountable for compliance with moral obligations, are "principle-dependent" rather than "object-dependent," in Rawls's terms (2000). And my claim is that second-personal relations and reactive attitudes quite generally address second-personal reasons in a way that presupposes that addressees have the capacity to be moved by these reasons through accepting principles to which their reciprocally recognizing participation in second-personal relations commits them.

Nothing depends, of course, on whether we use the words 'wrong' and 'moral obligation' in the way Mill and these contemporary thinkers say we do. We could use these words more broadly to include moral ideals or goals. However, if we did, we would still need terms to refer to the idea to which these thinkers point, namely, the part of morality that concerns that for which we appropriately hold one another responsible. And it seems clear enough that, as all these writers agree, this involves a notion of moral demands, that is, of standards of conduct that the moral community has the authority to demand compliance with, including through second-personal forms of accountability of the sort we canvassed in the last chapter. With this understanding, therefore, I henceforth use 'wrong' and 'moral obligation' in a Millian way as implying accountability-seeking demands.

Using 'wrong' in this way does not, we should note, require that there be an assignable victim who is wronged (hence, that what Mill regards as a right be in play), or even that that violations of norms of a community of mutually accountable persons directly threaten the interests of such persons. It is consistent with the idea that wrongdoing is essentially tied to accountability, even accountability to other moral persons, that what we are accountable for can extend, for example, to the treatment of nonrational animals, aspects of the environment, and nonrational human beings.[9]

8. Rawls calls these "object-dependent" desires in Rawls 2000: 45–48, 148–152.
9. See the discussion of this point in Chapter 2.

Making Moral Obligation's Second-Personality Explicit

Debates in moral theory rarely tie moral obligation to second-personal accountability explicitly, but they often implicitly assume such a connection nonetheless. In this section, we note this phenomenon in two familiar debates. One takes place within normative ethical theory between consequentialists and their critics over whether act-consequentialism is "too demanding." The other concerns morality's authority or, as it is sometimes put, "Why be moral?" In both cases, analysis of what most deeply underlies the debate reveals an assumption that moral obligation and standards of right and wrong are conceptually related to what the moral community, and we as members, can demand (second-personally).

Take the "too demanding" criticism first. Act-consequentialism's critics sometimes concede, *arguendo,* that an agent may always do best from the moral point of view by maximizing overall net good, for example, by always investing energy and resources at the margin to combat hunger, disease, and oppression worldwide. But they argue that even if this were so, it wouldn't follow that failing, say, to produce small marginal increases in overall value at very large personal cost is wrong. And they argue, furthermore, that a theory that requires that we do so is unreasonably demanding.[10] What underlies this objection?

The following formulation puts the criticism in a way that helps one to see what is going on:

> Perhaps we would admire someone who behaved in this way. But is it plausible to claim that those of us who do not are guilty of wrongdoing; or that we have a moral obligation to devote all our resources to charity?[11]

"Guilty of wrongdoing" is the revealing phrase. Wrongdoing is something one can be charged with and, lacking adequate account or excuse, be guilty of, where guilt is a verdict (an Austinian "verdictive") in some quasi-legal, second-personal form of accountability.[12]

10. A particularly good example is Scheffler 1982.

11. This formulation actually comes from someone who tries to defend consequentialism in the face of the "demandingness" objection (Mulgan 2001).

12. Compare Nietzsche's claim that, whereas in the aristocratic ethos, 'good' is the primary notion and 'bad' is defined as not 'good', in morality (in the pejorative sense), 'evil'

That one is guilty of wrongdoing is not simply a finding that what one did was less than the best one could have done (even when this is the normative standard of wrongdoing); it is the judgment that one did less than can be expected or demanded and that one can implicitly demand of oneself in a second-personal feeling that acknowledges guilt. What underlies the "demandingness" objection, therefore, is the worry that act-consequentialism's standard of right goes beyond what we can reasonably demand of one another (second-personally). A moral demand just is, *inter alia*, there being warrant to address a demand (second-personally) to someone as one person among others, "if not by law, by the opinion of his fellow-creatures; if not by opinion, by the reproaches of his own conscience" (Mill 1998: ch. 5). To make sense of the "demandingness" objection, therefore, we must see it as resting on the assumption that wrong and moral obligation are conceptually related to holding morally responsible, hence to second-personal demanding as it functions, for example, in the reactive attitude of guilt.

The other debate in which such a conceptual connection is implicitly assumed concerns morality's purported authority, that is, whether moral obligations are categorical imperatives in Foot's (amplified by Scheffler's) sense of always necessarily giving or entailing (conclusive) reasons for acting. In Chapters 10 and 11, I take on this question directly and argue that a conception of morality as equal accountability can be grounded in a theory of practical reason in a way that vindicates the claim that moral agents always necessarily have conclusive reasons not to violate moral obligations. At this point, however, I am concerned with what underlies this authoritative purport. Why does the statement "But it would be wrong" always purport to provide a conclusive reason?[13]

A number of writers, most prominently, again, Bernard Williams, have argued that holding someone accountable for wrongdoing through blame unavoidably carries the implication that she had conclusive reason not to

---

is the primary notion and 'good' is its contradictory (in our terms: 'wrong' and 'right' [not wrong]) (Nietzsche 1994).

13. Note that I say purport to provide conclusive reason. Richard Nixon evidently relied on this implication, according to H. R. Haldeman's testimony, when he said in response to the question of whether hush money could be raised to pay off the Watergate burglars: "There is no problem in raising a million dollars, we can do that. But it would be wrong." (The last "five crucial words" were not confirmed by John Dean's testimony.) ("Seven Charged, a Report and a Briefcase," *Time* 103 (March 11, 1974): 10–14.)

do what she is blamed for doing (Williams 1995: 40–44; see also Gibbard 1990: 299–300; Shafer-Landau 2003: 181–183; Skorupski 1999: 42–43; Wallace 1994).[14] Williams believes that this implication is "bluff," a bit of ideology that it is hopeless to try to vindicate or validate, since the only reasons for acting the person we blame can possibly have are internal reasons that are suitably anchored in her desires or other motivational susceptibilities, and, he thinks, nothing we could say on behalf of moral demands could possibly guarantee that. At this point, we need not concern ourselves with this latter claim. We will have occasion to return to the issue of what moral psychology we presuppose when we make demands and what its relation is to the validity of second-personal reasons at various points later.[15] At this juncture we need focus only on Williams's claim that blaming carries this implication, that is, that we cannot intelligibly demand that someone act in some way without implying that she has good and sufficient reason to do so.

Again, this just seems straightforwardly true. Try formulating an expression with which you might address a moral demand to someone. I doubt that you can find one that does not carry the implication that she has conclusive reason to do what you are demanding or reason not to have done what you are blaming her for. Certainly none of the obvious formulations will work. For example, you can hardly sensibly say, "You really shouldn't have done that," and then add "but you did have, nonetheless, conclusive reasons for doing it." And if you try to pull your punches, by saying "You shouldn't have done that, I mean, you know, morally speaking," although you may end up canceling the implication of conclusive reasons, it's hard to see how you can do that without also canceling an implication of blame or demand. Or to turn the point around, if someone were able to establish that she did in fact have good and sufficient reason for a putative violation of a moral obligation, then it seems she has accounted or answered for herself and shown she did no wrong.[16] When we charge her with wrongdoing, therefore, we must be implying that she can not provide such an account.

Or recall Philippa Foot's comparison between morality and etiquette

---

14. It is no coincidence that Williams is an original source of the "too demandingness" objection to consequentialism (Smart and Williams 1973).

15. The issue is addressed mainly in Chapter 7.

16. I am indebted to Christine Korsgaard for this way of putting it.

(1972). Norms of etiquette and morality are both categorical in form, and some norms of etiquette can be expressed in no less mandatory terms than can those of morality. One simply must not eat peas with a knife. But even so, we can cancel any implication that a 'must' of manners carries conclusive normative authority without thereby calling into question etiquette's customary normative purport. We can sensibly say that sometimes there is good reason not to do what etiquette requires without any suggestion that we are thereby somehow debunking manners. What explains this difference?

I believe that it is, again, moral obligation's essential tie to second-personal accountability. It is part of the very idea of a moral demand that we are accountable for complying. But such accountability seems no part whatsoever of the idea that etiquette requires something. That doesn't mean that manners are not, to some extent, "morals writ small," or that etiquette cannot be an important part of or supplement to equal respect.[17] And it is also obviously true that some people treat etiquette, or parts of it, as having an importance that is tantamount to morality's. The point is that accountability is no part of the concept of etiquette in the way it is of moral obligation. To the contrary, what etiquette usually calls for when its norms are violated is not accountability but something more like distracting attention from an otherwise embarrassing reciprocal recognition of a gaffe or, perhaps, third-personal disdain. Calling someone to account for bad manners is often bad manners itself.

Morality's Normativity and Second-Personal Reasons

The very ideas of wrong and moral obligation, therefore, are intrinsically related to the forms of second-personal address that, as we saw in Chapter 4, help constitute moral accountability. It follows that the fact that an action is wrong, or that it violates a moral obligation, must itself purport to be or entail a second-personal reason (or reasons). There can be no such thing as moral obligation and wrongdoing without the normative standing to demand and hold agents accountable for compliance. Of course, many of the reasons that ground claims of wrong and obligation are not themselves second-personal. That an action would cause severe harm, or even pain to your bunions, is a reason for someone not to do

17. On the latter, see Buss 1996a and Sherman unpublished.

it, whether or not anyone has any standing to demand that he not, and it supports, moreover, a relevant demand. But the action cannot violate a moral obligation unless such a standing exists, so any reason that is entailed by the moral obligation must be second-personal. Consequently, if moral obligations purport to provide conclusive normative reasons, other reasons to the contrary notwithstanding, then this must derive somehow from their second-personal character.

As I mentioned in Chapter 2, the projects of analyzing and vindicating morality's distinctive purported authority are generally framed in terms of "categoricality" and the normative weight of reasons to be moral. We are now in a position to appreciate why I there added that any attempt to account for moral obligation's distinctive bindingness must also explicate its distinctive tie to accountability. An adequate analysis of the concept of moral obligation must account for its conceptual connection to warranted demands. Even if it were possible, consequently, to account otherwise either for moral obligations' invariably purporting to provide superior normative reasons or their actually doing so, it would still be impossible thereby to explicate the distinctive hold or bindingness that moral obligations purport to have. This can only be done in second-personal terms.

This means that the project of analyzing morality's normativity is seriously incomplete as it has traditionally been conceived. I believe, moreover, that the significance of the fact that moral obligation's distinctive reasons are second-personal goes beyond even this. I have argued also in this chapter that appreciating moral obligation's tie to accountability provides the best explanation of morality's purported normativity as traditionally conceived. And I argue further in Chapters 10 and 11 that this normative purport can be vindicated as well when we see the place of second-personal reasons in an overall picture of practical reason. It follows that appreciating the second-personal character of moral obligation is necessary both to understanding its normative purport (both its putative normative weight and conceptual tie to moral responsibility) and to the most promising way of backing this hefty promissory note.

Morality as Equal Accountability

I have been arguing that being subject to moral obligations includes accountability to those with the normative standing to demand compliance. So far, this has been a conceptual thesis: *moral obligation as accountability*.

This abstract concept admits of different specifications or conceptions, however.[18] For much of the rest of this chapter, I discuss the early modern voluntarist version of morality as accountability: *morality as accountability to God*. According to the voluntarists' conception, only God has the ultimate authority to make moral demands. Even if human beings reciprocally benefit by complying with God's commands, we have no underived normative standing to expect compliance of one another or of ourselves. However, when voluntarists like Pufendorf thought through what is presupposed in addressing demands as genuinely second-personal reasons, they began to see that they were committed also to the idea that moral subjects must be assumed to be capable of imposing moral demands on themselves through recognizing that they validly apply to them as rational persons. And this put significant pressure on their thought in the direction of a different conception, one I call *morality as equal accountability*.

We can see a similar movement of thought in other thinkers as well. Although it is rarely appreciated, Adam Smith also makes accountability central to his picture of morality.[19] "A moral being," Smith says, "is an accountable being," who "must give an account of its actions to some other, and that consequently must regulate them according to the good-liking of this other" (1982a: 111). Although Smith says that man is "principally accountable to God," he quickly adds that each "must necessarily conceive himself as accountable to his fellow-creatures, before he can form any idea of the Deity" (1982a: 111n).[20]

Morality as equal accountability is the conception I defend in this book. According to this conception, moral norms regulate a community of equal, mutually accountable, free and rational agents as such, and moral obligations are the demands such agents have standing to address to one another and with which they are mutually accountable for complying. In Kantian terms, norms of moral obligation are "laws" for a "kingdom of ends," which structure and define the equal dignity of persons as beings who may not be treated in some ways and must be in others and who have equal standing to demand this second-personally of one another.[21]

18. For the general concept/conception framework, see Rawls 1971: 5.

19. I discuss this aspect of Smith's views in Darwall 1999b.

20. Note, however, that Smith does not retain this passage in the sixth edition. I am indebted to Vivienne Brown and Charles Griswold for reminding me of this.

21. "By a *kingdom* [*of ends*] I understand a systematic union of various rational beings through common laws" (Kant 1996b: 433). Also: "In the kingdom of ends everything has

So conceived, "morality is," as Kant puts it, "the condition under which alone a rational being can be an end in itself, since only through this is it possible to be a lawgiving member in the kingdom of ends" (1996b: 435).

Morality as equal accountability understands the moral point of view to be fundamentally *intersubjective*. It holds the moral perspective to be an impartially disciplined version of the second-person standpoint, in which, as anyone (or, as an equal participant in the first-person plural ["we"] of the moral community), one addresses someone (oneself or someone else) also as anyone (as another equal member).[22] It is useful to contrast this understanding of the moral point of view with the impersonal standpoint that Nagel, in *The Possibility of Altruism*, famously argued is the perspective from which one must be able to see others' interests, and ultimately one's own, as reason-giving (Nagel 1970). Such a point of view, Nagel maintained, is one from which one sees oneself simply as "one among others equally real."

However, an impersonal perspective *on* one among others is not necessarily the standpoint *of* one among others. It is not the intersubjective stance of someone relating to others as, and reciprocally recognizing his status as, one among others.[23] According to morality as equal accountability, the moral point of view is intersubjective in precisely this sense. It is an impartially regulated second-personal stance rather than a third-personal perspective on individuals, oneself included, as simply one among others.[24] In morality as equal accountability, agents relate to one

---

either a *price* or a *dignity*. . . . Morality, and humanity insofar as it is capable of morality, is that which alone has dignity" (434–435). As I stress in Chapters 6 and 10, Kant also says that the dignity of persons is that "by which [a person] exacts *respect* for himself from all other rational beings in the world" (1996d: 435).

22. For the claim that moral point of view is "first-person plural" see Postema 1995. It is also a theme of Korsgaard's writings.

23. This is also a theme of Christine Korsgaard's, in Korsgaard 1996d: esp. 275–276, 301. However, Korsgaard there seems to think that all reasons involve the making of claims (whereas I restrict this to second-personal reasons): "To say that you have a reason is to say something *relational,* something which implies the existence of another, at least another self. It announces that you have a claim on that other, or acknowledges her claim on you" (Korsgaard 1996d: 301). In my view, this conflates the general category of normative reasons with the distinctively second-personal reasons that figure in justifying ourselves to one another.

24. I believe this is also the right way of understanding Adam Smith's sentimentalist

another as one among others second-personally; they don't simply view each other that way third-personally.[25]

We should now recall the thought with which we began this chapter, namely, that, owing to the connection between moral obligation and accountability, Strawson's criticisms of consequentialist accounts of responsibility can be turned into a critique of consequentialist accounts of obligation. The problem with pragmatic approaches to responsibility, recall, is that they point to reasons of the wrong kind, since reasons of desirability are in themselves irrelevant to any standards to which we are committed from within the (second-person) stance we unavoidably occupy when we hold one another responsible. Since responsibility and obligation are conceptually tied in the ways we have noted, if this is a problem with consequentialist approaches to responsibility, it must be a problem also with consequentialist theories of moral obligation and wrongdoing. However desirable it might be from some external perspective that someone do something, this is a reason of the wrong kind to support a demand that he do it, and hence to support the claim that he would do wrong if he didn't. Unlike considerations of desirability (even moral desirability), demands are second-personal reasons; their validity depends not on the value of any outcome or state, but on normative relations between persons, on one person's having the authority to address the demand to another. It follows that claims of moral obligation or wrongdoing must be supportable from within the second-person standpoint and grounded in presuppositions to which you and I are committed when we reciprocally recognize one another as free and equal persons.

This line of thought tells fairly directly against act-consequentialist theories of moral obligation.[26] That explains why consequentialists who are influenced by Mill regarding obligation's tie to blameworthiness, like Brandt and arguably Mill himself, tend to hold some form of indirect consequentialism, such as rule-consequentialism (Brandt 1965, 1979; Hooker 2000; Johnson 1991). But indirect consequentialism just seems to postpone the difficulty, since even though it admits a distinction between the desirable and the obligatory, the only support it al-

---

metaethics of moral judgment, especially of judgments of justice. On this point, see Darwall 1999b.

25. On this, see Christine Korsgaard's important work (1996a).

26. For a related line of criticism, see Johnson 1985.

lows for claims of obligation are instrumental considerations regarding how a practice of obligation and accountability itself, structured by some candidate rule, serves to advance an external goal. And this still seems a reason of the wrong kind.[27] By contrast, morality as equal accountability understands standards of moral obligation as requiring support entirely within the second-personal standpoint itself—all the way down. In Chapters 10 through 12, I sketch how this might be done within a contractualism that is grounded in a theory of second-personal reasons.

Accountability and Second-Personal Reasons in Early Modern Natural Law

Morality as equal accountability is, again, only one interpretation (or conception) of the concept of morality as accountability. In the rest of this chapter, I discuss the early modern natural law conception of morality as accountability to God, as we find it in, for example, Suarez, Pufendorf, and Locke.[28] My purpose is twofold. First, it is useful to grasp in a detailed way accountability's role in some of the earliest attempts to articulate a distinctively modern concept of morality.[29] Second, I want to display tensions within early modern voluntarism that lead in the direction of morality as equal accountability. In these respects, it is helpful, I believe, to think of the conception of morality as accountability to God as an ancestor conception of morality as equal accountability. I present this discussion here, however, less for its historical interest and more

27. Of course, as I have noted before, most recently in note 1 above, an act- or rule-consequentialist theory of right might avoid this problem if it could be adequately grounded in an equal claim to happiness, welfare, or something similar.

28. In what follows, I draw on Darwall 2003a.

29. Here I follow Schneewind 1998 in thinking that the "Grotian problematic," that is, distinguishing between, and trying to appropriately relate, the idea of an individual's good and some other regulating idea (justice, right, or the morally obligatory) provides the distinctive backdrop for a "modern" concept of morality. I discuss this point in Darwall 1995a: ch. 1 and 1999a. Also relevant is Sidgwick's perceptive remark that "the most fundamental difference" between modern and ancient ethical thought is that, whereas the ancients believed that there is only one "regulative and governing faculty" to be "recognized under the name of Reason," "in the modern view, when it has worked itself clear, there are found to be two—Universal Reason and Egoistic Reason, or Conscience and Self-love" (Sidgwick 1964: 197–198). For a discussion of this claim, see Frankena 1992.

because it will enable me to provide some context for Pufendorf's Point, which will play a significant role in the argument of Chapter 10.

What can the idea of mutual accountability between equals owe to the early modern idea of morality as subjection to the will of superior authority? From the outset, the voluntarist natural lawyers combined two ideas that have central importance for morality as equal accountability. First, and most obviously, they held that morality essentially involves accountability. Moral norms don't say just what we are required to do, but also what we are answerable for doing. Morality requires us to account for our conduct in light of its demands, and unexcused violations can be imputed to our account. Of course, Pufendorf believed that morality essentially involves accountability to a superior authority, namely God. But, he also believed that being thus accountable is only possible for free rational agents who are able to hold themselves responsible—who can determine themselves by their acceptance of the validity of the demands, thereby imposing them on themselves.[30] I argue that this idea exerted a pressure on his thought in the direction of morality as equal accountability, although the latter is not, of course, a conception he accepted or likely would have accepted on reflection.

The second idea is that moral norms derive from demands one will has the standing to address to or make on another (free and rational) will and that moral obligation would not exist but for the possibility of reasons that can arise through, and that are presupposed by, this second-personal relationship. Again, the modern natural lawyers believe that the requisite relationship is asymmetric: morality involves, in its nature, being subject to God's authoritative will. At the same time, however, their view is that the relevant relation is essentially between rational wills and that it differs from subjugation, intimidation, or any form of non-rational control, as well as from the kind of reason-giving involved in rational coercion. Pufendorf makes an explicit distinction between being moved by an acceptance of an obligation rooted in God's authority and merely submitting to God's greater power (Pufendorf's Point).

---

30. Like Pufendorf, Locke also thought that " 'Person' is a Forensick Term appropriating Actions and their Merit; and so belongs only to intelligent Agents capable of a Law" (Locke 1975: 346). However, his moral psychology differed from Pufendorf's in important ways. For a discussion of relevant differences in this context, see Darwall 2003a.

Suarez on Moral Obligation

To provide background for Pufendorf, it will be useful to begin briefly with Francisco Suarez.[31] Suarez was in many ways a classical (Thomist) natural lawyer, but he thought that Aquinas's view left out an essential element: morality's distinctive power to bind or obligate those subject to it. To account for this, he argued, it is insufficient to show that acting immorally is against our end or nature as rational beings. Telling false-hoods may be "repugnant" in itself to rational nature, but this repugnancy is insufficient to lay us under a moral obligation to tell the truth (Suarez 1944: 181–183). Morality cannot therefore be identified with a teleological structure, as in Thomas's version of natural law, because nothing like this could explain morality's power to obligate. It does not provide a reason of the right kind.

To understand morality as obligating, Suarez believed, it is necessary to see its laws as commands that are addressed to us by a superior authority, that is, by God. Several ideas are packed into this. First, because "ordering pertains to the will," moral norms or laws must aim to direct a will (1944: 66). Only thus can morality have a "binding force" (66, 67). Second, moral norms are God's will as addressed to us. Suarez's idea is not that God simply wants or wills us to act in certain ways. If that were his will, we could not fail to comply ("all these precepts would be executed"), since God is omnipotent (55). Rather God wills "to bind" his subjects by addressing them in a certain way, by commanding them (55). Third, the commands that create morality are addressed to human beings as free and rational. Morality can exist "only in view of some rational creature; for law is imposed only upon a nature that is free, and has for its subject-matter free acts alone" (37). So, fourth, although moral norms "provid[e] motive force and impe[l]," they do so by providing a distinctive kind of reason that wouldn't have existed but for God's having addressed us and our wills in this distinctive way (in our terms, given us a second-personal reason) (54). Finally, fifth, this second-personal address makes moral obligations something we are accountable for complying with. If we do not "voluntarily observe the law," therefore, we are culpable ("legal culprits in the sight of God") (132).

31. Francisco Suarez (1548–1617) was an important late scholastic thinker in the tradition of moral and political thought that derived from Thomas Aquinas. For a useful introduction and selections, see Schneewind 1990.

It is thus essential to Suarez's picture that morality derives from a distinctive second-personal relationship between one rational will and another. Moral norms derive from claims that are made will to will and that purport to give the addressee a distinctive reason for acting he wouldn't otherwise have had, a second-personal reason, and to place him in the position of accountability for so acting. Of course, it is no less essential to Suarez's view that the requisite second-personal relation is asymmetric, that of a superior to an inferior will. There can be "moral government" only through the existence of rational creatures, that is, rational beings who, because they are created, are (in their nature, he thinks) subject to the authority of their Creator (1944: 37–38).[32] Still, morality exists only through the possibility of a second-personal address in which one rational agent can give another a distinctive kind of reason he wouldn't otherwise have had and which he is thereby accountable for acting on.

Pufendorf on Moral Obligation

We find these same themes in Pufendorf, but put more sharply and outside the Thomist framework.[33] The increased acuity comes from Pufendorf's distinction between physical and moral "entities": the difference, he claims, between how things stand in nature without the address of a commanding will and "superadded" moral features that result from this form of address (1934: 4–7). "Moral entities are produced" through God's "imposition" of his will in commands (5). Thus are "moral entities" superadded to the physical realm—the moral law and moral reasons are created.

Pufendorf calls the "active force" of moral entities its being "made clear to men along what line they should govern their liberty of action, and that in a special way men are made capable of receiving good or evil and

32. There is, of course, a deep tension between the idea that it is part of the nature of being created that one is subject to the authority of a creator and the idea that, as Suarez also thinks, accountability is essentially a second-personal relation for reasons that, if they are not clear by now, should become so by the end of our discussion of Pufendorf.

33. Samuel Freiherr von Pufendorf (1632–1694) was, along with Grotius, one of the two most important sources of the early modern theory of natural law. For a very useful introduction and selections, see Schneewind 1990. See also the important discussion of Pufendorf in Schneewind 1998.

of directing certain actions towards other persons with a particular effect" (1934: 6). The "special way" men can "receive" good or evil and "direct" actions toward others "with a particular effect" refers to accountability, specifically, the standing to address and acknowledge warranted (or legitimate) sanctions.

The key idea is that the distinctive second-personal character of God's relation to those he commands makes addressees accountable for obedience. Once God addresses us in this way, our actions and various of their effects are imputable to us. When, consequently, God makes us aware of an evil we will suffer if we violate his commands, he is not merely threatening or coercing us. He is putting us on notice of warranted sanctions in a way that is itself an authority-warranted expression of the same second-personal accountability relation that God presupposes in commanding us in the first place and that we presuppose when we acknowledge his commands. It is what his holding us accountable consists in.

When God addresses his will to free and rational beings, he makes us "moral causes," agents to whom actions and their effects can be imputed and for which we are thereby accountable. Of course, he must also have made us free and rational, since this is necessary for imputability. But it is not sufficient, since imputability, as Pufendorf thinks of it, entails accountability, and that requires imposition. The formal nature of a moral action, he says, "consists of its 'imputativity'," "whereby the effect of a voluntary action can be imputed to an agent." Whether the effects be "good or evil," Pufendorf continues, "he must be responsible for both" (1934: 68). This is the "primary axiom in morals": "a man can be asked for a reckoning" for anything in his power. Or, equivalently, "any action controllable according to a moral law, the accomplishment or avoidance of which is within the power of a man, may be imputed to him" (70). According to Pufendorf, then, when God addresses his will to us free and rational beings, he simultaneously creates the moral law and. makes us "moral causes" by making us accountable for following it.

Being under moral obligations, then, is not simply a matter of standing under categorical oughts, but, as well, of being obligated to (answerable to) someone for complying with these oughts. Moral obligation, consequently, depends upon the authority for a second-personal address that presupposes and can also generate the requisite accountability relations, as Pufendorf believes, to God. Pufendorf agrees with Suarez (and, he points out, with Hobbes), that this can only come from a will. He quotes with approval Hobbes's definition of law as "a precept in which the reason for obedience is drawn from the will of the person prescribing it" (1934: 88). And he also agrees that law can only be imposed on free and rational wills and, then, only by a form of second-personal address.[34] A law is "a decree by which a superior obligates a subject." And a "decree" comes into existence only in "being communicated to the subject in such a way that he recognizes he must bend himself to it" (89). Morality, with its distinctive form of accountability, therefore, can only exist because of the distinctive demands that one (kind of) free and rational will can make on another.

As Pufendorf's critics, notably Leibniz, pointed out, however, and as Pufendorf himself affirmed, even God's commands cannot create the whole structure of accountability *ex nihilo*. As Cudworth put the point, "It was never heard of, that any one founded all his Authority of Commanding others, and others Obligation or Duty to Obey his Commands, in a Law of his own making, that men should be Required, Obliged, or Bound to Obey him" (1996: I.ii.3).[35] Without its already being true that we should obey God's commands, these cannot obligate us to perform specific actions. Pufendorf acknowledges this point. We could not be obligated by God's command, he says, unless "we owed beforehand obedience to its author" (Pufendorf 1934: 89).

This is an instance of the general point we noted in Chapters 1 and 3 (and a consequence of Strawson's Point—this instance might be called Cudworth's Point). Since second-personal demands do not reduce to, and cannot be derived in any simple way from, propositions of value or non-second-personal norms of conduct, any obligation to God that results from his commands requires a normative second-personal accountability relation already existing in the background. As stated in Chapter 3: "Second-personal authority out, second-personal authority in."[36]

34. That law can only bind free rational wills is a major theme of Pufendorf 1934: 52–65.

35. Leibniz made similar arguments against Pufendorf in his *Opinion on the Principles of Pufendorf* (1989: 70–75).

36. I take this to be a problem for versions of the Divine Command Theory that attempt to ground God's authority to command in his goodness. That God is infinitely good could explain why we should be guided by his will as perfect advice. But it could not explain

But what can provide the required second-personal background, according to Pufendorf? The terms in which Pufendorf draws the distinction between moral and physical entities apparently prevent him from holding, with Suarez, that created rational beings are in their nature, and independently of imposition, the Creator's moral subjects in the sense of being rightly ruled by him. Moral entities "do not arise out of the intrinsic nature of the physical properties of things, but . . . are superadded at the will of intelligent entities" by imposition (Pufendorf 1934: 5–6). So there can't be a more fundamental obligation or accountability relation grounded in the natures of these different kinds of rational beings from which God's imposed will draws its authority over us. Without that, however, it remains unclear, by Pufendorf's own admission, how God's impositions can have the background authority needed to impose obligations (Cudworth's Point).[37]

Pufendorf tries to fix this problem by arguing that we are obligated to obey God out of gratitude, since we are indebted to him for our "very being" (101). But this creates problems of its own. If we are permitted to help ourselves to an independently standing obligation of gratitude in order to give authority to the structure of command, then why suppose that all other obligations require command for their moral force? What is special about gratitude? Once a voluntarist makes a concession on this obligation, why should he not make it also on others?

This was perhaps the most fundamental problem that voluntarists like Pufendorf faced. They wanted to hold that morality requires a distinctive form of accountability that derives from one kind of will's addressing a demand to another. But they also held that this is impossible without a normative structure in which two wills already have the requisite authority relations, independently of any second-personal interaction. This is what makes the relevant demand an order that obligates the inferior to obey as the superior's subject. But assuming this prior moral relation creates two kinds of problems. First, there is the problem just noted: assuming any prior moral relation raises the question of why other relations can't be taken for granted also, for example, promiser to promisee

---

our being accountable or responsible to God and, hence, God's having the authority to command us in this sense. For an example of such a version of theological voluntarism, see Adams 1999: 249–276.

37. I don't mean to imply of course that Suarez's position is at all plausible.

or parent to child. Second, as we shall presently see, in holding that any rational agent God addresses is thereby accountable for obedience, the voluntarists made their views subject to pressure from the idea of rational accountability in ways that can seem to cut against theological voluntarism.[38] God can hold free and rational agents accountable for following his commands, Pufendorf held, only if exercising the capacity for free and rational deliberation would lead agents to determine themselves by reasons for obedience, which reasons they recognize in this second-personal address. But this requires that free and rational (second-personal) deliberation already involves an acknowledgment of an independently established moral relation of inferior to superior that gives God's commands authority in the first place. And what might guarantee that?

Accountability, Moral Reasons, and the Second-Person Standpoint

Now we get to Pufendorf's Point, and here we have to consider a fundamental distinction that Pufendorf makes between the goods and evils that can attend moral violations and the way these enter into deliberation.[39] Many things can "influence the will to turn to one side" or the other, but nonmoral evils "bear down the will as by some natural weight." Obligation, however, "affects the will morally," so that it "is forced of itself to weigh its own actions, and to judge itself worthy of some censure, unless it conforms to a prescribed rule" (1934: 91). Obligation thus "differs in a special way from coercion."[40] Although both obligation and coercion "point out some object of terror," the latter only shakes the will with an external force," since what moves the will is only "the sense of the impending evil." "An obligation," however, "forces a man to acknowl-

38. In effect, they committed themselves to constraints of intelligible second-personal address that pushed their views in the direction of Grotius's doctrine that the law of nature expresses a "moral necessity, of any act from its agreement or disagreement with a rational nature" (Grotius 1925: I.x.i). A remark of Karl Graf Ballestrem's led me to see this.

39. There are subtleties here concerning a tension between Pufendorf's theory of the will as always having to aim at some good and his claim that "whatever we do from obligation," we do from "an intrinsic impulse of the mind" (1934: 8), which I cannot enter into here. I discuss them in Darwall 2003a.

40. This corresponds to Hart's famous distinction between being obligated and being obliged, which he makes in the course of criticizing the legal positivism of John Austin (Hart 1961: 6–8).

edge of himself that the evil, which has been pointed out to the person who deviates from an announced rule, falls upon him justly."[41]

This is an initial statement of Pufendorf's Point. It is not yet obvious, however, how, so stated, Pufendorf's Point can help solve his problem. How does the distinction between, as Hart would later put it, being obligated and being obliged, help to explain obligation's ability to move the will "of itself" differently from coercion? How does it help to note that in the former case one acknowledges that the evil that is threatened if one violates the moral law falls on one "justly"? (Hart 1961: 6–8). It seems that one could acknowledge that God, or anyone else for that matter, has the authority to make a demand of one without yet having to grant that this creates a reason for one to act as the other demands. How does this force the will "of itself" to give the demand intrinsic weight?

To see what Pufendorf must be getting at, we need to distinguish between merely external censure or blame, even censure that addresses a demand that one believes to be warranted from the other's point of view, and internal blame, that is, the self-reactive attitude of guilt. Blame is purely external when it comes from outside and is not accepted. It seems possible to accept even the fact that another is warranted in a demand she expresses as censure without yet accepting the blame or censure itself. When, however, one accepts and acknowledges blame or censure, one owns the blaming address of the censuring person second-personally; one credits that imputation, and thus also blames oneself.[42] One sees oneself as being to blame. One thereby holds oneself responsible in making the demand of oneself from a second-personal standpoint one shares with the other. Pufendorf's Point, then, is that *in holding people responsible, we are committed to the assumption that they can hold themselves responsible by self-addressed demands from a perspective that we and they share.* For us to blame them for noncompliance, we must see them as able to blame themselves from the same perspective, the standpoint of free and rational members of the moral community. So Pufendorf's Point can solve his problem only if violating the moral law threatens not merely evils that are only externally related to the violation, but also one's own censure.

41. Ibid. Cf. the discussion of the difference between coercion and second-personal address in Chapter 3.
42. Compare the remark of Hanoch Yerushalmi, quoted by Laura Blumenfeld: "Acknowledgment is . . . accepting responsibility. It's when you 'own your own guilt' " (2002: 292).

But cannot even internal blame be externalized? Is the worry supposed to be that I cannot avoid my own gaze, and so my own blame, in a way that I can avoid others' if I stay out of their sight? What if I could take a pill that would wipe out the memory of the violation? To solve his problem, Pufendorf's Point must be that although a pill might expunge the psychic state of internal blame, it couldn't expunge one's being to blame, as one acknowledges here and now (second-personally) one is.[43] In sincerely making this judgment of oneself, second-personally, one is already in the process of holding oneself accountable for one's conduct with respect to the relevant law. One sees not just that a demand of oneself is warranted from some other person's standpoint (say, God's). Taken by itself, even that might give one no motive; so far, it just concerns what that person can justifiably feel or do. Rather, in taking a second-personal standpoint on oneself and acknowledging blame, one makes the demand of oneself. And in making that judgment, one implicitly acknowledges an adequate motive, a conclusive reason, not to violate the demand. As we saw earlier in the chapter, it seems incoherent to judge that someone (whether oneself or someone else) is to blame for something that one thinks she has or had conclusive reasons for doing. When, consequently, a free and rational deliberating agent acknowledges she would be to blame for doing something, she thereby acknowledges conclusive reasons not to do it and, in a sense, holds herself accountable.

This picture links accountability centrally to the reasons free and rational beings have for living by the moral law. On this picture, recognizing moral reasons is itself part of moral agents' active participation in a scheme of accountability, part of their holding themselves accountable for guidance by the relevant norms.

Once we view things this way, significant pressures develop on the sort of voluntarism that Pufendorf put forward. Most obviously, accountability is no longer simply to God, but also, in a sense, to oneself. It may still be, of course, that God rightly claims, uniquely, the right to punish and to judge. Maybe only he has all the evidence or uniquely has the authority to render final judgments. But even these ideas may also come under pressure if this punishment itself includes self-condemnation

---

43. Cf. my discussion of Mill's distinction between internal and external sanctions from chapter 3 of *Utilitarianism* in Chapter 7 below.

and a sense of guilt, since these involve internal, and not just external, blame.

To the extent that we conceive of moral agents as capable of internal blame, we must think of them as capable of taking part in second-personal moral community. For Pufendorf, each agent forms such a community with God alone, with God being accountable to no one. But Pufendorf also thinks that agents can form such a community with God, and hence be truly accountable to him, only if they are capable of acknowledging God's censure internally, hence only if they can in this way hold themselves responsible and be accountable also to themselves. In relating to God, one takes a second-personal standpoint on oneself as a person, and one will have this capacity only if one is also capable of entering into a community of mutually accountable persons. Pufendorf does not himself draw the conclusion, of course, but it follows that only beings capable of entering into relations of mutual accountability can be moral agents. Or, as we might also put it, human beings can individually have moral community with God only if they have the capacity to be a moral community together themselves.[44]

We should view voluntarists like Pufendorf as putting forward but one *conception* of a more general *concept* of morality as accountability. Any interpretation of this general concept must see morality as grounded in the possibility of second-personal community. What characterizes a voluntarist conception is that it takes a moral hierarchy for granted and then derives the rest of morality (by fiat) from that. As we have seen, however, tendencies within the general idea of morality as accountability put heavy pressure on a voluntarist interpretation of that idea. To distinguish between moral obligation and coercion, Pufendorf required an account of moral agents' distinctive capacity for self-censure from a shared second-person standpoint and its role in free rational deliberation. But this effectively assumes that to be accountable to God, moral agents must also be accountable to themselves.

It is implicit in the very idea of one free and rational will addressing a claim to another (as free and rational) that the addresser is committed to the addressee's capacity, as second-personally competent, to accept the claim and freely determine herself by it. But what claims can one free and

44. It is important, again, that as Postema (1995) and Korsgaard (1996e) have stressed, this involves seeing the moral point of view as a first-person plural (and I here add, second-personal) standpoint, as one from which we address demands to each of us.

rational will make on another and reasonably expect reciprocation? I argue in Chapters 10 and 11 that the answer to this question is provided by morality as equal accountability, the idea that second-personal competence grounds an equal second-personal authority.[45] It follows that we human beings can enter (individually) into moral community with God only if we have the authority to form a moral community ourselves as mutually accountable free and rational persons: a Kantian "realm of ends."

CI and the Golden Rule as Second-Personal

I have been arguing that second-personal accountability is part of the concept of moral obligation. When we hold one another accountable for complying with moral requirements, moreover, the addressers presuppose that the addressees are second-personally competent to accept authoritative moral demands and freely act on them by making the demands on themselves second-personally. In Chapter 9, I argue that this is the deep idea underlying what Kant calls "autonomy of the will" and supporting his thesis that moral obligation must bottom out in a formal principle of the will, like the Categorical Imperative (CI), which moral agents can use to determine moral demands, and determine themselves to comply with them, in their own reasoning. To close this chapter, I would like briefly to illustrate that the CI and related injunctions like the Golden Rule are themselves most intuitively interpreted in second-personal terms.

Hobbes, for example, formulates a principle he claims to be "intelligible even to the meanest capacity," as follows: *"Do not that to another, which thou wouldst not have done to thyself"* (Hobbes 1994: XV.35). If we understand "thou wouldst not have done to thyself" in terms of desire or preference, we get very strange results. Jones, let us say, is in a position to peel me a grape (as I am to peel one for him). I prefer the state in which Jones peels me a grape to one in which he forbears to peel me a grape. In that sense, I would have him not (or in Hobbes's English:

45. This will turn Anscombe's famous claims in "Modern Moral Philosophy" (1958) on their head. Although I agree with Anscombe that morality is inconceivable without the idea of addressable demands, I maintain that her claim that they require divinely addressed demands ultimately overturns itself in the way I have indicated. I am indebted here to Kate Abramson.

"would not have him")[46] forbear to peel me a grape. Should we then understand Hobbes's Golden Rule as enjoining me not to forbear peeling a grape for Jones (as I am equally in a position to peel him a grape). That seems an obviously perverse way to interpret the principle. Clearly I do no wrong if I do not peel the grape for Jones, as he does no wrong also, if, having appropriately corresponding preferences, he does not peel the grape for me.[47]

It is clearly more intuitively plausible to interpret "wouldst not have done to thyself" in terms of what one would expect or demand that others not do to one or object to or resent their doing (or perhaps, what one would want to be able to claim or demand that they not do). Although I would prefer that others peel me grapes, and hence, that they not forbear doing so, I certainly don't object to their not doing so, or demand that they do so. As I wouldn't (want to) claim this from Jones, I do not violate the Golden Rule if I don't peel a grape for him.

A familiar way to think of the Golden Rule is in terms of *acceptance.* If you wouldn't or couldn't accept other people doing something to you, it is often said, then you shouldn't do it to them. But what does acceptance mean in this context? It is frequently pointed out in discussions of egoism that there is a theoretical sense in which an egoist can accept the totally self-regarding conduct of others even when it disadvantages her; she can accept that it is justified. That others are no less justified in their egoistic conduct than she is in hers just follows from egoism of this kind's being a universalistic position. All parties to the debate usually agree that she doesn't have to accept it in a more practical sense to accept it theoretically.

But what is it for someone to accept something practically? If it just means desiring or preferring it to alternatives, or at least not dispreferring it, then we are back in the same terrain we were two paragraphs ago with the same problems. Perhaps 'accept' means something like "not resist." But this also gives strange results. Whenever I play a competitive game, like ping-pong, there is a perfectly natural sense in which I am resisting

46. If we don't interpret Hobbes this way, we get an even stranger result, namely, that if I would not prefer him to forbear peeling me a grape (if, say, I were indifferent to that prospect), then I should not forbear to peel him a grape.

47. Scanlon makes a similar point (1998: 170), noting that this is Kant's objection also in *Groundwork* (1996b: 430n).

my opponent's efforts to win points. So should I not play to win points against her?

A moment's reflection shows, I think, that the most natural way to take 'accept' in "don't do to others what you wouldn't or couldn't accept their doing to you," is in terms of the second-personal circle of concepts we identified at the outset of this book. What I can accept in these terms is what I would not object to or claim or demand otherwise. On this natural interpretation, the Golden Rule is second-personal.[48] It asserts what we might think of as a fundamental principle of the reasonable, that is, as Rawls (1980) and Scanlon (1998) understand this idea. One should not act in ways that one demands or expects (or would demand or expect) that others not act, or equivalently, in ways that one would resent or object to. If I am going to object to others' stepping on my feet (and thus demand that they not do so), then I must not step on their feet either. Lincoln's famous remark, "As I would not be a slave, so I would not be a master" (1989: 484) is along the same lines: As I would not allow others a master's claim on me so should I not make a master's claim on others.

Or again, consider the Formula of Universal Law of the CI (FUL): "Act only in accordance with that maxim through which you can at the same time will that it become a universal law of nature" (Kant 1996b: 421).[49] There are delicate issues about how to interpret Kant's idea of a maxim and FUL in light of it, and about how to understand FUL, so interpreted, in relation to the Formula of Humanity (FH) and Formula of the Realm of Ends (FRE), which Kant says are equivalent. We can hardly sort this all out here. In Chapter 12, however, I argue that the best way of interpreting the CI in its various formulations is within a contractualist framework (grounded in the equal dignity of free and rational agents that we presuppose in the second-person standpoint). The intuitive idea is that,

48. For a fascinating study of Hobbes's moral philosophy that makes his version of the Golden Rule, what she calls Hobbes's "reciprocity theorem" central (understood in terms of what we would or would not blame or "fault" others for), and treats the desire to justify ourselves to one another as a central aspect of Hobbes's moral psychology, see Lloyd forthcoming.

49. A key difference with the Golden Rule (one Kant himself notes [1996b: 430n]) is that what one must be able to will is universal following of a maxim, not just a particular action.

when we regulate ourselves by the CI, we accept and comply with demands we think it sensible (reasonable) to make on everyone from the shared standpoint of a community of equal free and rational persons. This makes second-personal authority and competence fundamental. What is most basic is the dignity of free and rational persons, understood as their (second-personal) authority to make demands on one another as equals.

— 6 —

Respect and the Second Person

[f. L. *respect-*, ppl. stem of *respicĕre* to look (back) at, regard, consider, or ad. the frequentative of this, *respectāre*. Cf. F. *respecter* (16th c.), Sp. *respe(c)tar*, Pg. *respeitar*, It. *rispettare*.]

—THE OXFORD ENGLISH DICTIONARY ONLINE

A human being regarded as a person, that is as the subject of a morally practical reason, . . . possesses a dignity . . . by which he exacts *respect* for himself from all other rational beings in the world.

—IMMANUEL KANT, *METAPHYSICAL FIRST PRINCIPLES OF THE DOCTRINE OF VIRTUE*

Morality as equal accountability conceives of moral relations in terms of equal *respect*.[1] In seeing ourselves as mutually accountable, we accord one another the standing to demand certain conduct of each other as equal members of the moral community. In this chapter, I argue that recognition of this authority is an irreducibly second-personal form of respect. Conceived in Kantian terms as "common laws" for a "kingdom of ends" (Kant 1996b: 433), moral requirements structure and give expression to the distinctive value that persons equally have: *dignity*, a "worth that has no price" (1996d: 462). This chapter argues that both the dignity of persons and the respect that is its fitting response have an irreducibly second-personal character. Our dignity includes the standing to hold one another to our moral obligations toward each other, and respect for this second-personal standing is itself second-personal.

Dignity enters in two distinct places in morality as equal accountability. First, in holding ourselves accountable to one another at all, we give each other an authority to address demands to us as equal members of the moral community, even when the content of those demands extends be-

1. This chapter draws heavily on Darwall 2004b.

119

yond the treatment of persons. And second, we respect our dignity as persons more specifically when the demands concern how we must treat one another.

My method in this chapter is analytical. I simply draw out consequences I take to be implicit in our going moral conception. Later, I attempt to vindicate these aspects of our conception, arguing in Chapter 10 that we are committed to the common dignity (second-personal authority) of free and rational agents as a presupposition (normative felicity condition) of the address of any second-personal reason at all. Then in Chapter 11, I attempt to locate second-personal reasons in an overall theory of practical reasons.

Attitudes and Objects

Respect is the fitting response to dignity, as esteem is to the estimable, desire is to the desirable, and so on.[2] Just as reasons of the right kind for desire and esteem must be drawn from the distinctive ways these attitudes relate to their characteristic objects, the desirable and the estimable, respectively, so it is also with respect. The distinctive object of the kind of respect with which we are concerned, *recognition respect*, is dignity or authority.[3] Recognition respect differs from other attitudes, however, in that it can be mandated and not just warranted by its object. Someone who fails to esteem your estimable qualities may not give you the response you deserve, but esteem is nothing you or anyone else can expect or demand. Not so with respect of your dignity.

The dignity of persons, Kant says, is that "by which" we "*exac*[t] respect," that is, claim or, as Kant also says, "demand" it from one another as rational beings (1996d: 434–357).[4] But what is it to demand respect as

2. Just as in desiring something we see it as desirable, or in esteeming something we see it as estimable, so in respecting something we see it as having dignity or authority. Note that what I have been calling "reasons of the right kind" for an attitude concern whether the attitude "fits" its object in the sense that things are, evaluatively or normatively, as they seem from the perspective of that attitude. "Fittingness" reasons make it the case that an attitude is fitting to its object in this sense. See D'Arms and Jacobson 2000a and 2000b.

3. For the distinction between *recognition* and *appraisal respect*, see the next section.

4. Stress added to "exact" and removed from "respect." I should note that what I am presenting is only one interpretation of Kant's writings on dignity and respect. Kant sometimes writes as if dignity were a value that can be realized by rational beings only when

a person, and what enables us to make this demand? And what is respect for this dignity that it may be thus demanded? I maintain that the key to answering these questions is the irreducibly second-personal character of both our dignity and the respect that is its fitting response. The dignity of persons, I contend, is the second-personal authority of an equal: the standing to make claims and demands of one another as equal free and rational agents, including as a member of a community of mutually accountable equals. And respect for this dignity is an acknowledgment of this authority that is also second-personal.[5] It is always implicitly reciprocal, if only in imagination. As 'respect"s root '*respicĕre*' suggests, it is a "looking back" that reciprocates a real or imagined second-personal address, even if only from oneself.

To say that the dignity of persons is second-personal is to say that it cannot be wholly summed into (non-second-personal) values or norms, say, into a set of requirements on conduct that are rooted in our common nature as persons or even into certain ways that persons must and must not be treated (Kamm 1989, 1992; Nagel 1995). It also involves an equal authority as persons to claim or demand compliance with such requirements. It is worth recalling here Rawls's expression of this idea when he says that persons are "self-originating sources of valid claims" (1980: 546). Joel Feinberg makes a companion point, which I develop in this chapter, when he says that it is "the activity of claiming" that "makes for self-respect and respect for others" (1980: 155).

I believe, indeed, that it is our equal second-personal authority that is most fundamental and that substantive constraints on conduct derive from this authority. In my view, what we "owe to each other" as equal moral persons is best accounted for within a contractualist framework that, as I argue in Chapter 12, is itself grounded in the equal second-personal authority to which we are committed in the second-person standpoint.

---

they follow the moral law, as opposed to a value or standing they have by virtue of the capacity for moral action. For example, he writes of "the idea of the dignity of a rational being, who obeys no law other than that which he at the same time gives" (1996b: 434). I have been helped here by discussion with Oliver Sensen.

5. The second-personal character of (recognition) respect for persons has been overlooked by the discussion of respect over the last thirty-five years, including in my own work. See, for example, Buss 1999b; Cranor 1975; Darwall 1977; Dillon 1995, 1997; Downie and Telfer 1970; Hill 1997, 1998; Hudson 1980.

Appraisal versus Recognition Respect

It will help to begin by distinguishing the distinctive kind of respect we are concerned with, recognition respect, from other attitudes to which 'respect' can also refer and from other responses in the neighborhood. Consider, for example, the sense in which one can be said to have more or less respect for someone, either as a person or in some specific capacity (as a philosopher, say), or be said to have gained or lost respect for someone. In these contexts, 'respect' refers to a kind of *esteem*.

Of course, esteem can also take forms we would never dream of calling "respect." Pimples and unpopularity can wreak havoc with adolescent self-esteem, for example, without necessarily threatening self-respect. Esteem concerns what we admire, look up to, envy, or wish to acquire or emulate. Many such excellences cannot intelligibly be objects of respect of any sort, at least, not without some long and unobvious story. If the popular kids' imagined unblemished faces are seen to result from differences in conduct (hygiene, say) or seem an expression of their more sterling characters, then this can support a sense of differential respect.[6] But without some such connection, it cannot.

The esteem we call "respect"—henceforth, *appraisal respect*—is an assessment of someone's conduct or character or of something that somehow involves these.[7] Appraisal respect for someone as a person is moral esteem: approbation for her as a moral agent. We can have appraisal respect for people in more specific capacities as well, but even though this differs from moral esteem, it still concerns the person's conduct in the relevant capacity. Thus, although appraisal respect for someone as a tennis player differs from respect for her as a person, neither is it the same thing as esteem for her tennis-playing skills or achievements. If one thoroughly objects to how she conducts herself on the court, say, because she seeks to gain unfair advantage by manipulating the rules, this will tend to undermine respect for her as a tennis player. It will tarnish, even if it does not otherwise diminish, her victories and achievements.

Appraisal respect is esteem that is merited or earned by conduct or character. By contrast, the respect we can demand as persons regardless of

6. Another possibility is that, without assaulting my esteem for my conduct or character, such things can help undermine one's sense or feeling of one's worth or dignity as a person, despite a belief to the contrary. On this point, see Dillon 1997.

7. I take the terms "appraisal respect" and "recognition respect" from Darwall 1977.

our merit is no form of esteem at all. When we think that even scoundrels have a dignity that entitles them to respectful forms of treatment (say, in holding them accountable, as Strawson says [1968: 93]), we clearly have something other than esteem in mind. The idea is not that personhood is somehow an admirable quality: "Granted, he stole hardworking people's pension funds, but at least he's a person." What is in play here is not appraisal but recognition.

The object of recognition respect is not excellence or merit; it is dignity or authority. Recognition respect concerns, not how something is to be evaluated or appraised, but how our relations to it are to be regulated or governed. Broadly speaking, we respect something in the recognition sense when we give it standing (authority) in our relations to it. Since the authority that persons have as such is fundamentally second-personal, respect for it must be second-personal also; it must involve acknowledgment.[8]

There are forms of recognition respect, however, that are not fundamentally second-personal at all, namely, whenever the authority respect recognizes is not second-personal. In these cases, the relevant authority can be recognized without having to be acknowledged. In many of these instances, moreover, the authority can be merited or earned. But even when that is so, respect for the authority differs from esteem for any form of merit.

We saw in Chapter 3, for example, how when one person attempts to give another reasons to believe something through testimony, his (second-personal) standing to do so can depend upon or be defeated by his epistemic authority, by how reliable a witness he is or can be taken to be. To be sure, the standing we accord one another in collaborative theoretical reasoning is itself second-personal (Pettit and Smith 1996). But the epistemic authority that can defeat it is not. And my current point is that it is possible fully to recognize epistemic authority without any form of second-personal acknowledgment. One can respect the knowledge or wisdom one overhears in another person's solitary musings and regulate one's own private reasoning by them. Here one respects the other's epistemic authority without acknowledging any second-personal claim he makes, even implicitly.

---

8. I take it that, unlike recognition, acknowledgment is always to someone, if only implicitly and if only to oneself.

Even so, respect for someone's epistemic authority differs from esteem for his epistemic virtues. The latter shows itself in and partly just is a positive appraisal of him as a cognizer or of his contributions to collaborative inquiry. The former, however, is realized in our epistemic conduct in relation to him, for example, giving his views weight or authority in deciding what to believe ourselves.[9]

Or consider the authority that we give trusted advisors. This also can be merited or earned. We have recognition respect for an advisor when we give him standing in our deliberations about what to do or, at least, about what to believe we should do. The situation here is on all fours with the theoretical case. Even if there is a kind of second-personal authority involved in the giving and receiving of advice, especially when the advisor simply recommends a course of action without giving reasons, this authority is nonetheless taken to rest on and be defeasible by an authority that is not second-personal at all—the advisor's practical wisdom. If I come to believe that someone I had trusted is no longer a particularly good judge of reasons that bear on my practical situation, or that he is but that he can no longer be trusted to tell me what he really thinks, then I will no longer have any reason to treat his advice with recognition respect. But here again, my disesteem for his advising abilities is not the same thing as my resulting recognition contempt. The former shows itself in and partly just is a negative appraisal of him as an advisor. The latter is shown in how I conduct my own deliberations in relation to him and his advice, giving his views little weight in deciding what to do or in forming my beliefs about what reasons there are to decide one way or another.

Yet another example is the kind of implicit respect that, as Sarah Buss (1999b) has pointed out, is typically involved in the experience of shame. We experience shame, as we noted in Chapter 4, when we are brought

9. Here, however, is a problem case at the margins of the distinction between recognition and appraisal respect. Just as one can show recognition respect for something or someone in regulating one's beliefs, no less than one's actions, it would seem that one can in regulating one's esteem as well. So why isn't appropriately regulating one's thinking about what to feel by a proper appreciation of someone's character an instance of recognition respect? And if it is, then what is the difference between that and the resulting esteem (appraisal respect) for the person's character? Even here, we might want to distinguish the two, but the difference seems little if any in this case. I am indebted to Mark LeBar for this suggestion.

to see ourselves as others see (or might see) us, and this view is problematic for us in certain ways—say, because it involves disdain or something like it or because it reveals an aspect of ourselves that we would prefer to keep private.[10] Shame is not the fear of disdain; neither is it an awareness of being viewed with it or in a way that unveils. Rather, shame is feeling as if a view of oneself as shameful is to be credited. It is the experience of seeming to be correctly seen in some disturbing way by recognizing (though not necessarily acknowledging) the view of oneself one gets from the other's perspective. This is why Buss says that shame involves respect. Shame feels as if the other can see one as one really is—as if she has this competence and authority. So far, however, the authority seems entirely epistemic (in a sufficiently broad sense); it is like the authority one recognizes in taking another's epistemic attitudes seriously.

What makes respect for these different forms of authority structurally similar to, but still importantly different from, that for an authority to claim or demand is that they concern non-second-personal reasons. Respect for epistemic authority need involve no (even implicit) acknowledgment of any (even implicit) claim. To be sure, the contexts in which we normally show recognition respect for theoretical knowledge, practical wisdom, and similar forms of authority are frequently second-personal. Testimony, advice, mutual inquiry, and addressed criticisms all make a kind of claim on an addressee's attention, judgment, or reasoning. But in these cases, the relevant second-personal standing flows directly from a more basic epistemic or epistemic-like authority that is not itself essentially second-personal, one that can be respected in contexts that do not involve (even an imagined) acknowledgment of any (even imagined) claim or demand for respect.

Any standing to address second-personal reasons, however, is fundamentally second-personal. When a sergeant orders her platoon to fall in, her troops take it that the reason she thereby gives them derives entirely from their normative relations, from her authority to give them orders. That, again, is the point of Hobbes's famous distinction between "command" and "counsel" (1983: XIV.1). The sergeant addresses reasons that would not have existed but for her authority to address them in this way. And the only way that one can fully respect such a second-personal authority is second-personally.

10. On the importance of the latter, again, see Velleman 2001.

Similarly, I believe that recognition respect for someone as a person is also second-personal. It is an acknowledgment of someone's standing to address and be addressed second-personal reasons rooted in the dignity of persons, where this standing is also second-personal all the way down. 'Person' is a "forensic term," as Locke said; it is conceptually related to accountability (1975: 346). According to morality as equal accountability, to be a person just is to have the competence and standing to address demands as persons to other persons, and to be addressed by them, within a community of mutually accountable equals. This second-personal competence gives all persons an equal dignity, irrespectively of their merit. We therefore respect another as a person when we accord him this standing in our relations to him.

Respect versus Care

Recognition respect thus involves no evaluation or appraisal of excellence or merit, even of someone's merits as a person. It is, rather, a way of valuing someone intrinsically, in and for himself. In respecting someone's dignity, we respect and value him. But respect is not the only way of valuing someone in himself or for his own sake. Caring or benevolent concern is another.[11] It is important, therefore, to be clear about the differences between respect and care, since these ground importantly different moral philosophical ideas.

Like respect, care takes individuals as its object. But whereas respecting someone entails relating to her as a being with a dignity, caring for someone involves viewing her as a being with a welfare. In caring for someone, we want certain states—whichever will benefit her.[12] Respect, however, is attitude- or conduct-, rather than state-regarding. In respecting someone, we are disposed to regulate our conduct in relation to her—to do what is called for by her dignity.

11. By 'care' here I mean the sort of "sympathetic concern" I discuss in Darwall 2002b, especially chapter 3. There are other senses, for example, when we are enjoined by the law to take "due care," where what is involved is a form of respect. I am indebted here to an anonymous reader for the Press. Also, relationships of mutual concern, at least between those with second-personal competence, such as friendships, reciprocal love relationships, and so on, also involve an element of respect of part of what it is to relate to the other in that distinctive caring way. Here I am indebted to Joseph Raz and Susan Wolf.

12. This is a central theme of Darwall 2002b.

Reasons for acting that are rooted in respect are *second-personal, agent-regarding*, and *agent-relative*. Respect for persons is a responsiveness to what someone can claim by virtue of being an agent with second-personal competence. What we attend to here is not (at least, not primarily) what is for someone's welfare or good, but, among other things, what she herself values and holds good from her point of view as an equal independent agent. In so doing, we acknowledge her (and her authority) as free and equal. We may rightly think, for example, that unhealthy habits are harmful for someone and thus contrary to her welfare, but we may think as well that respect tells against exerting undue pressure to induce her to change. Concern for her and her welfare may lead us to want her to change, and to want to help her do so, even while respect for her dignity restrains us. A person's values and preferences can give others reasons of respect to permit her to promote them (and, I have elsewhere argued, give her reasons to pursue them herself), whether or not the resulting states would be beneficial or good in some other way from an agent-neutral point of view, or indeed, whether she has any other reason to promote them at all (Darwall 2001). And, because they are second-personal, respect's reasons are also fundamentally agent-relative.[13] They concern how others must relate to us and our authority to demand this.

Reasons of care, on the other hand, are *third-personal, welfare-regarding*, and *agent-neutral*. From the perspective of sympathetic concern, the cared-for's own values are regulative only to the extent they are represented in his welfare. If, for example, the person for whom one cares is sufficiently depressed, he may not value his own welfare or what would further it very much at all. In feeling sympathetic concern for him, one is regulated not by what he values or prefers (as in respect), but by what (one believes) would really benefit him. Of course, a person's welfare is bound up with his preferences and values, but the latter generate reasons of care only to the extent that this is so. And to one who cares, considerations of welfare present themselves as agent-neutral, rather than agent-relative, reasons. It seems a good thing agent-neutrally that the cared-for

---

13. See the discussion of this point in Chapters 1, 2, and 4. As I note there, the reason may itself be agent-neutral even though it is grounded in something fundamentally second-personal and agent-relative. Thus the principle of utility, which takes an agent-neutral form, might be thought to be based in the more fundamental idea that we must act toward one another (and ourselves) in ways that reflect our equal authority to make claims of one another.

benefit and, therefore, that there is a reason for anyone who can to bring that state about and not just a reason for those who have some particular relation to the cared-for or happen to care for her.[14] Finally, respect of one's dignity is something anyone can demand; but this is not so with sympathetic concern for oneself and one's welfare.

These differences between benevolent concern and respect can be brought out by reflecting on the relations between parents and children. Parents may legitimately give relatively little intrinsic weight to a sufficiently young child's protest against eating a healthful food, although they should take account of its bearing on the child's welfare, for example, the likelihood that eating it will be an unpleasant experience, the long-term effects on the child's psychic well-being of insisting that she eat it, and so on. At this stage, the parents may properly be guided by the child's welfare alone. When, however, their daughter returns to her former home in middle age, to take an extreme case, the situation is much changed. For parents not to take a middle-aged daughter's will as having intrinsic weight, indeed, as governing, would clearly be disrespectful, paternalism in the pejorative sense.[15] Now she has a second-personal standing she simply did not have near the beginning of her life. And were her parents to attempt to pressure her to eat "her broccoli" at this point, they would rightly be subject to reproach. Their failure of respect would invite a second-personal response calling for respect, second-personally, from them to her.[16]

Or think again of being in pain because someone is stepping on your foot. To someone who cares for you, it will seem as if relief of your pain would be a good state of the world and as if, therefore, there is a reason for anyone who can to try to realize it. Of course, since the person who is stepping on your foot likely has the best position in the causal network to do this, this will seem to be a particularly good reason for him to

14. For a further defense of these claims, see Darwall 2002b: 49, 69–72.

15. For a very insightful account of paternalism that is especially illuminating in this connection, see Shiffrin 2000.

16. We should note, however, that relations that we frequently call forms of care, like those between friends and loved ones, frequently involve respect as well as benevolent concern and have an ineliminable second-personal aspect. Friends, for example, understand themselves as supporting one another, including in their pursuit of their preferences, somewhat independently of considerations of each other's welfare. I am indebted here to Joseph Raz and Susan Wolf.

move his foot. But it will nonetheless be an agent-neutral reason. Your foot-treader's relation to you is just part of the causal structure that makes the agent-neutral normative fact that your being free of pain is desirable distinctively relevant to his deliberative situation. If, however, you see his taking his foot off yours to be dictated by mutual respect, you will see him as having a reason that is grounded in your authority to demand that he move his foot (indeed, to demand that he not have stepped on yours in the first place). This reason will be second-personal and agent-relative.[17] You will see his relation to you (his gratuitously causing you pain) as intrinsically relevant to how he should conduct himself toward you. Moreover, as I argue in Chapters 10 and 11, the relevance of this agent-relative relation (in the logical sense) can be seen to flow from what it is to relate to one another in the second-personal sense. It is second-personal relating that is primary. Agent-relative norms, like "one should not cause gratuitous pain to others," can be explicated within a contractualist framework that is grounded in what we are committed to in relating to one another second-personally at all.

Respect concerns how we are to conduct ourselves in relating to others, whereas care is sensitive to how things go for others, whether that involves relating to them or not. In itself, care neither is defined by nor necessarily involves any distinctive conduct toward or relating to its object. Insofar as we care for someone, our interest in our own conduct toward him is instrumental. Benevolent concern leads us to want to act in whichever ways are most conducive to his welfare. Recognition respect for someone, however, involves distinctive ways of conducting oneself toward or relating to him as a person, namely, those that are mandated by his dignity.

Given all this, it is entirely expectable that philosophical conceptions of morality as rooted in universal benevolence should take agent-neutral consequentialist forms and that conceptions like morality as equal accountability should spawn deontological moral theories with agent-relative constraints.[18] If morality is grounded in care or concern, then it

17. Again, what makes this norm agent-relative is that it cannot be stated without making ineliminable reference to the agent. Many moral norms, those sometimes called "deontological constraints," are agent-relative in this sense: for example, a person should keep her promises, other things being equal. On this point, see McNaughton and Rawling 1993.

18. Utilitarian theories from Hutcheson to Sidgwick are illustrations of the former, and

has a final agent-neutral aim, the welfare of all human or sentient beings, and moral evaluation of actions and social practices is therefore ultimately instrumental. Of course, it is possible to hold such a conception and maintain, as Mill did (1998: ch. 5), that the evaluation of conduct as wrong is not itself instrumental but dependent on accountability-structuring norms that are justified instrumentally themselves. But such evaluations are still instrumental at one remove; they treat private attitudes and public practices of responsibility as instruments for public good. And since they derive from a more fundamental agent-neutral aim, their normativity must ultimately be agent-neutral.

This last is, in effect, Strawson's Point about consequentialist approaches to moral responsibility extended to moral obligation. Conduciveness to an external goal differs from standards we are committed to within the second-person standpoint we take up when we address moral demands. By contrast, moral conceptions rooted in equal respect understand morality to concern most fundamentally how we should relate to one another—what demands we have standing to address and what standing we have to address them. This makes morality fundamentally a second-personal matter and, as a consequence, moral norms must be grounded from within the agent-relative/self-other standpoint of mutual respect. It is of course consistent with this framework (without further argument) that what we can demand from one another might include equal consideration of our welfare and, therefore, that respect for one another requires complying with, say, the agent-neutral principle of utility. This would be something like the reverse of Mill's position—getting an agent-neutral moral norm out of a fundamentally agent-relative conception of morality.[19] And the parallel point would seem to apply, namely, that according to such a conception, the normativity of such an agent-neutral norm would itself be fundamentally agent-relative (albeit, at one remove).

Kant on Respect

We shall consider respect's second-personal character in more detail presently. This can easily be missed. I missed it, for example, in my 1977

Scanlon's contractualism nicely illustrates the latter. For excellent discussions of the relation between deontology and agent-relativity, see McNaughton and Rawling 1993 and 1995.

19. I have been helped here by discussion with Allan Gibbard.

article, when I identified recognition respect for persons with "tak[ing] seriously and weigh[ing] appropriately the fact that they are persons in deliberating about what to do" (38).[20] This makes respect something one can realize outside of a second-personal relation; one need only adequately register a fact about or feature of someone: that she is a person.[21] In a similar vein, Iris Murdoch complains against Kant's view that Kant makes the object of respect not individual persons but "universal reason in their breasts" (Murdoch 1999: 215).[22] In this section, we consider Kant's views on respect. These have great interest in their own right, and they include a number of important points on which we continue to draw throughout the rest of the book. In what remains of this chapter, I argue that the key to seeing how recognition respect for persons actually is an attitude toward individuals, and not just toward a fact about or a quality in them, is to appreciate respect's role in mediating second-personal relations (that is, relatings) between individuals. And I suggest that the seeds of this view are in what Kant himself says about respect.

Respect *(Achtung)* figures in three distinct places in Kant's ethical writings.[23] First, in section 1 of the *Groundwork,* Kant argues that "respect for law" characterizes morally worthy conduct and that "duty is the necessity of an action from respect for law" (1996b: 400). Second, in the *Critique of Practical Reason,* Kant provides an empirical psychology of moral action and, within it, an account of the psychology of respect (1996a: 71–89). Third, in *The Metaphysics of Morals,* Kant discusses duties of respect, both to oneself and to others (1996d: 434–437, 462–468).

Kant does not explicitly distinguish between appraisal and recognition respect. Most of the time he is concerned with recognition respect for persons and their distinctive dignity, but there are places where what he has in mind is fairly clearly a form of appraisal respect, namely, compar-

20. In Hill 1998, Thomas E. Hill Jr. takes a similar view, writing that recognition respect for person is a "disposition to give appropriate weight in one's deliberations to the fact that someone is a person (whether meritorious or not)."

21. For a similar point, see Buss 1999a: 797.

22. I am indebted for this reference to Carla Bagnoli. See Bagnoli 2003.

23. I am very much indebted in this section to Peter Vranas's analysis of Kant on respect in Vranas 2001: 25–39. I follow Vranas in many aspects of his analysis, but not all (for example, his tendency to identify *reverentia* with a form of appraisal respect). I have been helped also by Dillon 2004 and Bernard Reginster's "The Moral Distinction of Self-Conceit," presented at the Kantian Ethics Conference, University of San Diego, January 16–18, 2003.

ative moral esteem: "before a humble common man in whom I perceive uprightness of character in a higher degree than I am aware of in myself *my spirit bows.*"[24] Just after this, Kant adds that *"respect* is a *tribute* that we cannot refuse to pay to merit" (1996a: 77). In our terms, respect that responds to merit and "uprightness of character" is appraisal respect.

Why Kant should be concerned to mark off instances of appraisal respect where another appears to have greater merit is somewhat unclear. Kant believes that the experience of respect invariably involves feelings of humiliation, as we shall see, and he may be thinking that this element would be lost unless we saw the other as having greater merit.[25] However, as we shall also see, Kant believes that recognition respect of the dignity of persons always involves a humbling acknowledgment of the moral law, which, according to his analysis, unavoidably "strikes down self-conceit" (1996a: 73). He repeats that analysis here, saying that the common person's example "holds before me a law that strikes down my self conceit" (77). But this will be true whether or not one sees the other as adhering more closely to this law.

The only distinction Kant explicitly draws within respect is that between *reverentia,* by which he invariably means a feeling of respect, and *observantia* or "respect in the practical sense," which he identifies with "the *maxim* of limiting our self-esteem by the dignity of humanity in another person" (1996d: 402, 449). Obviously, *reverentia* is what is involved in the comparative appraisal respect just discussed. But it is important to Kant's empirical moral psychology that recognition respect for the moral law and the dignity of persons *(observantia)* also gives rise to *reverentia.* Thus, in discussing the duty of self-respect, Kant remarks that a person has a worth that is "above any price, . . . an inalienable dignity *(dignitas interna)* which instills in him respect for himself *(reverentia)*" (436).

There is no duty directly to feel *reverentia* (1996d: 402). We can't have a duty to experience a feeling, Kant thinks. Rather, we have a duty of *observantia* to respect the dignity of humanity within ourselves and others,

24. See note 4 for some evidence that Kant sometimes runs together dignity as an object of recognition respect and dignity as an object of appraisal respect (moral esteem).

25. Kant doesn't say that we must believe or judge that the other has greater merit, rather, that in experiencing respect of this sort for another person, we see, feel, or experience the other as better than us. I know my own imperfections at first hand, but the other "appears to me in a purer light" (1996a: 77).

and the phenomenal experience or feeling of doing so is *reverentia*. Similarly, when Kant says that feelings of love and respect "accompany the carrying out" of the duties of love and respect, respectively, he is distinguishing simultaneously between pathological and practical forms of love and respect (448). Pathological love is what we feel when we carry out the duties of (practical) benevolence, and *reverentia* is what we feel when we carry out the duties of *observantia* or "respect in the practical sense" (448–468).

This brings us to Kant's explanation of how *observantia* gives rise to *reverentia*, how, that is, practical respect for the moral law and the dignity of persons involves distinctive feelings of respect. The framework for Kant's speculative psychology of respect is his transcendental idealism and "two standpoints" doctrine—Kant's distinction between the point of view we take on ourselves and our actions when we experience them as part of the causal structure of the "phenomenal" world of sense experience, on the one hand, and the intelligible perspective we adopt when deliberating about what to do, on the other (see 1996b: 451–462). From the deliberative standpoint (and, importantly, from the second-person perspective involved in holding one another accountable), our concern is not primarily to figure out what will happen or has happened. We are concerned, rather, with what we should do, with what we or someone else should have done, and with how appropriately to hold people accountable in light of what they actually did. From these perspectives, the phenomenal feeling of respect in us, *reverentia*, is not on the radar screen.

In deliberating about what to do, for example, we don't usually consider how, as a matter of psychology, we actually will, or will be able to, act on the reasons we come ultimately to accept.[26] Nor, in the course of deliberation, do we ordinarily contemplate how we feel in deliberating or acting. To deliberate intelligibly at all we must simply presuppose that we can act on good and conclusive reasons as we will come to see them.[27] Similarly, in holding someone accountable, we must proceed on the assumption that, without defeating evidence to the contrary, he could have acted as he was obligated. In addition to these practical needs, however, we also have the theoretical need to understand ourselves, one another,

26. Korsgaard 1996c is especially helpful here.
27. Of course, one may know of certain practical deficiencies and sensibly deliberate in light of these. But these must be relatively local and regulated by the global presupposition that one can act on what one takes to be good and sufficient reasons.

and our actions as part of the causal structure of the world we experience. This is where *reverentia,* the feeling a person has when she acts on the moral law and respects the dignity of persons in the "practical sense," enters the picture.

According to Kant, *reverentia* is a feeling that operates as a cause within our phenomenal psychology. Kant thinks that we can know *a priori* that we are subject to the feeling of respect, indeed, that any finite rational being must be. Assuming, as Kant believes, that recognition of the moral law is a condition of the possibility of pure practical reason, then so also is it a presupposition of the possibility of practical respect. This is the "fact of reason" (1996a: 30–31). In taking ourselves to be bound by the moral law, we perforce assume that we can comply with it. But morally obligatory action can be realized in the phenomenal realm only if its phenomenal counterpart has a phenomenal cause, and Kant takes it that this must be a feeling. So any finite rational being subject to moral imperatives must also be characterized by a psychology having something whose role, as the phenomenal counterpart of practical respect, is to cause the phenomenal counterpart of moral action. *Reverentia* is the feeling that plays this role.

We, however, are interested less in respect's functional role than in what Kant says about its distinctive phenomenology. Respect for the moral law, Kant says, "thwart[s]" and "restricts" *self-love,* but, more importantly, "humiliates" and "strikes down *self-conceit*" (1996a: 73). By "self-love," Kant refers to a "natural" "propensity" to take merely "subjective determining grounds" of the will to have objective normative significance. Like a naïve experiencer who takes an apparently bent stick in water to be really bent, a naïve agent may take his desire's object to be a source of reasons, oblivious to peculiarities of the perspective that his desire gives him. Things that are important to him seem to be important period. Self-love in this sense poses no deep threat to morality, however; in principle, it need be no more dangerous than the innocent mistakes of perspective that can be corrected once we are able to draw a subjective/objective distinction within our experience and accept some as mere appearances. Self-love, Kant thinks, needs only to be curbed by the moral law.

Self-conceit, however, assaults the moral law directly, and so it must be "humiliated." It is a form of arrogance *(arrogantia):* the presumption that one has a kind of worth or dignity oneself, independently of the moral law, through which self-love is made "lawgiving and the unconditional practical principle" (1996a: 73, 74). This is not just a naïve tendency to mistake seeming normative relevance from one's perspective with objective normative weight. It is rather the radical idea that something has objective normative significance because it is what one wills subjectively—first, that one has a unique standing to create reasons for acting independently of and unconstrained by the moral law, but also, second, that one can address these reasons to others and expect compliance, in other words, that one has a unique authority to address second-personal reasons: "lack of modesty in one's claims to be respected by others is *self-conceit (arrogantia)*" (1996d: 462).[28]

A person with "self-love" confuses what she desires with the objectively desirable. In desiring that her thirst be relieved, she takes it that there are reasons, in principle for anyone, to desire this state and bring it about. But she doesn't think that others should do this because this is what she wants or wills. Rather, in wanting it, it just seems to her that such reasons exist. Self-conceit, in contrast, is the idea that one's own will is a source of normative reasons (and is so uniquely). A thirsty person with self-conceit will take it that others have reasons to relieve his thirst because this is what he wills or wants (though he would have no such reasons if roles were reversed).

Self-conceit is thus a fantasy about second-personal status.[29] It is the conceit that one has a normative standing that others don't have to dictate reasons just because of who or what one is.[30] The idea is not that one has the kind of authority that an especially good advisor does, that one

28. Cf. Karen Horney's discussion of neurotic egocentricity: "a *wish* or *need*, in itself quite understandable, turns into a claim. Its nonfulfillment is felt as an unfair frustration, as an offense about which we have a right to feel indignant" (1970: 42; quoted in Swanton 2003: 190).

29. Compare here what Dillon says about the relation between self-conceit and "interpersonal respect" (2004). Dillon distinguishes another form of arrogance, "primary arrogance," that concerns not primarily interpersonal disrespect but an arrogation to oneself of rights one doesn't have. If, however, as I believe, the notion of a right itself involves the irreducibly second-personal authority to lay a claim or make a demand, then primary arrogance may itself be ultimately an interpersonal or second-personal notion also.

30. Cf. Bob Dylan's "Disease of Conceit" (2004: 534–535): "Whole lot of people seeing double tonight / From the disease of conceit / Give ya delusions of grandeur / And a evil eye / Give you the idea that / You're too good to die / Then they bury you from your head to your feet / From the disease of conceit."

sees better than others reasons that are there anyway. (Although it might involve this thought, if one took it to justify a special second-personal status.) It is rather the fantasy that one has a fundamental "lawgiving" standing that others simply don't have—as if one were king or God.[31] This is far from an innocent illusion, although Kant follows Rousseau in thinking that it is depressingly expectable whenever social comparison engenders *amour propre*.[32]

It follows that the moral law cannot simply curtail self-conceit or keep it in its place; it must "strike it down." It must declare "null and quite unwarranted" any "claims to esteem for oneself that precede accord with the moral law" (1996a: 73). We shouldn't be thrown off by Kant's use of 'esteem' here. The moral law must supplant self-conceit's presumptuous second-personal authority, the standing it presumes to demand recognition of the claims and demands it purports to address. Kant uses 'esteem' in a similar way when he defines *observantia* or "respect in the practical sense" as "the *maxim* of limiting our self-esteem by the dignity of humanity in another person" (1996d: 449). Obviously, in this context, 'esteem' must refer to recognition rather than to appraisal respect. Self-conceit is the fantasy that one has a claim to others' recognition respect but that they reciprocally do not have any against one.

The moral law substitutes the equal dignity of persons—the mutual accountability of the kingdom of ends—for the fantasized despotism of self-conceit.[33] The respect-creating encounter with a "humble common" person gives rise to a response to the common dignity that all persons share. This is no esteem (appraisal respect) that persons might differentially deserve,[34] but a form of respect that any individual can demand

31. "Arrogance (*superbia* and, as this word expresses it, the inclination to be always *on top*) is a kind of *ambition (ambitio)* in which we demand that others think little of themselves in comparison with us" (Kant 1996d: 465). For a fascinating discussion of the role of the "wish to be God" in Kant's philosophy generally, see Neiman 2002: 57–84.

32. For an insightful account of Kant's ethics that stresses the role of self-conceit, see Wood 1999.

33. I believe this also provides a useful framework within which to think of other self-serving ideologies, such as those of race and gender.

34. Although even this is an important idea, as Mill appreciated: "The principle of the modern movement in morals and politics, is that conduct, and conduct alone, entitles to respect: that not what men are, but what they do, constitutes their claim to deference; that, above all, merit, and not birth, is the only rightful claim to power and authority" (1988: 88).

simply by virtue of being a person (1996d: 434–35). And we recognize each other's equal authority to make demands as a free and rational agent by acknowledging our mutual accountability (for example, through reactive attitudes) and holding ourselves responsible to one another for complying with these. Respect for others thus involves making oneself accountable to others as equal persons, rather than simply taking account of any fact, norm, or value about one another as persons in our own private deliberations.

Kant divides "duties to others merely as human beings" into duties of love and duties of respect. Performance of duties of love is "meritorious" and therefore "puts others under obligation." Discharging duties of respect, however, gives rise to no reciprocating obligations since here we only do for others what is already "owed" them in the first place (1996d: 448). "No one is wronged if duties of love are neglected; but a failure in the duty of respect infringes upon one's lawful claim" (464). Indeed, "Every human being has a legitimate claim to respect from his fellow human beings and is *in turn* bound to respect every other" (462). Thus, "recognition [*Anerkennung*] of a *dignity (dignitas)* in other human beings, that is, of a worth that has no price," is something others can "require from me" (462).[35]

It follows that the duty of respect includes any specific duty, compliance with which persons have the authority to demand. Respecting others as equal persons requires that we discharge these duties. But it requires also that we recognize others' "legitimate claim" to our doing so, and this we can do only by recognizing their authority to claim or demand it. This is what brings in accountability and the second-person stance. In holding that the dignity of persons is that by which we can "demand," "exact," or "require" respect from others, that each thereby has a "legitimate claim" to respect, Kant is committed to the idea that the dignity of persons includes a second-personal authority to address demands for compliance with the first-order duties of respect. To respect that authority it is insufficient simply to comply with the first-order duties, even for the reason that duty requires it.[36] The standing to address demands can only be recognized second-personally, by making ourselves accountable to one another as equal free and rational agents for complying with the relevant

35. Note Kant's use of 'Anerkennung' here. As we see in Chapter 10, this is the term that looms so large in Fichte's discussion.

36. Unless the latter is given a second-personal reading.

first-order requirements. As Feinberg (1980) says, it is "the activity of claiming" that makes for self-respect and the equal dignity of persons. The kingdom of ends is a community of mutually accountable persons (Korsgaard 1996a).

Self-Conceit and Morality: The Case of Stalin

In Chapter 10, I argue that the fantasy of self-conceit is ultimately self-undermining since second-personal address commits us, quite generally, to an authority that anyone has just by virtue of second-personal competence. Briefly: addressing second-personal reasons always presupposes not just the addresser's authority and competence to hold the addressee responsible for compliance, but also the addressee's authority and competence to hold himself responsible. It is committed, therefore, to the authority of a perspective that addresser and addressee can occupy in common: the second-person standpoint of mutually accountable persons. Even when someone addresses reasons he takes to derive from an unreciprocated authority over his addressee, he can blame his addressee for not complying only from the very same standpoint from which his addressee can blame himself, a standpoint they share in common as free and rational persons. As Strawson noted, therefore, reactive attitudes involve a form of respect for their objects as persons with the very same authority to hold themselves and others responsible as well (Strawson 1968: 93).

A natural response to this argument may be to agree that if the presupposition that addressees can freely acknowledge and make authoritative demands of themselves from such a common standpoint is part of the very idea of second-personal address, then perhaps it does commit us to the equal dignity of free and rational persons, but then to deny that second-personal address, so understood, is anything we need have much of a stake in. Surely people can presume authority without having to think anything about whether those over whom they think they have it can be expected freely to accept it and comply on that basis. Alternatively, it seems that someone might be content with simply having power over others without any kind of authorizing narrative at all.

I agree that even Kantian self-conceit, the idea that one has an authority that no one else has, is coherent as an abstract proposition, and nothing I argue will assume otherwise. What I do argue is that taking up a second-person standpoint toward others and addressing second-personal reasons to them commits us to mutual accountability and, therefore, to denying self-conceit (however intelligible that proposition might otherwise be). I do not claim or assume that it is impossible to have or want power over others irrespective of any authority requiring second-personal reasons— would that it were so! Nevertheless, it is worth pointing out that neither self-conceit, at least in a pure form that excludes an underlying moralizing rationalization, nor the desire for power pure and simple, exclusive of an authorizing rationale, is at all common among human beings as we find them.

Consider Stalin, for example. Stalin would seem to have been as hungry for power or as liable to self-conceit as they come, but at least in Edvard Radzinsky's riveting biography (1997), he also appears to have been some-one who was motivated by richly elaborated reactive attitudes, which, to be sure, he marshaled for his own ends. As Radzinsky describes him, Stalin's self-conceit was not pure. His emotional life was replete with episodes, frequently staged, in which a justified authority over others seemed manifest to him, justified in ways that, as it seemed to him, others should be able to appreciate. And even his cruelest murders were accom-panied, indeed fueled, by self-justifying emotions and narratives. It seems no exaggeration to say, in fact, that Stalin's distinctive form of evil essen-tially employed a cynical and distorted form of moral self-justification that he manipulated for his own purposes. Thus, Radzinsky tells us, a standard ploy of Stalin's was to catch someone he wished to "eliminate" in a lie, after which Stalin "felt entitled to feel a moral hatred for the liar and traitor" (237). Radzinsky describes a poignant scene from Stalin's boyhood in which, when fellow students in the Gori Church School "made a back" to enable an elderly teacher to cross a wide and turbulent stream, Stalin was overheard to say: " 'What are you then, a donkey? I wouldn't make a back for the Lord God himself.' " To which Radzinsky adds, "He was morbidly proud, like many people who have been humil-iated too often" (29).

I, for one, find it impossible to read Radzinsky's accounts of Stalin's fury-fueled, but coldly calculated, in-fighting, purges, murders, and willing sacrifice of his own innocent citizens without seeing in it a form of *ressentiment* that takes itself to be seizing and wielding power, not nakedly, but righteously. In my view, this sort of distorted self-serving moralizing is actually quite common, although not, thankfully, on Stalin's scale. People frequently manipulate aspects of the moral framework in narratives that rationalize their special exemptions and departures. It is actually quite rare, I think, for human beings to reject the second-person standpoint outright, since, for one thing, our emotional lives are full of reactive feelings and attitudes that essentially involve it. Although "hypocrite" is perhaps not the first epithet one would use, even Stalin seems to instantiate Rochefoucauld's dictum that "hypocrisy is the tribute that vice pays to virtue" (Rochefoucauld 1973: 79).

Respect as Second-Personal

We are now in a position to see that respect for persons is second-personal in two distinct, but related, senses: it involves recognition of a second-personal authority and the recognition itself comes from a second-person standpoint. Consider the former aspect first. Someone might accept the first-order norms that structure the dignity of persons and regulate himself scrupulously by them without yet accepting anyone's authority to demand that he do so. He might even accept these as mandatory norms without accepting any claim to his compliance. I hope it is now clear that although such a person would thereby respect the duties with which persons can demand compliance, in failing to respect their authority to demand this, he would also fail, in an important sense, to respect them. He would fail to acknowledge their equal authority as free and rational and so fail to relate to them on terms of equal respect.

In *The Realm of Rights*, Judith Thomson says that respect for persons can have no foundational role in morality if "respect for persons just is respect for their rights" (1990: 210–211).[37] But is respect for someone simply respect for her rights? If we think of respecting someone's rights as according her the specific things that Thomson maintains we have a right to—forbearing trespass, coercion, and causing undue harm and distress; keeping promises; and so on, then respect for her as a person cannot consist just in that. For we could respect persons' rights in this sense without respecting these as their right, as anything they have the authority to claim or demand from us.

This is the first way in which respect is second-personal: a fundamentally second-personal authority. But this form of authority is itself some-

---

37. I am grateful to Judith Thomson for discussion of these points.

thing that is appropriately recognized second-personally also, through relating to others in a way that acknowledges this authority. And this is the
second way in which respect is second-personal. Not only is the authority
it recognizes second-personal, but its distinctive form of recognition is
second-personal also. We accord authority within the second-personal
relations that structure mutual accountability by relating to one another
in ways that acknowledge each other's standing to demand, remonstrate,
resist, charge, blame, resent, feel indignant, excuse, forgive, and so on.
Since accountability is, in its nature, second-personal in both senses, respect for persons is as well.

It seems possible to respect the fact that someone has second-personal
authority—for example, that she can claim certain conduct as her right—
without relating to her in the way that genuine respect for her as a person
involves.[38] To see this, consider, first, an analogous case in theoretical
reasoning. Suppose you are disinclined to trust someone's judgment in
forming your own beliefs, but that, on reflection, you reject your distrust
and think you should take his testimony as evidence. When he says, "p,"
this does not increase your inclination to believe p or to give his testimony
evidential weight until you recall your considered view about his relia-
bility, which corrects your distrust. Here it seems natural to say that
although you respect the fact that he is a reliable witness and so the fact
that he has a claim on your beliefs, you do not, yet anyway, fully trust
and respect him and his judgment.

Consider now a fully second-personal case. Suppose it is a parent who
is not yet disposed to regard his college-age daughter as a fully independent person with full second-personal authority, at least, not to do so
wholeheartedly. We can well imagine that he believes, on reflection, that
he should so regard her, that is, that she has the same claim to respect
that he does. But parental habits die hard. When she says she doesn't
want to do something within her discretion that he believes to be for her
greater good, he is disinclined to defer to her in his own reasoning about
what to do and feel with respect to her until he reminds himself of his
considered conviction. When she calls him on his paternalism, he is neither naturally nor second-naturally disposed to see and hold himself responsible as from her authoritative perspective (for example, by feeling
guilt or shame) but defends himself until he recalls that she is right; she

38. In what follows, I am indebted to Amanda Roth.

really is no less entitled to respect than he is. Here again, it seems that although the parent respects the fact that his daughter has the same dignity he does, he does not yet relate to her on terms of equal respect; he does not yet accord her full second-personal authority in relating to her.[39] Respect of this kind is an irreducibly second-personal way of relating to someone *de re*. It is the relation to individual persons that is primary. Indeed, the fact that someone has second-personal authority just *is* her having the standing to claim to be related to in this way.

To respect someone as a person is not just to regulate one's conduct by the fact that one is accountable to him, or even just to acknowledge the truth of this fact to him; it is also to make oneself or be accountable to him, and this is impossible outside of a second-personal relation. This, I believe, is what most deeply underlies the sense of 'respect''s root, '*res-picĕre*' (to look back). To return someone's address and look back at him is to establish second-personal relationship and acknowledge the other's second-personal authority. To look someone in the eye is to make oneself and one's eyes, the "windows" of one's soul, vulnerable to him, and in both directions. One gives the other a window on one's responses to him but also makes oneself vulnerable to his attitudes and responses by empathy.[40] When the address is an attempt to hold one responsible, returning the other's address, being open to his claims, including by giving him this window, is itself part of holding oneself accountable to him.[41]

39. Cf. Sarah Buss on "respect in its primitive, prereflective mode" (Buss 1999b: 539).

40. At the most primitive level, by mimicry and contagion, but also by imaginative projection, since one must already be doing that in relating to him second-personally, as we saw in Chapter 3.

41. When I gave an earlier version of this chapter as a Presidential Address to the Central Division of the American Philosophical Association in April 2004, I preceded it with a video clip from *The Blues Brothers* in which the character played by Aretha Franklin attempts to hold Matt "Guitar" Murphy accountable with a rendition of "Think (You'd Better Think What You're Doin' to Me)," much of which she sings in a wonderful eye-to-eye dance with Matt. The conceit was that the view of respect expressed in my (1977) article was like that of Aretha Franklin's famous "Respect" and that the view expressed in the address (and this book) was (is) like that of her *Blues Brothers'* "Think." The earlier was a first-personal, giving someone "her propers" view; the second took respect for persons to be essentially second-personal.

Bernardo Strozzi's painting, *The Tribute Money*, illustrates the same point. As Matthew tells the story (in the King James version of the Bible), the Pharisees attempt to entrap Jesus and ask him whether or not it is lawful to give tribute to Caesar. "But Jesus perceived their wickedness, and said, Why tempt ye me, ye hypocrites?" (Matthew 22:18). I imagine this to be the moment that Strozzi's painting depicts. Jesus is addressing the Pharisees and

Manners, Honor, and Public Space

We respect someone as a person when we acknowledge her dignity. Of course, this acknowledgment need not always be explicit. Part of what we claim from one another is a space of personal privacy or discretion within which we can be left more or less alone if we want. If respect for persons always called for explicit acknowledgment, it would be impossible for this claim ever to be realized. Moreover, in a social situation in which the demands of personal dignity are sufficiently well established and generally reciprocally recognized, explicit acknowledgment is less commonly called for. But think of situations in which the dignity of persons, say of some group in particular, is under attack, not just in the sense that they are subjected to various forms of injury, but also in the sense that that their claim to dignity, their second-personal status as persons, is threatened or not generally recognized. To maintain, in such a situation, that one respects the dignity of members of this group without being willing to acknowledge it publicly will be difficult.

Another aspect of the shared public space in which respect figures centrally is etiquette. Sarah Buss argues that expressing respect is "the essential function of good manners" (1999a: 795).[42] Her point is not simply that respect frequently calls for politeness. This we learn at our parents' knees. It is rather that conventions of etiquette are at least partly public rituals of respect in something like the way that religious rituals enact the idea of the sacred. By treating one another cordially and courteously, we give an "outward and visible sign of an inward and spiritual" *reverentia* for the dignity of persons that is itself second-personal.

Of course, etiquette can, and perhaps frequently does, also reinforce

---

attempting to hold them accountable. But look closely at the Pharisee on the right—he is not looking back at Jesus, but past him to another Pharisee on the other side. I like to think that this shows that Strozzi appreciates Pufendorf's Point: even God must gain our recognition to hold us accountable. I am grateful to Will Darwall for noticing this and to both Julian and Will Darwall for helpful conversation on this point.

42. Sarah Buss (1999b) quotes a remarkable passage from Hume in which Hume says that the function of manners is to check self-conceit: "As the mutual shocks, in *society,* and the oppositions of interest and self-love have constrained mankind to establish the laws of *justice;* in order to preserve the advantages of mutual assistance and protection: In like manner, the eternal contrarieties, in *company,* of men's pride and self-conceit, have introduced the rules of GOOD-MANNERS or POLITENESS; in order to facilitate the intercourse of minds, and an undisturbed commerce and conversation" (Hume 1985a: 261). See also Sherman, unpublished.

divisions and hierarchies that are in conflict with equal respect. Even calls for "common courtesy" and "decency" can blunt and subvert challenges to an established unjust order that are necessary genuinely to respect others as equals.[43] Nonetheless, properly conceived, manners are an important supplement to a morality of equal respect.

It is useful to compare the way respect for one another as persons is mediated in a mutually accountable public space with the way a superficially similar, but fundamentally different, kind of recognition respect and disrespect are enacted in a culture of honor. Insults are paradigmatic expressions of disrespect of this latter kind. But although insults are invariably addressed,[44] when they assault someone's honor, the standing they threaten differs from second-personal authority, since, unlike the dignity of persons, it is socially constituted.[45] In traditional honor societies, insults like Bolingbroke's "pale trembling coward" address to Mowbray in Shakespeare's *Richard II* put in question the ability to receive the honor of others' favorable regard and acceptance as someone of merit. Honor may present itself as merited, but it is nonetheless "bestowed on people by society," as Avishai Margalit puts it (1996: 24). Whether Bolingbroke's insults and charges are groundless or not, Mowbray is right to believe that he will nonetheless be dishonored unless he can successfully defend his good name in a way that convinces people to restore their faith and credit in him.

Sufficiently wide disrespect destroys honor by constituting dishonor. But not even universal disrespect can destroy the dignity of free and rational persons, at least, not directly. Equal dignity is nothing anyone can bestow, so neither is it anything any person or group can remove through disrespect. Humiliations that aim to degrade, depersonalize, and dehumanize must work differently. They must seek not simply to lower someone's standing in others' eyes, but to demean someone in his own

---

43. William Chafe (1980) gives many compelling illustrations of how "civility" was appealed to by white North Carolinians in resisting attempts to desegregate schools long after the Supreme Court held segregation to be unconstitutional in *Brown v. Board of Education*.

44. One can feel insulted and be offended without being addressed, even indirectly, in an insulting way. And it is possible also for someone to express things that are genuinely insulting to one without addressing one, even indirectly. It is not, however, possible to insult someone without addressing her, at least indirectly.

45. And it is also, I would further argue, not fundamentally about accountability at all.

eyes so that he loses self-respect. Even this doesn't directly destroy the dignity to which respect for persons and self-respect responds. Still, we know that it is possible for domination by violence and threats of violence, and even by relatively nonviolent, disrespecting relations or institutions that are, in Goffman's term, sufficiently "total," to beat down, dispirit, and undermine self-confidence and self-respect so that the very second-personal capacities necessary for accountable living can atrophy (Goffman 1961).

There are important differences between the ways in which attitudes of respect and disrespect support and reinforce a regime of honor and the manner in which reactive attitudes function in a second-personal economy of mutual respect. Disrespect (contempt) that dishonors is disdain—an attitude that is addressed not so much to its object as to those with the standing to bestow honor or dishonor upon that person. Disdain does not demand, nor even really invite, response from its object; it is exclusive rather than inclusive. And what a person loses when he is dishonored is not a standing within a mutually accountable community, but "face," a social place (where one can show one's face without having to justify oneself to others).[46]

Reactive attitudes through which we hold one another accountable, however, have an inclusiveness that follows from their second-personal character. Blame, indignation, resentment, remonstrance, and so on, are, as it were, reciprocally addressed to their objects. In calling for acknowledgment, they have an implicit mutuality or reciprocity. As Strawson says, "the partial withdrawal of goodwill which *these* attitudes entail . . . is, rather, the consequence of *continuing* to view [their object] as a member of the moral community" (1968: 93). Reactive attitudes engage their targets second-personally and aim to draw them into an exchange that will constitute their being held accountable.[47] Their address comes with an implicit RSVP.

46. Relevant here is the deep connection I noted before (Chapter 3, note 31) between honesty and the search for truth, on the one hand, and public accountability, on the other. By reckoning people at "face value," cultures of honor actually pose an obstacle both to public inquiry and to public accountability and encourage evasion and keeping up appearances. A request for justification is itself an insult in such a social framework.

47. This, I believe, provides a basis for responding to Annette Baier's (1993) criticisms of the Kantian approach.

Whence Dignity?

Morality as equal accountability thus presupposes that every free and rational agent has a dignity for which he can demand respect. But what can support this idea? I argued in Chapters 3 and 4 that moral obligation is essentially tied to second-personal accountability. This was the thesis of *morality as accountability*. The very idea of moral obligation presupposes that of a second-personal authority or dignity, whether as in the early modern natural law conception of *morality as accountability to God* or as in the Kantian/contractualist conception of *morality as equal accountability*.

But what can support or vindicate any of these ideas? Much as Kant says of his argument at the end of section 2 of the *Groundwork,* our method to this point has been to analyze assumptions and presuppositions of moral obligation as these latter ideas are "generally accepted" (1996b: 445). As Kant points out, however, it is entirely consistent with these analytical results that the ideas of morality and moral obligation are nothing but a "figment of the mind" (2002: 445).[48] And if that were so, so also would the ideas of second-personal authority that I have argued are conceptually or analytically contained within them be illusory as well.

To vindicate moral obligation and the dignity of persons and show that they are not mere figments, Kant says that a "critique" of practical reason is necessary (1996b: 445). In Chapter 9, we consider how Kant pursues such a critique in *Groundwork* 3 and in *The Critique of Practical Reason.* Ultimately, Kant abandons the strategy he broached in *Groundwork* 3 of trying first to secure the idea of freedom or autonomy in a critique of practical reason and then to show how the other central moral ideas can be derived from that. In the *Critique of Practical Reason,* Kant is content to treat acceptance of the moral law as a central undeniable aspect of our practical lives and to defend it from that perspective.[49] Kant was right ultimately to reject his *Groundwork* approach, but as I argue further in Chapter 10, however, Kant was wrong to give up on the attempt to provide a more substantial vindication of morality than is possible with the defensive strategy he was later content to take.

We have already seen that the lesson of Strawson's Point is that an

---

48. This is Allen Wood's translation of *Hirngespinst.*
49. This is the method Rawls (2000) refers to as "philosophy as defense."

adequate theory of moral responsibility must invoke standards that are internal to the second-person standpoint. And I have argued that moral obligation's conceptual tie to accountability yields the further consequence that an adequate theory of moral obligation must also be available within the second-person point of view. But this line of argument has proceeded by analyzing "generally accepted" concepts of moral responsibility and obligation to reveal their irreducibly second-personal character, and so it is impotent by itself to vindicate the very ideas it analyzes. In Chapter 10, however, I proceed in the opposite direction and argue that the presuppositions of the second-person standpoint, when fully worked clear, include the dignity of persons and the moral law. For any kind of second-personal reason, based on a second-personal relation of whatever form, both addresser and addressee are committed by the terms of their relation to presupposing that they have a common normative standing simply by virtue of being (second-personally competent) rational persons. This vindicates moral obligation and the dignity of persons on the assumption that second-personal reasons exist at all.

But why suppose that any second-personal reasons are valid? Chapters 10 and 11 also develop Fichte's Point that second-personal interaction gives us an awareness of the distinctive character of our own agency and of a kind of freedom—autonomy—that distinguishes practical reasoning fundamentally from theoretical reason. In second-personal engagement, we see that we have a kind of freedom we simply could not have if reasoning about what to do were like reasoning about what to believe. And this helps us to locate second-personal reasons within an overall theory of practical reason.

— PART III —

— 7 —

The Psychology
of the Second Person

We respect persons when we give them standing in our relations with them and recognize their second-personal dignity. But what psychic mechanisms are involved in respect and the second-person standpoint? How is it possible for a capacity that is sensitive, in principle, to claims of free and rational agents as such to be realized in human psychology, naturalistically conceived? Whether there is such a thing as dignity and what it takes to have that status are not, of course, matters of empirical psychology. The thesis of morality as equal accountability is moral-philosophical, not psychological. Still, rival consequentialist moral theories can be lent an air of apparent empirical support and realism by the familiar Humean moral psychology with which they are often associated and hence an apparent default plausibility that Kantian theories rarely seem to enjoy. There is, for some, a lingering sense that any moral theory claiming *a priori* foundations and faculties cannot possibly apply to human beings as we actually are.

This chapter discusses aspects of human psychology that are relevant to morality as equal accountability and to the second-person stance more generally. We have already seen (in Chapters 4 and 5) how familiar reactive attitudes have an implicitly second-personal structure that fits them to practices of mutual accountability. In this chapter, we consider how these interact with other psychic mechanisms that also play crucial supporting roles, most notably, empathy and what Gibbard calls our "normative psychology," namely, the distinctive human capacities concerned with accepting and regulating behavior and feeling by norms (1990: 55–82).

Two caveats are necessary at the outset. First, I should stress again that nothing I say in this chapter is intended to provide direct support for morality as equal accountability or for the existence of second-personal reasons. Any arguments for these ideas must be normative and philosophical.[1] Nonetheless, to the extent that human behavior can be shown to involve capacities in which second-personal moral notions are psychically realized, so also can these ideas be seen to fit with our psychology, or at least not to be in conflict with it.

Second, although I draw on a steadily increasing literature in experimental psychology, some of my psychological hypotheses are abstract and speculative. To some extent, this is unavoidable. And it is worth noting that the Humean framework similarly employs a more abstract conception of desire than any that can be found in common sense or experimental psychology. In fact, the Humean theory's notion of desire is sufficiently abstract that the phenomena I point to here are likely consistent with the basic "law" of the Humean theory of motivation—which states that all intentional action results from appropriately paired desires and beliefs (Davidson 1980; Smith 1994). The fact remains that the mechanisms I discuss are implicated in desires that are, in Rawls's helpful terms, "principle-dependent" rather than "object-dependent."[2] Here there will be two crucial points. First, sometimes, perhaps frequently, the desires that help to explain our intentional behavior are among those we have because we accept certain norms of action. And second, some of the

1. For these, see Chapters 10–12.

2. On the basic Humean idea, see Smith 1987 and 1994. For Rawls's distinction, see Rawls 2000: 45–48, 148–152. See also Freeman 1991. For further discussion of these points, see Chapters 9, 10, and 11.

Rawls's distinction is similar to, but also importantly different from, Nagel's distinction between "motivated" and "unmotivated" desires (Nagel 1970: 29–30, 38). For Nagel, a desire is motivated if it is based on a reason, if, that is, there is something that is the agent's reason for so desiring. Unmotivated desires are those one brutely has, like the desire for a cool drink, as we say, "for no reason." However, a desire could be motivated but still be object-dependent, namely, if the agent's reasons are drawn from properties of the desire's object or if the agent desires that thing because she think it is intrinsically good. Such desires would be "object-dependent" and "heteronomous" in Kant's sense, since they would come not just from the will's being a "law to itself independently of any property of the objects of volition." (See Kant 1996b: 440 and Chapters 9 through 11 of this book.) "Principle-dependent desires," by contrast, derive from norms of action to which one is subject simply as a rational will and independently of the properties, hence independently of any value of any object of volition, that is, of any representable state of affairs or possible state of the world.

norms we evidently accept essentially involve the idea of second-personal authority.

Finally, we should keep in mind a point I made at the end of Chapter 5, namely, that the familiar forms of moral reasoning that are involved in such principles as the Golden Rule and the Categorical Imperative have an intuitive second-personal interpretation. The thought that people ought not to act in ways that fall short of their expectations or implicit demands of others reveals itself in our psychology in all sorts of ways, from the reactive attitudes to more principled moral reasoning of the kind that psychologists of moral development like Kohlberg (1981) have studied. Any denial that these forms of reasoning and the feelings that draw upon them are deep and pervasive aspects of human psychology would seem to be, to quote Bishop Butler, "too glaring a falsity to need being confuted" (1983: I.8).[3]

Desire and Norm

We can begin by considering the respective motivational roles played by desire, as philosophers normally understand it, and norm acceptance, as Gibbard describes it. I claim, again, that second-personal competence essentially includes the capacity to be guided by norms, especially by second-personal norms that concern the authority to claim and demand. Ultimately I argue that there is yet a further essential element: the ability critically to evaluate second-personal norms one accepts, and competing alternatives, from the standpoint of one mutually accountable person among others and to be guided by those one would endorse from that standpoint.[4] One way of viewing the argument of this book is as an attempt to show that this is but a more developed version of what is implicit in any second-personal thinking, for example, in reactive attitudes.

Gibbard introduces the idea of norm acceptance through a discussion of cases of weak will. Suppose, for example, that you can't get yourself to stop eating nuts at a party (1990: 56).[5] On the one hand, you desire

3. The context is Butler's claim that conscience is natural to human beings.

4. As Gibbard would understand it, this would be a capacity to be guided by relevant higher-order norms. See Gibbard on the "authority" of normative judgments (1990: 177–183).

5. This case has the same structure as the one Plato discusses in the *Republic* of the

to keep eating them. On the other, you think you shouldn't. It doesn't matter for present purposes why. The reasons might relate to health, avoiding boorishness, not taking more than one's share, or whatever. The point is that some conflict exists between your desire for nuts and your normative conviction regarding what there is most reason for you to do. We know, of course, that frequently the nuts win out. But the point is that they don't always and that even when they do, there is usually some conflict. At least some motivation seems to come from accepting that there are weightier reasons to stop eating.[6]

This is not sufficient to establish that the motivation does not derive from further independent desires, of course. Perhaps it comes in this case from the desire to be healthy or from the desire not to be or to seem a boor. However, there are many reasons for thinking that this cannot always be so in general, that our accepting norms and normative reasons must exert some influence on our behavior that cannot be reduced to that of independently existing desires that are not themselves principle-dependent.[7]

One reason is that beliefs and desires can themselves explain behavior as intentional only on the hypothesis that we are usually instrumentally rational, and this will be so only if norms of instrumental rationality play a regulating role (Korsgaard 1986). Lewis Carroll (1895) famously made the analogous point about inference as it applies to belief. Without guidance by some norm of inference, a set of beliefs or believed premises is impotent to yield conclusions. (Of course, beliefs might simply cause further beliefs in some nonrational way, but this wouldn't explain the transition of thought as rational.) If, for example, someone believes p and if p, then q, she cannot conclude q unless she follows a norm of inference, *modus ponens*, that takes her from (her beliefs that) p and if p, then q, to (a belief that) q. Trying to add a further *modus ponens*-like belief—(if p and if p, then q, then q)—will not help, since it will still take following *modus ponens* to get rationally even from these augmented beliefs to a

---

person who restrains thirst by seeing that there are better reasons not to drink (437d–439d).

6. For an argument that motivation always comes from reasons to which desires and normative judgments respond, and never from the psychic states of responding to them, see Dancy 2000.

7. There are too many issues to enter into fully here. For relevant discussion, see, in addition to Dancy 2000, Darwall 1983, Nagel 1970, and Smith 1994.

belief that q. The rational formation of new beliefs through inference cannot be fully explained by belief, therefore; it also requires regulation by a norm of inference.

The situation is exactly analogous with instrumental reasoning from ends to necessary means.[8] To reason to a conclusion to take the necessary means to an end, it is required, not just that one have the end and believe some means to be necessary to achieve it, but also that one be regulated by a norm of practical inference that takes one from this desire and belief to the practical conclusion to take the necessary means.[9] And the only way the end and belief can rationally give rise to a desire to take the means is via a norm of instrumental reasoning that is analogous to *modus ponens*. A further desire to take the necessary means to one's ends will be impotent in itself, for the very same reason that Lewis Carroll pointed to in the theoretical case.

Regulation by norms of these theoretical and practical kinds is thus necessary to explain rational behavior, even in the terms of Humean desire-belief psychology. As important as this phenomenon is, however, it doesn't yet fully capture the way in which norm acceptance is involved when an acceptance that one should or has reason to do something tends to motivate doing it, and such tendency, as in Gibbard's nuts example, conflicts with occurrent desires. The reason is that this necessarily includes accepting not just norms of inference but also norms that can supply premises in practical reasoning, that is, substantive normative reasons for acting. *Modus ponens* and the norm of instrumental reason, as well as such associated norms of coherent theoretical and practical reasoning as the law of non-contradiction and formal decision theory, are best interpreted as norms of "relative rationality" (Darwall 1983: 14–16, 44–49, 66–67; also Darwall 2001). If one has good reason not to believe p and if p, then q, then the fact that one believes p and if p, then q cannot (by *modus ponens*) give one any reason to believe q. Rather *modus ponens* transfers whatever rational support there is for the first two beliefs to the third. Believing q is rational "relative to" there being reason to believe both p and if p, then q, respectively.

8. The point is especially well made in Broome 1999. See also Blackburn 1995 and Railton 1997: 76–78.

9. At this point, I am abstracting from the difference between having something as end, which presumably involves intention, and desiring it, which need not, since it doesn't matter for present purposes.

Here again, the situation is exactly analogous in instrumental reasoning. If one has no reason to have an end (and/or no reason to believe that some means is necessary to achieving it), then the mere facts that one has the relevant end and belief can give one no reason whatsoever to take the means. The most that instrumental rationality can require is that one either take the means or give up either the end or the belief about the means' indispensability. The practical analogue of *modus ponens* transfers rational support from the end and the belief to the means. Taking the means is rational relative to there being reason to have the end and to believe that the relevant means is indispensable.[10]

Our beliefs, desires, and intentions must be more than merely coherent to be supported by reasons. It follows that when we sincerely judge that there is reason to do something or that we ought to do it, we must accept substantive normative claims that go beyond any that follow from norms of coherent belief, desire, and action. And there is good reason to think, moreover, that the influence of accepting such normative judgments, like that of accepting norms of practical inference, cannot be reduced to the influence of independently existing desires.

Particularists like Dancy may insist at this point that the normative reasons we accept frequently resist formulation in universal norms, whereas universalists may hold that if I judge, say, that I should forego the nuts because that is for my good, this commits me to a universal norm of prudence. But these differences don't matter for our purposes. Whether motivational influence comes from acceptance of particular or universal normative claims, what matters is its irreducibility to independently existing desires.[11] I therefore use "normative acceptance" to refer to the acceptance of either.[12]

10. The intuitive idea is that what rationality rules out here are incoherent combinations of attitudes. It does not rule in any particular attitude or action on the condition that one has certain others. On this point, see Broome 1999; Dancy 2000; Darwall 1983, 2001; Greenspan 1975; and Hare 1971.

11. Dancy, again, holds that, strictly speaking, any motivational influence must come from normative reasons themselves, not from their acceptance or from any desires that might respond to them. If 'motivation' refers to agents' reasons, that is, to (believed) facts or features of the situation that the agent counted in favor of acting, this seems surely correct. However, we also frequently use 'motivation' to refer to a subjective motivational state. When, for example, we say that someone was motivated by fear, we do not mean that fear was his reason. What the agent had in view that counted in favor of his action was not the fact of his fear, but scary facts his fear "lit up" for him.

12. For a discussion of the psychic state of norm acceptance, see Gibbard 1990: 55–82.

Presently, I point to what I think are important psychic differences between desire and normative acceptance. First, however, we need to note an important logical difference. Desire, as conceived within the Humean framework, takes propositions or possible states of affairs as objects.[13] Desire and belief are defined by their differing "directions of fit" with respect to a common propositional content or possible state of the world (Anscombe 1957; Platts 1979: 256–257; Smith 1994: 111–119). A belief that p represents the world as being such that p, and if the world is not such that p, the belief is mistaken and should be changed. Beliefs are thus said to have the "mind-to-world" direction of fit; they seek to fit the mind to the world. Desires work the other way around, in a "world-to-mind" direction. A desire represents a possible state of affairs that the world should contain (viewed, as it were, from the desire's perspective).

So conceived, desires are *state-of-the-world-regarding* in their nature. To have a desire is to be disposed to bring some state of the world about. It is, we might say, to be *teleologically* disposed. Even when the desired state includes one's performing a specific action as an essential part, even when performing the action comprises the state in its entirety, the motivational influence of the desire is still entirely teleological. One is moved to perform the action as an essential (or the sole) constituent of the state.

Normative acceptance, however, has a different logical structure.[14] What practical norms and normative reasons for action call for is action pure and simple or, perhaps, a choice or intention to perform an action. Similarly, norms for belief recommend this or that belief; norms for feeling recommend this or that feeling; and so on. Call anything that can be regulated by a norm an "attitude."[15] And call any being whose attitudes can be normatively regulated, and thus to whom norms can apply, a "subject." Attitudes are states of subjects that subjects can have for reasons, that is, where not only is there some non-rationalizing, say causal, explanation (explaining reason) of their having the attitude, but there is also something that is *the subject's reason* for having it, namely, some

---

See also Hart's discussion of taking an "internal" perspective on rules or law (Hart 1961: 55–57).

13. The Humean view, in this context, is not necessarily the same as Hume's. For an interpretation of Hume along these lines, however, see Bricke 1996.

14. For some similar claims, see Scheffler 2004: 231.

15. For present purposes, we can identify doing A with the intention or choice to do A.

consideration or considerations the subject herself takes as a normative reason or reasons and acts on.

So whereas desires are state-of-the-world-regarding, normative acceptance is *attitude-of-a-subject-regarding;* and practical norms are intention- or action-regarding.[16] Normative acceptance thus motivates intention and action directly, not out of a desire for some state.[17] Perhaps we should say that it motivates "deontologically." Even when the norm is teleological, like "Bring it about that *p*," normative acceptance does not motivate teleologically. It can only motivate one to act in conformance with applicable norms or normative reasons, even when these dictate the very same acts one would be moved to by a desire that *p*. And this logical difference gives rise to a psychic difference: unlike the acceptance of a norm recommending that one bring *p* about, a desire that *p* can show itself in disappointment that *p* did not occur, whether or not one was in a position to realize it.

The psychic difference between desire and norm acceptance also reveals itself in our experience in various other ways. One is in the phenomenon of *regret.* Failing to satisfy a desire can give rise to regret only if one thinks there was some reason to have done something to have satisfied the desire.[18] The most familiar experience is regretting doing something one thinks one shouldn't have done, all things considered—continuing to eat the nuts, for example. But it is also possible to experience regret for things one thinks there was only some reason not to do, but overbalancing reason to do. In these cases, we are likely to say we regret "having" to do what we did rather than that we simply regret doing it, since the latter would imply regret, all things considered. The important

16. Since states of affairs do not themselves admit of normative regulation, there can be no (unreduced) normative reasons for states—no brute ought-to-be's. (I argue for this claim at greater length in Darwall 2003b. Roughly, when we say that there is reason for something to obtain, all we can defensibly mean is that there is reason for having some attitude toward that state.)

17. Of course, desires can be normatively regulated also—the desirable is what there is reason or we ought to desire. But reasons for acting cannot be reduced to reasons for desiring (although Humeans and non-Humeans alike can accept the principle of instrumental reason—that there is reason to do what will bring about desirable states of the world). For a discussion of this point, and of a fundamental disagreement between Sidgwick and Moore about whether the basic concept of ethics is ought (normative reason) or intrinsic value, see Darwall unpublished.

18. More precisely, my remarks are meant to apply the form of regret that philosophers call "agent-regret." See, for example, Williams 1973: 170–205 and 1981b: 31, 74–75.

point is that failing to act on a desire can move us to regret only to the extent that it engages what we take to be normative reasons for acting.

An additional, second dissimilarity involving regret follows in the wake of desire's and normative acceptance's different logical structures. Both regret and unsatisfied desire are "con attitudes," broadly speaking, but whereas regret is against or "con" some action (or omission), unsatisfied desire is "con" some state. Thus, consider the case where the object of regret is the omission of an action whose performance was an essential constituent of a state you intrinsically desired. Suppose you think that you should have done A and you desire (or wish) that you had done A. Even in this case, regret at not having done A is different from feeling displeased that your doing of A didn't take place. The first naturally tends to give rise to dissatisfaction with yourself (as an agent). Displeasure that the state of affairs of your doing A did not obtain, however, can occasion dissatisfaction with yourself only if you took it you had some reason to do A (even if only because you thought your desiring to do A gave you such a reason).

Third, whereas accepting a norm regulating an attitude typically involves some tendency to acquire the relevant attitude in the conditions specified by the norm (Gibbard 1990: 55–82), a desire that one have that attitude does not itself involve a tendency to acquire the relevant state (at least, not directly). Thus, a desire that I believe something cannot itself give rise to the relevant belief, although it can motivate me to look for reasons that would support the belief, on the basis of which I might then acquire it. Desire is a normatively regulable attitude with its own distinctive (right kind of) normative reasons. In desiring that I believe something, it will seem to me that my having the belief would be desirable, that there are reasons for me to desire the state of the world in which I have that belief and reasons therefore to bring that state of the world about. But these are not reasons of the right kind to make the belief credible, nor is it possible by accepting them to form the belief. I can only form the desire that I have the belief. This is another reflection of the "wrong kind of reasons" problem that noted in Chapter 1. Were I, however, to believe that there are epistemic reasons for the belief, then I would accept that this is something I should believe. And it is possible to form a belief on these grounds (even when one can't say more specifically what the reasons are).[19] Similarly for practical norm acceptance:

---

19. The significance of this point for practical reason is somewhat masked by the fact

thinking there is some reason to do something (even when one is unsure what the specific reasons are) involves some tendency so to act or intend. Attitudes that can be regulated by norms, again, are precisely those mental states that subjects can form for reasons—their reasons—that is, considerations they take as normative reasons to have the relevant attitude.[20]

We should not, however, draw too bright a line between desire and normative acceptance. Desires, again, are among the attitudes that can be normatively regulated. And to play the right role in motivating intentional action (even on the Humean picture) desires can hardly be just brute urges.[21] They must be more like what Scanlon calls favorable "directed attention." When someone desires P in the "directed attention sense," "the thought of P keeps occurring to him or her in a favorable light . . . the person's attention is directed insistently toward considerations that present themselves as counting in favor of P" (Scanlon 1998: 37). But this just means, and Scanlon takes it to mean, that when one desires P it seems to one as if there are (normative) reasons to desire P and hence, owing to the principle of instrumental reason, to bring P about.[22]

Even though this brings desire within the scope of the normative, there is a remaining important difference with normative acceptance, namely, that desires involve seeming normative reasons, whether or not we accept, on reflection, that the reasons actually exist. In the nuts example, your desire to keep eating the nuts conflicts with your acceptance that you have better reasons to stop. You could accept that, of course, and still think there is some reason to keep eating, other things being equal. But to desire to keep eating, you don't have to accept even that *pro tanto* normative judgment. It is enough for desire, even in the directed attention

that the desire that one do A does seem to give rise to one's doing A. However, I believe that the reason why this seems to be so is that we accept as an obvious norm of practical reason that we should do what brings about desirable or valuable states, and what seems to us to be true when we have a desire to do A, is that doing A would be good or valuable. Even here, I think, the desire gives rise to an action (that is, something done for some [apparent] normative reason) only thanks to this additional normative acceptance (or, at least, apparent normative acceptance).

20. Rabinowicz and Ronnøw-Rasmussen (2004) argue that attitudes implicitly contain the distinctive attitude-relevant reasons as part of their content and that appreciating this phenomenon is the solution to the "wrong kind of reasons" problem.

21. This thesis is defended in Quinn 1991.

22. Also in this same vein are: Bond 1983; Dancy 2000; Darwall 1983; Hampton 1998; Pettit and Smith 1990; and Quinn 1991.

sense, that eating the nuts seem good in some way, that there appears to be some reason to do so. That can be so even if you reject that there is any reason to keep eating. This kind of case is perhaps clearer in sensory experience. Once you are familiar with the illusion, the fact that a stick looks bent in water may not give you any reason to think that it is really bent. The illusory character of the experience doesn't outweigh a still existing reason; it defeats what would otherwise be a reason. And the same thing can happen with desire. The very things that seem attractive to you about eating the nuts might be features or considerations that you reject as any reasons at all, even as they continue to seem attractive.

A related phenomenon can happen with normative acceptance itself when, in Gibbard's words, we are "in the grip of a norm" (1990: 60). Gibbard discusses the phenomenon in connection with Milgram's famous experiments about obedience, which occupy us for different reasons presently. Subjects in the Milgram experiments were told by an authority figure to administer shocks to another subject to test how people learn. The "teacher" was told to respond to "learner"'s mistakes with shocks of increasing severity, beginning at 15 volts and continuing up to 450 volts. In fact, no shocks were actually given, and the learners were really confederates. But this was not, of course, what the subjects believed. And distressingly, a substantial majority of the subjects in the initial setup (approximately two-thirds) administered all the shocks they were ordered to, up to and including 450 volts, with the highest several levels being labeled, "Danger: Severe Shock." Many, however, were obviously upset, conflicted, and obeyed at the higher levels only under protest.[23]

We naturally respond to these experiments with dismay, judge that the subjects should not have administered the shocks as they were ordered, and hope we wouldn't have done so ourselves were we in their shoes. Gibbard points out, however, that, given the results, we should assume that we well might have, albeit with conflict and reservations. After all, 80 percent of the subjects administered shocks to at least 225 volts (halfway up the shock generator). Gibbard analyzes this case as involving the acceptance of conflicting norms—against harming others and against disobeying authority. But though subjects genuinely accepted norms of both kinds, many were also "in the grip" of a norm of authority in the

23. The experiments are described and analyzed at length in Milgram 1974. For an excellent discussion, see Sabini and Silver 1982: chs. 3–5, 9–11.

sense that, in the circumstances, the norm seemed to override and ground weightier reasons than the norm against harm, although this was the reverse of what many of the subjects (on reflection) actually accepted. And it seems possible, moreover, to be, as it were, in the grip of a norm entirely, that is, for it to seem to provide normative reasons, even though we reject it on reflection and judge that it gives no normative reasons whatsoever.

The sort of normative acceptance that is revealed in the Milgram experiments is psychically different from desire. We can say, of course, that the subjects wanted not to disobey, that they wanted not to harm, and that, in the circumstances, they evidently wanted the former more than they did the latter. And in the directed attention sense of desire, at least, we can say that, in having these desires it seemed to them that there were reasons to desire, and thus to bring about, states of the world in which they did not harm. But it seems obvious that the Milgram subjects didn't just want these latter states pure and simple; they wanted them, at least partly, because they thought they shouldn't harm.[24] Their desires followed their norms; they were principle-dependent rather than object-dependent. And because of this, their psychic conflict, caught between norms dictating conflicting actions, was palpably different from that of someone who merely has conflicting object-dependent desires, that is, desires for two outcomes that cannot simultaneously be realized. It showed itself in forms of agitation, upset, and emotional distress that are quite different from the conflict of someone forced to choose between two alternatives to which she is averse, but which otherwise violate no norm that she accepts or that grips her.

Accepting Moral Norms and the Second Person

I have been pursuing the evidence, both speculative and empirical, for the human capacity for norm acceptance because it is an essential aspect of second-personal competence. When you and I address second-personal demands to one another, we presuppose that we both have the capacity to accept and act on second-personal norms that ground relevant second-personal reasons irrespectively of our (object-dependent) desires for states of the world. That was an essential aspect even in our first example, when

24. Of course, they might also have wanted this out of, say, sympathy.

you addressed a demand to someone to get off of your feet. The reason you purported to address to him came not from the badness of your being in pain (as this might be represented in a desire that you be free of it) but from a norm proscribing foot treading. And in addressing the reason to him, you consequently assumed that he could accept and act on it irrespectively of any (object-dependent) desire that your feet be free of pain, or even of pain caused by foot treading (that was the agent-relative aspect of the reason).[25]

What I have said in this chapter so far has concerned (practical) norm acceptance in general. It seems possible, however, to have that capacity while lacking psychic mechanisms that are involved in accepting and recognizing norms that relate to second-personal reasons in particular. To instantiate second-personal competence, the human repertoire must include something, like reactive attitudes, that mediates second-personal accountability, along with the capacity to reflect on and revise these in critically accepting second-personal norms and reasons.

In this connection, Gibbard notes that the emotional manifestations exhibited in the Milgram experiments show not just any norms were in play, but that peculiarly social ones were operating. Violating a prudential norm is unlikely, by itself, to give rise to the sorts of feelings of embarrassment, shame, and guilt that the Milgram subjects evidently felt. If I keep eating the nuts, the thought that I shouldn't because it is bad for me cannot support feelings like these unless I somehow connect it to some ideal of a presentable or morally decent self, so that I am embarrassed by publicly displayed intemperance, or ashamed even when I keep eating the nuts in private, or feel remorse that I never seem to leave enough for others.

Most importantly for our purposes, the norms that seem most obviously involved in the Milgram experiments are second-personal, moral norms. They concern what people have the authority to demand. Norms of obedience are second-personal by their very nature, and I have argued that any moral obligation not to harm is second-personal also. Moreover,

---

25. Recall that in saying you presupposed these things, I am not making a psychological claim. I am not saying that you actually thought, or that I can reasonably take you to have thought these things (although you may have). I am saying that the second-personal competence of your addressee was a normative felicity condition of your address: the reason you purported to address can be validly addressed only if your addressee has second-personal competence.

an analysis of the experimental setup and results reveals that there were second-personal aspects at play in the responses of subjects that went beyond even the second-personal character of the implicated norms. For example, that the subjects were under instructions they had some obligation to comply with as consenting participants in the experiments was not just made evident to them as an abstract proposition. The authority figure was actually there in the same room with them, and he ordered them. When subjects questioned whether they "had" to go on, or protested about being ordered to, the apparently authoritative experimenter responded with a sequence of increasingly forceful "prods": (1) "Please continue" or "Please go on," (2) "The experiment requires that you continue," (3) "It is absolutely essential that you continue," and (4) "You have no other choice, you *must* go on" (Milgram 1974: 21).

Presently, we shall consider how these prods might have worked psychically. First, however, we should note that they were not the only second-personal element in the experiment.[26] In the initial setup, the learner was in an adjoining room. He could not be seen and, up until the point when he was administered a shock level of 300 volts, he could not be heard. At this point, however, the learner began audibly pounding on the wall. The pounding continued through 315 volts, after which there was no sound at all coming from the room and, indeed, the learner stopped responding in the learning exercise (which the subjects were instructed to treat as mistakes). In the initial experiment, none of the forty subjects stopped administering shocks before they heard any protest. Five, however, stopped at the first expression of protest. Four stopped on the next round (315 volts), two on the next, and one on each of the next two. So thirteen out of forty subjects (32.5 percent) stopped the shocks within five rounds of the first protest. Moreover, these were 100 percent of the subjects who stopped at all.[27]

A second setup was identical, except that vocal protests could be heard through the walls throughout. In this version, almost the same number continued until the end—twenty-five instead of twenty-seven. But eight stopped obeying orders to shock in the "Strong Shock" range (135–180 volts), well before the 300 volts that drew the first disobedience in the first setup.

26. The details that follow come from Milgram's description of the different setups of the experiment, together with the data (1974: 32–43).

27. The rest (twenty-seven) continued administering shocks until the end (450 volts).

In a third setup, the learner was placed in the same room, a few feet from the subject, and could be both seen and heard. Here thirteen subjects stopped obeying by the end of the "Strong Shock" range, and only a minority, sixteen, administered the full series of shocks (almost 40 percent less full compliance than in the initial setup).

A fourth, and final, setup was identical to the third, except that the learner received a shock only when his hand rested on a shock plate. At the 150-volt level, the learner demanded to be set free and refused to place his hand on the shock plate, whereupon the experimenter ordered the subject to force the victim's hand onto the plate so that he could receive the shocks the subject administered. Remarkably, in this setup twelve subjects continued to the end, but even so this was less than half of the number that did so in the first version. More importantly, twenty (or half the subjects) stopped in the "Strong Shock" range, long before, again, there was any disobedience in the first setup.

Clearly, having protests addressed to them made a significant difference in the subjects' behavior. There was no disobedience in the first setup before any audible protest, and almost 80 percent of the disobedience that did occur took place during or just after the protest (eleven out of thirteen). In the second, protest was audible earlier, and there was also significantly greater disobedience earlier. In the third, protest (and its grounds) were both visibly and audibly evident, and this also significantly increased earlier disobedience. And in the fourth, in which subjects were ordered not just to administer shocks despite the protest but also to enforce a denial of learner's demands to be set free (and arguably to punish them for their demands), the disobedience was greatest of all.

The conflicts that the Milgram subjects experienced were not just between conflicting norms, but between conflicting second-personal norms that grounded demands. Moreover, these demands were at some point or other actually addressed by those the subjects took to have the authority to address them. Both their acceptance of the norms and the address of normatively grounded demands seemed to have psychic consequences. The norms were constant throughout the various setups, as was the experimenter's addressing of orders. What was variable was the evidence and salience of the learners' protests.

But why focus on protest? What varied was not just that but also evidence and salience of pain and of causing pain. Why not say that it was the increasing amount and vividness of the learners' suffering that explained the increased disobedience? But consider: how was the pounding on the wall likely to have been experienced by subjects in the first setup? Presumably, the pain was now getting to be so bad that the learner was asking the subject and the experimenter to stop. As one subject said, "I think he's trying to communicate, he's knocking" (Milgram 1974: 32).

Think about it from the subject's perspective. The learner is, you believe, someone like you who has volunteered to take part in the experiment. You might think that, like you, he feels obligated to take part. You might even think (if only as a rationalization) that it would be unfair to him not to play your role so long as he does. At the least, you certainly would think that whether he has consented to being caused pain is relevant to whether you should cause it to him. These are all second-personal matters. They concern your respective claims and how you and he have the authority to interrelate as mutually accountable equals.

The most significant change in the overall rate of disobedience came when the learner was moved into the same room with the subject. The subject could then see the effects of what he was doing. But also importantly, he was aware, for the first time, of the learner's awareness of him. Even if audible protests were experienced as claims in the first two setups, the conditions made reciprocal recognition impossible. Bringing the learner into the room gave him a presence as someone to whom the subject was accountable—a second-personal advantage the experimenter had in all the setups. Milgram himself notes the possible relevance of this factor:

> Possibly, it is easier to harm a person when he is unable to observe our actions than when he can see what we are doing. His surveillance of the action directed against him may give rise to shame or guilt, which may then serve to curtail the action. Many expressions of language refer to the discomfort or inhibitions that arise in face-to-face attack. It is often said that it is easier to criticize a man "behind his back" than to confront him directly. (1974: 38–39)

The other was present now not just as someone with the standing to demand compliance with a norm requiring that he not be harmed but also as someone with some standing to judge one's compliance with it.[28]

28. Another relevant study was conducted by John Thibaut and Laurens Walker, who were interested in assessing psychological aspects of adversarial systems of criminal justice. Subjects were read a set of facts about an assault case, half incriminating, half exculpatory, and asked to assess guilt or innocence. In one setup, the facts were read to the subjects by

That second-personal aspects of the situation make a psychic difference seems obvious enough.[29] But how does this work? And how do the mechanisms involved interact with norm acceptance? No doubt we are, to some extent, moved by desires for others' approval or esteem, or by desires not to be in disagreement with them, even when we care nothing for the standards they employ or have no inclination to share their views. But we are so moved only to some extent. Aristotle noted that we care more about honor and esteem from those we honor and esteem ourselves, and he concluded that this must be because we care independently (and more) about meriting the esteem of those whom we accord the authority to judge us (1980: I.5).

This seems clearly on the mark. When subjects in the Milgram experiments were troubled by the protests of those they were shocking in the same room with them, it seems incredible that they were simply experiencing the discomfort of being regarded in demanding ways. It seems much more likely that, to varying degrees, empathy took them inside their victims' perspectives and that at least some subjects experienced emotions such as shame and guilt in which they empathically regarded themselves as warranting disdain (shame) and/or blame or some other

---

one person. In another, they were read by two people, with one "representing" the accused by reading only exculpatory facts, and the other "representing" the prosecution. Subjects who were read the facts in the second setup were significantly likelier to think the defendant innocent than in the first (1975: 42–53).

29. In another Milgram experiment, subjects were subway riders who were asked to give up their seats without any reason that might justify such a request. When Milgram first asked his students to conduct this experiment, he was surprised by their reluctance and the difficulty they reported in executing it. He decided to conduct some trials himself. A newspaper account reports his experience: "But when he approached his first seated passenger, he found himself frozen. 'The words seemed lodged in my trachea and would simply not emerge,' he said in the interview. Retreating, he berated himself: 'What kind of craven coward are you?' A few unsuccessful tries later, he managed to choke out a request. 'Taking the man's seat, I was overwhelmed by the need to behave in a way that would justify my request,' he said 'My head sank between my knees, and I could feel my face blanching. I was not role-playing. I actually felt as if I were going to perish.' " (Michael Luo, " 'Excuse Me. May I Have Your Seat?': Revisiting a Social Experiment, And the Fear That Goes With It," *New York Times*, September 14, 2004.) Years later, one of Milgram's students who ran the experiment remembered a response of one of the subjects whose seat he requested. "The woman snapped: 'If I were standing and you were sitting, I think it'd be very reasonable to ask you for your seat, but I'm not going to give you my seat.' " This seems clear evidence of second-personal psychic phenomena. I am indebted to Tristram McPherson for reminding me of this experiment.

form of second-personal accountability.[30] How else can we explain the depth and variety of psychic conflict that must have been involved, at least for some? The conflicting external demands of experimenter and victims would likely have been replicated, to varying degrees, empathically within the subjects' own outlooks on themselves.

This fits, again, with what we learned about the role of empathy in second-personal thought in Chapter 3. When I am engaged by another's address second-personally, I inevitably gain a second-personal perspective on myself. I can grasp the other's responses as second-personal only if I see them in relation to my own. And I can do that only if I can see my address as from the other's point of view. By being vulnerable to the other in this way, I am susceptible to appearances as from the other's standpoint. Thus blame can be felt as guilt.[31] Of course, blame also elicits defensive responses, but that simply proves the same point. If we weren't vulnerable to seeing ourselves as others see us empathically, and hence to blaming ourselves, there would be nothing to defend against.

It is useful to compare here what Mill says about moral sanctions in chapter 3 of *Utilitarianism,* in which he considers the normative (or, as he interprets this, the motivating) force of the principle of utility. "What is its sanction?" he asks. "What are the motives to obey it? Or more specifically, what is the source of its obligation? Whence does it derive its binding force?" (1998: ch. 3, §1). Mill first discusses "external sanctions,"

30. Compare here Adam Smith on the natural disposition to defer to superiors owing to empathetic projection into their standpoint: "Upon this disposition of mankind, to go along with all the passions of the rich and the powerful, is founded the distinction of ranks, and the order of society. Our obsequiousness to our superiors more frequently arises from our admiration from the advantages of their situation, than from any private expectations of benefit from their good-will. . . . The strongest motives, the most furious passions, fear, hatred, and resentment, are scarce sufficient to balance this natural disposition to respect them" (1982b: 52–53).

31. A related phenomenon is the familiar experience of simply being persuaded by a vivid representation that another person forcefully makes. (An example: One day I went to my local pool to swim laps. Because work was being done on the glass door connecting to the outside deck, and it was the dead of winter, the water was colder than usual. An elderly woman before me in line turned to me and said, "It's 75 degrees. You can't possibly swim in that." Because she had spoken so authoritatively, I was persuaded. I saw things as she painted them. When I got back to my car, I thought: "You know, 75 degrees isn't *that* cold. I've often swum in 75 degrees and colder." By then, however, I was in my warm car, full of rationalizations about why it was really a better thing that I not swim that day anyway.)

within which he includes "hope of favour and the fear of displeasure" from others and from God, whether selfishly or from sympathy or "awe" that inclines us to accord with their will. But Mill gives these short shrift. His chief interest is in the "internal sanction." This "ultimate sanction," Mill says, is "conscience": "a feeling in our own mind; a pain, more or less intense, attendant on violation of duty, which in properly cultivated moral natures rises, in the more serious cases, into shrinking from it as an impossibility" (ch. 3, §3).[32]

But what makes conscience an internal rather than external sanction? The desire to avoid the displeasure of others is no less internal to the psyche than are feelings of conscience. Why does it make a difference whether the displeasure originates with others or with oneself? Perhaps one can avoid others' displeasure more easily than one can one's own, but Mill's discussion puts no weight on that possibility. What he stresses is the way conscience makes one feel toward the action itself. When moral norms have been internalized, the thought of an action the norms require "presents itself to the mind with the feeling of being *in itself* obligatory" (1998: ch. 3, §1). In a "properly cultivated moral nature," the thought of violating a central norm, strikes one "as an impossibility." What makes conscience an internal sanction, therefore, is not its psychic location. Pain resulting from others' displeasure is no less an internal state than that of being displeased with ourselves. What makes conscience an internal sanction for Mill is rather its object. When we consider that we have done something we think wrong, we don't just have a painful feeling. We have a painful "appearance" that we shouldn't have done what we did, that not doing it was "*in itself* obligatory." We have a putative awareness of having acted contrary to what members of the moral community (and we ourselves as such members) justifiably demand.[33]

Second-personal address that appeals to shared norms, like remon-

---

32. Mill argues that although conscience's dictates naturally give the "intuitive" "customary morality" of common sense an advantage, this can be eroded by the "dissolving force of analysis" over time if accepting it is not socially beneficial. Utilitarian morality, on the other hand, has another psychological support that tends to mold conscience in its direction, namely, "the desire to be in unity with our fellow creatures" (1998: ch. 3, §9, 10) Ultimately, time is on utilitarianism's side, and when it becomes widely accepted, conscience will dictate complying with it.

33. Here I draw on Mill's analysis of 'wrong' and moral obligation, which I discussed in Chapter 5.

strance or blame, can give rise empathically to conscientious feelings that are tied to those norms. Milgram's subjects most likely experienced conflicting normative feelings whose vividness depended on the salience of others' second-personal authority to demand their compliance. Of course, such forms of address can trigger defensive responses also. But part of the reason they can, again, is to defend the self against blame's hitting home and being experienced as guilt. Through empathy we can feel not just others' blame but also that we are to blame.

Thus, one way in which empathy and second-personal address can interact with normative psychology is in the exchange of reactive attitudes and the engendering of conscientious feelings and even normative acceptance. I argued in Chapter 4 that reactive attitudes have a second-personal conceptual structure that calls for a reciprocally recognizing response of which it presupposes its (implicitly addressed) object to be capable. For ordinary human beings, empathy provides the psychological mechanism that funds this presupposition.

To conclude this section, I shall briefly mention one other way in which empathy and second-personal address can figure in our normative psychology, namely, in critical normative discussion, both about individual cases and about norms themselves. Gibbard speculates that norm acceptance has a distinctive evolutionary role that enables human beings to use language and linguistically encoded motivations to solve coordination problems (1990: 64–80). Norm acceptance manifests itself not just in regulating conduct but also in tendencies to avow the norm in contexts of "unconstrained normative discussion" (74). By normative discussion, Gibbard means not just the sort of thing that moralists, moral philosophers, or writers to editorial pages engage in but also something that is virtually ubiquitous in human life, from gossip, to discussion of novels, movies, and sitcoms, to "I was like . . . ; He was like . . ." conversations in which participants display their reactions to others' actions and feelings.[34] In all of these instances, people negotiate questions of how it makes sense to respond to what people do and what norms for evaluating conduct it makes most sense to accept. And as they do, empathy works to bring others' views inside our perspective so that they can be part of our own critical reflection and not just recorded as what others think. Second-

34. On the relevance of gossip to shared moral reflection, see Sabini and Silver 1982: ch. 5 ("A Plea for Gossip").

personal accountability is not the only form of social criticism, of course, but surely much of what human beings discuss concerns what they and we can warrantedly expect and demand of one another.

Cooperation and Second-Personal Motivation

Other experiments demonstrate and illustrate the involvement of second-personal psychic mechanisms in human cooperation. Why do people cooperate when it is against their interests to do so? Cooperation is any organized pattern of interaction in which, although the overall pattern advances the cooperating individuals' interests, it nonetheless requires actions from the participants that are less than optimal individually. The classic example is Prisoner's Dilemma, in which the parties do better if both pursue a cooperative strategy, but where the individually optimal strategy is non-cooperative.[35] Two people face a Prisoner's Dilemma when each profits most by an outcome of their respective actions by which the other profits least (for example, by arming while a hostile foe disarms), but when both profit more if they both do something that is individually suboptimal (say, both disarming). Each party orders his outcomes thus: first: I arm, she disarms; second: we both disarm; third: we both arm; and fourth: I disarm, she arms. In such a situation, advancing one's interests seems unambiguously to recommend arming, since, whatever the other does, one comes out better. But this leads both to an outcome that is worse for both than would have resulted if they had done what is collectively best but individually suboptimal (both disarming).

Because the orthodox view in much contemporary social science, not to mention practical philosophy, has been that self-interested behavior is rational by default, the problem has been to explain why human beings cooperate as much as we evidently do. No motivation beyond preference satisfaction or self-interest is required to explain cooperation in cases with the structure of an "iterated" Prisoner's Dilemma, in which "tit for tat" or some other strategy requring actions that would be suboptimal in a "one shot" game may be most optimal for players even individually (Axelrod 1984). When there are repeated plays, it will pay individually to cooperate now to draw out reciprocating cooperation from fellow players

35. For a short introduction to the Prisoner's Dilemma, see Barry and Hardin 1982: 11–12, 24–25.

later. But many studies have revealed much human cooperation that cannot be explained by self-interested strategies even of this sort.

There is growing empirical evidence that normative acceptance, including of a distinctively second-personal kind, is frequently involved.[36] Some especially interesting experiments conducted by Ernst Fehr and Simon Gächter suggest that reactive attitudes are often implicated. Fehr and Gächter (2002) gave groups of four subjects 20 money units (MUs) each, from which each could contribute any amount to a group project and keep any amount she didn't contribute. For every MU invested in the project overall, each of the members earned 0.4 MUs, regardless of her own investment. Thus the investor's return from investing one additional MU was 0.4 MUs (and the expected return of not investing it was 1 MU). If, however, all group members invested no MUS, each would end up with 20 MUs, whereas if all of them invested all of their 20 MUs, each subject would earn 32 MUs.

The variable condition manipulated by the experiment was whether the round of contributions was (known to be) followed by a round in which subjects could anonymously "punish" noncontributors. In this condition, the subjects were given a profile of the others' contributions in the first round without attribution. Each could then assign from 0 to 10 points to any other individual, at a cost of 3 MUs per point to the "punished" subject and 1 MU to the "punishing" subject, respectively. Thus individuals could punish only at cost to themselves.[37]

Unsurprisingly, when the cooperative contribution rounds were run before subsequent punishment rounds (and this was known in advance), there was a higher level of cooperation than without expected punishment (approximately 13 MUs to 11 MUs). This also increased over time,

36. Especially good is Fehr and Schmidt 1999. Much of this literature is discussed in Ben-Ner and Putterman 1998. For an excellent critical review, see Anderson 2000. See also Mansbridge 1990. For an excellent argument that punishment-based accounts of human cooperation are significantly better than reciprocity-based accounts within an evolutionary framework, see Sripada 2005.

37. The experiment consisted of six contribution rounds, one set run with paired punishment rounds, one without. To rule out repetition creating cooperation or punishment through tit-for-tat reciprocity or reputation, the group composition continuously changed so that no subject ever met another subject more than once. On the "evolution" of reciprocity in iterated activity, see Axelrod 1984 and Trivers 1971. On reputation effects, see Alexander 1987; Leimar and Hammerstein 2001; Lotem, Fishman, and Stone 1999; Nowak and Sigmund 1998a, 1998b; Wedekind and Milinski 2000.

whereas later cooperation levels without punishment were lower. By the sixth round, the mean cooperation with punishment was above 14 MUs, whereas without punishment, it declined to below 6 MUs. Considered so far, however, these results might be explained simply by a self-interested desire to avoid sanctions.

The more interesting and important finding is that the subjects were prepared to punish at cost to themselves, sometimes at significant cost.[38] A total of 84.3 percent of the subjects punished at least once during the six periods, 34.3 percent punished more than five times, and 9.3 percent punished more than ten times. Fehr and Gächter term the punishment "altruistic," but by this they evidently mean just that subjects were prepared to hold non-cooperators responsible even at cost to themselves. Subjects reported that they responded with negative emotions to failures to cooperate and that they expected others to respond to them with these same attitudes when they failed to cooperate. Asked how they would feel in hypothetical scenarios in which they are taken advantage of by free riders, subjects predicted they would respond with significant "anger and annoyance," as they predicted others would respond to them if they free rode.

It seems clear enough that reactive attitudes like resentment and indignation were involved that appeared to subjects to be warranted by others' failure to cooperate. Subjects who had these reactive responses would have seen themselves as having a reason, a second-personal reason, to hold the non-cooperators responsible quite independently of reasons of other kinds, self-interest, for example. And evidently enough, these reasons were not only independent of self-interest; for almost 85 percent of the subjects, they apparently outweighed it.[39]

But if subjects were susceptible to reactive attitudes in responding to others, these feelings would have been no less available by empathic projection in their imagined and actual responses to themselves. And this would then have given them motivations to cooperate themselves that

38. Of course, it can be said that in these cases subjects also got the benefits of satisfying their resentment, but while this is no doubt true, this seems to be a principle-based desire in the sense that resentment involves at least the appearance of a second-personal reason.

39. There were also likely self-interested considerations that were related to the second-personal reasons involved in the reactive attitudes, for example, the desire not to have to live with the painful awareness of being taken advantage of. But these would have been parasitic on the second-personal reasons.

are quite distinct from a desire to avoid sanctions.[40] For example, such feelings could have functioned as a vivid reminder of a second-personal norm they accepted, which their apparently warranted reactive attitude itself "enforces." Alternatively, or in addition, putting themselves in the shoes of imagined punishers could have given rise empathically to reactive attitudes directed toward themselves.[41] And in feeling, for example, that they would be to blame for freeloading, they would, in effect, be addressing to themselves a second-personal reason to cooperate.

In any or all of these ways, subjects implicitly saw themselves and others as having, in our terms, the authority to address the second-personal demands that were implicit in the "punishment" they meted out and, therefore, second-personal reasons to comply with these demands. If the threat of resentment provides an important support to cooperation, as these experiments suggest, then the implicit presupposition of second-personal standing must play an important role as well. Indeed, there is evidence that the perceived legitimacy of sanctions, that is, whether they are seen as genuinely authoritative and applied in good faith or simply strategic threats, is itself a significant determinant of levels of cooperation. Fehr and Rockenbach have shown that when sanctions are believed to be applied self-interestedly rather than as expressing valid demands in holding others responsible, this actually diminishes cooperation, that is, makes it less than it would be even in a no-punishment condition.[42] This is a remarkable result, since from the strategic point of view, (second-personally) unjustifiable sanctions are no less undesirable and sensibly avoided than are justified ones.

Second-personal psychic mechanisms evidently run sufficiently deep that people are willing to forego benefits or incur costs not only to address

40. Except, of course, a desire to avoid justified sanctions (as in Pufendorf's Point). But these also would have been parasitic on the second-personal reasons that justify the sanctions.

41. On the importance of "empathic anger" in moral development, see Hoffman 2000: 96–102.

42. Fehr and Rockenbach explain this difference as follows: "Our results suggest that the moral legitimacy of the sanction is a crucial factor. In the public good context the punishment of 'free-riders' is an altruistic act that is considered as morally legitimate. . . . In the present context, punishment serves the punisher's self-interest and, if it is used to enforce an unfair payoff distribution in favour of the punisher, it decreases altruistic responses" (2003: 137–140). Again, Fehr and his colleagues tend to use 'altruistic' to mean 'cooperative'.

justified demands but also to defy unjustified ones. And human beings are not the only species in which a response of this sort has been observed. Brosnan and de Waal have found that capuchin monkeys who had been receiving equal rewards for equal effort in an experiment refused to participate further when they saw others beginning to receive more. Noting that there is substantial evidence that "a sense of fairness" is a human universal,[43] they describe their findings as "supporting an early evolutionary origin for inequity aversion" (2003: 297). But if equity is, as seems clear, a matter of justified claims and demands, it follows that their research supports an early evolutionary origin for second-personal or proto-second-personal psychic mechanisms.

The relevance of the second-person stance to cooperation is further supported by another study by Robert Frank (1988) of the ability to discriminate between cooperators and non-cooperators. After a thirty-minute conversation about whether to cooperate in a one-shot Prisoner's Dilemma in which their subsequent plays were mutually blind, subjects predicted whether their interlocutors would cooperate or not. They were remarkably successful. Sixty percent of the participants who had been predicted to defect did so, and 75 percent of those who had been predicted to cooperate did so (134–145). The likelihood that such a high overall accuracy rate would happen by chance is less than one in a hundred. Moreover, subjects had substantially greater confidence in predictions that subsequently proved correct than in those that turned out to be incorrect. Simply on the basis of a thirty-minute conversation and with no knowledge or experience of their interlocutors' record of cooperation, participants manifested an extraordinary ability to predict whether another person would cooperate for mutual advantage or defect in his own individual interest.

What explains this success? Frank hypothesizes that it has to do with the detection of involuntary bodily symptoms, for example, facial expressions, of emotions that can motivate cooperation. This certainly seems correct. However, his candidates, evidence of sympathy, and emotions like shame and guilt would, in principle, be equally available to anyone who was watching the conversation from a third-person perspective as to those participating in it. And there is experimental evidence that people are not particularly good at detecting lying in general

43. They cite Henrich 2000 and Henrich 2001.

(Ekman, O'Sullivan, and Frank 1999; Good 1999). There is evidently something about the authenticity of conversation, perhaps especially conversations about whether to cooperate, that enables people to detect it more readily.

I speculate that people in these situations are sensitive to reciprocal recognition, that is, they can detect whether they are being engaged in a serious second-personal deliberation about whether to cooperate in which someone is already according them second-personal authority in that very interaction. Consider: there is an important difference between the motivations that cooperators and defectors respectively have in discussions about whether to cooperate in a one-shot Prisoner's Dilemma. Since a self-interested defector's choice is entirely independent of whether he believes his interlocutor will cooperate or defect (since it will pay him to defect regardless), he has no stake in determining his interlocutor's intentions or motivations.[44] His only motive in talking is to try to convince his interlocutor to cooperate. A cooperator, however, is motivated both to convince her interlocutor to cooperate and to determine whether he will actually follow through if he says he will, since even a cooperator reasonably wishes to avoid being taken advantage of. In scanning her interlocutor, she must determine whether he is similarly scanning her, that is, whether their scanning is mutual. When she looks into her interlocutor's eyes, does she see him looking back into hers to see whether she is looking into his to see whether she is looking into hers, and so on? A moment's reflection suggests that reciprocal interest of this sort is something we do quite frequently detect. Think of detecting reciprocal romantic or sexual interest. If that is so, cooperators can help assure one another in this way of their willingness to cooperate. In effect, each enables prediction of her willingness to respect an agreement to cooperate by evidently respecting one another in a conversation about whether to cooperate.

A related experimental result is the finding that when subjects converse about what to do in one-shot Prisoner's Dilemmas, cooperation is roughly doubled (Orbell, Dawes, and van de Kragt 1988, 1990). This is notable in itself, of course, since non-cooperation is still evidently the dominant strategy of rational self-interest, even after such a conversation has taken

---

44. Unless, that is, he is sophisticated enough to realize that a sophisticated cooperator will be trying to determine whether he is trying to determine this.

place. After all, the other person will either act as agreed or not, and either way one will do better by defecting. So why is cooperation increased? It seems from these studies that it is not because such discussion heightens moral sensitivity generally, since it evidently does not increase cooperation with strangers. Again, something essentially second-personal seems to be going on. Conversants are likelier to cooperate with each other.

A natural explanation is that such cooperation is simply a further expression and extension of a reciprocal recognition that is already implicit, in some form, when two interlocutors have a serious conversation about what to do. We earlier noted Pettit and Smith's observation (1996) that serious conversation involves some measure of mutual respect and recognition of one another's authority. In discussing, moreover, what they are to do, either individually or together, each purports to recognize the other's authority to participate in such a practical discussion, in effect, a joint deliberation, and hence, to be a source of reasons to act (and not just of reasons to think that certain reasons for acting exist). They recognize one another as a source of claims on their respective wills and conduct and not just on their beliefs, even about what would be sensible action for either or both. They see each other as sources of second-personal reasons. Of course, this could all be simply illusion. I could be trying to get you to believe that I am a cooperator, including to believe that I am looking into your eyes to determine whether you are looking into mine to determine whether I am looking into yours, and so on. But that may not be so easy to fake.

A related possibility is that at least some such conversations give rise to a genuinely collective intention to cooperate, that is, that the conversants come to deliberate together from a "first-person plural" perspective: What shall we do? From this standpoint, cooperation clearly dominates over any other (collective) strategy. In discussing this possibility, Dawes notes that many of the conversations in his studies do indeed take the form of collective deliberations (Orbell, Dawes, and van de Kragt 1988, 1990). But this hypothesis does not conflict with the explanation that cooperation results from reciprocal recognition. According to Margaret Gilbert's "pool of wills" theory (1990, 1996a), in order for two people to decide, say, to take a walk together, each must communicate her willingness to the other (second-personally) to form a plural subject (a "pool of wills") for this purpose. But this means that they must already be reciprocally recognizing each other second-personally. In a slogan: The way to "we" runs through "you" and "I."[45]

Adam Smith on Judgments of Justice

In Chapter 3, I briefly laid out Adam Smith's anticipation of the contemporary simulationist idea that attributing mental states to others frequently involves an empathic projection into their shoes, as well as Smith's remarks about the distinctively human disposition to "truck, barter, and exchange" and its relation to mutual respect. In the final section of this chapter, I wish to discuss briefly the role of empathic projection (and what Smith called "sympathy") in his theory of moral judgment, specifically, his theory of judgments of justice, since this supports the reflections of the last two sections.

According to Smith, when we judge an agent's action or motive, we do so by projecting (impartially, as though we were anyone) into the agent's perspective and viewing the practical situation as we imagine it to confront her in deliberation. If the person's actual decision and motive match those we simulate under these ideal conditions, then we judge them to be "proper." And when we judge someone's feeling or reaction, we do so from her perspective as a patient, viewing the situation, as we imagine it to face her, as someone responding to it.

It is important that Smithian moral judgments involve an implicit identification with others as having an independent point of view. This already pushes Smith's thought away from the observer-based virtue ethics of Hutcheson and Hume.[46] Although Smith is a metaethical sentimentalist, like Hume and Hutcheson, it is an important difference between his view and theirs that Smithian judgments of propriety are made not from a third-person perspective but from idealized (impartially disciplined) versions of personal and interpersonal standpoints. What takes Smith even farther from Hutcheson and Hume, and into the second-person standpoint, is his metaethics of justice.[47]

Injustice, for Smith, is essentially tied to warranted resentment. It is not simply improper conduct but improper conduct to which the proper

45. I discuss Gilbert's ideas in this connection in the next chapter.
46. For discussion of this aspect of Hume and Hutcheson's views, see Darwall 1995a.
47. For another interpretation of Smith that emphasizes interpersonal aspects, see Tugendhat 2004.

response is a second-personal reactive feeling to challenge or hold the agent accountable in some way. So on Smith's view, injustice can be judged only by projecting ourselves impartially into the agent's and, crucially, the affected parties' points of view and then considering whether to feel resentment from that perspective. This individual-patient-regarding character of justice leads Smith to oppose utilitarian tradeoffs and to hold that resistance to injustice is warranted not by considerations of overall utility but by concern for the "very individual" who would be injured (1982a: 90, 138). Moreover, what we consider from the standpoint of affected parties is whether to respond with a distinctive feeling that itself presupposes mutual accountability between persons. Sympathy with victims' sense of injury involves, according to Smith, not simply a sharing of their sense of having been wronged. It also involves recognition of their authority to challenge the wrong by resisting it, or, failing that, to demand some form of compensation or punishment. It recognizes their second-personal authority to address demands of justice.[48] We can only judge whether something is properly resented or resisted, therefore, by imagining being in the shoes of the affected parties and considering whether any of us, if reasonable, would feel a reactive, accountability-seeking sentiment that implicitly lodges some second-personal challenge or complaint and addresses a second-personal reason to respect this challenge.

I bring Smith in at this point to buttress and give a framework for the experimental results of the preceding two sections. When subjects in the Milgram experiment experience emotional conflict between the conflicting claims of an authority figure, on the one hand, and their victims, on the other, it seems implausible that they simply experience these as incompatible external demands. To some extent or other, they likely project into their addressees' respective standpoints and feel the justice of their claims and their authority to blame and hold them accountable. There is experimental evidence, as we have seen, that sanctions increase cooperation when they are seen to be legitimate, but actually decrease it when they are believed only to be applied only strategically (Fehr and Rockenbach 2003). In the one situation, the sanctions are seen to be just,

---

48. Consider in this connection what Smith says about those who feel guilt for having unjustly injured others. Even when their victims are ignorant of the crime, the guilty may be moved to confess their guilt and submit "themselves to the resentment of their offended fellow-citizens," in the hopes of some form of reconciliation (Smith 1982a: 118–119).

as subjects might judge in Smithian fashion by simulating the resentment and indignation of their (potential) punishers. In the altered situation, the subjects' simulation must lead not to resentment but to some self-interested motive that cannot support a judgment of justice and the authority to hold accountable, that is, to a reason of the wrong kind.

What armchair moral philosophical and psychological speculation suggests, experimental psychology confirms. That we have distinctively second-personal normative psychological capacities seems, to quote Bishop Butler now in different context, to "be as strongly and plainly proved in all these ways, as it could possibly be proved, supposing there [were these psychic mechanisms] in our nature" (1983: I.6).[49]

49. Butler was describing the empirical case for disinterested benevolence.

— 8 —

Interlude: Reid versus Hume on Justice (with Contemporary Resonances)

It will help to fill in our picture of second-personal aspects of cooperation and justice, and also set the stage for the constructive arguments of Part IV, if we pause at this point to consider Thomas Reid's critique of Hume's well-known claim that justice is an "artificial" or convention-based virtue and reflect on some contemporary implications of this critique. Hume famously argues that justice is conventional in the sense that it depends upon a self-interested agreement in intention among individuals, perhaps inexplicit, to regulate their conduct by certain rules (the rules of justice) so long as others do. In fact, Hume uses 'convention' to refer, in part, to such a set of shared intentions.[1] Without a convention in this sense, he argues, nothing can be just or unjust. Neither, he claims, is there any intrinsic obligation to be just, even once rules of justice are established. The obligation to justice arises entirely from the usefulness of the convention. The "natural obligation" and "original motive to the establishment of justice" is a self-interested desire for the personal advantages that established practices of justice can bestow (Hume 1978: 498, 499). And the "moral obligation" to be just resides in a sentiment of approbation we feel by sympathy with the public interest that justice, as a rule, promotes (498–500).

It is important to Hume's analysis that the agreement that establishes rule-structured practices of property, promise, and contract is not itself any sort of promise or contract, explicit or implicit. Hume thinks that there can't really be any promises or contracts at this pre-conventional

---

1. As we will see, Hume has a minimalist view of what is necessary for the intentions to be appropriately shared, more like that of Bratman (1993) than Gilbert (1990).

stage. But neither is any such explicit joint undertaking necessary, in his view. It is enough that individuals communicate to one another both their common interest in establishing practices of justice and their respective conditional intentions to follow the rules if others do. The agreement (or "convention") that results is not so much between the individuals as it is one that arises among them. It is a "coming together" of their individual wills.

Against these claims, Reid argues, first, that sentiments and motives related to justice emerge in normal human development without any "artificial" agreement no less than do those implicated in Humean "natural virtues" like benevolence. In effect, Reid sides with present-day explanations of cooperation and justice in terms of reactive attitudes (e.g., Fehr and Gächter's)[2] as opposed to a Humean model that anticipates the "emergence of cooperation" or "reciprocal altruism" theories of Axelrod (1984) and Trivers (1971). Second, he claims that the idea of moral obligation is intrinsic to that of justice and is irreducible to justice's general usefulness (a version of Strawson's Point). And third, Reid argues that Hume's account misses key second-personal elements of justice, especially, the obligation to keep promises and contracts.[3]

Reid's critique of Hume resonates with themes we briefly noted in Margaret Gilbert's ideas about the agency of "plural subjects" (1990, 1996b), as well as with Scanlon's well-known critique of practice-based accounts of the obligation to keep promises (1990, 1998: 295–327). Exploring the connections to Gilbert's work helps clarify the relation between the second-person and first-person plural standpoints. And developing the links with Scanlon's helps prepare the way for my claim that a second-personal vindication of moral obligation, dignity, and autonomy of the sort I advance in Chapters 10 and 11 can also provide a foundation for Scanlon-style contractualism, as I argue in Chapter 12.

Central to Reid's critique of Hume is a distinction that Reid makes between "operations of the mind" that are "solitary" in the sense of being able to "exist, and be complete, without being expressed" or "known to any other person," and "social" operations, which "cannot exist without

2. Although not cast explicitly in terms of reactive attitudes, I believe that Sripada (2005) can also be seen within this tradition.

3. I was initially set thinking about these topics by Luca Parisoli's, "Hume and Reid on Promises" (2001), which I commented on at the David Hume Society Meetings, University College, Cork, Ireland, July 1999.

being expressed by words and signs, and known to the other." Without social operations, Reid says, a person might still "think, and reason, and deliberate, and will." But "it would be impossible for him to put a question, or give a command, to ask a favour, or testify a fact, to make a promise or a bargain" (Reid 1969: 438). Social mental operations are, in our terms, second-personal.[4]

Hume on Justice

The main lines of Hume's theory of justice are well-known, so we can be relatively brief.[5] Unlike "natural virtues" like benevolence and compassion, justice is socially useful (and therefore, Hume argues, morally virtuous), not instance by instance, but only in the aggregate; and not in every circumstance, but only in certain specifiable conditions—moderate scarcity and limited generosity—that, to be sure, characterize the main of human life. If goods or benevolence were in much greater supply than is usual or drastically scarce, justice would be either unnecessary or unavailing. And nothing is intrinsically admirable about the "cautious, jealous virtue" even when it is called for (Hume 1985b: 183). We approve of benevolence and compassion in themselves and regardless of their contexts, whereas with justice our approval derives from the fact that the "whole plan or scheme," the overall practice structured by the rules of justice, promotes the interests of all in normal human circumstances (1978: 497).[6]

Were we to rely only on our own resources or on the goodwill of

4. Reid's *Essays on the Active Powers of the Human Mind* was published in 1788, twelve years after Adam Smith's discussion of the human disposition to "truck, barter, and exchange" in *Wealth of Nations* (1776), and eight years before J. G. Fichte's *Foundations of Natural Right* (1796), which established recognition *(Anerkennung)* as a central philosophical category of post-Kantian German philosophy.

5. Hume lays them out in book 3, part 2 of *A Treatise of Human Nature* (Hume 1978) and section 3 of *An Enquiry Concerning the Principles of Morals* (Hume 1985). Discussions include: Baier 1991; Cohon 1997; Darwall 1995a; Gauthier 1979, 1992; and Haakonssen 1981.

6. The central idea here can be put by saying that Hume is operating with a "practice conception" rather than a "summary conception" of rules, in Rawls's sense (Rawls 1955). Justice is realized in rule-structured practices whose participants regard the rules as "sacred and inviolable" (Hume 1978: 533) rather than heuristics or "rules of thumb" for producing social good.

others, we would be left, although not perhaps in a Hobbesian state of nature, in a substantially less secure state than we can have with established practices that protect property and make promises, contracts, and the rule of law possible. Normally, human beings act to bring about some good to self or others: "The WILL exerts itself, when either the good or the absence of the evil may be attain'd by any action of the mind or body" (Hume 1978: 439, also 399). But though people act to benefit others as well as themselves, they naturally favor those who are near and dear (488). Without established rules of justice, we can have no warranted common expectations from friend, stranger, and foe alike to counter these natural human partialities.

The problem (at least, ultimately) is that rules of justice can play this role only if it is possible for individuals to undertake actions that cannot themselves be justified either by private or by public benefits, however long-term. The first phenomenon will be familiar from Prisoner's Dilemma. The "whole plan or scheme" of justice can benefit all only if the rules require individual sacrifice. Indeed, Hume writes, "it is easily conceived how a man may impoverish himself by a signal instance of integrity, and have reason to wish, that, with regard to that single act, the laws of justice were for a moment suspended in the universe" (1978: 497). But the same point applies to public benefit, as Hume appreciates. "A single act of justice is frequently contrary to public interest," as, for example, when a law, promise, or contract requires the restoration of "a great fortune to a miser, or a seditious bigot" (497).[7] Without, however, individuals regulating themselves by rules of justice even when these require sacrificing long-term self-interest and public interest, the collective benefits of the "whole plan or scheme" cannot be achieved.

But how does Hume think it is possible for human beings to establish, sustain, and actually regulate themselves by rules of justice? Since the general benefits of established practices of justice are clear, there is no problem in understanding how individuals could want to live under rules of justice and, indeed, want to do whatever is necessary to see that they

7. Actually, context suggests that Hume does not really mean here that acts required by rules of justice can be harmful on balance when we take full account of their effects on the general practice. And his view in the *Treatise* may be that this never happens. However, he clearly has this possibility in mind in the famous "sensible knave" passage from the second *Enquiry* (1985b: 282–283). For our purposes, we can ignore these complications. I discuss them in Darwall 1995a: 284–318.

are established and generally followed. The problem is how to go from the desire that rules of justice be in good working order, or even from the desire to regulate conduct by them or accept them oneself if that is necessary for public or private benefit, or from, that is, the thought that any or all of these would be desirable, to actually accepting or regulating conduct by them. It should be clear that this is simply another version of Strawson's Point and an instance of the "wrong kind of reasons" problem. Considerations of the desirable are reasons of the wrong kind to justify claims of justice or to warrant anything as a norm of justice.

Hume's solution is that the rules can be established by a *convention*, "a general sense of common interest" in everyone's regulating conduct by the rules and a consequent general "resolution" or "agreement" to do so (1978: 490). Everyone sees the benefits for himself and those he cares about of widespread obedience to justice's rules, which understanding all then "express to one another" along with the "resolution" each has "of squaring his actions by [them], on condition that others will do the same" (490, 498). This is enough, Hume says, to give whoever has the "first opportunity" an adequate motive to perform an act of justice as "an example to others" (497), who are then likelier to follow the rules and become models themselves. So far, so good. The likely desirability (good) of establishing conventions of justice is a reason of the right kind for trying to establish them. "And thus justice establishes itself by a kind of convention or agreement" (497). But the issue is how to establish a convention in such a way that participants themselves can then act for reasons of justice, that is for reasons of the kind that are distinctively relevant to enforcing claims of property, promises, and contracts—in our terms, for the relevant second-personal reasons.

A Humean convention is a "coming together" of individual wills, each resolving to follow the rules provided that others do too, in order to acquire the benefits of the cooperative endeavor of an established regime of justice.[8] Hume's famous example of how it is possible for individuals

8. For a different reading, see Postema 1995. Postema's "first-person plural" interpretation puts great weight on a distinction between the "common sense of interest" and "sense of common interest" that Hume himself does not consistently mark. Moreover, sympathy, which Postema is right to stress for its role in the first-person plural standpoint, evidently plays no role in Hume's explanation of the formation of the convention that establishes rules of justice. On the contrary, Hume quite clearly says that the original motive to establishing justice is self-interest.

to do this simply out of self-interest is that of "two men, who pull the oars of a boat by an agreement or convention, tho' they have never given promises to each other" (1978: 490). The convention, again, is simply the coincidence in their prudential conditional intentions to row so long as the other does. For this, it can be enough that they both want to get to the same place in the same boat.

We should note again explicitly, because it will be important later, that a Humean convention does not require anything like what we might more naturally call an "agreement" (either explicit or implicit) in what Margaret Gilbert calls the "everyday" sense in which, when two people agree to do something, they normally regard themselves as creating some resulting claim on one another, however weak.[9] This is the sense in play, Gilbert (1990) argues, when, without anything as formal as a promise, people decide to do something, like take a walk, together. Doing something by agreement in this more robust sense is more like Smithian exchange. It involves at least an implicit invitation and acceptance in a second-personal space in which both parties understand the normative context. Both must presuppose that neither may simply force or rescind the agreement unilaterally and that each will have some resulting reason, however defeasible, to honor it, and to object, if the other doesn't.

Of course, two people might row a boat together as the result of an agreement of this kind also, but Hume's point is that they need not.[10] Nothing second-personal is required. Without even implicit communication of the sort necessary for an "everyday" agreement, two people for whom it is common knowledge that both want to get from one shore to the other can simply approach the same rowboat, pick up a salient oar, begin to row, and not stop until they reach the opposite shore. If one or the other wants at any time to take a break, she can stop rowing, with some confidence that the other will likewise stop, and resume at whatever time it is mutually convenient, remaining confident that, since both want to get across, that will be sooner rather than later. Of course, things may not be so simple.

9. As against Gilbert, however, I argue that this reason is not simply overridable; it is defeasible—so defeasible, in fact, that it may never have any force at all if, for example, the agreement is coerced.

10. Gilbert's point, of course, is that Hume's oarsmen are not really rowing the boat together. If one stops, and the other says, "Hey, I thought we were rowing together," the first could quite reasonably reply, "What do you mean, 'we'?"

The same features are present in iterated Prisoner's Dilemma where tit-for-tat or some more complex strategy is evidently better for both players, both collectively and individually, than the non-cooperative strategy that dominates in a one-shot Prisoner's Dilemma (Axelrod 1984). In fact, rowing until the other stops and stopping until the other rows just is tit-for-tat. Hume's view is that the situation facing individuals who have not yet established practices of justice will be substantially the same from the "first opportunity" for compliance. If it is common knowledge that it is in everyone's interest that justice be established, then the situation is relevantly similar to that of two people approaching a boat that can take them both to the opposite shore. Perhaps the first complier takes more of a risk than someone does in making incipient rowing motions. Nevertheless, so long as she is in a position to survey others' future compliance and to withdraw her compliance if others do, and so long as that is sufficiently evident and of sufficient concern to others, this may be similar enough to the rowing case and iterated Prisoner's Dilemma to make it sensible for individuals to comply with rules of justice in their own interest.

But Hume acknowledges that this reasoning can work only on a relatively small scale. When society becomes sufficiently "numerous," the interests at stake are "more remote; nor do men so readily perceive, that disorder and confusion follow upon every breach of these rules" (1978: 499).[11] At this point, people can no longer rely on the general sense that individual violations put the "whole plan or scheme" at risk. With large enough numbers, therefore, self-interest is no longer an adequate motive to justice. Self-interest continues to recommend acting justly when this is necessary to sustain the practice, but when it isn't, and when the gains to self are sufficiently great, it recommends that one act unjustly.

We should note, again, that the same point holds for benevolence of any form, however partial or universal. Once numbers are sufficiently large, and the connection between individual violations and the health of the practice is sufficiently remote, then concern for the welfare of particular individuals, or groups, or even for everyone's welfare, can likewise

---

11. This passage suggests, as I mentioned in footnote 7, that in the *Treatise*, Hume believes that breaches of the rule actually are against violators' interests. The problem he is pointing to here, however, is that, even if it were more for violators' long-term interest to comply, they can't be relied upon to perceive this. Again, we need not worry about this complication.

recommend injustice. "Donating" a seditious bigot's property to Oxfam may, if kept sufficiently secret, better advance the overall welfare even when due account is taken of its effect on practices of justice. In such a case, universal benevolence recommends injustice rather than justice. And it seems clear that for benevolent motives targeted on groups of whatever size or character, similar examples could be found.

It follows that when rules of justice are meant to bind together sufficiently large groups, neither self-interest nor any sort of benevolence can provide the necessary bond. It is at this point, Hume believes, that a moral obligation to be just must come into play. However, if matters have been relatively straightforward to this point, they now begin to get very complicated, for two chief reasons. One is that Hume's is a virtue ethics; consequently what he generally calls "moral obligation" is a sentiment of approbation or disapprobation whose object is never, in the first instance, an act, but always some motive or trait of character of which an act is, at best, a "sign." "When we praise any actions, we regard only the motives that produced them, and consider the actions as signs or indications of certain principles in the mind and temper" (Hume 1978: 477).[12] The second is that what makes justice an artificial virtue in Hume's view is precisely that there is no "natural" motive (e.g., neither self-interest nor benevolence of any kind) that invariably recommends justice. So the question arises, if moral obligation consists in or rests on the moral sentiment, and if the moral sentiment takes motives or traits as its proper objects and is directed toward acts only as signs of these, then what is the motive or trait of justice? In other words, which motive is the object of the approbation in which the obligation to justice consists?

The answer cannot be self-interest precisely for the reason we have just seen; when the numbers are sufficiently large, self-interest no longer invariably recommends justice. But neither can it be any sort of benevolence for a reason of the very same kind. Of course, Hume might argue, as Hobbes has sometimes been interpreted in his response to the fool, that since the stakes of having well-functioning practices of justice are so large, and since people are notoriously so bad at knowing when their actions will actually have deleterious effects on the practice (or their own repu-

12. Any inclination to think that Hume is talking about a species of merit here that is different from that involved in justice should be dispelled by the fact that he makes this claim at the beginning of Part III ("Of Justice and Injustice") as part of an argument that justice is an artificial virtue.

tation), the correct self-interested strategy is never to violate the rules of justice (Hobbes 1994: XV.4; Kavka 1995). And a similar argument might be made from benevolence, either partial or universal. But although these strategies are logically open, they don't seem to be Hume's.

In his reply to a "sensible knave" who questions what reason there is to be just when it is not advantageous, Hume does point out that even the most careful knave risks being hoisted by his own petard.[13] (1985b: 283). But Hume also says that the knave's challenge cannot adequately be met in its own (self-interested) terms: "If a man think, that this reasoning much requires an answer, it will be a little difficult to find any, which will to him appear satisfactory and convincing. If his heart rebel not against such pernicious maxims, if he feel no reluctance to the thoughts of villainy or baseness, he has indeed lost a considerable motive to virtue." This says that self-interest is by itself an inadequate motive to justice and that it requires supplementation by moral disapproval of injustice. Hume ends his response, moreover, by saying that the knave misses the greatest satisfactions in life, which involve moral approbation: "the invaluable satisfaction of a character" and "peaceful reflection on one's own conduct" (283). This means that, if justice ends up coinciding with self-interest, it is only because moral reflection on one's own just motives and character closes the gap. But if that is so, the motive of justice of which moral sentiment approves cannot itself be self-interest, since, without the gap being closed already by moral approbation, self-interest does not invariably recommend justice.

Before we return to considering what Hume thinks is the motive of justice, we should note a fundamental difference between what Hume means by 'moral obligation' (the moral sentiment), on the one hand, and second-personal reactive attitudes as these figure in moral accountability, on the other. This can be obscured by Hume's frequent use of 'blame' as a synonym for disapprobation and his discussion of a kind of responsibility in relation to freedom of the will. I cannot discuss these topics adequately here, but, as I noted briefly in comparing Hume to Smith at

---

13. Thus, the virtuous have "the frequent satisfaction of seeing knaves, with all their pretended cunning and abilities, betrayed by their own maxims; and while they purpose to cheat with moderation and secrecy, a tempting incident occurs, nature is frail, and they give into the snare; whence they can never extricate themselves, without a total loss of reputation, and the forfeiture of all future trust and confidence with mankind" (Hume 1985b: 283).

the end of the last chapter, approbation and disapprobation for Hume are *third-personal* responses rather than second-personal reactive attitudes like resentment, as it figures in Smithian judgments of justice, or indignation or second-personal blame.[14] Hume does frequently use the word 'blame,' as I've said, but it is clear that he doesn't have anything essentially second-personal in mind, since he speaks of blame for involuntary flaws and famously criticizes the distinction "usual in all systems of ethics" between moral virtues and vices and natural abilities and disabilities.[15] And although he thinks that moral evaluation involves attributing a kind of responsibility, it is one concerned with identifying "durable and constant" traits of character as a solid basis for esteem rather than with second-personal moral accountability as we have been conceiving it (1985a: 98).[16]

So what, then, does Hume think is the motive of justice? One possibility, which I have explored elsewhere and that is suggested by various passages, is that Hume supposes that the trait of justice involves accepting rules of justice as valid norms.[17] And moral approbation of justice consists in approval of this trait.[18]

This proposal supplies a motive for moral sentiment to approve of and reasons of the right kind to be just, but there are several reasons, rooted in deep philosophical commitments of Hume's, why he cannot easily

14. For more extensive discussion see Darwall 1994, 1999b, and 2004a.

15. "I would have any one give me a reason why virtue and vice may not be involuntary, as well as beauty and deformity. These moral distinctions arise from the natural distinctions of pain and pleasure; and when we receive those feelings from the general consideration of any quality or character, we denominate it vicious or virtuous" (Hume 1978: 608–609). See also appendix 4, "Of Some Verbal Disputes," to Hume 1985b, where Hume argues that the distinction between moral vice and virtue, on the one hand, and other merely natural abilities and disabilities (such as wit and dullness), on the other, is merely verbal.

16. On this point, see Watson 1996. Watson distinguishes between something's being ethically attributable to a person (for the purposes of what he calls eudaimonistic evaluation) and the person's being morally *accountable* for it in the sense of being liable to blame or moral sanction. Watson argues that accountability requires a form of control but attributability does not.

17. Thus, Hume says that individuals "lay themselves under the restraint of such rules" (1978: 499) and that rules of justice are "immediately embraced" (1985b: 192). See Darwall 1995a: 284–318.

18. Another possibility is that the trait of justice is not so much tied to a distinctive motive or reason of justice as to the useful habit of following the rules of justice. This fits better with Hume's text in various ways, but seems not to give us a distinctive motive of which to approve. I am indebted to Remy Debes for this suggestion.

accept it. But so much the worse, I'm inclined to think, for Hume's framework. The tensions are these: First, if someone accepts rules of justice as valid norms, then she will think she has normative reasons to do something simply because it would be unjust not to (or because it would violate the norm). But this means that the idea that the moral obligation to justice consists in an approval of the trait or motive of justice gets things backwards. The trait of justice of which we approve involves already taking justice as intrinsically obligating.[19]

Second, on Hume's official view, as we have seen, voluntary action seeks to bring about some good (Hume 1978: 439, also 399). This is a source of the contemporary "Humean" theory of motivation, according to which action always results from desires (which have some apparently good [desirable] state of the world as object). As we noted in the last chapter, however, normative acceptance is irreducibly attitude-of-a-subject-regarding rather than state-of-the-world-regarding. In accepting a norm of justice requiring me to restore a seditious bigot's property, I take there to be a reason for doing so that cannot be reduced to a reason for (desiring) the existence of any state, even the state of the money's being returned. Perhaps the world would be a better place if the money went to Oxfam; that might be a more desirable state of affairs. And even if I think that a property-restoring act's being done is a better state, the reason I will credit in accepting a norm of justice requiring me to restore the property will differ from any deriving from (or consisting in) the value of that state. Imagine, again, that I can bring about more such valuable states by the shocking spectacle of violating the norm myself thereby causing, say, two other would-be violators not to go through with their previously intended violations. The (agent-relative, second-personal) reasons for acting that derive from a norm of property would not recommend that I do so. Reasons for action cannot, in general, be reduced to reasons to desire states, and, in particular, a reason of justice to return a seditious bigot's property cannot be. Or so someone who has the motive of justice must think if she is to regulate her conduct in the way she must for a whole plan or scheme to be collectively beneficial. But, again, this conflicts with Hume's general theory of motivation.

Finally, were Hume to accept the suggestion, it would open a yawning

---

19. A similar "externalization" is involved in Mill's remark, quoted above, that the feeling of conscience is a motive to act rightly. As Mill himself notes, when we accept "customary morality" as a matter of conscience, a morally required action "presents itself to the mind with the feeling of being in itself obligatory" (1998: ch. 3, §1).

gap in his account of how the rules of justice are established. In Hume's story, individuals recognize that it is in their common interest if everyone follows the rules of justice, and they communicate this sense to one another. Suppose, however, that the rules of justice will be established in a sufficiently large society only if enough people actually accept the rules as binding norms. This will then support a desire in each individual that enough people so accept the rules. But this recognition and desire cannot itself directly motivate acceptance of the rules as valid norms of justice in any individual. It provides a reason of the wrong kind. Suppose that you are convinced that beneficial rules of justice will be established only if you accept the rules as valid norms of justice. You then have a reason of the right kind to want to be someone who accepts the rules as valid norms, but not yet a reason of the right kind actually to accept the norms as norms of justice. You cannot accept the norms for this reason.

This, again, is a consequence of Strawson's Point and another instance of the "wrong kind of reason" problem. I might want to be someone who believes that things are getting better in the world, but that fact and my reasons for wanting to be optimistic can't give me a reason of the right kind for thinking that the world isn't going to hell in a handbasket.[20] Or I might want to be someone who isn't afraid of flying, but the reasons to which that desire responds do not speak to my fear. Similarly, I might think it would be better (and so want) to accept the rules of justice as norms of action. But to do that I must accept certain agent-relative, second-personal practical reasons. And I can't do that simply on the grounds that it would be better for me, or even for society, to do so.

Reid's Critique of Hume on Justice

We come now to Reid's critique of Hume's conventionalist account of justice. Reid concedes that a "conception of the virtue of justice" is impossible until people "have lived some time in society," but he denies that this shows that justice is conventional, since reason itself depends on development and maturation within a social context (1969: 405). In any case, Reid argues, the sense of justice arises simultaneously with the capacity for moral judgment in general. And this sense already involves, moreover, the apprehension of "an obligation to justice, abstracting from the consideration of its utility" (406).

---

20. Of course, it might motivate me to look for reasons of the right kind.

As evidence of these claims, Reid cites the fact that the concepts of *favor* and *injury* come with normal human (social) development, independently of Humean conventions, and that these concepts presuppose those of justice and injustice. The very idea of a favor is of an intentional benefit that goes beyond anything its beneficiary has the standing to expect or demand as her just due. And the notion of an injury is of a harm that violates a norm of justice.[21] It is one thing to see ourselves as benefited or harmed by others, even intentionally, and another to regard another's act as a favor or injury. The latter only makes sense in relation to warranted expectations that Reid collects under the concept of justice. What justice requires and allows, as he puts it, "fills up the middle ground between these two" (1969: 410).

Reid explicitly connects these notions, moreover, to (second-personal) reactive attitudes: "A favour naturally produces gratitude. An injury done to ourselves produces resentment; and even when done to another, it produces indignation" (1969: 410).[22] Before we have the concepts of favor

21. Obviously, what Reid means by 'injury' is nothing physical or medical, but something that is appropriately resented, as in "Sir, you do me an injury."

22. It is instructive to compare a passage from Hume's second *Enquiry*: "Were there a species of creatures, intermingled with men, which, though rational, were possessed of such inferior strength, both of body and mind, that they were incapable of all resistance, and could never, upon the highest provocation, make us feel the effects of their resentment; the necessary consequence, I think, is, that we should be bound, by the laws of humanity, to give gentle usage to these creatures, but should not, properly speaking, lie under any restraint of justice with regard to them, nor could they possess any right or property, exclusive of such arbitrary lords. Our intercourse with them could not be called society, which supposes a degree of equality; but absolute command on the one side, and servile obedience on the other. Whatever we covet, they must instantly resign: Our permission is the only tenure, by which they hold their possessions: Our compassion and kindness the only check, by which they curb our lawless will: And as no inconvenience ever results from the exercise of a power, so firmly established in nature, the restraints of justice and property, being totally *useless*, would never have place in so unequal a confederacy" (1985: 190). For justice to be in play, according to Hume, the parties must be sufficiently close in power to make abiding by its rules genuinely advantageous. This would not be so, he thinks, if our power were sufficiently great in relation to certain creatures that we could use them for our ends with impunity.

Hume's reference to resentment is notable, as Kate Abramson has pointed out to me. But it is important also that Hume takes its relevance not to be intrinsic (or even as evidence of injustice), but to be indirect via mutual advantage. Issues of justice arise only if creatures can make us "feel the effects of their resentment" in a way that makes it in our interest to establish conventions that establish obligations toward them.

Hume is here subject to the same kind of Strawsonian criticism that I have frequently

and injury, we can, of course, be pleased when we are benefited, especially so when it is intentional, and displeased when we are harmed. To have the concept of a favor or injury, however, we must have some notion of what we can warrantedly expect or demand from others. Favor and injury are thus second-personal concepts. They concern our standing to have expectations and make demands of one another and are connected to second-personal responses that presuppose this authority. As Strawson points out for negative reactive attitudes like resentment, "the making of the demand *is* the proneness to such attitudes," and, we might add, vice versa (1968: 92–93).[23]

Reid also anticipates Strawson's Point. To see something as an injury, Reid observes, it is necessary to "have the conception of justice, and perceive its obligation distinct from its utility" (1969: 406). Regarding something as required by justice "carries inseparably along with it, a perception of its moral obligation" (413). It is inconceivable, therefore, that the distinctive sentiments of justice could arise simply through a mutually advantageous convention.

Reid's Critique of Hume on Promises

Among the most interesting of Reid's criticisms for our purposes are those he makes of Hume on the obligation to keep promises. Hume's account of promising is notoriously byzantine,[24] and it would take us too far afield

---

mentioned and specifically lodged against Bernard Williams in Chapter 5 (footnote 4). Like Williams, Hume wants to accommodate the category of justice (or rights, for Williams), but without the second-personal moral psychology necessary for us to be able to accept "reasons of the right kind" for challenging injustice. It is one thing, again, to think that it would be desirable, whether from anyone's individual point of view or from some common standpoint, to hold someone accountable for doing something, or even to think that a habit of doing so is desirable or even worthy or esteem, but quite another to think that the action is of a kind that warrants resentment along with the authority to demand forbearance. Like Williams, Hume only admits reasons for challenging injustice that are outside any we accept within the second-person standpoint when we hold another accountable. I am indebted here to discussion with Simon Blackburn.

23. Note also the following passage from Reid: "He perceives that injury is done to himself, and that he has a right to redress. The natural principle of resentment is roused by the view of its proper object, and excites him to defend his right. Even the injurious person is conscious of his doing injury; he dreads a just retaliation; and if it be in the power of the injured person, he expects it as due and deserved" (1969: 416–417).

24. Or, as Hume might have put it, "Romish," since he says that promising is "one of

to attempt to master all its intricacies. Suffice it to say that although Hume sensibly understands promising to involve the voluntary under-taking of an obligation ("the willing of that obligation, which arises from the promise"), his moral psychology and virtue ethics require that the obligation be understood via the moral sentiment's role in an individual's psychic economy (1978: 517). Against this, Reid points out that the ideas of promise and its resulting obligation are essentially social, they are *to* others, and, therefore, involve "social operations of the human mind"; in our terms, second-personal psychic mechanisms, must be involved. Nei-ther, Reid argues, can the obligation to keep promises depend on the usefulness of a conventional social practice of promising, as Hume sup-poses is true of the moral obligation to justice generally, since children are capable of understanding, and naturally accept, the basic fairness and reciprocity involved in keeping faith long before they have any conception of its social utility (1969: 444).

Reid stresses throughout the necessity of a pre-conventional, second-personal form of reciprocal obligation that individuals must already im-plicitly recognize in order for them to come to have genuine conventional obligations at all. For this point, it doesn't much matter whether or not we reserve the words 'promise' and 'contract' for undertakings that re-quire specific conventional contexts. If we do, then the point will still remain that we could not come to have the conventionally established obligations of promise and contract unless we were capable of the pre-conventional second-personal obligations that make conventional obli-gations generally possible in the first place. Suppose we reserve 'promise' for a conventionally defined obligation that is undertaken with tokens of 'promise' and its synonyms, and we reserve 'contract,' for those that re-quire as context the law of contract. So defined, promise and contract will be essentially conventional, and whatever distinctive obligations they carry will depend in some way on their respective conventional contexts. They will depend, as Hume puts it, on a certain "form of words" and therefore on employing "symbols and signs instituted" by "the conven-tions of men" (1979: 522). However, if Reid is right, these will nonetheless

---

the most mysterious and incomprehensible operations that can possibly be imagin'd, and may even be compar'd to *transubstantiation,* or *holy orders,* where a certain form of words, along with a certain intention, changes entirely the nature of an external object, and even of a human creature" (Hume 1978: 524).

also depend on the possibility of voluntarily undertaking second-personal obligations that are not conventional. To anticipate, it must be possible for individuals to create binding conventions by a kind of agreement that is itself neither conventional (in the usual sense) nor simply a coordination of self-interested conditional intentions, as in Hume's boat-rowing example or in iterated Prisoner's Dilemma.

Reid faults Hume for failing to grasp promising's "social" or second-personal character. Commanding, testifying, requesting, bargaining, and promising are all irreducibly "social": "they cannot exist without being expressed by words or signs, and known to the other party." It is impossible, moreover, "to resolve" social operations "into any modification or composition of the solitary" (1969: 438). (This, we should note in passing, is a consequence of the circle of irreducibly second-personal concepts that we described in Chapter 1.[25]) It is consequently impossible to understand promising in terms of such "solitary" Humean mental acts as "willing an obligation" (understanding 'obligation' as Hume does) or as the expression of "a resolution of performing" the promised act (Hume 1978: 518, 517).

Additionally, even if the distinctive forms that contract and promise take in established practices depend on "human invention," these nonetheless presuppose a second-personal sociality that makes conventional practices possible in the first place. Reid makes a similar claim about language. No doubt much of language is conventional also, but without a background of natural, nonconventional dispositions to respond second-personally, conventional linguistic discourse would be impossible: "This intercourse, in its beginning at least, must be carried on by natural signs, whose meaning is understood by both parties, previous to all compact and agreement. . . . The power which man has of holding social intercourse with his kind, by asking and refusing, threatening and suppli-

25. As Searle famously argued in "How to Derive an 'Ought' from an 'Is'" (1964), giving rise to an obligation to the promisee is part of the very idea of a promise. As we noted in Chapter 3, however, we can't really get an 'ought' from an 'is', Searle to the contrary notwithstanding. Either a genuine obligation follows from a promise, in which case whether someone actually promised is itself a normative rather than a factual question, or if it is a factual question, then the only thing that follows is a *de facto* authority to demand that it be kept, not the authority *de jure* that a genuinely normative obligation involves.

cating, commanding and obeying, testifying and promising," cannot be human invention, but must rather be a distinctive "part of our constitution, like the powers of seeing and hearing" (1969: 439).

Contemporary epistemological discussion has drawn from related Reidian claims about *testimony* (Burge 1993; Coady 1992; Foley 1994; Moran 2005).[26] Reid argues that unless we are disposed to give others authority in theoretical reasoning by treating their testimony as providing reasons for belief that extend beyond any reasons others can themselves offer in support of what they say, our practices of reason-giving cannot get off the ground. This is a version of the point we noted from Pettit and Smith (1996) in Chapter 3. When we conduct serious "conversation of an intellectual kind," we must impute to one another a second-personal authority to give us reasons to believe things.[27] Burge endorses an "acceptance principle" along what he presents as similar Reidian lines: "A person is entitled to accept as true something that is presented as true and that is intelligible to him, unless there are stronger reasons not to do so" (1993: 467).

Reid notes that "as soon as they are capable of understanding declarations," children "are led by their constitution to rely on them." And "they are no less led by constitution to veracity and candour, for their own part" (1969: 444). This rings true. Were children not naturally disposed to trust what they are told and to avow candidly their own beliefs, it is difficult to see how they could possibly be inducted into practices of theoretical reason-giving or even to learn a language. Of course, even if trust and veracity are natural defaults, that does not mean that this presumption cannot be defeated by a record of unreliable testimony. Indeed, it will be crucial to my argument later that second-personal theoretical authority is ultimately defeasible in this way and so different from the kind of authority we presuppose in addressing and acknowledging second-personal practical reasons. Nonetheless, even common inquiry must presuppose some presumptive (theoretical) authority.

Reid argues that the analogous points must hold also with practical trustworthiness. Fidelity must be the natural default in the practical realm no less than in the theoretical. Children naturally trust others' assurances

26. I have been much helped by discussion with Edward S. Hinchman, and by Hinchman 2000.

27. As we saw in Chapter 3, however, these reasons are defeasible third-personally.

about their future actions no less than what they say about other matters (Reid 1969: 444). It would be impossible, moreover, for us to make agreements, promises, and contracts, unless we already took ourselves to be accountable to one another and accorded each other the second-personal authority to undertake these distinctive obligations.[28] Of course, violations of agreements or promises do not simply give the lie to declarations of future actions. They are distinct forms of injustice with their own characteristic remedies. If I agree or promise to do something, then I am obligated to make that happen in a way that I am not normally obligated to make what I assert true. I am obligated only to assert what is true, or what I believe to be true.

Again, it doesn't matter if we reserve 'promise' and 'contract' for distinctive conventionally defined methods of voluntarily undertaken second-personal obligations. Reid's point is that such conventional obligations will be possible only if we can presuppose an authority to make claims of one another and undertake voluntary obligations at all that does not itself depend upon antecedent conventions. We can hear in Reid's words echoes of Smith on exchange:

> One boy has a top, another a scourge; says the first to the other, if you will lend me your scourge as long as I can keep up my top with it, you shall next have the top as long as you can keep it up. Agreed, says the other. This is a contract perfectly understood by both parties, though they never heard of the definition given by Ulpian or by Titius. And each of them knows, that he is injured if the other breaks the bargain, and that he does wrong if he breaks it himself. (Reid 1969: 437)[29]

What Reid calls "contract" here is the sort of agreement in the "everyday" sense that Margaret Gilbert (1990) argues gives rise to plural subjects. When two individuals agree in this way, it is then possible for them to do something together, in the first-person plural.

Reid and Gilbert insist that agreements of this sort result in voluntarily assumed obligations to one another. Once the agreement has been made,

28. Compare Nietzsche's remark at the beginning of essay two of *On the Genealogy of Morals* (1994): "To breed an animal with the *right to make promises*—is not this the paradoxical task that nature has set itself in the case of man?"

29. According to the *Oxford English Dictionary*, a scourge was a whip or a lash used to spin a top. Ulpian was a third-century Roman jurist, and Titius evidently appears in an example of restoring property in Blackstone's *Commentaries*.

each is obligated to do his part, unless released by the other.[30] These obligations are thus second-personal. People who have made an agreement are obligated to one another not just in the sense that they have an obligation with respect to each other but in the further sense that they are accountable to each other. Failure to discharge the obligation gives the other grounds for second-personal reactive attitudes, such as resentment, and perhaps grounds for redress of some kind. Presently, we consider how it is possible for such second-personal obligations to arise voluntarily. Before we do so, however, we should note that if it is possible for obligations of justice to arise in this way, that would close the gap in Hume's account.

Hume says, recall, that individuals who lack conventions of justice can bring them into existence by communicating their common interest in regulating their conduct by its rules: "I observe, that it will be for my interest to leave another in the possession of his goods, *provided* he will act in the same manner with regard to me." When this is "mutually express'd" and common knowledge, "it produces a suitable resolution and behavior" (1978: 490). This may be enough to start a convention when numbers are sufficiently small, but it will be ineffective, again, when numbers grow larger. There is a point beyond which expressions of common interest will be insufficient to establish or sustain any convention to regulate by rules of justice, because, as we've seen, following the rules in individual cases will no longer invariably promote, or be seen to promote, individual and public interest.

If, however, the individuals could make an agreement in the "everyday" sense to follow the rules of property, promise, and contract, they could establish these rules by convention. To do so, each would not simply tell the other that it will serve his interests to follow the rules if others do. Rather, like the two boys in Reid's example or like Smithian barterers, one might propose that she follow the rules on the condition that others do so also, and others might accept this proposal. Assuming it possible to obligate themselves by a voluntary agreement in this way, all would then be obligated to one another to treat the rules as authoritative. The specific rules of property, promise, and contract would then be established by "a convention or agreement" that is "not in the nature of a promise"

---

30. For interesting differences between agreements in this "everyday" sense, and mutually exchanged promises, see Gilbert 1996a.

(reserving 'promise' as Hume does for distinctive forms of second-personal assurance that involve "symbols and signs instituted" by "the conventions of men").[31] But neither would it be the sort of coordinated prudential conditional intentions that Hume calls "convention." Rather, the agreement would be of the "everyday" kind that does not itself pre-suppose antecedently agreed rules.

Gilbert on Agreement and Obligation

Of course, Hume was not prepared to take the possibility of everyday agreement for granted. So why should we? How, indeed, is it possible for individuals to obligate themselves to one another by an agreement? I believe that the answer is to be found in the presuppositions of second-personal engagement in general. Whenever someone addresses a second-personal reason of any kind, including just proposing an offered agreement for another's consideration (which itself involves the implicit address of a reason to consider), he presupposes that the other has the second-personal standing of a free and rational agent. He commits himself, as I argue in Chapter 10, to the equal dignity of persons, that is, to their common authority to make claims and demands of one another as mutually accountable equals. Even if each cannot be specially obligated to the other in the ways specified by the terms of their agreement until the agreement has actually been made, it is a presupposition of their mutual address that they are already obligated to one another in general as free and equal rational persons.[32]

Recall the experiments we considered in the last chapter in which subjects play Prisoner's Dilemma after a conversation about whether or not to cooperate. In one setup, individuals showed a significantly enhanced ability to predict their interlocutors' plays (Frank 1988). In another, the

31. Of course, this might still not be effective. My point is simply that if the parties took one another to have second-personal competence and authority, it would be possible for the conventions to become thus established. Unlike Hume's story, the parties could regard one another as having (and regarding themselves as having) reasons (of the right kind) to comply.

32. This is a consequence of the instance of Strawson's Point we called "Cudworth's Point" (see Chapter 5 above). Just as God cannot obligate us by his commands without it already being the case that he has second-personal authority with respect to us, so also would it be impossible for two individuals to obligate themselves especially to one another by an agreement unless they already had the second-personal standing so to obligate one another in this way. Again: "Second-personal authority out, second-personal authority in."

amount of cooperation roughly doubled (Orbell, Dawes, and van de Kragt 1988, 1990). I speculated that we could explain these results if we notice the role of second-personal recognition in the experimental setup. The distinctive ability to determine another's sincerity in conversation about whether to cooperate involves, I claimed, sensitivity to reciprocal respect. Suppose someone tells you he will cooperate. Is he telling the truth? Is he really willing to do the collectively beneficial thing so long as you do? Or does he just want you to believe that he is? Well, if you are discussing whether to cooperate, the question really becomes, Is this a serious conversation? Is he discussing this question in earnest and giving you a second-personal authority, or is he simply going to decide what to believe and do unilaterally? If the latter, then not only will there be nothing reciprocal about his choice, but also there will be nothing genuinely reciprocal about the conversation; it will not be serious. He will have no particular need to determine what you are going to do, say, by listening carefully, because his choice will be unilateral. If he is an egoistic non-cooperator, he will not cooperate whatever you say or do. He has nothing at stake in the conversation and need give you no authority in it, either to answer the theoretical question of what (to believe) you will do, or to answer the practical question of what to do himself. No genuine co-deliberation, either theoretical or practical, will occur.[33] I speculated that part of normal human social development involves the capacity to detect the presence or absence of reciprocal attention and, hence, of serious engagement.

Similarly, experimenters note that, in the second setup, which showed substantially increased cooperation, conversations about what to do frequently proceeded in the first-person plural, with subjects deliberating about what they ("we") would do collectively. This suggests that, in some cases at least, a genuine co-deliberation was going on that ended in an agreement to cooperate "together" in Gilbert's sense. If Gilbert is right, however, these conversations must have had a serious second-personal aspect. Two individuals can agree to do something together in Gilbert's sense only through interactions that are at least implicitly second-personal.[34] For the decision to cooperate to constitute a Gilbertian agreement, there must be both invitation and uptake, if only implicitly (Gilbert

33. I take this helpful term from Scanlon 1998: 268.

34. Note, however, that it seems to be possible for individuals to share intentions, if not to agree in the everyday sense, without the full satisfaction of Gilbert's conditions. On this see, Bratman 1992 and 1993.

1990: 6–8). It would hardly be surprising that this would increase co-operation, since, as Gilbert points out, the cooperators would have appropriately felt some obligation to one another to comply with their agreement. The (second-personal) reasons to comply that any such obligation involves find no adequate representation in rational self-interest models, but according to those models, increased cooperation should not have occurred anyway. Even after serious conversation, the dominant self-interested strategy is not to cooperate.

I believe that the capacity of individuals to make agreements and form plural subjects depends upon their already presupposing one another's second-personal standing in seriously addressing each other in the first place. So any resulting obligation depends both on what they presuppose, namely, that they both have the requisite authority, and on their addressing one another on terms that presuppose this. It is the terms of this standing as mutually accountable persons in general that then gives them the authority to obligate themselves especially to one another through the terms of their agreement.[35]

The standing to make and be obligated by agreements at all is a second-personal authority that entails mutual accountability. This, again, is a consequence of Cudworth's Point (which is itself a version of Strawson's). Just as God cannot create by command the second-personal authority necessary to give his commands normative force, so also is it impossible for obligations to come from agreements all the way down. Unless you and I already have the authority to bind ourselves by an agreement, as we presuppose when we address one another, we cannot create a resulting obligation. Before you and I consummate an agreement to do something together, then, we are already obligated to one another as equal free and rational persons (as we presuppose in any serious conversation about whether to agree), although not yet specially obligated as we would be

35. Gilbert (1996b) maintains that parties to an agreement are obligated to comply even if the agreement is coerced. She grants that there may be no moral obligation to keep coerced agreements, but holds that there is an obligation that creates a normative reason for acting nonetheless. But if, as I believe, the parties to an agreement presuppose that they have an equal dignity as free and equal persons in addressing one another second-personally at all, then it is hard to see how this can be so. Any second-personal reasons for acting that agreements normally give rise to would seem to be defeated if the agreement is coerced. Of course, there might be other reasons for keeping a coerced agreement, such as self-interest. But without a second-personal reason, there can be no obligation to keep the agreement.

by a consummated agreement. The second obligation cannot be created without the existence already of the first. Again we see: "Second-personal authority out, second-personal authority in."

So far, this may seem just to get the parties into the space of the reasonable and mutual accountability. Their (presupposed) common second-personal authority is sufficient for that and necessary for them to bind themselves by an agreement. But it may seem that it is nonetheless not sufficient for a binding agreement. However, some demand of good faith has to be built into the very idea of second-personal authority, since that concerns address by its very nature.[36] The very existence of the category depends on there being a distinction between serious representations or undertakings, on the one hand, and those that are not, on the other. But for that distinction to be maintained, individuals must be accountable to one another for the seriousness of their representations and undertakings; they must have a claim against one another that they not present themselves as making serious representations and undertakings when they are not (with, of course, the usual escape clauses about play, humor, irony, and so on). So if two parties present themselves as having a serious conversation about whether to agree to something and then agree, then both have a resulting claim that the agreement be kept. Both already had a claim that any address on the matter of whether to agree be in good faith. And since it is a presupposition of a serious conversation about whether to agree that the parties will be bound if they agree, then some claim actually to keep the agreement must follow also from their common authority to demand good faith.

Scanlon on Promising

Another contemporary resonance of these and related points can be found in Scanlon's recent writings on the obligation to keep promises. As against the Humean claim that there is no obligation of promise-keeping outside of an established practice, Scanlon defends the Reidian thesis that promissory obligations do not require conventions (1990, 1998: 295–327). Scanlon's account may not, however, be sufficiently sensitive to the second-personal aspects of promising that Reid emphasizes.

---

36. Along similar lines, one might say that a warranted demand for honest dealing is built into the very idea of relating accountably to others.

Scanlon's explicit target is Rawls's view that the obligation to keep promises is an instance of the general requirement to do one's fair share in mutually advantageous practices (Rawls 1971: 344–350). He presents cases where there is no ongoing practice of promise-keeping and argues that it is possible in such cases for people to undertake to give one another assurances of future conduct that create obligations of fidelity, whether or not we choose to call such extra-conventional acts "promises." Scanlon's basic line of argument strikes me as largely successful, although less than it might be were it to be more sensitive to the second-personal character of promising, namely, that promises are forms of address that presuppose a second-personal authority of promiser and promisee.[37]

Scanlon's argument depends on the claim that it would be unreasonable to reject *Principle F:*[38]

> If (1) in the absence of objectionable constraint, and with adequate understanding (or the ability to acquire such understanding) of his or her situation, *A* intentionally leads *B* to expect that *A* will do *X* unless *B* consents to *A*'s not doing so; (2) *A* knows that *B* wants to be assured of this; (3) *A* acts with the aim of providing this assurance, and has good reason to believe that he or she has done so; (4) *B* knows that *A* has the beliefs and intentions just described; (5) *A* intends for *B* to know this, and knows that *B* does know it; and (6) *B* knows that *A* has this knowledge and intent; then, in the absence of special justification, *A* must do *X* unless *B* consents to *X*'s not being done. (245)

We may stipulate that these conditions are all satisfied in standard promises. Scanlon's claim is then that the wrongness of breaking promises is to be explained by the wrongness of violating Principle *F*. Unless, however, we interpret the idea of "providing assurance" in a second-personal way that already presupposes the authority of the assured to claim compliance, or assume, at least, that assurer and assured present themselves to one another as presupposing this in common, I doubt that this is so.

Consider, first, cases where one intentionally or negligently causes someone to expect that one will do something. Scanlon argues persuasively that in such cases the person whom one has led to have the ex-

37. In what follows, I draw on Darwall (2006).
38. I refer to Scanlon's presentation (2003). A very similar account is provided in 1998: 295–317.

pectation acquires a claim on one. If she has not yet relied on the expectation, then she has a claim to one's correcting the expectation if it is mistaken. And if she has relied on it, then she has some claim to compensation. But if she has not relied on the expectation, she has no claim that one fulfill the expectation, only that one correct any mistake in it. Promises are, of course, different. If one promises to do something and the other hasn't yet relied on an expectation that one will do it, one cannot simply disabuse her of the expectation if one wishes not to do what one promised. The other has a remaining valid claim to one's doing what one promised and not just to due notice of nonperformance or to compensation in the case of reliance.

Principle *F* attempts to capture this through a complex set of conditions connected to providing assurance. But this idea can be interpreted in two different ways. A *causal* interpretation of providing assurance would be: causing someone to be assured that something will happen, say, that one will do something. On a *second-personal* interpretation, however, providing assurance would involve an act of *assuring,* that is, a putatively claim-giving address to another of the same species as promise (maybe the very same thing as a promise).

Scanlon could avail himself of a second-personal interpretation of providing assurance without rendering Principle *F* idle. We know from the literature generated by Searle (1964) that it is one thing to show that the idea of promise cannot be understood except in terms of putative undertakings of obligation and another to establish that a genuinely binding obligation is created in fact.[39] However, if we interpret providing assurance in causal terms, Principle *F* is not compelling.

To show this, we have to imagine a fairly elaborate case in which all of the conditions in *F* are satisfied. Suppose you want me to attend your party. If I were to promise to do so, then I would give you by that distinctive form of second-personal address a claim to my doing so; you would warrantedly expect this *of* me, and not just justifiably expect that I would do so. But suppose, first, that I simply intentionally cause you to expect that I will do so, say, by telling your friends that I will. In that case, if you have not relied on that expectation, I can discharge any claim you have of me by simply telling you in a timely fashion, before you rely on the expectation, that I am actually not going to come, if that is my

39. See, for example, Hare 1967.

intention. But again, that is not so if I promise or assure you that I will come. In that case, you will have a claim that cannot be discharged by telling you of my real intentions should I decide not to come, even if you have not yet relied on the expectation that I will come. But what if Principle *F* is satisfied with the various assurance conditions being interpreted in causal terms?

Suppose it is common knowledge between you and me that you have access to my email and that you check it regularly. (Let's not worry about why *that* would be!) On Monday, I send an email to a friend saying that I firmly intend to go to the party unless you wish me not to (the consent dimension of clause (1)), but that I will not promise or assure you myself, since I desire that, *were* I, counterfactually, to change my intention, you would have no remaining claim to my coming to the party. My complex desire for this extremely unlikely counterfactual situation notwithstanding, my firm intention is still to come to the party unless you wish otherwise. This satisfies clause (1). Since I know that you want to be assured that I will come unless you wish otherwise, (2) is satisfied. I send the message in order to cause you to be assured, and since I know you will read the message and, let us assume, believe it, I have good reason to believe that you will be thus assured. You believe of course that *were* I to change my mind I would not regard you as having any claim to my coming (therefore, that I am not *assuring you,* second-personally, that I will come), but you also believe that the probability that I will change my mind is negligible, so (3) is satisfied.

Suppose, then, that on Tuesday, I send a second email to my friend saying that because you have likely read and believed my first email, as I had hoped, you are therefore likely now to be assured that I will come to the party unless you wish me not to. Since you read this second message, you come thereby to know that I wrote the first message with the aim of causing you to be thus assured and that I believe you have been, so (4) is satisfied. Since I wrote the second message with the intention that you would read and believe it, and I know that you will read it, condition (5) is satisfied.

Suppose, then, that on Wednesday, I send a third email to my friend saying that because you have likely read and believed my second email, as I had hoped, you must now know that I had written the first with the intention of causing you to be assured and that I know that you have been. You read my third email, so you now know that I had this knowledge and intent; so condition (6) is satisfied.

Suppose now that I *do* change my mind and decide not to go to your party *and* that you have in no way yet relied on the expectation that I will go. You have, of course, a claim that I notify you of this in a timely fashion before you rely on it. But do you have a claim to my actually going unless you consent to my not going? It seems that you do not. After all, although I intentionally created in you the expectation that I would go, because I had a firm intention to do so, I also intentionally created in you the expectation that in the utterly unlikely instance that I were to change my mind, I would not in fact come nor regard you as having any claim to my coming. In the relevant respects, therefore, this seems to be like a case in which I intentionally create an expectation and in which you have a claim to compensation if you rely and to timely notice of my real intentions if I come to change them, but not to my actually doing what you had been led to expect if you have not yet relied on that expectation and if I have given you timely notice of my changed intention.

Even though conditions (1) through (6) are satisfied, then, it nonetheless seems that, if I have informed you otherwise and you haven't relied, you have no remaining claim to my actually coming to your party. I conclude that there is a case where it would not be wrong to violate Principle *F* on a causal interpretation. And although I have not directly argued that Principle *F*, interpreted causally, is one someone could reasonably reject, I hope it is reasonably clear that whether that is so or not, it's not being so would not explain why it is wrong to violate promises.

Promises have an essentially second-personal character that Principle *F* cannot capture when it is interpreted in causal terms. It is part of the very idea of a promise or an assurance that the addresser gives the addressee to understand that she thereby has a claim to the addresser's following through. Moreover, when I promise or assure someone that I will do something, I must already be authorizing the other to presuppose that she and I share a second-personal authority to make claims of, and be accountable to, one another. In this last section, I have been arguing that Principle *F* is impotent to explain the wrongness of breaking promises unless we interpret it in second-personal terms.

The lesson, I believe, is that the obligations of promise-keeping have an essentially second-personal character that cannot be fully accounted for outside the second-person standpoint. There is no way to construct the distinctive claims and authority over ourselves that we can give to another by a second-personal assurance out of non-second-personal materials, for example, by reckoning benefits and harms our actions have caused and obligations that derive from these. Here again, "Second-personal authority out, second-personal authority in."[40]

The need to explain the distinctive forms of accountability involved in promising gives us a glimpse of a point discussed in Chapter 12. A contractualist theory of moral obligation, like Scanlon's, must seek to link norms that no one can reasonably reject to mutual accountability in the right way. Justification to one another as mutually accountable equals is a fundamental idea in the contractualist framework. But what commits us to this idea? Not all rational justification is to others in the way that the mutual accountability of contractualist morality requires. Rational thought is frequently and appropriately solitary rather than social, in Reid's sense. It is true that most human beings have a desire to be able to justify themselves to one another, at least in certain areas of their lives (Scanlon 1982). And it is true also that mutual accountability is an ineliminable aspect of relations, like friendship, that most of us value highly (1998: 148–168). But as important as these facts are, they give us reasons of the wrong kind for thinking that we actually are accountable to one another in the way contractualism supposes. They ground no authority to make claims and demands of one another. This, again, is Strawson's Point. In Chapter 12, I argue that contractualism cannot have the foundations it requires, therefore, unless it is grounded in the second-person standpoint. Second-personal practical reasoning involves justification to by its very nature.

In Part IV, we turn to the constructive arguments with which such a foundation must be built. What I hope to have established by this point,

---

40. Judith Thomson argues that the capacity of promises to obligate requires no special explanation: "There is nothing deeper that needs to be or can be said about how word-givings generally and promisings in particular generate claims. Their moral force lies in their generating claims; and the fact that they do generate claims is explained by the fact that issuing an invitation is offering to bind oneself, so that when the invitation is accepted, the offer is accepted, and one therefore *is* bound" (1990: 303). But this explanation seems already to assume the (second-personal) authority to bind and be bound by accepted invitations; without that, even if we assume that an offer to bind oneself to another is an invitation and that if other accepts this invitation, she will have accepted one's being bound to her, it is unclear why one couldn't simply cancel that by taking it back (as one could not if there were a genuine obligation, as there would be if one and she had the relevant second-personal authorities to be bound and to bind in the first place). I am indebted to Gary Watson for this passage from Thomson. (See Watson unpublished.)

and in these last two chapters in particular, is that the second-personal concepts these arguments will employ have a firm footing in human psychology as well as in powerful moral ideas and arguments. In what remains, I attempt to show that second-personal authority is not just an essential element of deeply held moral ideas and feelings. It is also something we presuppose whenever we take up a second-person perspective to address claims or demands of any kind at all. And, the second-person standpoint is a central element of practical reason *überhaupt*.

— PART IV —

— 9 —

Morality and Autonomy in Kant

We have been concerned since Chapter 3 with the second-person stand-point's involvement in our moral conceptions and psychology. In this and the following two chapters, we turn to questions of more fundamental justification. What can vindicate these aspects of our moral thought? How can we account for the normativity that a law proclaiming equal dignity purports to have?

We owe the most compelling and systematic account of morality as respect for the equal dignity of persons to Kant. In this chapter, we consider Kant's own defense of the moral law's supreme authority, both his constructive argument in the *Groundwork* and the "fact of reason" in the *Critique of Practical Reason*. Each gives a central role to the distinctive freedom that Kant calls "autonomy"—"the property of the will by which it is a law to itself independently of any property of the objects of volition" (1996b: 440)—and to a claimed equivalence between morality and this freedom that Allison calls the "Reciprocity Thesis." As Allison formulates this Kantian doctrine, "freedom of the will is not only a necessary but also a sufficient condition of the moral law"(1986: 395). The moral law, and hence the dignity of persons, entails autonomy and vice versa. In the *Groundwork,* Kant puts this equivalence claim to constructive use, arguing that autonomy is a necessary presupposition of the deliberative stand-point and that we can infer the supremacy of the moral law from this independent premise. In the *Critique of Practical Reason,* Kant abandons this strategy and argues that the awareness of autonomy comes itself only through the recognition that we are bound by the moral law (the fact of reason).

In my view, both approaches fail to satisfy completely. The most we can get from the fact of reason is not an account of, nor any warrant for, the purported authority of moral obligation, but only the reassurance that we do not need such an account since we are convinced of morality's authority already. That may be, but stilling skeptical worries is not the only purpose that such an account might serve. We might also reasonably wish for a better understanding of what Korsgaard (1996e) calls the "source" of the moral law's normativity. The constructive arguments of the *Groundwork* aim to provide such an understanding, but I shall argue that Kant's official argument in *Groundwork* 3, as well as arguments that philosophers have recently constructed from materials in *Groundwork* 1 and 2, all ultimately break down. (e.g., those of Korsgaard 1996b, 1996e, 1996f; Wood 1999). I believe they all fail for a common reason, namely, because they aim to derive the moral law from presuppositions of a (first-person) deliberative standpoint alone.

As I see it, any such argument is bound to fail, since nothing in the bare project of acting for reasons, first-personally, commits a deliberating agent to autonomy as Kant defines it. I sketch this diagnosis in a preliminary way presently. First, however, we should note that even if Kant's argument were successful in these terms, it would still not fully capture, and therefore would not adequately vindicate, the distinctive normativity of moral obligations. The reason, as I have stressed in earlier chapters, is that moral obligation's purported normativity includes an irreducibly second-personal element. Moral obligations do not simply purport to provide supremely authoritative reasons. They are also what we are responsible for doing, what members of the moral community have the authority to demand that we do. And even if an argument of some other kind could show that moral obligations invariably provide overriding reasons, there is no way to establish accountability except within a second-personal framework. That is the lesson of Strawson's Point, or, as I have consistently put it: "Second-personal authority out, second-personal authority in." It follows, I believe, that the normativity of moral obligation cannot possibly be vindicated outside a second-person point of view.

Moreover, I believe that it is also impossible, outside the second-person standpoint, to establish that moral obligations are binding in the more familiar sense of providing supremely authoritative reasons.[1] Kant's

1. Alternatively, if it is held to be a conceptual thesis that moral obligations provide overriding reasons, I believe it is likewise impossible to establish that we actually have any moral obligations.

strategy in *Groundwork* 3 is to argue that autonomy is an inescapable presupposition of deliberation and then to derive the validity of the moral law from that assumption. I agree with Kant that autonomy of the will is a deep feature of practical reason. But I disagree with his claim in *Groundwork* 3 that autonomy (as Kant understands it) must be presupposed in any intelligible (first-personal) deliberation. As I see it, autonomy and the dignity of persons, in the form of second-personal competence and second-personal authority, are presuppositions we are committed to from a second-person point of view.

The basic problem for Kant's argument in *Groundwork* 3 stems from the fact that as Kant defines autonomy of the will, it has no structural analogue in theoretical reason. This means that if Kant is to argue that autonomy is an inescapable presupposition of the practical standpoint, he must show how deliberation about what to do unavoidably presupposes a kind of freedom that other types of reasoning do not presuppose.[2] But the only kinds of freedom that he plausibly identifies as inescapable presuppositions of practical reasoning in *Groundwork* 3 are ones that are common also to theoretical reasoning. As Kant there puts it, reason cannot "receive direction" from outside in making "judgments" in any area in which it is employed (1996b: 448).

If there were a theoretical analogue of autonomy of the will, there would have to be formal norms (like the Categorical Imperative) that ground reasons for belief that are no less substantive than moral reasons concerning the dignity of persons. Some norms of theoretical reasoning do apparently derive from the "form" of belief. For example, because belief necessarily aims at the true, beliefs are subject to formal norms of consistency and coherence. But these just rule out combinations of belief as incoherent or inconsistent; they do not rule in any beliefs in particular, even *pro tanto*.[3] As Kant understands autonomy of the will, however, it has normative implications that go significantly beyond norms of practical coherence and consistency, like principles of instrumental reasoning and the formal theory of rational choice. If that were all it involved, autonomy could not entail the moral law.

Similarly, logical beliefs are also arguably grounded in the form of

2. And that is not, moreover, simply the capacity to "set ends." Even if this also has no obvious analogue in, say, reasoning about what to believe, it is clearly not what Kant means by autonomy of the will.

3. For discussion of this point, see Chapter 7.

belief. But these are significantly less substantive than the moral law also. To be sure, it is central to Kant's critical theoretical philosophy that a critique of pure reason can yield synthetic *a priori* truths such as the principle of universal causation. But if we look for practical analogues of theoretical principles like the causal principle, or inference to the best explanation, even these fall short of the CI except, perhaps in its truistic form: "Act only on universal laws (or on maxims that could be universal laws)." This is significantly weaker even than "Act only on maxims you could *will* to be universal law," not to mention the Formula of Humanity. What's more, a convincing argument for autonomy should not rest on controverted questions of Kant's transcendental idealism.

If Kant is to argue successfully that the practical standpoint unavoidably presupposes autonomy, then, he must show that it presupposes a kind of freedom that is unlike any we inescapably presuppose in theoretical reasoning. I argue that he fails and, moreover, that any such attempt must fail since, so far as the presuppositions of intelligible (first-personal) deliberation go, reasons for acting might all derive from the features of the objects of the will rather than from its form. To make this possibility vivid, I consider what practical reasoning would be like from a *naïve (first-person) practical standpoint*.

Suppose someone desires some state, *p*.[4] In (intrinsically) desiring *p*, she sees *p* as (intrinsically) desirable; she takes features of *p* as warranting a desire that *p* and, *pro tanto*, as warranting actions that might bring *p* about (Bond 1983; Dancy 2000; Darwall 1983; Hampton 1998; Pettit and Smith 1990; Quinn 1991; Scanlon 1998: 41–55). From the practical point of view, desires are "backgrounded," as beliefs are from the theoretical (Pettit and Smith 1990). Suppose that *p* is relief of your pain. To someone who desires this, it will seem as if there are aspects of your being in pain and being relieved from it, respectively, that are reasons to desire your relief. And these reasons will also seem reasons to do *A*, if *A* will bring that about. In a case of this kind, reasons for doing *A* seem to come not from the form of the will but from "propert[ies] of the object of volition," since they apparently come from the object of desire (although not, again, as desired; like belief, desire is in the background).

A *naïve practical reasoner* deliberates about what to do from the per-

---

4. As I noted in Chapter 7, it is consistent with *A*'s being instrumental in the relevant sense that *p* is the state of *A*'s being done.

spective of (critically revised) beliefs and desires. For such an agent, desires (and related mental states like pleasure and enjoyment) seem responsive to the value or desirability of outcomes or possible states of affairs. The agent reasons from premises drawn from the content of her beliefs and desires, not from anything about their form. Moreover, for such an agent, practical reasoning is structurally analogous to theoretical reasoning. When we reason from our beliefs, what we take as premises are putative facts about the world as they seem to us from the perspective of our beliefs. And when we reason from our desires (understood as involving evaluations of possible states of the world), our premises are putative facts about how it would be desirable for the world to be, as this seems from the perspective of our desires.[5]

I do not, of course, accept this naïve picture of the will. But the question remains: What rules it out? I argue that nothing in the conditions of intelligible first-personal deliberation does. In my view, it takes second-personal address to dispel the naïveté. This is an aspect of Fichte's Point. It is what we come simultaneously to presuppose and discover about the nature of our agency from a second-person standpoint that excludes the heteronomy of naïve practical reasoning. The full implications of Fichte's Point are, first, that the second-person perspective invariably presupposes autonomy and the dignity of persons understood, respectively, as second-personal competence and second-personal authority (Chapter 10), and, second, that this standpoint reveals a fundamental difference in the kinds of freedom that theoretical and practical reason respectively involve (Chapter 11).

If the arguments of Chapters 10 and 11 can be made out, then, we will

---

5. It takes some care to show that presuppositions of the practical standpoint do not rule this picture out. The biggest challenge is to show that nothing in the way reason-grounding norms of conduct must figure in practical conduct does so. It is an important insight of Kant's that agents act for normative reasons, as they see them, and that this involves the implicit acceptance of universal norms of conduct as applying necessarily to any rational agent. In Chapter 7, I argued that norm acceptance is state-of-a-subject-regarding rather than state-of-the-world-regarding. Moreover, it is an important, further consequence of the "wrong kind of reason" problem that norms of conduct differ conceptually from norms for desire. But although that is true, nothing in the terms of intelligible deliberation rules out the possibility that all reasons for action might nonetheless derive from reasons for desire, so that all reasons for action are instrumental. A second issue, again, concerns the necessity of rational norms and its relation to desire. I argue that a Moorean (consequentialist intuitionist) version can address this worry.

have a vindication of the normativity that the moral law purports to have. The burden of this chapter, however, is to show why arguments that remain within a first-person standpoint alone, like Kant's, are bound to fail.[6] Only by being enriched second-personally can a more "sophisticated" first-personal deliberation arise within which the key Kantian concepts of autonomy and dignity can play the deliberative roles Kant gives them.[7]

The Need for a Vindication of Morality/Autonomy

At a remarkable juncture in the *Groundwork,* at the end of section 2, Kant notes that it is consistent with his arguments to that point that morality might be nothing but a "figment of the mind" (2002: 445).[8] He believes that he has already shown in sections 1 and 2 that morality is "grounded on . . . autonomy of the will" (1996b: 445). Morality's fundamental principle is, he has argued, the CI, and that holds only if the will can be subject to a law solely by virtue of its form and independently of any properties of its objects (its content or "matter"). Conversely, he has argued that autonomy implies the CI. By the end of section 2, then, the Reciprocity Thesis has been established.

But so far Kant's arguments have been entirely analytic. He has ana-

6. I mean, of course, a "non-second-personal first-person standpoint." As I've noted before, second-person standpoints are always versions of first-person standpoints.

7. Although it plays no obvious foundational role, we should note that there are many places in Kant's writings where the second-personal character of the moral law is implicit. I noted already in Chapter 6 passages in which Kant mentions second-personal aspects of dignity, respect, and self-conceit (Kant 1996d: 434–435, 462). In addition, Kant has remarkable discussions of conscience as replicating a judicial scene, with prosecutor and so forth (e.g., 1996a: 98–100; 1996d: 400–401, 437–440). More foundationally, Kant holds that "I can recognize that I am under obligation to others only insofar as I at the same time put myself under obligation" (1996d: 417–418). (I am indebted to Robert Johnson for reminding me of this passage.) And from the *Critique of Pure Reason:* "[E]veryone also regards the moral law as commands, which however they could not be if they did not connect appropriate consequences with their rule *a priori,* and thus carry with them promises and threat." (1998: A811–812, B839–840). (I am grateful to Jacob Ross for pointing me to this passage.) For example, as David Velleman has pointed out, Kant says in the Preface to the *Groundwork* that "the command 'thou shalt not lie' " holds for all rational beings (Kant 1996b: 389; Velleman 2005: 116–121).

8. This is Allen Wood's translation of this passage, which seems superior to Mary Gregor's.

lyzed the "generally accepted" concept of morality and found it to involve autonomy of the will (1996b: 445). And conversely, he has argued that the very idea of a will bound only by its form entails the CI (402, 420–421). All this shows, however, is that if there is such a thing as morality, then the will must have autonomy, and if there is such a thing as autonomy of the will, then the moral law (the CI) must be the will's law. It is thus consistent with the arguments in sections 1 and 2 of the *Groundwork* that the moral law, the dignity of persons, the CI, and autonomy of the will are all "chimerical idea[s]" (445). Neither autonomy nor morality follows from the Reciprocity Thesis. All that follows is that they stand or fall together.

Autonomy of the will and the CI both require "a possible synthetic use of practical reason," so neither can be established analytically. Both require a "critique" of practical reason of the sort that Kant embarks on in *Groundwork*'s section 3 (1996b: 445). Before we examine this, however, we should get some of the chief elements of Kant's action theory before us.

Kant's Action Theory

"Desire," according to Kant, "is the faculty to be, by means of one's representations, the cause of the objects of these representations" (1996a: 9n; 1996e: 211). Desire and belief both involve representations of possible states of the world. Belief, we might say, is the "faculty" to be, by means of the world, the cause of one's representations' fitting the world. And desire is the faculty to be, by means of one's representations, the cause of the world's fitting one's representations.[9]

Not all behavior that results from beliefs and desires involves rational agency or the will. Indeed, by Kant's lights, not even all behavior that results from beliefs and desires in a "rationalizing," teleological way necessarily involves rational will.[10] Kant defines the will as "the capacity to act in accordance with the representation of laws" or "principles." Willed action is invariably undertaken, therefore, on some (putatively) rational principle or norm; it must involve normative acceptance (1996b: 412).[11]

9. On "direction of fit," see Anscombe 1957; Platts 1979; Smith 1994.

10. See Donald Davidson's classic paper (1980).

11. This doctrine should be interpreted in a way that allows for the possibility of weakness of will. One way of doing so is to take Kant to hold that nothing counts as a genuine

By the same token, however, an act's resulting from a desire does not preclude it from being an instance of genuine agency nor, indeed, from involving pure practical reason (and, as Kant believes, autonomy). If the principle on which an agent acts is itself "precede[d]" by a desire that furnishes "the condition of its becoming a principle," then the principle is "empirical."[12] It is unable to "furnish a practical law," and the will is heteronomous (1996a: 21, 33). Autonomy of the will, pure reason's being "of itself practical," is realized only if "reason can determine the faculty of desire as such" (1996e: 213).

Thus, Kant grants that all actions result from desire. What he denies is that all desires are "object-dependent;" some are "principle-dependent" (Rawls 2000: 150–151). Some desires arise not as apparent responses to represented possible states of the world or outcomes but because the agent accepts some norm or principle of action independently of the properties of any desired or desirable state.[13] Autonomy is realized only when an activating desire is thoroughly principle- rather than object-dependent, that is, when the desire depends on a principle and that principle is not itself "empirical" (based on a prior desire) or derived from the value (e.g., the desirability) of an independent outcome or state.[14] Autonomy thus depends on the possibility of an agent's accepting and acting on a normative principle that grounds substantive reasons for action independently of her regard for any object or state that might be an

---

action unless the agent does it for some reason, hence that she must see her action as recommended *pro tanto* by some rational norm. It is consistent with this that the agent nonetheless simultaneously believes (accepts) that her act is contrary to what she has most reason to do, all things considered, hence contrary to what valid rational norms would most recommend. On "normative acceptance," see Chapter 7.

12. Kant here seems to ignore the possibility that normative reasons might not be conditional on desire, but still dependent on features of the object of desire, as these might be given in a Moorean intuition that some possible state of the world is intrinsically good, that is worthy of desire.

13. For the interaction between this distinction and Nagel's distinction between motivated and unmotivated desires, see Chapter 7, note 2. Note also that autonomy requires not only that the will is governed by its own principles (laws), which apply to it independently of a desire for any state (i.e., are not "empirical" in the sense laid out in the last paragraph), but also that it is governed by norms that apply to it independently of the (apparent) value (e.g., desirability) of any outcome or state. On this point, see below.

14. This condition is necessary, but not sufficient, for autonomy. There is one further condition, which is described in the paragraph after the next.

outcome of her action. Most obviously, the agent's acceptance of the principle must be independent of any desire for some state or outcome, even one as cognitively rich as sympathetic concern. Less obviously, but no less importantly, autonomy requires that the agent's acceptance of the principle be independent also of any putative evaluation of some outcome or state (like a Moorean intuition that a possible state is intrinsically good or "ought to exist for its own sake" [Moore 1993: 34]).

We can put this point by saying that the agent's valuing an outcome and even the outcome's having value, say, its being desirable, are reasons of the wrong kind to ground accepting a principle if that acceptance is to manifest autonomy. Or, equivalently, instrumental reasons are reasons of the wrong kind. "*Good* or *evil*," Kant says, "always signifies a reference to the *will*" (1996a: 60). Autonomy requires reason-grounding norms of action "all the way down," that is, principles that are binding on the agent at the most fundamental level simply as a rational agent (among others), independently of the value of any possible state of the world. Only so can the will be "a law to itself independently of any property of the objects of volition" (1996b: 440).[15]

There is one other essential aspect of Kantian autonomy, which will occupy us more later, that can be appreciated by contrasting Kant's idea with rational intuitionism of the deontological sort held by Richard Price (1974) and W. D. Ross (1930).[16] Deontological intuitionists differ from consequentialist intuitionists like Moore in holding that there are fundamental norms of action that do not derive from the value of outcomes. Consider, for example, a Rossian who holds that there is a *pro tanto* moral duty to keep promises that is self-evident *a priori*. Can the acceptance of this principle after a deontological intuitionist fashion manifest Kantian autonomy? I think the answer has to be "no." To be sure, such an acceptance is not based on features of any object of the agent's desire or on the independent desirability of any possible state of the world. So any desire an agent acts on because she accepts this principle as self-evident *a priori* will be principle-dependent rather than object-dependent. But

15. It is important to see that autonomy, as Kant defines it, has both a normative and a metaphysical component. The normative component is the claim that there are valid (reason-grounding) norms that apply to the rational will as such, independently of any property of the objects of volition. And the nonnormative, metaphysical component is that the will can act on this law.

16. Rawls 1980 and Korsgaard 1996e are helpful here.

her acceptance of the principle will nonetheless be based on "propert[ies] of the objec[t] of [her] volition," independently of anything about the form of the will (Kant 1996b: 440). She accepts the principle because (as she believes) promise-keeping is (self-evidently) intrinsically right (pro tanto). She doesn't accept the principle of keeping promises because it follows from some formal principle of the will like the CI. Her acceptance derives rather from intrinsic features of promise-keeping and the property of rightness that she takes to supervene upon these.

Having noted this deontological intuitionist form of heteronomy, I want to set it aside. We return to it later when we consider Kant's account of the "fact of reason." If Kant is to vindicate autonomy as non-illusory within a critique of practical reason, he must argue that the practical standpoint rules out broadly intuitionist views of both consequentialist and deontological varieties. To show that Kant's own attempted vindication fails, therefore, it will be enough to show that it does not rule out the consequentialist variety, and this is what I focus on.

A few final clarificatory remarks. First, I should stress again that I am not defending the consequentialist picture. I am arguing that the materials that Kant brings to bear in *Groundwork* 3 do not rule it out and that it takes the second-person standpoint to do so. So, second, although I agree that autonomy is a deep feature of practical reason, I deny that it can be established in the way Kant tries in *Groundwork* 3. And third, I agree with Kant that autonomy is a presupposition of moral obligation and the dignity of persons. But again, I do so because I think these ideas have an irreducibly second-personal element that presupposes autonomy.

Vindicating Morality/Autonomy in *Groundwork* 3

Kant begins section 3 with interrelated definitions of will and freedom: "*Will* is a kind of causality of living beings insofar as they are rational," and freedom is "that property of such causality that it can be efficient independently of alien causes *determining* it" (1996b: 446). Kant points out that this defines freedom only negatively, so it must be inadequate. A random "choice"-generating device might operate independently of external causes, but it would not be a free will. The will is, or includes, practical reason, so it must involve guidance by "practical laws" ("laws of freedom"), that is, by valid norms of practical reason (448).[17] There-

17. Of course, Kant cannot simply assume that norms of practical reason involve autonomy (and so are "laws of freedom" in that sense), without begging the question.

fore, although freedom is "not a property of the will in accordance with natural laws," it "is not for that reason lawless but must instead be a causality in accordance with immutable laws of a special kind" (446). An adequate definition of the will must therefore include both a negative and a positive concept of freedom. A will determines itself independently of alien causes (negative freedom) and in accordance with rational norms (positive freedom).

Kant realizes that it doesn't follow from these reflections that we actually are free, in either a negative or a positive sense. What we have so far is actually just another reciprocity thesis, this time between the will, on the one hand, and negative and positive freedom, on the other. If the will exists, then so do negative and positive freedom, and vice versa. It is consistent with that being the case, however, that the will and negative and positive freedom are all "chimerical ideas."

What gets us inside this circle of concepts, according to *Groundwork* 3, is the idea of an inescapable presupposition of the deliberative standpoint:

> I say now: every being that cannot act otherwise than *under the idea of freedom* is just because of that really free in a practical respect, that is, all laws that are inseparably bound up with freedom hold for him just as if his will had been validly pronounced free also in itself and in theoretical philosophy. (1996b: 448)

Kant's strategy is as follows. We assume the Reciprocity Thesis as already established, hence that autonomy entails the bindingness of the moral law. And then we attempt to show that any deliberating agent must presuppose autonomy. It will then follow from the Reciprocity Thesis that any deliberating agent must also presuppose that she is bound by the moral law. And, if that is so, then, for practical purposes, she *is* bound by the moral law. The possibility that she might not be bound by it, or that she is bound by some conflicting alternative practical law (say, one that counsels her to produce more valuable states of affairs even when this conflicts with the moral law) is something she must reject as a condition of the intelligibility of her own deliberation.

This would be an excellent strategy, if it could be pulled off. It is, indeed, difficult to see how a norm that a deliberating agent is bound to accept as a condition of the intelligibility of her own deliberation could fail to apply to her validly. And it may seem an initially promising strategy also. It seems quite plausible that presuppositions of negative and positive freedom in at least some of the senses that Kant mentions are indeed necessary for deliberation to be intelligible.

Take negative freedom, for example. To be negatively free, I must be able to deliberate about what to do and to act on my deliberations "independently of alien causes determining" me. Whether I am negatively free in this sense, I cannot, of course, say. But if we interpret "alien causes" as causes that might interfere with my reasoning, it certainly seems that I must deliberate under the assumption that I am. Serious practical deliberation just is the attempt to work out what there are reasons to do for the purpose of acting on them. To count as deliberating at all, I must proceed under the assumption that my thinking rationally, or acting on practical reasons, is not precluded by "alien causes" in this sense.[18]

The situation is identical with positive freedom, understood as the internal capacity to deliberate in accordance with and to act on rational norms. Here again, for me sensibly to deliberate about what to do, I must presuppose that I can do so in accord with rational norms and act on the upshot of my deliberation. To understand myself as deliberating at all, I must proceed on the assumption that I can think about what to do rationally.

Now so far, it is important to see that the relevant presuppositions of negative and positive freedom are in no way unique to or distinctive of practical reasoning. Whether one is deliberating about what to believe, what to feel, or what to do, one must assume that one can think free of alien causes and in accordance with rational norms. And Kant says as much: "One cannot possibly think of a reason that would consciously receive direction from any other quarter with respect to its judgments, since the subject would then attribute the determination of his judgment not to his reason but to an impulse" (1996b: 448). This is true of reason in all its employments. Whenever we make normative judgments concerning what there is reason to believe, feel, or do, we must presuppose negative and positive freedom in the sense that our judgments are free of alien causes and in accordance with rational norms.

So far, so good. However, Kant also claims that the positive freedom

18. The emphasis here must be on "alien" causes. I can't see that the argument, at this point anyway, requires the presupposition that one's rational thinking is not itself a causal process. I set aside the question of whether Kant believed that a deliberating agent must assume incompatibilist freedom as irrelevant to our concerns.

he has identified is the same thing as autonomy of the will. "What, then, can freedom of the will be other than autonomy, that is, the will's property of being a law to itself?" (1996b: 447). But why should we suppose that? The only sense in which Kant has vindicated a presupposition of positive freedom is one that is common to both practical and to theoretical reason. And, as we have seen, autonomy of the will has no structural analogue in theoretical reasoning. So the kinds of freedom that theoretical and practical reasoning presuppose in common cannot entail autonomy.

Perhaps, however, there is something about the practical standpoint in particular that requires a deliberating agent to presuppose autonomy. Consider, then, how deliberation might proceed from a naïve (first-person) practical perspective. The primitive deliberative phenomenon is taking some fact about the world as a reason to do something. Wondering how to spend a free evening, I scan the newspaper to find an attractive possibility, say, going to watch a film. What I take as reasons for desiring to go, and for actually going, are aspects of the possible state of seeing the film on whose basis I might want to see it, or, if I cannot articulate these, the fact that, as it might seem to me, seeing the film would be good or desirable, a possible state or outcome that there is some reason to bring about.[19] Evidently enough, then, if I decide to go for that or these reasons, my reasons for going will derive from properties of the object of my desire (and so my volition); it will depend on good-making features of the possible state of the world that would be the outcome of my action as these seem from my perspective. Equally evident, I have not had to suppose that these reasons come from the form of the will.

But do we yet have genuine agency and a will? For Kant, rational action involves not just beliefs and desires, but also some norm or principle the agent accepts and implicitly make her own in acting on it (1996b: 412; 1999: 23–24). For intelligent pursuit of an outcome I desire to involve my will, I must deliberate on the basis of some rational norm, one I take to apply validly to any possible rational agent. And I must presuppose that I am bound by such norms as a condition of the intelligibility of my own deliberation. But does this require me to presuppose autonomy? For

19. Of course, these might include facts about myself, my expected mood, how I would expect to enjoy the film, and so on, that I take as reasons for going, and for wanting to go. But these are still facts about the objects of my desire most properly understood, not the fact of my desire itself.

this assumption to amount to autonomy, I would have to be required by the logic of my deliberative situation to presuppose that (at least some) reason-generating norms are valid independently of any properties of the objects that I am counseled by them to bring about. What in the deliberative context forces me to assume this?

Consider what norm I might accept in deciding to go to the film because I expect the state of seeing it to be good (for whatever good-making reasons my consideration of the state presents me with). The state of my seeing the film will seem to me to be an intrinsically good thing,[20] a state that, in Moore's words, ought to exist for its own sake.[21] So a natural answer to the question what norm I might accept is Moore's answer. I might accept the act-consequentialist norm of always doing whatever promotes good or desirable states or outcomes, and think, in accepting that, that any rational agent should do likewise.

Now I am not saying, I should make clear, that anything in the deliberative context would force the acceptance of this norm. I am just saying that nothing seems to preclude it and that accepting it would seem quite natural from a naïve practical standpoint. Just as belief aims at accurate representation of the world as it actually is, so from the naïve practical standpoint of an agent with desires might action seem to be for bringing about intrinsically desirable states or outcomes, as these seem from the perspective of her desires.[22]

20. Compare Kant's remark in *Reflexionen* 6660: "The expression 'it is good' expresses a relation to desire as the expression 'it is true' a relation to belief" (Kant 1900–   ). I am indebted here to Timothy Rosenkoetter, "A Semantic Approach to Kant's Practical Philosophy," presented at the APA Central Division 2003 meetings in Cleveland, Ohio. The translation of the above passage is Rosenkoetter's.

21. On reflection, the idea that a state simply ought to be cannot be made fully coherent. I develop this point at greater length in Darwall 2003b. I argue that Moore's conception should be rejected, mainly because it is inconsistent with the autonomy of the will we can appreciate from the second-person standpoint. For a sympathetic discussion of the idea that deliberation from the practical standpoint is best interpreted in Moorean terms, see Regan 2003a.

22. Compare also Kant: "Theoretical knowledge may be defined as knowledge of what *is*, practical knowledge as the representation of what *ought to be*" (Kant 1998: A633). This is Moore's approach in *Principia Ethica,* although he doesn't identify judgments of what states have intrinsic value ("ought to exist for what for its own sake") with desires for those states. Moore does, however, draw the consequence that action on such a view is essentially instrumental and that normative reasons for action derive entirely from the intrinsic value of states.

This was Moore's view in *Principia*. Indeed, he there held that there is only one fundamental ethical concept, the notion of intrinsic value or of something's being such as "ought to exist for its own sake." And he concluded that the concept of an action's being right (or what one ought) to do is conceptually reducible to that of intrinsic value and empirical causal concepts: "To assert that a certain line of conduct is, at a given time, absolutely right or obligatory is obviously to assert that more good or less evil will exist in the world, if it be adopted than if anything else be done instead" (Moore 1993: §17, 77).

Now Moore's (conceptual) definitional claim is surely a mistake, as his famous open question argument can be employed to show. Anyone who, knowing that one course of action will produce the best states, asks whether there might nonetheless be better reason to do something else (say, not to repay a loan to a seditious bigot), clearly asks an open question.[23] And someone who asserts that there is an overriding reason to repay the loan, even at the cost of producing less desirable states, clearly does not contradict himself. So the concept of there being reason to do something is distinct from the concept of the action's being one that will bring about the most desirable feasible states. Even so, someone might quite coherently and, from a naïve deliberative standpoint, quite naturally, think that although these are distinct concepts, considerations of the desirability of outcomes provide the only reasons for action. She might accept the Moorean doctrine not as a definition of right or ought to do but as a fundamental normative principle.[24]

Practical reasoning on the consequentialist principle is in an important sense formally analogous to theoretical reasoning about what to believe. It can be factored into two parts, along the lines of Moore's definition. One part is theoretical reasoning pure and simple, working out everything one can do and the long-term consequences, that is, determining for every feasible act, how the world would be if it were done.[25] The other is ethical, evaluating all possible states of affairs to determine which "ought to exist" and to what degree. But although the thought that a possible state is good or ought to exist differs, of course, from the thought

23. So long, that is, as we evaluate states independently of their relation to valid norms of action.

24. As, indeed, Moore later did (1966).

25. Obviously, I am abstracting from epistemological issues. I assume this model can be modified to take account of probabilistic information, uncertainty, and so on.

that a state actually exists in fact, it has the same structure. Both are state-of-the-world-regarding. We can think of thoughts of the former kind as given in desire and thoughts of the latter kind as given in belief. Naïve deliberation under the influence of desire and belief, regimented with the Moorean principle, then becomes the determination of which available action would bring about the most valuable states, with this being determined under the influence of the agent's (critically informed) beliefs and desires.

But do we have an agent even yet? Obviously, a creature who deliberates about what to do simply from the perspective of her current desires and beliefs, and who is incapable of stepping back and critically revising these, is not an agent in any sense we should be interested in here. A deliberating agent must, as Korsgaard says, both be, and be able see herself as, "something over and above" her desires who "chooses which desire to act on" (1996e: 100). But it is quite possible for a naïve agent to do that without assuming Kantian autonomy of the will. Although she will, of course, have to assume autonomy in the familiar sense of being able to act on critically revised desires and so to make her actions "her own" (e.g., Dworkin 1988). As we have been thinking of it, the naïve agent's desires are identified with her current evaluations of the value of the possible states of the world that are their objects. She can certainly step back from these and reevaluate, getting a better conception of the features of these states on which she takes their value to supervene and, hence, of their value.

Just as a theoretical reasoner can bring experience and reflection to bear on the dispositions to belief involved in her current experiences, for example, overriding or defeating any tendency to believe that an apparently bent stick in water before her really is bent, so also can a naïve practical reasoner analogously critically revise her desires. A naïve deliberating jogger encountering a charging dog, for example, might draw on past experience and reflection to override a strong tendency of fight or flight and form a desire to continue at his leisurely pace while keeping his hands relaxed with palms down and feigning indifference.

Plainly, this picture of deliberation is still much too naïve. For one thing, although an implicitly realist epistemology can seem quite plausible for theoretical reasoning, it can be difficult to see how to understand the intrinsic desirability of states metaphysically and how to guarantee the right kind of epistemic relation between desires (or intuitive evaluations of desirability) and the intrinsic value of states so understood. For another, this picture assumes that rational deliberation is in its nature instrumental, and we have no good reason to believe that. But my point in providing this consequentialist sketch is not to defend it, but to suggest that it bears at least some resemblance to the way things seem from a naïve deliberative standpoint and to ask what in the presuppositions of any intelligible practical reasoning rules this picture out. So far as I can see, nothing does. Deliberation on this basis is surely intelligible, even if it is mistaken.

Thus, although intelligible deliberation must presuppose positive freedom of some form, it need not presuppose autonomy of the will. If it is sufficiently naïve, it can coherently proceed by assuming a kind of positive freedom that is formally analogous, in the sense I've illustrated, to what we must presuppose in theoretical reasoning. A naïve practical reasoner may intelligibly assume that her reasoning is guided by norms that derive ultimately from the nature and value of its objects (the world as it ought to be), just as a theoretical reasoner must assume that his reasoning is guided by norms that depend on its relation to its objects (the world as it actually is). It follows that Kant's argument for autonomy in *Groundwork* 3 fails.

Other Arguments in the *Groundwork*

Perhaps, however, other arguments in the *Groundwork* can vindicate autonomy and the moral law. One that has been much discussed recently is Kant's "derivation" of the second formulation of the CI, the Formula of Humanity (FH): "So act that you use humanity, whether in your own person or in the person of any other, always at the same time as an end, never merely as a means" (1996b: 430; see especially Korsgaard 1996f and Wood 1999: 124–132). Although Kant himself explicitly notes that the argument for FH in section 2 depends on assumptions that he will only later attempt to prove in section 3 (in the argument just canvassed) (1996b: 429n), it is sometimes put forward as a freestanding argument.

Christine Korsgaard and Allen Wood present Kant's argument for FH as a "regress of conditions."[26] The argument takes two somewhat different

---

26. Korsgaard gives a streamlined version of her interpretation of Kant's argument for FH in Korsgaard 1996e: 122.

forms. One proceeds from a premise about the kind of valuation of ends in general that any practical reasoning necessarily involves (the "value of ends" argument). And a second proceeds from the kind of value that any deliberating agent must attribute specifically to her own rational agency (the "value of agency" argument).

The "value of ends" argument begins with the premise that when an agent acts for a reason, she must act for some end that she regards as objectively valuable (Korsgaard 1996e: 122; Wood 1999: 129). It then claims that an end can have objective value only if something is the source of its value (or, as it is also sometimes put, if the "conditions" of its having objective value are realized).[27] In one way this claim is uncontroversial. If there are conditions on some end's being valuable, and if whether there is reason to do something depends on the value of that end, then in acting for that reason, the agent must presuppose that the relevant conditions hold.

The argument then shifts to what an agent must presuppose to be the condition or source of the value of her ends and what follows from this. Korsgaard puts Kant's argument as follows.

> He asked what it is that makes these objects good, and, rejecting one form of realism, he decided that the goodness was not in the objects themselves. . . . Kant saw that we take things to be important because they are important to us—and he concluded that we must therefore take ourselves to be important. (1996e: 122)

Wood puts a similar formulation by saying that "we can regard this goodness [i.e., the objective goodness that we must see our ends as having] as originating only in the fact that we have set [the] en[d] according to reason . . . Rational choice of ends is the act through which *objective* goodness enters the world." Wood concludes on Kant's behalf that "the source of all such value is nothing but the value of rational willing itself, which can confer objective value on other things only if it is presupposed that it has objective value" (1999: 129–130).

Now in one sense it is uncontroversial that an end an agent sets for herself has objective value only if choosing the end accords with reason. Consequentialist realists like Moore can agree, since they will take it that

---

27. Korsgaard favors the latter formulation in 1996f (originally published in 1983) and the former in more recent formulations, for example, 1996e.

a valuing fails to accord with reason when it fails to accord with facts about the value of possible states of the world that provide reasons for choice.[28] What they are bound to reject is that laws of practical reason are formal (have their source in the form of the will) and hence that the desirability of outcomes and the choiceworthiness of actions depends on whether they can be desired or willed in accordance with such formal laws. What they assert is heteronomy: the laws of practical reason are given by the independent value of outcomes or possible states of the world, to which desires and evaluations of states apparently respond.

It is clear, however, from Korsgaard's opposing the premise to a form of realism that Kant meant to reject ("substantive realism" of the sort Moore is generally thought to represent), that the premise of her argument already rules out heteronomy, and so simply assumes autonomy of the will.[29] But if, as Kant believes, nothing can warrant that assumption other than a critique of practical reason of the sort he undertakes in *Groundwork* 3, then, so far as the materials of the *Groundwork* go, the resulting argument for FH must ultimately depend on the argument for autonomy in *Groundwork* 3, which we have already found wanting.

Again, I should stress that I can agree with the premise of the Korsgaard/Wood argument for FH. My point is that we don't have an argument for it in the materials provided either by *Groundwork* 3 or by contemporary attempts to buttress these. I believe that it takes materials provided by the second-person standpoint to establish all three of the following: the dignity of persons, the CI, and autonomy.[30]

It follows that without an argument for autonomy already on hand, the "value of ends" argument cannot establish FH. What, then, about the "value of agency" argument? This version finds better support within Kant's own text.

28. See also Parfit 1997.

29. "Substantive realism" is Korsgaard's term in Korsgaard 1996e.

30. Actually, even if we were to assume the first premise in the sense that entails autonomy, that is. that a condition or source of value is being willed rationally (in accord with formal laws), it is very unclear how anything like FH would follow as a conclusion. The basic problem, as various commentators have pointed out, is that it is not obvious why a condition or source of value must itself have value in order for anything else to derive value from it. Samuel Kerstein (2001) points out that there would be no less reason to say that rational agency is the source of disvalue (if, that is, something's being objectively bad is thought to depend on its being rationally rejected as an end), but no one would think to conclude that rational agency is therefore disvaluable.

The human being necessarily represents his own existence [as a rational agent] in this way [as an end in itself]; so far it is thus a *subjective* principle of human actions. But every other rational being also represents his existence in this way consequent on just the same rational ground that also holds for me; thus it is at the same time an *objective* principle from which, as a supreme practical ground, it must be possible to derive all laws of the will. (Kant 1996b: 429)

This passage directly precedes Kant's statement of FH, so it can reasonably be interpreted as intended to support it.

Now there are uncontroversial senses in which a deliberating agent must treat her own rational agency as an end in itself. For purposes of her deliberation, she has no rational alternative but to value thinking and acting rationally, at least implicitly. If this has no value, then she should be doing something else rather than deliberating. And she must also assume the value of reasoning well. Deliberation is something one can do at all only by trying to do it properly. In these senses, a presupposition of the value of rational practical thinking is simply built into deliberation. Moreover, serious deliberation, by its very nature, attempts not just to answer, as it were, the advisor's question: "What is the best advice to give myself about what to do?" It attempts also to direct the will rationally. In all these senses, a presupposition of the value of rational agency is simply part of serious deliberation.

But that seems to be as far as the presuppositions that are necessary for first-personal reasoning go.[31] I could quite intelligibly deliberate under the assumption that, although my rational thought has great value now, it might not some time from now (a reason for me to deliberate now rather than then).[32] It is not obvious, of course, how I could possibly

31. For an excellent discussion of this argument to which I am indebted, see Regan 2003b. David Sussman (2003) argues that Regan's arguments don't work as criticisms of Kant, although they might as criticisms of Wood's and Korsgaard's interpretation of the regress argument. Sussman argues, plausibly, that Regan, Wood, and Korsgaard all conflate objective value with practical necessity, and that Kant's arguments depend on the way in which, when a rational agent commits herself to an end, she is then under a practical necessity to take the necessary means. As he points out, this follows a line that Korsgaard herself pursues in Korsgaard 1997. I criticize this line in Darwall 2001. One problem is that, so far as instrumental reason is concerned, the agent is under a rational necessity only to take the necessary means or to give up the end. So instrumental reason is insufficient, by itself, to provide a source of reasons for acting.

32. The relevant value might be at least partly instrumental.

justify such an assumption. But there is nothing incoherent in it, and the assumption would be perfectly compatible with intelligible deliberation. And I could certainly think that the value of my thinking and acting rationally in the future is overridden by other values if, for example, I were given a Hobson's choice in which I could continue as a well-functioning rational agent only at the cost, say, of my children's lives.

Moreover, in none of these senses, it is important to see, does valuing my own rational agency (now) commit me to valuing others'. For example, when I deliberate, I authorize my own rational thought and agency, in the sense of presupposing that I am (now anyway) competent to judge reasons and to act on them.[33] But nothing in that authorization commits me either to thinking it present in others, or even to thinking that it will continue through time in me. I am, of course, bound to recognize that others are committed to their own rational authority insofar as they deliberate, but that doesn't mean that I must authorize them, or even that they are committed to authorizing themselves in the future. I might think that I or they, or that both of us, are simply not to be trusted as practical reasoners in the future. Neither is it the case that to deliberate intelligibly now, I must think that I have reason to promote or respect their, or even my own future, rational agency. Again, I am not saying for a moment that there is any justification for thinking any of these things. I am just saying that they seem not to be ruled out by any norms that are constitutive of the very activity of rational deliberation. Someone would certainly still count as deliberating if she accepted them, though she wouldn't, for example, if she didn't seek normative reasons for acting or assume that she can think rationally for purposes of her own current deliberation.

These possibilities can all be made vivid by considering the Moorean picture that I have been suggesting is the natural way of seeing things from a naïve first-person deliberative standpoint. From this perspective, rational authority is fundamentally epistemic; anyone's title, one's own or anyone else's, ultimately depends on how reliably his or her thinking reflects an independent order of facts about the world and the intrinsic value of possible outcomes. So viewed, rational authority can be defeated or earned just as epistemic authority is in theoretical reasoning. Clearly

33. Wood makes an argument that is relevant here. See Wood 1999: 130. The kind of authority under discussion here differs from other forms of valuing in play in the preceding paragraphs.

enough, taking one's own powers of inquiry to warrant trust in the present moment does not commit one now to trusting one's past or future judgment or to trusting now the judgment of any other would-be inquirer. Engaging another in a serious conversation about what to believe does implicitly grant epistemic authority to the other, as we saw in Chapter 3. But first-personal theoretical reasoning need not grant such authority, and neither must first-personal practical reasoning if it takes a naïvely consequentialist, Moorean form.

It is significant, therefore, that when Kant says that every "rational being also represents his existence on just the same rational ground that holds for me," he remarks in a footnote that he "here put[s] forward this proposition as a postulate" and that "the grounds for it will be found in the last Section" (1996b: 429n). This shows a recognition on Kant's part that in order for a rational agent's claim of the value of his own rational nature to entail the Formula of Humanity, it must itself be grounded in autonomy of the will. But if that is so, any such claim that does not already presuppose autonomy will be insufficiently strong to entail the moral law, and, as we have already seen, Kant doesn't think that anything he has said in sections 1 and 2 proves autonomy. He believes that the arguments he provides before section 3 are consistent with the moral law and autonomy of the will both being chimerical ideas.[34] Consequently,

___

34. In Korsgaard 1996e, Korsgaard puts forward a different argument for the Formula of Humanity that is rooted in the self-reflective character of the deliberative standpoint. Korsgaard notes that agency requires some degree of self-reflection, that the agent must see himself as "something over and above all [his] desires" who "*chooses* which desire to act on" (100). This commits the agent to a "practical identity," a normative conception of himself, which he draws on in deliberation. She argues that there is one practical identity I cannot question as a deliberating rational agent, namely, my identity as a deliberating rational agent. I am committed from within the deliberative standpoint to my "identity simply as *a human being,* a reflective animal who needs reasons to act and to live" (121). This means, she argues, that I must treat my own humanity or rational agency as somehow a source of normative reasons for me. To vindicate the bindingness of the moral law, however, we need to be able to conclude that I am committed to treating rational agency in others as normative for me also. Korsgaard's argument from here is complex, drawing primarily on Wittgensteinian themes about the impossibility of a private language (131–136). The basic idea is that the claim that rational nature is a source of *agent-relative* reasons—that is, that the agent's rational nature gives reasons distinctively to him—treats these reasons as the kind of essentially private phenomenon that Ludwig Wittgenstein showed to be incoherent. The moral of the private language argument for practical philosophy, Korsgaard argues, is that all reasons must be "public and shareable" (136). Con-

the *Groundwork*'s case for the vindication of dignity and the moral law ultimately hangs on the argument of *Groundwork* 3, and, as we have seen, that argument does not work.

The Fact of Reason

By the time he wrote the *Critique of Practical Reason*, Kant had apparently given up on the strategy of *Groundwork* 3. In the second *Critique*, he holds that there is no access to the concept of freedom except through that of the moral law:

> [W]hereas freedom is indeed the *ratio essendi* of the moral law, the moral law is the *ratio cognoscendi* of freedom. For, had not the moral law *already* been distinctly thought in our reason, we should never consider ourselves justified in *assuming* such a thing as freedom (even though it is not self-contradictory). But were there no freedom, the moral law would *not be encountered* at all in ourselves. (Kant 1996a: 4n)

Were the deliberative standpoint not to involve an "encounter" with the moral law, it would require no presupposition of autonomy. When, however, we become conscious of being morally bound, we acknowledge "a

---

sequently, whatever reasons an agent's normative identity as rational gives him must be public and shareable too. Therefore, the rational nature of others is no less normative for him than is his own.

The problem with this strategy is that any lesson that can be drawn from Wittgenstein's private language argument is quite general and applies in theoretical reasoning no less than in practical reasoning. Moreover, theoretical inquiry is no less self-reflexive than is practical deliberation. A rational believer, like a rational agent, must be able to see herself as "something over and above" her inclinations (in this case, to beliefs as these are given in experience). And, as we have seen, she must also see her reasoning as free of determination by alien causes and guided by rational norms. Finally, in inquiry we are guided by a rational conception of ourselves as theoretical reasoners no less than we are by a practical identity in deliberation. We must give ourselves a kind of authority in our own reasoning about what to believe no less than we must in deliberation. It follows that these considerations, taken by themselves, are insufficient to establish autonomy or anything that is equivalent to it, since they are consistent with the sort of heteronomy that characterizes theoretical reasoning. For example, they are consistent with the Moorean realism of the naïve deliberative standpoint. Of course, Korsgaard would reject realism of this form, as would I. But the point is that nothing in the argument from practical identity or the impossibility of a private language itself rules Moorean realism out. So the argument cannot establish autonomy or the moral law.

determining ground" that cannot "be outweighed by any sensible conditions" and that is "quite independent of them." And this "leads directly to the concept of freedom" (29–30).

Kant makes his point with a pair of vivid examples. The first involves someone who claims to be subject to an irresistible lust. Kant's comments here are in a compatibilist vein: such a person could surely control his lust if he were threatened with hanging on a gallows "erected in front of the house where he finds this opportunity" (1996a: 30). That he can control his lust in this sense, however, is consistent with his behavior's being determined entirely by his currently strongest inclination or object-dependent desire. It just shows that in altered circumstances, some other object-dependent desire would have been stronger. And maybe he has some such desire, perhaps the desire for self-preservation, that would override, not just his lust, but also any other desire, including any principle-dependent desire that is necessary to motivate genuinely moral action.

Kant's second example is addressed to this very possibility. Here we are to imagine someone whose prince demands "on pain of the same immediate execution, that he give false testimony against an honorable man whom the prince would like to destroy under a plausible pretext." Whether this person would refuse to do such a thing, Kant writes, "he would perhaps not venture to assert." But whether he would or he wouldn't, he "must admit without hesitation that it would be possible for him."

> He judges, therefore, that he can do something because he is aware that he ought to do it and cognizes freedom within him, which, without the moral law, would have remained unknown to him. (1996a: 30)

Once he acknowledges that he should refuse to comply with his prince's demand even on pain of execution, he cannot coherently think it impossible for him to refuse owing to an irresistible desire for self-preservation. The point seems to follow from the nature of a deliberative (normative) practical judgment. Were he to suppose his desire for self-preservation to be literally irresistible, he would be forced, in reasoning practically in light of that, to conclude that he should do something else— after all, he can't give up his life. But Kant evidently thinks that nobody really believes there is anything else he should do in this case other than refuse to betray an honorable man. When we're being honest with ourselves, we acknowledge that we shouldn't give in to a corrupt tyrant to destroy an honest person, perhaps even at the pain of our own death. And if we acknowledge that, then we are also forced to assume that that is something we can refuse to do.[35]

Kant is here simply drawing out the logical consequences of what he takes to be already involved in accepting the bindingness of the moral law. The consciousness of the moral law is, he says, a "fact of reason"

> because one cannot reason it out from antecedent data of reason, for example, from consciousness of freedom (since this is not antecedently given to us) and because it instead forces itself upon us of itself as a synthetic *a priori* proposition. (1996a: 31)

Kant clearly believes that his readers will agree with his moral phenomenology if they will just be honest with themselves, and we can read the example as being offered in that spirit. We put ourselves into the shoes of the person in the example, simulate practical thought from that perspective, and agree that in those circumstances the thing to do is to refuse the corrupt tyrant's offer and not have an honest person's death on our hands. Do we think we would do that? Surely we hope so, but alas, we also know the results of the Milgram experiment. But we must accept that we could.

Obviously these reflections are impotent to establish that the moral law

---

35. Recall, at this point, Foot's point (1972) that suitably qualified ought claims, like those of etiquette, are not necessarily practically normative; they do not entail supremely authoritative, or even necessarily any genuinely normative, reasons for acting. There is no incoherence in thinking that one is utterly incapable of doing what etiquette requires or recommends. Even apart from psychic obstacles, there may be physical bars that make it impossible to set a proper table. One may simply lack enough forks. Similarly, there may be ways of attempting, at least, to cancel the normative force that moral oughts and obligations typically purport to have and qualify them in the way that those of etiquette already seem to be. Inverted commas or a suitable inflection may enable one to express the thought that although refusing the prince's demand is what one should do, "you know, morally speaking," one is unable to comply. But Kant's point is that it is simply deliberatively incoherent to think that the prince's offer is irresistible in the sense of being literally impossible to refuse *if* one also thinks one should refuse it as a deliberative thought, that is, as a conclusion of a chain of practical reasoning. After all, if it is impossible, then it is nothing you can coherently consider doing and so you must conclude that what you should do is something else. For a very helpful discussion of 'ought' implies 'can' in this vein, see Vranas unpublished. Vranas argues that it 'ought implies can' is conceptually necessary, where 'can' has the sense of 'has the ability and the opportunity'.

is binding, however, since they already presuppose that we accept that (although they might inspire a cynic who has sought to evade what he himself most deeply believes). But Kant is no longer attempting to give a positive argument that morality is not illusory. He is employing a strategy that Rawls calls "philosophy as defense," showing how we need not give up our acceptance of the moral law once we already have it. In a way, this strategy is like Strawson's in "Freedom and Resentment." Is the possibility that the will is not free (or autonomous) a threat to morality? Well, it might be if we had to establish autonomy as a premise before we could defensibly think we are morally bound. But we don't have to worry about that. We begin already accepting certain moral claims and ideas including, Kant thinks, the bindingness of the moral law. And once we have that, we must accept autonomy on pain of deliberative incoherence. Of course, if someone could establish that we lack the very condition that our being morally obligated presupposes, then we'd have a problem.

However, even if we don't need a philosophical argument to convince us that the moral law is supremely authoritative, we still have a philosophical interest in understanding why it is.[36] I believe, as I begin to show in the next chapter, that the answer is to be found in the second-person standpoint. To conclude this chapter, however, let me note a way in which the second-person perspective is actually required to underwrite the use to which Kant puts the "fact of reason" in the second *Critique*.

Just after the passage we have been discussing, Kant presents what he calls the Fundamental Law of Pure Practical Reason (FPP): "So act that the maxim of your will could always hold at the same time as a principle in a giving of universal law" (1996a: 30). This is, in essentials, the same as the more formal versions of the CI from the *Groundwork*: FUL (Formula of Universal Law: "Act only in accordance with that maxim through which you can at the same time will that it become a universal law") and FLN (Formula of the Law of Nature: "Act as if the maxim of your action were to become by your will a universal law of nature") (1996b: 421). But why, we should ask, does Kant think that the fact of reason supports a formal principle like FPP? The reasoning in the Remark that follows

36. Or, if one supposes it to be a conceptual truth that the moral law is supremely authoritative, we have an interest in understanding what makes something we take to be a moral law one in fact. The conceptual truth would only be that if anything is a moral law, then it is supremely authoritative.

FPP appeals essentially to autonomy of the will: "The will is thought as independent of empirical conditions and hence, as a pure will, as determined by the mere form of law." Then Kant says, again, "Consciousness of this fundamental law may be called a fact of reason . . . because it forces itself upon us of itself as a synthetic *a priori* proposition" (1996a: 31).

But what exactly is the connection between the claim that since one should do what the moral law requires and refuse the prince's demand, one can so refuse, on the one hand, and either autonomy of the will as Kant understands it or FPP, on the other? The connection between autonomy and FPP seems clear enough. But what does the "fact of reason" example have to do with either autonomy or FPP? A Rossian deontological intuitionist could easily grant what Kant says about the example and generalize from it that whatever a person morally ought to do must be something she can do. But why should he conclude FPP from that? Couldn't he deny that any principle like FPP underlies the list of duties he accepts or that such a formal principle is required to explain why it would be wrong to give in to the prince? Couldn't he even deny the FPP?

If he agrees with Kant about the example and about 'ought' implies 'can', why should he be led from that to autonomy of the will? Deontological intuitionists deny autonomy, as we noted earlier, since they hold that actions (objects of volition) can be intrinsically right or wrong and that the law derives from that. Nothing in what Kant says about the example should lead them to abandon this position. And if Kant adds that we are directly conscious of the CI as a synthetic *a priori* principle, then it seems he is simply fighting deontological intuitionists on their own turf and just disagreeing about whether moral duties can be summed into a single principle. In any case, there seems no obvious route from the "fact of reason" to autonomy of the will or FPP.[37]

The Fact of Reason: A Second-Personal Interpretation

Now I believe that there actually is an argument for FPP and the CI that can be made from intuitive examples like the one Kant presents. However, such an argument would rely on the second-personal aspect of moral obligation: its conceptual tie to accountability. Recall, first, that the

---

37. Of course, if the "fact of reason" itself includes awareness of the CI, then there is no step to take.

sense of 'can' that is in play in Kant's own discussion is simply that of an open deliberative alternative, that is, something such that one's abilities and opportunities with respect to it do not preclude intelligible consideration of whether to do it. That is why 'ought' implies 'can' in that sense is so obviously true. 'Ought' has the sense of a deliberation-concluding normative judgment: This, of the things I can do, is what I ought to do. But now note that the fact that someone can do something in this sense is entirely consistent with her not knowing that she ought to do it, with her not being able to know it, and with her lacking any formal process of practical reasoning (involving a principle like FPP) through which could she could determine that this is what she should do and determine herself to act accordingly. A Rossian intuitionist, for example, can hold that someone (call her "Citizen") ought to refuse the prince's demand even if she doesn't know she should do so, couldn't know she should, and had no process of reasoning, like FPP or the CI through which she could discover this or determine herself to do so. Even so, the Rossian can agree with Kant that, since Citizen ought to refuse the prince's demand, she can do so. But, again, that doesn't entail anything about the CI or autonomy.

It is common ground that Citizen is morally obligated to refuse the prince's demand, that it would be wrong for her not to do so, and that that is therefore what she should do and, consequently, what she can do. As I argued in Chapter 5, however, if this is what Citizen is morally obligated to do, then it is also what she is accountable or responsible for doing; it is what the moral community (and she as a member) has the authority to demand that she do. Now if we, as members of the moral community, accept second-personal norms that support these demands, and, on this basis, address this proposition to Citizen,[38] we are not simply informing her of how things are "in the moral community," as an anthropologist might inform someone of mores he does not himself accept. We implicitly address the demands to Citizen and put them forward as authoritative, as, indeed, does Citizen herself when she acknowledges the moral obligation.

We relate to Citizen through "moral address" (Watson 1987: 263, 264). In so doing, moreover, we are subject to Watsonian "constraints of moral address," that is, conditions that must be satisfied for the addressing of

---

38. Or, indeed, if Citizen addresses it to herself.

demands, holding responsible, blaming, and so forth, to be intelligible in their own terms. (As I have alternatively been putting it, these are normative felicity conditions of the second-personal reason we attempt to address existing and, hence, of the success of our address.) Thus, although there is no conceptual pressure to hold that the mere existence of good and sufficient reasons for someone to do something entails that he knows or even can know this (would that it were so!), it does seem to be a conceptual requirement of blaming and holding Citizen responsible for not refusing the prince's demand (if she fails to) that we presuppose that she must have been in a position to know that she should have refused and that she could have determined herself to refuse by the relevant reasons.

When we hold people responsible, we imply that they had it within them to act as they should, not just in the sense that the alternatives were open to them or that they weren't physically prevented, but that there was a process of reasoning they could have engaged in by which they could have held themselves responsible and determined themselves to act as they should have. We imply that they could have decided to do it by, in Bernard Williams's words, a "sound deliberative route" (1981a). (Recall that Williams himself [1995] argues that blame presupposes this (Williams thinks illicitly).) But what reasoning process can we assume that those subject to moral obligations must have available to them? Kant's idea is that it would have to be a procedure that is itself tied to what it is that makes us subject to moral obligation in the first place, our being rational wills, and therefore that it must be tied somehow to the "form" of the will. The CI and the FPP are Kant's proposals for the requisite reasoning process, in effect, *the form that moral reasoning would have to take if it is to lead us to conclusions that we can intelligibly be held responsible for reaching.* And autonomy of the will follows as a corollary. But my point is that it takes a focus on the second-personal aspect of moral obligation to appreciate the connection between thinking that Citizen is morally obligated (responsible for refusing) and thinking that there must be a process of reasoning (the CI or FPP) through which she could have determined her obligation and determined herself to refuse. A second-personal interpretation of this Kantian claim is that (something like) CI reasoning is part of second-personal competence.

We get to substantially the same conclusion if we think through the role of second-personal competence in holding one another accountable.

When we hold each other responsible for complying with moral obligations as fellow members of the moral community, we imply that we each
can also hold ourselves responsible. But this requires us to regiment moral
demands by what anyone could accept as a sensible demand of everyone
as equal members of a community of mutually accountable equals, and
thereby demand of herself. In Chapter 12, I argue that the CI, especially
in the Realm of Ends formulation (FRE), is an interpretation of this
intuitive idea, that is, CI is a formulation of the reasoning process that
constitutes the second-personal competence we presuppose when we hold
one another responsible for complying with moral demands.

    What is fundamental in this way of thinking is the second-personal
authority that I have been claiming is an essential aspect of the dignity
of persons: the (equal) authority that persons have, as such, to make
claims on and demands of one another at all. Autonomy of the will and
the necessity of a formal deliberative process derive from this more fundamental idea—as necessary conditions for the possibility of second-
personal authority and as necessary to mediate second-personal relations—rather than vice versa. There can be second-personal authority
only if there is second-personal competence. And persons can be assumed
to have second-personal competence only if we can assume autonomy
and some form of moral reasoning like the CI. People can sensibly be
held accountable for complying with norms only if they can themselves
accept and determine themselves by them (Pufendorf's Point). But that
can be guaranteed to be so only if what makes the demand-warranting
norms valid is their issuing from a process that people can, at least in
principle, go through in their own reasoning and thereby make the relevant demands of themselves.

    If, however, the dignity of persons, conceived as equal second-personal
authority, is the fundamental moral notion, what commits us to that idea?
Why should we accept that it is not a chimerical idea itself? We now have
almost all the materials we need to answer that question.

— 10 —

Dignity and the Second Person: Variations on Fichtean Themes

> A human being regarded as a *person,* that is as the subject of a morally practical reason, . . . possesses a *dignity* . . . by which he exacts *respect* for himself from all other rational beings in the world. . . . Humanity in his person is the object of the respect which he can demand from every other human being.
>
> —IMMANUEL KANT, *METAPHYSICAL FIRST PRINCIPLES OF THE DOCTRINE OF VIRTUE*

In this chapter, I argue that the key to validating our dignity as persons is to appreciate what might be meant by saying, as Kant does in the passage above, that dignity is something by which we "exact" or "claim" respect "from every other human being." Respect that acknowledges the validity of a claim is, as we saw in Chapter 6, second-personal, as are also the claim and the authority to make it. And the dignity of persons, I there argued, is the second-personal standing of an equal. It is the status of an equal member of the moral community (the "realm of ends") to hold one another accountable for compliance with the mandatory norms that mediate relations between free and rational persons. When, consequently, someone respects another's dignity as a person, she gives him the second-personal standing of an equal in her relations with him.

As we noted in Chapter 1, dignity partly involves there being constraints on the permissible treatment of persons, ways one must act toward persons and ways one must not (Kamm 1989, 1992; Nagel 1995). But that is only part of it, since there can be requirements on us that no one has any standing to require of us.[1] The latter is what being in a position to claim or "exact" respect brings in—the authority to demand compliance with dignity's requirements through mutual accountability.

---

1. Logical requirements, for example. See the discussion of this point in Chapter 1.

Thought of in this way, dignity includes equal status in the moral community, understood as a cooperative of mutually accountable free and rational agents.[2] The dignity of persons, we might then say, is the complex whole that comprises all three of the following: the substantive mandatory norms regarding conduct toward persons, the standing to demand compliance with these as one among mutually accountable equals, and valid demands that are grounded in this authority.[3] (Again, I argue in Chapter 12 that the content of specific moral requirements can be explicated within a contractualist framework that is itself grounded in the second-person standpoint. The present chapter seeks to show that the second-person perspective is committed to dignity conceived as shared basic second-personal authority. Chapter 12 argues that procedural versions of the CI, including a contractualist interpretation of the Realm of Ends formulation (FRE), can be grounded in this authority.)

But what commits us to this standing? Why should we suppose that we have the authority to claim anything from one another simply as equal persons? If the reasoning of the last chapter is correct, then even if the moral law, the dignity of persons, and autonomy of the will are all reciprocally related to one another, nothing within first-personal practical reasoning alone requires us to accept any of these. An agent might deliberate intelligibly (from a naïve first-personal standpoint) on the assumption that all are chimerical ideas. In the current chapter, I lay out reasons for thinking that dignity and autonomy (second-personal authority and competence) are inescapably presupposed in the second-person stance, and I begin to make the case, the main part of which is presented in the chapter following, that an account of second-personal practical thought is central to a fully adequate account of practical reason.

If, however, the moral law is essentially tied to the dignity of persons,

2. Moreover, there may be moral obligations that extend beyond the treatment of persons, for example, the treatment of other animals who are not persons and the treatment of the environment. The dignity of persons shows itself in these cases also, since it involves membership in the moral community to whom all are accountable for complying with these demands.

3. Moral obligations must thus be understood as involving implicit demands that are "in force," as I noted in Chapter 1, even when actual individuals have not explicitly made them. As Strawson points out, "the making of the demand *is* the proneness to [reactive] attitudes" (1968: 92–93). This, again, is like Hart's interpretation of Bentham's account of law (1990: 93–94) involving "quasi-commands." See the discussion of this point in note 17 of Chapter 1.

and if dignity includes an irreducibly second-personal standing, then it should not be surprising that the second-person perspective is essential to appreciating the bindingness of the moral law. No authority to address second-personal reasons of any kind is reducible to propositions of value or normative principles of right that can adequately be appreciated either first- or third-personally, since nothing of this sort will itself include the irreducibly second-personal element of claim or demand.[4] If, consequently, persons have the standing to make claims of one another as free and rational, this must be something we are committed to from within the second-person perspective. Moreover, in my view, it is a commitment to the equal dignity of persons in this irreducibly second-personal way that brings along with it a commitment to autonomy of the will and the CI, rather than vice versa.

Prelude: Assembling the Materials

Our goal in this chapter, then, is to construct an argument for the claim that the dignity of persons, conceived of as a shared basic second-personal authority, is inescapably presupposed from the second-person standpoint as a normative felicity condition of addressing second-personal reasons and, therefore, that autonomy of the will is as well. We hope to conclude that addressing any second-personal reason whatsoever will necessarily commit one to these two assumptions. By now, we have in hand many of the materials we need for such an argument, including Strawson's and Pufendorf's Points. In this section, we briefly survey these so that we can, in succeeding sections, combine them with ideas of Fichte's about second-personal address in general to produce a convincing argument. Fichte claims that second-personal address always presumes, as such, to direct an agent's will through that agent's own free choice. It attempts to make a claim on her through an address to her as a free and rational agent. We can call this *Fichte's Analysis* of second-personal address.

Fichte's Point, then, is that there are two conditions that must be satisfied for second-personal address, so analyzed, to succeed; hence there are two assumptions that any attempt to address someone second-

4. Obviously, I mean here to exclude such third-personal propositions as that *A* has the authority to demand that *B* get off his foot (which essentially includes the idea of a claim or demand that is addressable second-personally). And as well, first-personal propositions that are also second-personal.

personally is committed to making.[5] The first is that the addresser and the addressee share an equal authority to make claims of one another as free and rational. And the second is that they share a freedom to act on claims that are rooted in this authority. Fichte's Point, as I am interpreting him, is that any second-personal address whatsoever must simultaneously presuppose this second-personal authority and second-personal competence.[6] Indeed, being second-personally competent is what we should understand 'free' in the phrase 'free and rational' to refer to.[7] In effect, then, our aim in this chapter is to construct an argument for Fichte's Point. I believe that this can be done by combining Fichte's Analysis with Strawson's and Pufendorf's Points.

STRAWSON'S POINT.   Holding someone responsible always addresses a demand, and the only way to justify any such demand is with second-personal reasons, that is, from within the standpoint we must occupy to address it. Otherwise, we will be invoking "reasons of the wrong kind." This gives us the framework of four interdefinable, irreducibly second-personal notions we have identified: (1) addressable demands, (2) the authority to address them, (3) second-personal reasons that are implicit in their address, and (4) accountability to others. Any one of these four notions implicitly involves the other three, and there is no way to reduce the distinctive normativity of any one of them to norms and values that can be appreciated fully without a second-person standpoint.

Strawson makes these points about moral responsibility in particular, but nothing restricts their application to the moral case. Whenever someone puts forward a putatively valid claim or demand of any kind, she purports to initiate a second-personal relation that inevitably involves all four concepts. Two elements of this framework are especially relevant to

5. As always throughout this book, I mean: for it to succeed normatively, that is, as I have put it, that there are two "normative felicity conditions" of second-personal address. This means, again, that there are two conditions that second-personal address must satisfy for the (normative) reasons it attempts to address actually to exist and be given. Second-personal address may succeed in conventional (Austinian) terms by contrast, for example, a speech act may constitute a command, if relevant authority exists *de facto,* whether or not it exists *de jure.*

6. Here again, I mean that this is a presupposition to which the address is conceptually committed, not that the anyone who addresses another second-personally actually presupposes it.

7. As in "equal authority to make claims of one another as free and rational."

the argument of the current chapter. One is the connection between addressing demands and accountability. To address a demand is invariably to attempt to initiate a relation whereby the addressee can be presumed responsible for complying with the demand. (Conversely, holding someone responsible invariably addresses demands.) As we have seen, it is impossible for any such attempt to succeed unless a more general accountability relation already obtains between addresser and addressee, which relation both presuppose in addressing and acknowledging the demand respectively. This is the version of Strawson's Point we called Cudworth's Point, which we saw in Cudworth's critique of theological voluntarism and which I appealed to in discussing Gilbert and Scanlon at the end of Chapter 8. God cannot obligate us by specific commands unless we are already accountable to him in general, and it is impossible for you and me to agree to take a walk together, or for either of us individually to promise unless we already have the second-personal authority to make or refuse agreements or to give or receive promises, as we presuppose when one of us issues an invitation or attempts to make a promise and the other accepts or declines.

The second element is the distinctive kind of reason for acting that authoritative demands invariably address taken together with the capacity to act on a reason of this kind (second-personal competence) that we presuppose when we address any such demand. Second-personal reasons are authority-regarding rather than outcome-regarding or state-of-the-world-regarding. Recall our initial example, in which you are in pain because someone is stepping on your foot. The fact that you are suffering pain that might be relieved by someone's moving his foot is, in itself, an agent-neutral, outcome-regarding, non-second-personal reason for him to move it. Such a person is simply in an especially good position to bring about a better state of the world; this reason for him to do so is one that is also had, in principle, by anyone who can bring about this state. If, however, you address a demand to him that he move his foot (since he had no right to step on yours in the first place), the reason you attempt to give him is authority-regarding rather than state-of-the-world-regarding; it is agent-relative and second-personal. In addressing the demand, you need not presuppose that he has a reason to bring about the relief of your pain because it is a better state. What you presuppose is rather that you have the authority to demand that he move his foot, that there is therefore a reason for him to do so (whether he wants to or thinks that would be a particularly good thing or not), and, finally, that he is accountable for doing so.

Now as we saw at the end of the last chapter, when we hold one another morally responsible, we presuppose that we can each comply with moral requirements, not just in the weak sense of having the ability and the opportunity to do so, but in the stronger sense of having the capacity to recognize and (freely) act on the distinctive second-personal reasons they involve. And we saw also that this requires us to presuppose that we have the capacity to act on reasons that are rooted simply in the second-personal authority of a free and rational agent as such and that are consequently independent "of any features of the objects of volition."[8] Moral accountability thus presupposes autonomy of the will. We can be held morally responsible only for what we can hold ourselves responsible for by making moral demands of ourselves from the perspective of one free and rational agent among others.[9]

I contend that one consequence of Fichte's Analysis is that these presuppositions are not limited to the moral case; they are invariably implicated in second-personal address. Any second-personal reason whatsoever is authority- rather than outcome-regarding, and any address of a second-personal reason purports to initiate an accountability relation in which both parties are responsible to one another as rational and free (second-personally competent). In effect, then, it is a consequence of Fichte's Analysis that second-personal address must always presuppose autonomy and the dignity of persons. If the address of any second-personal reason is to an agent as free and rational, then being accountable for compliance must involve the addressee's capacity freely to determine herself by reasons that are grounded in a second-personal competence and authority that addresser and addressee must be presumed to have in common.[10]

8. There are two elements here. First, we must presuppose that we can act on the relevant agent-relative norm (say, not to step on one another's feet). Second, but no less important, we have to assume that we can hold one another, and ourselves, responsible for so complying. So we must assume that in being subject to moral demands, we have these two interlocked motivational capacities, which assumption amounts to autonomy of the will. I am indebted to Ryan Preston for discussion of this point.

9. As Kant puts it, "I can recognize that I am under obligation to others only insofar as I at the same time put myself under obligation" (1996d: 417–418).

10. With second-personal reasons other than those deriving from moral obligations, however, the presupposition is only that the agent can freely determine herself to act on these reasons *pro tanto*, that is, other reasons to the contrary notwithstanding.

Second-personal address must always presuppose shared second-personal authority and second-personal competence.

PUFENDORF'S POINT.   The second element we will need for our argument is Pufendorf's Point, which Pufendorf puts forward as a claim about moral motivation. In order for God's commands to create obligations, we must be able to distinguish between someone being moved to comply by fear of, or by the desire to avoid, God's sanctions, on the one hand, and his being moved by the conviction that the sanction "falls upon him justly," on the other (1934: 91).[11] We can be genuinely obligated to comply with God's commands only if we have the capacity to accept his authority and to determine ourselves freely by this acceptance. We must have second-personal competence.

One way we have been putting this point is by saying that to be subject to an obligation and be, consequently, responsible for compliance, the obligated agent must be capable of holding himself responsible. To do this, he must be able to see the addresser's claim or demand not just as externally imposed even as imposed justifiably from the addresser's perspective, but as something he, the addressee, justifiably demands of himself from a standpoint that he and his addressee can share. He must be able to think not just that someone else might have reason to reproach him were he not to comply but also that he would be to blame, that there would be warrant for him to blame himself.

This is Pufendorf's Point from, as it were, the addressee's perspective. But it has two corollaries from the addresser's perspective. First, although special authority may carry distinctive forms of accountability of an addressee to a specially authorized addresser, there must always also be an underlying presupposed authority to hold responsible that addresser and addressee have in common. Any special authority must still presuppose that an addressee's failure to comply would be an appropriate object of blame and other reactive attitudes, and these, as Strawson pointed out, always implicate the perspective of second-personally competent persons as such (the moral community). For the addresser to think that an addressee would be to blame for not complying with her demand, she must think, not just that she (the addresser) would have standing to complain,

11. Not just in the Hobbesian sense that God does no wrong in applying it, but that God has the authority to apply it.

but that her addressee would be to blame, that is, the addressee would be appropriately blamed by anyone.[12] She must think that her addressee has the same basic authority to blame himself that she has to blame him.

Second, Pufendorf's distinction from an addressee's perspective between acting on a desire to avoid sanctions and acting on a second-personal reason generates a complementary distinction from the addresser's point of view. Any addresser of a second-personal reason is committed to there being a difference between relating to someone in "demanding" (directive) ways in making a valid demand or holding him responsible for complying with it, on the one hand, and merely forcing him to comply, for example, by threatening some evil, on the other. Part of the very idea of accountability is that there must be something (call it a "sanction" or "consequence") that someone with the authority to hold a person responsible can demand that the person accept if he fails to do what he is responsible for doing. Exactly what an appropriate consequence would be is a normative rather than a conceptual question. In theory, it could consist in no more than having to be the object of a reactive attitude, to listen to a charge, to acknowledge responsibility or guilt, or maybe even something weaker. But what is not left open by the concept is liability to a consequence of some kind, that is, that some consequence would "fall upon" one justly so that accepting it would help constitute one's taking responsibility for what one has done.

The idea of accountability therefore requires a distinction between the authority to put someone on notice of a sanction as part of holding him accountable, on the one hand, and illegitimately threatening the very same evil without this authority, that is, coercion, on the other. It follows that someone who addresses a demand or puts someone on notice of a purportedly valid sanction presupposes that, although she may act toward the other in this directive or "demanding" way because of her authority, she could not legitimately do so if she lacked the relevant authority. Without that authority, what would have been a valid notice of sanction becomes coercion, and this would violate the addressee's authority. Indeed, without the relevant authority, even the attempt to direct the agent's will by making the demand in the first place would be coercion.[13] She is

---

12. One way to see this is to ask what otherwise the complaint could consist in. Having the standing to say, "You shouldn't have done that" will simply be empty unless the complaint itself is something the addressee can be expected to accept.

13. I am indebted to Jacob Ross for this point.

committed, therefore, to the idea that *it takes second-personal authority to have a justification of the right kind (second-personal reasons) to direct the will of another free and rational agent.*

We can see this in the phenomenon of blame itself. Reactive attitudes exert a kind of directive pressure on their objects. We naturally resent therefore being the object of resentment we think unwarranted. But blame is not influence pure and simple. Blame purports to be a second-personally warranted form of influence, to be justified, that is, by an authority its object can accept because it springs, ultimately, from the same authority he himself has, and must accept himself as having, in being an accountable agent at all. When we blame someone, we "view him as a member of the moral community; only as one who has offended against its demands" (Strawson 1968: 93). So in blaming him, we acknowledge his authority and implicitly acknowledge that if we didn't have second-personally adequate grounds for blame, then our directive influence would be illegitimate; it would be a violation of his authority.

Pufendorf's Point mirrors our analysis of the second-personal features of Kant's example of the "fact of reason." Citizen, from our example in Chapter 9, must choose between complying with her moral obligation not to betray an honest person (and collude with a tyrant), on the one hand, and saving her skin, on the other. Part of Kant's point is that we recognize that we can do as we morally ought, our fear and desire for self-preservation to the contrary notwithstanding. And I argued that, if we attend to the presuppositions of moral responsibility, we will agree not just that complying with moral obligations is always deliberatively open to us but that we can act as we are obligated for the very reasons that we are obligated. And this commits us to Pufendorf's distinction between being moved by fear of some evil consequence and being moved by our acceptance of the moral obligation (in our terms, by accepting the moral community's authority to demand compliance and, identifying with this perspective, making the demand second-personally of ourselves).

Pufendorf's Point and this second-personal analysis of the "fact of reason" are both advanced, like Strawson's Point, with respect to moral obligation and responsibility in particular. But a lesson of Fichte's Analysis is that whenever we address demands and assume the authority to hold one another responsible, we commit ourselves to Pufendorf's distinction in both its addressees' and addressers' versions. We presuppose a distinction between being moved by desires for goods or evils, on the one hand,

and being moved by an acceptance of the relevant second-personal reasons (and thereby making the relevant demands of ourselves), on the other. And we commit ourselves to the complementary distinction between legitimately attempting to direct someone's will with the relevant second-personal authority and illegitimately imposing our will on him, thus violating his authority as a free and rational person.

Fichte's Analysis: Second-Personal Address and Free Practical Reason

We can begin to work toward an argument for Fichte's Point by attempting first to understand Fichte's Analysis. Fichte calls any second-personal address a "summons" *(Aufforderung)*. And he argues that issuing or acknowledging a summons commits addresser and addressee alike to recognizing what he calls the "principle of right": "I must in all cases recognize the free being outside me as a free being, i.e., I must limit my freedom through the concept of the possibility of his freedom" (2000: 49).[14] Considerations of the right are thus second-personal reasons that are rooted in a common authority that you and I have as free and rational. And Fichte argues also that any summons presupposes the freedom of both addresser and addressee to act on these reasons. His claim, as I interpret it, is that any summons commits both parties to recognizing the principle of right as well as the freedom of addresser and addressee to act on the second-personal reasons it encodes.

I should emphasize that I extend Fichte's claims and arguments farther than he does or would himself.[15] For reasons I cannot adequately discuss here, Fichte distinguishes between moral duty and the right, and he understands enforceable constraints of right as "technical" or "practical," that is, as hypothetical requirements that agents are committed to only

14. It will ease exposition if I sometimes say that it "presupposes" or "assumes" this. I mean this in the sense I hope is now familiar, namely, that the presupposition is a normative felicity condition of a second-personal reason's being successfully addressed, whether or not the addresser presupposes this in fact.

15. So Fichte might himself reject what I am calling "Fichte's Point." I argue, however, that the point is implicit in his arguments. Whether he would be convinced and accept the credit I am attempting to bestow upon him I cannot of course say. (Second-personal relations are especially complex when spread out over two centuries.)

insofar as they aim to live together.[16] I believe, however, that Fichte's ideas support, indeed that they require, the stronger proposition that second-personal address invariably presupposes categorical requirements rooted in the dignity of persons (second-personal authority) along with autonomy of the will (second-personal competence).

Fichte connects his analysis of second-personal address to a fundamental distinction he makes between the kinds of freedom that are involved in theoretical and practical reason, respectively. When you and I reason about what to believe, we aim to construct representations of a common world, to "represent . . . objects" as they are "apart from any contribution by us" (2000: 19). In theoretical reasoning, our perspectives are the way the world is, according to each of us respectively.[17] If, consequently, you have reason to think that my view of things is mistaken or skewed, you may discount my beliefs as mere appearances when forming yours.

From the second-person standpoint, however, we see that nothing analogous can hold in practical reasoning (naïve first-personal deliberation to the contrary notwithstanding). When you and I make claims on one another's will, we take ourselves to be free to act on reasons that are grounded not in our relations to an independent ordering of the value of different outcomes or possible states of the world but just in our authority with respect to each other. Our respective practical perspectives are thus not simply standpoints on an independent something and discountable when they reflect it poorly. Fichte's Point is that they are the perspectives from which we lead our lives as free and independent rational agents and relate to one another on terms that respect this status. When we make claims on each other second-personally, we acknowledge a source of reasons and a kind of freedom—second-personal authority and second-personal competence—that make practical reason fundamentally different from theoretical reason.

Like Kant, therefore, Fichte is committed to practical reason's embodying a form of freedom that goes beyond any species, positive or negative, that is presupposed in theoretical reasoning (or in naïve first-personal practical reasoning). Agency itself involves, Fichte claims, a "positing" of

16. For a more extended discussion, see Darwall 2005, from which I here draw. See also Frederick Neuhouser's introduction to Fichte 2000 and Neuhouser 1994.

17. This is a conceptual point about the nature of belief that needs to be accounted for even within an idealist framework like Fichte's.

oneself as an agent, and an agent cannot "posit itself without ascribing free efficacy to itself" (2000: 4, 18). Fichte stresses, moreover, that the "free efficacy" we assume in practical reasoning differs from any we must presuppose in rationally representing or "intuiting a world." Any such representing is "*constrained* and *bound* with respect to its content."[18] Belief, by its very nature, aims to represent the world as it actually is. The activity involved in an agent's self-positing, by contrast, is "opposed to such representational activity" and "*free* with respect to its content" (19). In the terms we developed in the last chapter, it involves a kind of freedom that goes beyond any a naïve agent must assume.

But neither, and again like Kant, is practical freedom for Fichte simply the capacity to set ends.[19] (For Kant, recall, it also includes autonomy.) Fichte does say that "what is contained first and foremost in the concept of freedom is nothing but the capacity to construct, through absolute spontaneity, concepts of our possible efficacy," or "the concept of an *end*" (2000: 9, 20). However, Fichte adds: "But if a rational individual, or a person, is to find himself as free, then something more is required" (9). What free agency involves beyond the ability to set ends (formal freedom) is a "positing" of our own free agency. And Fichte maintains, as we see in the next section, that we posit ourselves as free agents from a second-person standpoint.

For Fichte, it is second-personal engagement that makes us aware of a kind of freedom we have that is fundamentally unlike any that is involved in theoretical reasoning or in practical reasoning from a naïve first-person standpoint. Fichte believes that second-personal engagement commits addresser and addressee alike to limiting their "external freedom" through the "principle of right."[20] In so doing, each "lets his own external freedom be limited through inner freedom" (2000: 10). "Inner freedom" must thus include second-personal competence. Addresser and addressee freely restrict their external freedom when they accept one another's authority and impose demands on themselves (the principle of right) that either person would make on both from a standpoint they can both share as rational and free (second-personally competent). As I interpret it, there-

18. Again, I take Fichte to be making a conceptual point here that even an idealist framework must respect.

19. For a contrary view, see Neuhouser's introduction to Fichte 2000: iv.

20. Like Kant, Fichte uses "external freedom" to refer to a legally protectable sphere of free movement or action (1996c: 214).

fore, Fichtean "inner freedom" (second-personal competence) is the formal analogue of Kant's autonomy of the will.

Fichte's Analysis: Positing Agency and Second-Personal Reasons

But why does Fichte suppose that we "posit" ourselves as free agents from a second-person standpoint? In the first-person perspective, agency is "backgrounded" and no part of the agent's "deliberative field."[21] A deliberating agent's focus is on the alternatives she faces along with their supporting reasons. So unless the reasons are of a special agency-regarding sort, like second-personal reasons, it will not be on her own agency (Pettit and Smith 1990; Regan 2003a, 2003b). Consider, again, an agent occupying a naïve first-person standpoint, deliberating on the basis of her preferences, desires, or Moorean evaluations of possible outcomes. She sees possible states or outcomes as more or less desirable (worth bringing about) and possible actions as more or less likely to effect them. Her deliberation is instrumental and transparent with respect to her own agency—it looks through her will to what valuable outcomes she can achieve.[22]

When we deliberate second-personally, however, in the light of a "summons" from one rational agent to another "calling upon it to resolve to

21. I take these illustrative terms from Pettit and Smith 1990 and Herman 1996.

22. Perhaps, however, this is only true so long as we conceive of deliberation in consequentialist terms. What if the agent accepts agent-relative principles of conduct, such as that each person should keep her promises? Won't that give her a deliberative purchase on her own agency? We know from the "fact of reason" that in supposing she is bound by an agent-relative principle, an agent must presuppose that she can act on it. But as we also saw, this only requires her to suppose that this action is deliberatively open. It doesn't involve any presupposition of autonomy. Moreover, Kant believes that such a principle applies to one only on the condition of autonomy. So the question remains, What within the deliberative standpoint commits the agent to that assumption? On the instrumental conception of action, see Schapiro 2001.

In a somewhat similar vein, Scheffler argues that the very idea of holding oneself to a standard requires one to conceive a source of reasons, a norm of action, that is not itself instrumental or outcome-based. As Scheffler acknowledges, however, this is consistent with the norm itself being consequentialist (like the Moorean norm to produce optimal outcomes I mentioned in the last chapter). Scheffler argues that this consequentialist possibility is, however, in tension with our normal human patterns of holding one another responsible through reactive attitudes. To credit these latter responses, however, is implicitly to credit the second-person standpoint. (See Scheffler 2004.)

exercise its efficacy,"[23] we are required to posit the free agency of addresser and addressee alike as part of our reasoning (Fichte 2000: 31). Although agency is no doubt assumed in the background somehow in any deliberation, it is only from a second-person standpoint that the addresser's free agency (and that of addressees) must be posited, that is, brought into their reasoning as a premise. And when it is, addresser and addressee alike must also assume that both have the capacity to act on second-personal reasons, that both are second-personally competent.

The summons is to someone as a free agent (including as second-personally competent), so in being aware of it, the summoned is aware of herself as thus regarded. Taken only so far, however, this might be no different from an observer's awareness. That someone sees one as a free agent is but another aspect of the way things are in the world anyway, part of the causal order of things that might be made better or worse. What makes all the difference is that a summons addresses one second-personally; it comes with an RSVP. In taking it up, even in publicly considering whether to take it up, one per force relates-to-the-other-relating-to-one-as-a-free-agent. One deliberates within a second-personal relationship in which each reciprocally recognizes the other as a "you" to whom she is a "you" in return. The presuppositions of intelligible second-personal deliberative thought require that one deliberate on the assumption, that is, on the premise, that one and the other are both agents with second-personal competence. Through responding second-personally to a summons, "the subject acts in such a way that the concept of itself as a free being and the concept of the rational being outside it (as a free being like itself) are mutually determined and conditional" (Fichte 2000: 40). This gives us a practical perspective on our own agency that is irreducible to any consciousness we might have of ourselves as part of a causal order. One simultaneously "posits" oneself and the other as free and rational agents within one's own deliberation (9).

The most perspicuous interpretation of Fichte's idea is in terms of second-personal reasons. A summons is any attempt to address second-personal reasons to some free and rational (second-personally competent) agent. Only by addressing a second-personal reason can one agent attempt to direct the will of another through the other's free choice. "The rational being's activity is by no means to be determined and necessitated by the summons in the way that . . . an effect is necessitated by its cause;

23. This could also be from the agent to herself (second-personally).

rather the rational being is to determine itself in consequence of the summons" (2000: 35). A summons attempts to give another agent (second-personal) reasons by which she can freely determine herself, and it does this by addressing the other as rational and free.[24] This is Fichte's Analysis of second-personal address.

If one person attempts to give another reasons for acting that are not second-personal, then no second-personal address in the current sense is involved; no claim is made on the other's will and only epistemic authority is presupposed. In pointing to non-second-personal reasons for acting, an advisor does not aim to direct an advisee's will as such: "I'm not telling (demanding, requesting, etc.) you to do anything. I'm just giving you advice."[25] Advice makes a claim not on an advisee's will or actions but on her beliefs about what there is reason for her to do. An advisor summons an advisee, not to act in some way or other, but only to believe that certain considerations are reasons for her to act. So an advisor addresses an advisee directly, not as an agent, but as a cognizer of practical reasons.

If, however, someone issues a request, order, or demand, say, if you ask someone to move his foot from on top of yours, then you address your addressee directly as an agent who is capable of freely determining himself to act on the reasons you address. And if he takes up your address (which he cannot avoid doing if it is common between the two of you that he has listened and heard), then he reflects back a reciprocal address (as someone who has, like you, the standing and competence to address and act on second-personal reasons as well). Even a bare request addresses a second-personal reason that is additional to any non-second-personal reasons that might stand behind it, since it presupposes the normative standing to make the request.

Fichte's Point: The Principle of Right and Equal Dignity

Now the kind of case Fichte has most especially in mind is a summons addressed to someone simply as one free and rational agent among others,

---

24. Even if the only reason it explicitly addresses comes from a request so to determine herself.

25. Of course, this is only true with respect to the advice itself. There is presumably an implied claim on the advisee's will in presuming on her time and attention in listening to and considering the advice. But then these would themselves presuppose second-personal reasons.

that is, as an equal. Thus, a request or a demand to another that he move his foot from on top of yours might most naturally be presented and interpreted as grounded in normative relations presumed to hold between free and rational persons as such. In interpreting your request as an address of such a (second-personal) reason, your addressee must presuppose that you are claiming a second-personal authority simply as a rational person with second-personal competence, which status you must assume he has also.

Presently we consider Fichte's claim that second-personal recognition commits both parties to the principle of right. It may seem no surprise that reciprocal recognition as an equal should lead to this conclusion, however, since it seems already to be packed into the premises framing such mutual respect in the first place. But what about an address that presupposes an unequal, unreciprocated authority of addresser over an addressee? On Fichte's Analysis, even hierarchical forms of second-personal address are fundamentally to another as a free and rational agent, since they address (second-personal) reasons by which the addressee can freely "determine [himself]" (2000: 35), and that is possible only if the addressee can accept the authority the addressee presupposes (simply as free and rational). So even the addresser of a demand that is presumed to be based in an unreciprocated, hierarchical authority must assume that the authority on which the demand is based is one the addressee can freely and rationally accept. Otherwise, we don't have a case of Fichtean second-personal address, but rather an attempt to influence or cause compliance in some other way that "depriv[es him] of [his] ability to act freely" (41).

In supposing, moreover, that an addressee is responsible for complying with a demand, an addresser is committed to a number of other assumptions that imply a second-personal authority issuing from second-personal competence. First, the addresser can intelligibly hold an addressee responsible for compliance only if she assumes that he can hold himself responsible. But the addressee can do this only if he can blame himself for not complying, that is, only if he can make the demand of himself from the same perspective from which he accepts the addresser's authority, that is, the standpoint of a free and rational agent. Likewise, second, to hold the addressee responsible, an addresser must assume that the addressee would be blameworthy for failing to comply with the demand. So the addresser must also assume that her own authority to blame the addressee for noncompliance comes ultimately from the very same point of view. She must think that were the addressee not to comply without excuse, he would be to blame period, that is, from a perspective that the addresser and addressee can share as free and rational. Third, in assuming that an addressee is responsible for complying with a demand, the addresser must presuppose that she has an authority to relate to the addressee in "demanding" ways that would be illegitimate were she to lack the authority.

Each of these assumptions commits an addresser to a second-personal authority deriving from second-personal competence. The first two illustrate the Strawsonian point that reactive attitudes like blame always involve an aspect of mutual accountability, since they are always addressed from the perspective of someone as a second-personally competent person (a member of the moral community) to someone as a(nother) second-personally competent person (and thus an equal member) (Strawson 1968: 93). They thereby ultimately derive their authority to address their implicit demands from this perspective. The third assumption makes explicit a point that is implicit already in the first two, namely, that the authority to hold responsible implies a distinction between legitimately relating to someone in "demanding" ways that, however directive, do not amount to coercion because they are warranted by second-personal reasons (reasons that, it is assumed, an addressee could himself freely accept and that holding himself responsible would require him to accept), on the one hand, and relating to him in the very same ways without the relevant authority, which would then be coercion and therefore an illegitimate violation of the addressee's authority as free and rational, on the other.

Consider, for example, an order delivered by a superior to an inferior within a military chain of command. If a sergeant orders a private to do ten pushups, she addresses a reason to him that presupposes her authority to give the order and the private's obligation to obey it. So far, the only relevant normative presupposition is of unequal authority; the sergeant has the standing to give orders to the private, whereas the private has no standing to give orders to the sergeant. But an order doesn't simply point to a reason holding in normative space; it purports to address it second-personally and thereby to hold the addressee responsible for compliance. As second-personal address, an order presupposes that its addressee can freely determine himself through accepting the reasons it addresses and the authority in which they are grounded and hold himself responsible for complying with it. Any second-personal address whatsoever calls for reciprocal recognition of the authority it presupposes (in this case the sergeant's authority). It attempts to direct an addressee's will through the addressee's own free acceptance of that authority.

This ups the ante on the presupposed authority and consequent second-personal reasons, since it requires that the authority be one that the addressee can accept as free and rational. This is what follows when we combine Fichte's Analysis with Pufendorf's Point from the addressee's perspective. There must be a distinction between the addressee's (the private's) complying with a demand because of a desire to escape some evil, on the one hand, and his complying because he freely accepts the addresser's (second-personal) authority and therefore the addressed second-personal reason, on the other. So although the sergeant, of course, addresses her order to not just any rational person but to the private, there is an important sense in which her addressee must be conceived to be a-person-who-happens-to-be-a-private. Second-personal address is always to a free and rational agent. That is why an order can constitute a summons the taking up of which requires an addressee to posit both himself and his would-be superior as free and rational agents. In presupposing, therefore, that the private can accept her authority, the sergeant cannot simply assume that he can be expected to accept this as a private. Nothing about actually occupying that role can be relevant to whether to accept the norms and authority relations that define it. Rather the sergeant must presuppose that the private can accept the authority she claims as a person, that is, from the (second-person) standpoint they both share as free and rational, and that, as a person, he can accept the specific normative requirements she attempts to place on him for the hypothetical case of occupying the role of private.

In assuming that the private is responsible for complying with the order, the sergeant is committed to thinking that the private would rightly be blamed if he didn't comply without adequate excuse. But reactive attitudes like blame address demands from a perspective they presuppose their addressee can share. So although the sergeant assumes she has a distinctive authority to hold the private accountable, which goes with her special authority to issue the order in the first place, any such specially authorized standing must ultimately be grounded in an authority she must assume that the private shares with her (to hold himself accountable). Otherwise, threatening a sanction, even one he couldn't complain about, would give him a reason of the wrong kind to comply. The reason would not be a second-personal reason to do the pushups whether or not he could escape the sanction, one the acceptance of which is part of holding himself responsible.

So, finally, in making a claim on the private as free and rational in this way, the sergeant must also presuppose a distinction between making a legitimate claim on the private's will in a way that respects his authority as free and rational, on the one hand, and, on the other, attempting illegitimately to direct his will by simply imposing her will on him in some way that "depriv[es him] of [his] ability to act freely" (Fichte 2000: 41), that is, by coercion. However hierarchical, therefore, any address of a second-personal reason also implicitly presupposes a common second-personal authority as free and rational. This is Pufendorf's Point from the addresser's perspective projected through Fichte's Analysis into the second-person framework in general.

Suppose, for instance, that the sergeant believes that if the private disobeys, she will then be entitled to put him in detention. Seeing what she regards as signs of incipient disobedience, she reminds the private of this fact; she puts him on notice of a sanction that she would be authorized to apply in holding him responsible. In so doing, she necessarily presupposes a distinction between the justified threat of this sanction, which she must suppose to be consistent with the addressee's freely determining himself by the second-personal reasons provided by her order, on the one hand, and attempting unjustifiably to determine him to do the same act by the mere threat of the very same unwanted alternative in which the sanction consists, that is, without the relevant authority, on the other. To use Hart's helpful terms, she must presuppose a distinction between obligating the private by an order and obliging him illegitimately by coercion (1961: 6–8). She must assume that although the private is subject to her orders, it would nonetheless be a violation of his normative standing to attempt to direct his will by threatening the very same evil if she lacked the requisite authority (and other things were held equal). And this commits her to presupposing his authority as a free and rational agent.

Similarly, from the addressee's perspective, if the private is responsible for compliance and being placed in detention by the sergeant is a second-personally justified way of holding him responsible, then the private must accept a distinction between any reason to comply with the order in order to escape the sanction (whether justified or not) and the second-personal reason to comply that the sergeant attempts to give him in issuing her order. Holding himself responsible requires accepting the latter reason and acting on it. If he fails to comply, moreover, then accepting the sanction is not simply acquiescing in something he deserves; it is a way of holding himself responsible, which, again, he can do only from the standpoint that he and the sergeant share as free and rational. So both the sergeant and the private are committed to recognizing their common second-personal competence and second-personal authority.

We come now to Fichte's claim that reciprocal recognition between rational agents commits both parties to the principle of right: "I must in all cases recognize the free being outside me as a free being, i.e., I must limit my freedom through the concept of the possibility of his freedom" (2000: 49). In this abstract form, the principle of right is already implicit in the line of thought we have just traversed. If the argument of this section has been correct so far, then second-personal engagement invariably commits both parties to presupposing that their relations are properly governed by their common standing as rational persons, more specifically, that each will seek to "determine" the other only in ways that are consistent with, and do not undermine, the other's self-determination as a free and rational person. Fichte draws the further consequence that this requires recognizing "spheres of freedom" within which individuals have enforceable rights to do as they will and with respect to which others are required to forbear interference (10, 40–41, 44). If any legitimate interference must be able to be justified to others by second-personal reasons they can themselves accept as rational persons, then this will circumscribe a sphere within which individuals have an enforceable claim to non-interference.[26]

26. As I mentioned, Fichte insists that the principle of right is distinct from and independent of the moral law. And he sometimes claims that any obligation imposed by the principle of right must be voluntarily assumed, indeed, assumed individual by individual, through an "arbitrary" positing of the other and simultaneous making of a law not to violate his external freedom (2000: 81). For this reason, Fichte calls the concept of right a "merely technical-practical," rather than moral, concept (10). "The law of right," he asserts, "says nothing to the effect that a particular person should limit his freedom" (14). It simply says what follows from the voluntary self-limiting that is part of positing oneself in opposition to another individual whom one simultaneously recognizes.

On this "voluntarist" interpretation, it takes an individual's voluntary participation in a "reciprocal declaration" to be obligated to (and with respect to) a particular individual

An Objection: Slavery

In the next and final section, I formalize the argument for Fichte's Point that I made informally in the last section. First, however, I want to con-

---

by the principle of right (2000: 15). I don't believe, however, that Fichte can hold to a voluntarist interpretation if he is to maintain that the conditions for self-awareness are sufficient to validate the principle of right. Fichte sometimes seems to be aware of this, for example, when he says that although one cannot complain that another does one an injury in refusing recognition, nonetheless one can claim that the other "must then remove himself from all human community" (12). (Cf. "[W]hen human beings are to live alongside one another, each must limit his freedom, so that the freedom of others can also exist alongside that freedom" [14].) This suggests that the only way an individual can avoid the obligations imposed by the principle of right is to avoid other people altogether. It is unclear, however, why this should be so on a voluntarist interpretation. Why wouldn't there simply arise various voluntary communities of right, associations within which individuals are obligated by the principle of right, with no obligations of right to outsiders? It is hard to see how a voluntarist interpretation can avoid this consequence.

Other things Fichte says fit no better with a voluntarist interpretation. First, Fichte asserts that agents demand continued recognition of themselves and their freedom "for all the future" when they reciprocally recognize one another (2000: 48). But again, why should this be so on a voluntarist interpretation? It would seem that individuals would be as free voluntarily to obligate themselves for a temporally limited period as to do so indefinitely. However, if, as I have been suggesting, reciprocally recognizing individuals are committed to the second-personal standing of rational persons not as a matter of voluntary agreement but as a presupposition of second-personal address, then such a demand would be expected. A demand for continued recognition from a particular individual "for all the future" would simply be part of a general demand for respect from all persons for all times, a demand to which one is committed as a presupposition of second-person claim making. The situation would be exactly as Kant describes: a rational person "possesses a *dignity* . . . by which he exacts *respect* for himself from all other rational beings in the world" (1996d: 435, emphasis added to "exacts").

Second, Fichte frequently says that reciprocally recognizing agents recognize one another as rational beings and that they are thereby committed to treating one another as rational beings (e.g., 2000: 42, 43). But these claims presuppose that there are ways of (properly) treating and mistreating rational beings as such and, therefore, that failing to recognize a rational being is not just forbearing to make a voluntary commitment one is free not to make. They presuppose that rational being is itself a normative status, that there are ways of respecting or mistreating people just by virtue of their nature as rational, and that, therefore, one is not free not to recognize and respect them. Again, this makes perfect sense on the "presuppositional" interpretation I am proposing. The dignity of rational persons as such, and of the individual before one as a rational person, is what one is committed to as a presupposition of the intelligibility of recognizing him second-personally.

Finally, the most significant problem with the voluntarist interpretation is that unless we assume a background normative relation that obligates agents (to one another) to keep

sider what may seem an obvious objection to the line of thought I have
sketched thus far.

---

their voluntarily made commitments, it is powerless to explain how a voluntary agreement
can give rise to any obligation to respect spheres of freedom. (This was the version of
Cudworth's Point we encountered before in discussing Gilbert on everyday agreements and
Scanlon on promises in Chapter 8.) Fichte clearly assumes that individuals have warranted
claims against each other if they violate the other's sphere of freedom once reciprocal
recognition has transpired. If I have conformed to the law my co-respondent and I both
committed ourselves to in reciprocally recognizing one another, and he subsequently violates that law, then I am in a position to charge him with a violation of my right: "I . . .
appeal to a *law* that is valid for us both, and apply that law to the present case. I thus
posit myself as judge, i.e. as his superior. . . . But, insofar as I appeal to that common law
in my opposition to him, I invite him to be a judge along with me; and I demand that in
this case he must find my action against him consistent and must approve of it, compelled
by the laws of thought" (2000: 47). But what gives the "law" we committed ourselves to
normative force? The fact that we committed ourselves to it, as if adopting it together?
That could be so only if there exists a further background normative relation that gave us
the authority so to bind ourselves voluntarily and whose authority does not itself depend
on a voluntary commitment (Cudworth's Point again). My co-respondent and I can be
obligated by our "reciprocal declaration" only if we already had the authority to commit
ourselves by it, so whether we had that authority cannot itself depend on our voluntary
commitment. We must already have had the normative standing to address second-
personal reasons, as we presupposed in addressing them to one another.

Suppose, alternatively, that we interpret Fichte as saying that I appeal, not to the fact
that my co-respondent and I committed ourselves to the law, but to the law itself to which
we then committed ourselves. But this seems to provide no help if my co-respondent now
rejects it and refuses to recognize me. Of course, Fichte might argue that he can't simply
refuse to recognize me. All I have to do to get him to recognize me is simply to summon
him, second-personally, with a charge, remonstrance, or any other address. ("I can compel
him to acknowledge that he knows that I am one [a rational being] as well" (2000: 42).)
This means, however, that I must be in a position to demand or "exact" respect, just as
Kant says, from "all other rational beings in the world," whether they have voluntarily
recognized me before or not, simply by summoning them second-personally. And, on
reflection, this seems precisely what Fichte should believe. A second-personal summons
can be sufficient to give a rational being an awareness of being free and rational agent
only if to be a person is to be in a position to exact respect.

Fichte might agree at this point but nonetheless claim that even if it is true that a
rational person is always in a position to exact respect from any other, it is the fact of
recognition that obligates. At this point, however, the idea that recognition is voluntarily
given is seeming substantially less plausible. Moreover, and this is the final important point,
recognition of someone as a person seems itself to involve the recognition of a normative
standing, a dignity, that it responds to and does not confer. This is Cudworth's Point in
another form. Ultimately, therefore, the voluntarist interpretation provides no coherent

When we think about familiar cases of subjection and domination that take an apparently second-personal form, it can seem quite incredible that second-personal address must presuppose anything even remotely like a shared dignity. Surely the argument proves too much. It is one thing to say, for example, that slavery is immoral. It is quite another to say that slavery involves conceptual confusion or some sort of pragmatic contradiction. Something must be wrong, certainly, with any argument that would require us to conclude anything like that.

Nothing I have said, either in Fichte's voice or my own, however, entails that slavery or similar practices are necessarily conceptually confused or pragmatically contradictory. What I have said does imply that the addressing of a demand or order by a slaveholder to a slave, *qua* purporting to be second-personal address, does indeed presuppose that the slaveholder and the slave share a common normative standing as free and rational persons. Unlike subjection or subjugation, any second-personal address seeks reciprocal recognition by its very nature. However, several observations are necessary to avoid misunderstanding on this point, so it will be useful to consider the example of slavery in some detail.[27]

First, I am not saying that it must be the case that slaveholders actually accept that their slaves have equal standing in any respect. For one thing, even if a slaveholder purports to address a slave second-personally, his address may be inauthentic or insincere. This is like the kind of violation of a speech act's felicity conditions that Austin calls an "abuse" (1964: 18). Even if a slaveholder purports to address a pure second-personal reason to a slave, the most I would claim is that if the slaveholder does not accept that the slave has a normative standing as an equal free and rational person, then he addresses the slave "abusively." His belief conflicts with what the slave is given a claim to expect by the terms of the slaveholder's address, and it is contrary to what would have to be true in order for any second-personal reason to be successfully addressed, hence for any more specific such reason to be addressed to the slave. (Again, my claim in this case, as in others, concerns "normative felicity condi-

---

alternative to the idea that the reciprocal recognition involved in second-personal address presupposes, rather than somehow creates, the normative standing persons have to address second-personal reasons.

27. Although my discussion has some resonance with Hegel's famous section on "Lordship and Bondage" in *The Phenomenology of Sprit* (1977), most of my points are substantially different. I have been helped here by discussion with Matthew Smith.

tions" for the reason's actually existing and being successfully given, not a conventional, Austinian condition of his speech act's constituting an order. The former presupposes authority *de jure,* the latter, only authority *de facto.*)

For a second thing, the slaveholder's approach to the slave may not even purport to be second-personal address in our sense. He may simply be attempting to force the slave's submission or compliance in one way or another that doesn't even purport to address a second-personal reason. To be sure, the most interesting and disturbing cases of domination include second-personal traces or simulacra, such as a humiliating mutual acknowledgment of the slaveholder's power to subjugate the slave.[28] But even here, if there is nothing that purports to be authentic second-personal address of the kind we have been concerned with, the argument simply does not apply. As I pointed out in Chapter 6, however, even tyrants like Stalin rarely reject the second-person standpoint outright. To the contrary, they generally manipulate it for their own purposes.

---

28. I am indebted to Nir Eyal for the following example. (What follows is, in the main, Eyal's description and analysis.)

> In Sergio Leone's *Once Upon a Time in the West,* the malicious villain, played by Henry Fonda, rapes the heroine, played by Claudia Cardinale, with the intention of causing her maximal suffering and humiliation. As the villain leans on top of her, the heroine averts her eyes and looks the other way. The villain grabs her chin and turns it back in order to look her in the eye whilst raping her. The villain does so because a "You are raping me" situation is even more humiliating to the victim than a "He is raping me" situation. And looking one's rape victim in the eye in real time makes the situation into a second-personal in an obvious sense, i.e. a "You are raping me" situation. The reason that a "You are raping me" situation is more humiliating than a "He is raping me" one seems to be that the former situation includes mutual acknowledgment of salient features of the situation, including the humiliation of the victim.

While Eyal's analysis seems clearly correct, the situation does not involve second-personal address in the sense in which we are interested; it does not involve the address of a second-personal reason that presupposes a normative standing. What the rapist forces to be mutually acknowledged seems to be something like "I can do this to you and you can't stop me" or "I can treat you as someone to be raped," not anything normative such as "I am entitled to rape you." This is humiliating subjugation rather than a second-personal address grounded in the addresser's presupposed authority. It is worth noting, however, that only rarely is even attempted subjugation merely a matter of exerting force without at least some fantasy or self-narrative of authority. On this point, see my discussion in Chapters 4 and 6.

And for a third thing, even if the terms of second-personal address commit a master addressing claims to his slaves to presuppose their second-personal authority, that does not mean that he presupposes it in fact.

Second, I am not saying that if a slaveholder claims to the world at large that he has authority over his slaves, this commits him to recognizing his slaves' dignity either. In this case, he addresses his claim not to his slaves but to others, and whereas my argument would then require us to conclude that he must presuppose their dignity, it would not entail that he must presuppose that of his slaves. He might simply be claiming that his slaves are his property, like his cattle, and that he therefore has, within certain limits, rights to do with them as he will, which claims his addressees must accept. Such a claim would clearly not commit him to his slaves' dignity as persons any more than he would be committed to any such doctrine with respect to his cattle. My claim is rather that if he purports to address a second-personal reason based on this claim to his slaves, then this second-personal address would commit him to the presupposition that he and they share an equal (second-personal) standing just as free and rational persons.[29]

Third, even if this were true, it still wouldn't follow that any purported second-personal address to a slave as a slave, that is, as having a normative status that is (as we believe) incompatible with being a free and rational person, must be conceptually confused or pragmatically self-contradictory. Indeed, it doesn't *follow* that it must be unsupported or false. After all, there are many forms of unequal authority that we believe to be quite consistent with the equal dignity of rational persons as such. Imagine a sergeant in a citizen army that a fully just society of equals maintains entirely for defensive purposes. In issuing an order to a private, the sergeant addresses a second-personal reason based on relations of superior authority she can quite reasonably expect the private to accept and be guided by from the perspective of one free and equal person among others.

Now we, of course, may believe that a condition of involuntary servitude cannot be endorsed rationally for any conditions, but it is surely possible for someone to believe otherwise. For example, someone might

29. Of course, many things we call "orders," for example, "Heel" said to a cocker spaniel, do not necessarily involve the purported address of a second-personal reason in the sense we have been interested in.

believe, without any obvious incoherence, that such a practice could be justified for the case of imprisoned soldiers of a defeated army of conquest. Indeed, it seems possible for a slaveholder in the antebellum South coherently to have believed, however mistakenly or unjustifiably, that his slaves could be expected rationally to endorse his claim to authority over them. After all, he might have thought, he had rightfully acquired them in accordance with procedures that could be rationally endorsed, from a perspective of freedom and equality, by anyone! He had bought their "contract" in something like the way baseball teams did before the abolition of the "reserve clause" in major-league baseball. (Never mind that the slaves did not consent to their enslavement in the first place.) All this seems absurd to us because it seems obvious that these putative normative relations simply cannot be rationally endorsed from the perspective of one free and rational person among others. But if someone were to believe otherwise, she might think it possible for the equal dignity that a slaveholder's second-personal address implicitly presupposes to be consistent with the superior authority that the slaveholder would explicitly claim in something like the way a sergeant in a just society can explicitly claim authority to command a private whom she must implicitly presuppose to have the same dignity as a free and equal rational person that she does.

It is, consequently, no objection to the argument of this chapter that the argument would entail that practices like slavery are impossible, necessarily conceptually confused, or pragmatically self-contradictory. The argument does not have these consequences or presuppositions.[30] In fact, I am not even here claiming that slavery is immoral. Although I certainly endorse that substantive normative thesis, my argument in this chapter does not depend on it. My claim, again, is only that any address of a second-personal reason, including any from a master to a slave, is committed to the presupposition that addresser and addressee share an equal normative standing as free and rational persons.

---

30. Many slaveholders likely tried to have it both ways, rationalizing their slaves' subjugation by fantasies of a superior authority their slaves could rationally accept that they themselves could not possibly have accepted on reflection. For a fascinating discussion of the ways in which thinking through the legal standing of slaves revealed presuppositional contradictions in antebellum slavery, see Oakes 1990. Oakes discusses a North Carolina Supreme Court Case, *State v. Will,* that found that "there were not only limits to the master's authority but that the slave had a right to resist the master who stepped beyond these limits (161). I am indebted to Elizabeth Anderson for this reference.

Formulating the Argument

We are now in a position to lay out the argument more formally, continuing to bear in mind that the premises all concern second-personal address as such.

1. *Addressing second-personal reasons always presupposes that addressees can freely and rationally determine themselves by the addressed reasons.* This follows directly from Fichte's Analysis. To address a second-personal reason of any kind is to attempt to direct an agent's will through her own free self-determining choices. That is why the issuing and taking up of any second-personal summons whatsoever requires both addresser and addressee to deliberate on the assumption that both are free and rational. Both must assume that both have the capacity to determine themselves by the relevant second-personal reasons.

2. *Addressing second-personal demands or claims always presupposes that the addressee is responsible for compliance.* Accountability of some kind is built into the very idea of a demand or claim, and vice versa (Strawson's Point). The concepts of valid claim or demand, second-personal reason, and responsibility (accountability) all share the same irreducible idea of the authority to claim or demand. If *A* has the standing to demand certain conduct from *B*, then *B* not only thereby has a reason to do what *A* demands; *B* also has a responsibility, including to *A*, such that if *B* does not freely comply, *A* may hold *B* responsible in some way. Exactly what way will vary with the case. *B* may be responsible only for giving some account of his failure to comply, that is, for justifying himself to *A*. Or various reactive attitudes or even legal coercive sanctions may be appropriate. But in any case, it is part of the very idea of *A*'s making a valid demand of *B* that *A* has the authority to relate to *B* in "demanding" ways that: (1) *B* might not want or choose, (2) *A* thereby has justification for, whether or not *B* wants or chooses, and (3) *A* would not have justification for without the relevant authority.

3. *Addressing second-personal reasons always presupposes that addressees can rationally accept these reasons (and the authority relations in which they are grounded). Thus, although second-personal reasons are frequently addressed to someone standing in some more specific normative relation, the addressee is more properly conceived of as a-person-who-happens-to-stand-in-that-normative-relation. Second-personal justification is thus always ultimately justification to another as free and rational.* Here there are two

points. The first, which is that second-personal address presupposes that the addressee can rationally accept the addressed reasons and the authority relations in which they are grounded, follows from premise 1. The only way an agent can freely and rationally determine himself by a reason is by rationally accepting and acting on it. And the only way an agent can accept a second-personal reason is by accepting the authority relations in which it is grounded.

The second point is that the addresser must also presuppose that the addressee can be expected to accept these things as a free and rational person and, therefore, that although second-personal reasons frequently invoke more specific normative relations, the reason is more properly conceived of as addressed to a-person-who-happens-to-stand-in-that-putatively-normative-relation. It is not enough for the sergeant to presuppose that the private she addresses actually accepts her authority. The private cannot freely and rationally determine himself by the reason the sergeant purports to give him unless he rationally accepts it. And that he is himself a private, or that he actually accepts the sergeant's authority over him, is irrelevant to whether he can accept this role rationally. That depends, rather, on whether, as a rational person, he should accept this normative relation in general and, as a consequence, accept the sergeant's authority should he occupy, as he does, the position of private.

It is important that premise 3 concerns second-personal reasons in particular. Whether or not practical reasons are subject to any test of rational acceptance or motivation in general,[31] there are special reasons for thinking that second-personal reasons must be owing to the relation between second-personal address and accountability. We have noted before Gary Watson's point that holding someone morally responsible carries such presuppositions as constraints of "moral address" (1987: 264–265). But Fichte's Analysis shows that there is no relevant difference in this respect between moral address and second-personal address in general. Any second-personal address whatsoever purports to initiate a relation in which an addressee is accountable to an addresser. And the lesson of Fichte's Analysis is that second-personal reasons are always ultimately addressed to agents as free and rational. So an addresser can intelligibly hold an addressee accountable for acting as a second-personal address directs only if she can presuppose that her addressee can ration-

31. That is, whether "existence internalism" is true (Darwall 1983: 54–55).

ally accept the reason and determine himself by it in his own deliberation. Even though second-personal reasons frequently invoke more specific normative relations, therefore, they are always ultimately addressed to a-person-who-happens-to-stand-in-that-specific-putatively-normative-relation. And whether that specific relation actually is normative for the addressee, whether it is one whose specifications he is genuinely responsible for complying with, depends on whether he can accept it as a rational person, that is, from a perspective that he and his addressee share as free and rational.

When we address second-personal reasons and hold addressees accountable for complying, we are committed to the presupposition that they are appropriate objects of reactive attitudes, therefore blameworthy, when they fail to comply without excuse. But even when reactive attitudes involve some distinctive person's perspective (that of an injured party, as in resentment, or the perspective of the wrongdoer, as in guilt), they always also involve the generalized or impartial perspective of any person with second-personal competence. Blame, in particular, is felt not as from some particular point of view; rather, it implicitly addresses demands as from the perspective of any free and rational person. So in addressing any demand and holding an addressee responsible, the addresser is committed to an authority he has in common with his addressee to address demands in blaming and holding responsible simply as a person with second-personal competence.

We have sometimes put a corollary of this last point by saying that to hold someone responsible for complying with a demand is to be committed to the presupposition that the addressee of our demand can hold herself responsible for complying with it. To do this she must be able to make the demand of herself from the perspective that she and we can share: the generalized perspective of second-personally competent persons. In presupposing she can do this, therefore, the addresser is committed to the authority of this perspective.

4. *Addressing a demand always presupposes a distinction between legitimate (second-personally justified) ways of relating to someone directively ("demandingly") that respect him as a free and rational person, on the one hand, and illegitimately coercing him, on the other.* The last two paragraphs of commentary on premise 3 already asserted that second-personal address invariably commits us to a common authority of addresser and addressee alike, as second-personally competent, to hold themselves and

one another responsible for complying with whatever demands can be authorized from this perspective. This is already a significant result. But for it to have real teeth, we need that second-personal address is in general committed to there being some such latter demands (and hence, by the argument in 3, to second-personally competent agents having the authority to hold one another responsible for complying with these).

This is what premise 4 gives us. In making or holding anyone responsible for complying with a demand of any sort, we are invariably committed to a distinction between relating to that person directively ("demandingly") in a way that nonetheless respects him as a free and rational person, on the one hand, and treating him simply coercively, that is illegitimately coercing him, and so failing to respect him as a free and rational person, on the other. This, again, is Pufendorf's Point from the addresser's perspective projected into general second-personal space (as a consequence of Fichte's Analysis). Holding someone responsible with reactive attitudes, as Strawson emphasizes, simultaneously makes demands of the other as second-personally competent and respects him in recognizing his having an authority in having this competence (1968: 93). And this commits us to the proposition that relating to someone in a demanding way (even if only by making someone the object of a reactive attitude) requires warrant by the requisite second-personal reasons, that is, that simply demanding conduct or attempting to coerce it from someone is illegitimate, a violation of the other's authority as second-personally competent.[32] *It follows that one demand that anyone has the authority to make is that he not be subject to demanding (coercive) conduct that cannot be justified by second-personal reasons.*[33]

Call any form of relating to someone that one has standing to realize toward him by virtue of his failure to comply with a justified demand, whether or not he wants or chooses, a "sanction."[34] Then, by definition, the address of any second-personal reason will presuppose the standing

32. I have been helped in this paragraph by Jacob Ross.

33. Note the similarity between this and Fichte's principle of right: "I must in all cases recognize the free being outside me as a free being, i.e., I must limit my freedom through the concept of the possibility of his freedom" (2000: 49).

34. Although I pursue the argument here in terms of sanctions, it could as well be put in terms of the initial demand, which an addresser must also assume is a properly authorized way of relating to another "demandingly" that would be illegitimate without the requisite authority.

to exact sanctions should the addressee fail to comply. We have from Fichte's Analysis that any such address is ultimately to another as a free and rational person. It follows that the addresser is committed to a distinction between making a legitimate demand on someone's conduct (including with the notice of sanctions for unexcused noncompliance) in a way that (rightfully) recognizes the addressee as a free and rational person, on the one hand, and attempting illegitimately to determine his will by a mere threat of the unwanted alternative in which the sanction consists (that is, by coercion, which notice of the sanctions would be if she lacked the relevant authority), or to impose her will by some other illegitimate means, on the other.[35]

Now it might be thought that even if, say, the sergeant of our example would be committed to thinking that without authority her demands and sanctions would lack legitimacy, it would not follow that they would then be illegitimate in the sense of violating the private's authority.[36] She might think that, even if she were to lack a (Hohfeldian claim-) right to sanction the private, which would entail a corresponding duty of the private not to resist, she would nonetheless have a (Hohfeldian) liberty to impose her will on him, including by threatening the very same evils in which, as thing actually stand, her justified sanction consists.[37] But this is not a possibility she can contemplate from a second-person perspective for all but one of the reasons we mentioned in the last paragraph. In holding the private responsible at all, she is committed to respecting his authority as second-personally competent. She is committed, therefore, to thinking that any second-personal authority at all, which itself partly is a standing to hold free and rational agents responsible, must be complemented by

35. Alternatively, the initial demand presupposes a distinction between addressing the demand in a way that respects the addressee's authority (because it is justified second-personally) and trying to get him to do it by simply demanding that he do it, which would be illegitimate and disrespectful.

36. I am indebted to Gerald Gaus and to Eric Mack for raising this concern. The argument in the text to this point recalls Hart's "to assert a general right is to claim in relation to some particular action the equal right of all men to be free in the absence of any of those special conditions which constitute a special right to limit another's freedom; to assert a special right is to assert in relation to some particular action a right constituted by such special conditions to restrict another's freedom" (1955: 188). The objection I consider in this paragraph is one that Mack (1976) raises against Hart.

37. Alternatively, perhaps it would simply violate someone else's authority. I am indebted here to Ira Lindsay. What follows responds also to this possibility.

a second-personal authority that anyone can have just in being second-personally competent.

We can get the conclusion that anyone has the authority to demand that she not be subjected to non-second-personally-justifiable demands more directly from premise 3 as follows: Any second-personal authority at all can exist only if it can be rationally accepted by free and rational agents as such. But for that to be true there must be grounds for such an acceptance, and whatever interests free and rational agents have as such would have to be among such grounds. It is conceptually necessary, moreover, that free and rational agents have an interest in not being subject to others' arbitrary will since that would, by definition, interfere with the exercise of their free and rational agency. As this interest must be among the grounds that free and rational agents have for accepting any authoritative demands at all, it necessarily supports a demand, as free and rational, against being subject to demands that cannot be so justified. It follows, again, that second-personally competent agents have the authority to demand that they not be subject to mere impositions of will, that is, to demanding (coercive) conduct that cannot be justified second-personally.

5. *Addressing second-personal demands always presupposes, therefore, that the addressee has a second-personal authority as free and rational and, consequently, that addresser and addressee share a common authority to make claims on one another.* In presupposing that coercing or simply imposing her will on her addressee would be illegitimate, an addresser must therefore presuppose that this would violate her addressee's authority as a free and rational person. So any address of second-personal reasons must presuppose that addresser and addressee share a (second-personal) authority to make demands of one another as free and rational persons.

It is important to see that not just any distinction between appropriate and inappropriate conduct toward someone as rational commits one to shared second-personal authority. Someone might undertake a kind of rational therapy or training, applying "sanctions" as a corrective when someone fails to act rationally. This would commit a rational trainer to some distinction between appropriate and inappropriate "correction" of the other as rational, but it wouldn't be the distinction I am pointing to here, and so it wouldn't commit him to recognizing that the other has a second-personal authority.[38] Similarly, Plato's argument against Thrasy-

---

38. I am indebted here to discussion with Shelly Kagan.

machus in the *Republic* that there must be a distinction between correct and incorrect rule in the sense of proper versus improper care of the governed does not entail such authority either, any more than a gardener must assume that her vegetables have any claim against her if she tends them poorly. It is the assumption of legitimate authority understood as the standing to address second-personal reasons that generates this presupposition.

6. *Addressing second-personal reasons always, therefore, presupposes a common basic dignity of persons.* If, as I suggest, we understand the dignity of persons to consist or be grounded in the second-personal authority of rational and free (second-personally) competent agents, then this follows by definition from premise 5 (assuming, of course, the "forensic" character of the concept of person as involving accountability (second-person competence)) (Locke 1975: 346).

7. *Addressing second-personal reasons always presupposes autonomy of the will (second-personal competence).* Taking premises 3 and 5 (or 6) together, we have that any second-personal address whatsoever presupposes an addressee's capacity to accept and act on reasons that are grounded, ultimately, in an authority that addresser and addressee share as free and rational. We are now back in the same terrain we traversed when we analyzed Kant's "fact of reason" in second-personal terms. When we hold people responsible, we imply that they have it within them to act as they should, not just in the sense that the obligatory alternative was deliberatively open to them, or that they weren't physically prevented, but also that they had a process of reasoning available to them through which they could, in principle, have determined the validity of relevant second-personal reasons and been motivated to act on them. Since second-personal reasons are not outcome-regarding, we need therefore attribute no particular (object-dependent) desires to those we aim to hold accountable. But we must assume that they have access to a source of reasons simply in being rational wills who are apt for second-personal address, hence, a source that is "independent of any features of the objects of volition." It follows that we must assume autonomy of the will, that is, that the will can be "a law to itself" independently of object-dependent desires or any outcome-value of their objects. As I argued at the end of Chapter 9, this is the most promising line of support for Kant's claim that the validity of the CI (a "formal" rather than "material" principle [Kant 1996b: 19–31]) is a necessary condition for the possibility of moral obligation.

Second-personal competence, moreover, is what autonomy of the will must be if we are accountable to one another simply as rational agents who are apt for second-personal address. The requisite process of reasoning must itself be one that expresses, and enables us to specify, respect for the common second-personal authority we presuppose whenever we address second-personal reasons and hold one another accountable. Chapter 12 argues that what can fill this role is contractualist reasoning interpreted through Kant's idea of the "Realm of Ends"—in our terms, a pattern of reasoning that is grounded in the common (second-personal) authority that all second-personally competent agents share. Roughly, we hold ourselves morally accountable to others when we impose demands on ourselves that we think it sensible to impose on anyone from a perspective that we can all share as free (second-personally competent) and rational. And we presuppose that anyone we hold thus accountable is someone who can in principle also accept and impose these same demands on himself by taking up this impartial second-person perspective and seeing the sense of imposing them on anyone.[39]

39. We might, as I mentioned before, see the relevant impartial perspective as one we share and that demands made from that standpoint are ones we make as the moral community in the first-personal plural. As I also emphasized, however, the perspective is no less second-personal for that, since it essentially involves address.

— 11 —

Freedom and Practical Reason

The last chapter argued that the dignity of persons and autonomy of the will not only entail one another as the Reciprocity Thesis asserts, but also that they are presupposed by the second-person standpoint. Both are transcendental conditions for the very possibility of second-personal reasons (or "normative felicity conditions," as I have called them). So we must presuppose them when we address second-personal reasons of any kind.

Even if this argument succeeds in its own terms, however, it might seem to have only limited vindicatory force, since it appears just to widen the circle of reciprocity. What can assure us that the notion of a second-personal reason and its companion ideas of valid demand, accountability, and the authority to claim and demand are not all themselves empty? Even if taking up the second-person stance commits us to equal dignity and autonomy, that is consistent with that standpoint and its associated commitments being no more than rationally optional, or worse, illusory.

In this chapter, I respond to this challenge by placing second-personal reasons within a more comprehensive understanding of practical reason and our freedom as rational agents. Developing Fichte's insights, I argue that the second-person standpoint gives us a perspective on our own agency that enables us to appreciate a fundamental difference between theoretical and practical reason and so improves our grasp of reasons for acting. Were someone somehow to avoid taking it up, consequently, she would fail to appreciate what we, who have taken it up, can validate as reasons from a more comprehensive view that includes it.

Before I begin to lay out this line of thought, however, we should note that there is no obvious way simply to refuse to see things second-personally. The force of Strawson's original arguments in "Freedom and

277

Resentment" partly derives from the fact that reactive attitudes, along with their second-personal presuppositions, are aspects of the human condition that are not optional in any realistic psychological sense. Recognizable human life without second-personal thought and experience is simply unimaginable, as the example of Stalin helps confirm as an extreme case.[1] In itself, however, this has only limited philosophical significance. The philosophical question is whether we should see things in this way. As Hume noted in another context, that we find ourselves naturally taking up this perspective when we leave our studies does not settle the reflective philosophical question we raise within them (1978: 455). And after all, the capacity for philosophical reflection is no less distinctively human than is the disposition to reactive attitudes.

Or again, a Fichtean summons from another free and rational agent will usually be enough to set us to thinking second-personally, if only in considering how to respond.[2] But even if we can't avoid such acknowledgment and its accompanying presuppositions when we take up a summons, we can step back from these and ask whether, on reflection, we should still accept them. And nothing suggests that fundamental philosophical reflection on practical reason must be second-personal itself.

All the same, it is worth noting that even though the argument of the last chapter amounts to a reciprocity thesis, it is a significantly wider one than that concerning morality and autonomy of the will. So the argument of the preceding chapter may have significant vindicatory force even without the argument of this one. There have been serious philosophical critiques of the "morality system" and principle- or obligation-based conceptions of morality, not to mention rejection of moral obligations' claim to provide universal categorical reasons, but there has been little if any attempt to reject or question the whole range of second-personal concepts we have identified.[3]

1. See the discussion of Stalin in Chapter 6. Compare Scheffler's remark about the attempt to regiment reactive attitudes along consequentialist lines: "[T]he idea that it would be wrong for the innocent woman and her associates to resent the man for harming her in order to make optimal use of his causal opportunities, but appropriate for them to resent or be indignant with him for not harming her, seems psychologically and humanly absurd" (2004: 230).

2. Cf. Korsgaard: "It is impossible to hear words of a language you know as mere noise. In hearing your words as *words,* I acknowledge that you are someone" (1996e: 143).

3. Thus, we should note that one of the most influential critics of the "morality system," Bernard Williams—who coined the phrase "morality system" itself in *Ethics and the Limits*

Normativity and the Open Question: Belief and Truth

In this chapter, I deepen and extend the contrast between theoretical and practical reason that I began to develop in the last two chapters. I take it to be uncontroversial that the question of practical reason is what we have reason to do and that that of theoretical reason is what we have reason to believe. Using Velleman's terms, we can say that the "formal aim" of action is to do whatever there is (normative) reason to do and that the formal aim of belief is to believe whatever there is reason to believe.[4] These formal aims are explicitly normative (as, indeed, any such formal aim would have to be). Equivalently, we could say that the formal aims of belief and action are, respectively, to believe and act as we should, as is warranted, as would be apt or correct, as is best supported by normative reasons (and so, in this sense, as is best), and so on.

In addition to its formal aim, Velleman says that belief also has a "substantive aim": to believe (only) what is true. What makes truth, or believing only truths, a substantive aim of belief is that satisfying it is conceptually distinguishable from satisfying belief's (explicitly normative) formal aim: being what one should believe, or being warranted, apt, or correct (to believe). "What should I believe?" is a different question from "What is true?"

Trivially, we should believe whatever we should believe, whatever would satisfy belief's formal aim, just as, trivially, we should do whatever we should do, hence whatever would satisfy action's formal aim. But with belief we can say something more substantive owing to the nature of belief. Belief is the mental state of representing the way things are with the aim of getting it right, that is, aiming to represent things as they actually are or to believe only truths. Consequently, that we should believe only what is true (or what is likeliest to be true relative to our evidence) follows from the nature of belief. True beliefs are correct, where being correct is conceptually distinct from being true. If someone makes a counterfactual supposition just to see what would follow from it, it is a

---

of Philosophy—nonetheless defends the idea of "basic human rights" (1985: 192). For an earlier important criticism of law-based moral conceptions, see Anscombe 1958. See also Slote 1992 and Baier 1993. The classic critique of the claim that moral obligations are categorical is Foot 1972.

4. Velleman 2000. I am much indebted to Velleman's work on the aim of belief in what follows.

bad joke to say that his supposition is mistaken or incorrect. False beliefs, like false answers, are mistaken or incorrect, however.

The notions of normative reason for belief or action, or of a belief's or action's being correct, warranted, apt, appropriate, fitting, and so on, are all normative concepts. Moore's "open question" argument is often taken to be a useful test of whether a concept is normative or not (1993: 67).[5] So long as we bear in mind that we cannot infer identity or distinctness of properties, and, as well, that our grasp on a concept may be imperfect in various ways, we can take the fact that certain questions seem conceptually open as an indication that distinct concepts are in play (Railton 1989: 158). For example, if a philosopher uses 'good' as a synonym for 'pleasure', we can take the fact that it seems possible to ask, without conceptual confusion, "I grant that the experience would be pleasurable, but is that any reason to bring it about, desire, or have any other particular attitude toward it?" as showing that 'good', as this philosopher is using it, does not express a normative concept. By the same token, however, we must be careful not to conclude too quickly from the fact that a question of apparently the right form is logically closed that the relevant concept is a normative one. Thus, from the fact that it is not logically open to ask without conceptual confusion, "I grant that p is true, but is there any reason to believe p?" it would be a mistake to conclude that truth is a normative concept or, even more, to conclude that a 'p is true' means the same as 'p is something one should believe.' What closes the question is not that these have the same meaning, but what we noted above about the concept of belief. We simply don't count a way of representing or regarding p as true as a belief that p, unless it is a species of representing or regarding with the aim of so representing p only if p. For example, supposing that p differs from believing that p for this very reason.

Normativity and the Open Question: Action, Desire, and Outcome Value

We get leverage on the formal question of what there is reason to believe by directly considering what is true, or what is likeliest to be true given

5. On this point, see Darwall, Gibbard, and Railton 1997: 3–4.

our evidence.[6] Consider, then, a picture of the theoretical standpoint that is analogous to that of the naïve practical standpoint that we briefly discussed in the last two chapters. Experience purports to be of an independent order of fact and involves inclinations to beliefs that putatively represent that order. As we gain more experience, we correct our representations with the aim of representing things more accurately, believing only what is true. What makes it possible for experiences to confirm or conflict with one another is their objective purport. I see what seems to be a straight stick lying on the bank of a pond and notice that, when it is placed in the pond, it looks bent. Perhaps I initially believe that it is bent. But as I gain more experience with sticks and ponds, I come to the conclusion that sticks retain their straightness in ponds; they only look bent.

On this picture, the rational formation of beliefs about an independent order of fact like the empirical world is guided by responsiveness to that order, that is, to states of the world as they actually are. There is, of course, no such thing as pure responsiveness in experience—that is the "myth of the given" (Sellars 1997). Any experience that can bear on what to believe must already be conceptualized and taken within some theoretical framework. By the same token, however, unless the formation of beliefs about independent facts involved an element of receptivity (in empirical belief, responsiveness to the world as it actually is), it would be hard to see how belief formation, at least about the world, could proceed rationally.

This is just another form of a point we encountered in Chapter 9, namely, that although there are varieties of freedom, negative and positive, which even a theoretical reasoner must presuppose, nothing analogous to Kantian autonomy of the will seems to be among them. When it comes to forming beliefs about independent facts, reasons for belief cannot be found independently of properties of the objects of belief. To the contrary, rational beliefs of this kind must be guided by the very world that provides their objects. They must be object-guided and thus object-dependent.[7]

6. Evidence is a relation between propositions. Evidence that p (is true), provides reason to believe that p (is true).

7. This doesn't mean that they must not also be to some degree principle-dependent, but given the substantive aim of belief they can hardly be principle-dependent in the way autonomy of the will requires.

Now, in practical reason, the question is not what to believe but what to do. Nevertheless, there is a way of thinking of the practical standpoint, what I have been calling the naïve (first-person) practical standpoint, according to which it is formally analogous to the standpoint of theoretical reason as we have just pictured it. This, again, is the way that Moore conceives of practical reasoning in *Principia Ethica*. According to Moore in *Principia*, there is a single fundamental ethical concept, the concept of good or intrinsic value, or, as Moore also puts it, of something's being such as "ought to exist for its own sake" (1993: 34). So far as this concept goes, anything whatsoever might instantiate it: experiences, objects, relations, states of affairs, or, indeed, actions. Something has intrinsic value in this sense if, and only if, it ought to exist or, as we might alternatively formulate it, if the state of its existing ought to be.

What suits Moore's conception of intrinsic value to the naïve practical standpoint is that it provides a conception of the value of possible states of the world and hence of the value of outcomes. But this means that it also provides a way of seeing action as having, like belief, a substantive aim. Whereas belief's substantive aim is to represent the world as it actually is, action's substantive aim, on this Moorean picture, would be to bring about intrinsically valuable outcomes—the world as it ought to be, so far as this is feasible.

Actually, in *Principia*, Moore's position is that bringing about intrinsically valuable outcomes is action's formal aim, since he there maintains that the concept of being what one should do is definable in terms of the concept of intrinsic value and empirical causal concepts concerning the outcomes of possible actions. To assert that a given act is what one should do, Moore says, "is obviously to assert that more good or less evil will exist in the world, if it be adopted than if anything else be done instead" (77).[8] This claims an identity of meaning between "what one should do" (alternatively, "what action is best supported by normative reasons," "what is the correct, most warranted, or best act, etc."), on the one hand, and, on the other, "which action is the one, of those available to the agent, that would produce the most intrinsic value." And it characterizes action's formal aim in explicitly instrumental terms. Even if an act has intrinsic value just in virtue of the kind of act it is, Moore believes, the

---

8. Moore formulates this in terms of what is "absolutely right or obligatory," but it is clear enough that this is what he has in mind.

concept of the act's being what one should do, all things considered, is nonetheless identical with the concept of its having the most instrumental value of any act available to the agent (where that instrumental value might include its "bringing about" the intrinsically valuable state of the act's being performed).

Intrinsic value for Moore is value as an existent: "When we assert that a thing is good, what we mean is that its existence or reality is good" (1993: 171). The idea that an act is intrinsically valuable, therefore, is that its existence or reality is good.[9] Moore takes this to imply that the concept of there being a reason to perform the act is the same idea as its being the case that, if the act is performed, the world will then contain something that is intrinsically valuable as an existent; a state of the world will be brought about that ought to be simply by virtue of what it is (or would be). It is no exaggeration therefore to say that this understanding of reasons for action identifies them with action's instrumental value— its capacity to produce intrinsically valuable outcomes, including, perhaps, the outcome of the act itself being performed. The concept of an action's value as an action is thus identified with that of the act's capacity to produce things with intrinsic value as existents (including, perhaps, the act itself), outcomes that ought to be just by virtue of what they are.

Thus in *Principia*, Moore held that the formal aim of action is to produce intrinsically valuable outcomes. In this, however, Moore was clearly mistaken, as he himself gave us the conceptual tool to see: the open question argument. We can suppose it to be a fact that a given action will produce the most valuable outcomes and still sensibly, that is, coherently, ask whether one should perform that act (alternatively, whether it is the act best supported by normative reasons, the best act, and so on).[10] Identifying the formal aim of action with its capacity to produce intrinsically valuable outcomes thus fails the open question test.[11] Similarly, one can deny that an act with the most intrinsically valuable outcomes is what one should do without self-contradiction or conceptual confusion. So the Moore of *Principia* to the contrary notwithstanding,

9. On this point, see Moore 1993: 197. I discuss what Moore says there in Darwall 2003b.

10. I hope this will strike the reader at this point as understatement. Otherwise the claim that any second-personal reasons exist would be not just false but incoherent!

11. As W. D. Ross noted (1930: 8–9).

action's formal aim cannot be identified with the bringing about of intrinsically valuable outcomes.

But this opens up the possibility that bringing about intrinsically valuable outcomes might nonetheless be action's substantive aim. Perhaps, that is, just as accurately representing the world as it actually is is belief's substantive aim, so analogously might action have the substantive aim of bringing about the world as it ought to be, subject to constraints of feasibility. Moreover, as I have been suggesting over the last two chapters, this will indeed seem a plausible thing to think if we consider action from the naïve (first-person) practical standpoint of an agent with desires deliberating about what to do.

Desires, like beliefs, involve representations. Just as a belief is always a belief that p, for some p, so also, on a familiar philosophical picture, at least, is a desire always a desire that p, for some p.[12] If, for example, I want a chocolate ice cream cone, what I want is that I eat such a cone. But belief and desire differ in their directions of fit. Beliefs have the mind-to-world direction of fit—they are correct when they fit the world; however, desires have the world-to-mind direction of fit—from their perspective, at least, the world is "correct," as it should be, when it fits them (Anscombe 1957; Platts 1979: 256–257; Smith 1994: 111–119).

Care is required, however, in interpreting this familiar idea. We should not take it to mean that desires dictate to the world in the sense that a desire that p somehow makes it the case that p has value or ought to obtain. That would be getting normative reasons on the cheap, deriving an ethical 'ought' from a psychological 'is'; and it would fail also to appreciate the "backgrounding" of desire from the agent's point of view (Darwall 1983; Pettit and Smith 1990). The point is rather that in desiring that p, an agent regards p as valuable, as a state of the world that ought to be.[13] She takes it that there is normative reason to bring p about.

12. Although I make use of this familiar picture of desire here, I think there are good reasons for being suspicious of it, some of which I discuss in Darwall 2002b: 47–49, 92–94. First, benevolent desires have not just a propositional "direct object" but also an "indirect object": the being for whose sake the (beneficial) state of affairs is desired. Second, there are many desires for objects (e.g., to engage in a certain activity) that cannot adequately be characterized as desires for a state in which one engages in that activity.

13. More carefully, we should say that in desiring that p, it seems, or it is to the agent as if, p is valuable or a state that ought to be. One can, of course, desire that p and judge there is no reason whatsoever to bring p about, just as one can have an experience that is as of a bent stick in a pond and judge that there is no reason to think that the stick is really bent. I discuss these points at greater length in Darwall 2001.

From the naïve practical standpoint, therefore, an agent will take herself to have normative reasons to bring about the objects of her desires not because her desires create or are a source of reasons but because in desiring these objects, she sees them as states she has reason to bring about. From this perspective, the agent looks, as it were, through her desires and agency to how the world might better be and to what she can do to bring this about. Her desires seem to provide a form of "practical experience" that is analogous to experience of the world as this operates in reasoning about what to believe about the world as it actually is.[14] They present themselves as a form of epistemic access to the intrinsic value of the states that are their objects, and hence, to normative reasons for bringing these states about. They will not seem the only form of access; neither will they seem incorrigible. Being pleased that p also involves seeing p as something good or as a state that ought to be.[15] And since pleasure differs from desire precisely in the fact that pleasure's objects are conceived to obtain in fact and desire's are conceived not as actual but only as possible, pleasure may seem to provide more credible evidence that its object is valuable and ought to be.

Thus, just as a theoretical reasoner takes his experiences as evidence of the way the world actually is and attempts by comparing and extending his experiences in various ways to come to beliefs that are likeliest to satisfy belief's substantive aim, so likewise does a naïve practical reasoner treat her practical experiences, her desires and other like responses, as evidence of what possible states of the world would be intrinsically good, hence, of how the world should be. And in so doing, she effectively treats action as having a substantive aim—bringing about the world as it should be—that is analogous to belief's: representing the world as it actually is.

Now if the idea of intrinsic value is itself a normative notion, it may seem puzzling that it could figure in a substantive rather than a formal aim. However, we saw above why bringing about valuable outcomes cannot be the formal aim of action. The concept of an act one ought to do is a distinct concept from that of an act that would bring about the most valuable outcomes, that is, possible states of the world that ought to be, or even from the concept of an act's being the sole constituent of a state of the world that ought to be. We need not worry about whether intrinsic value is an explicitly normative concept or, if it is, precisely what

14. For a defense of this conception of desire, see Stampe 1987.
15. As Sidgwick's view of pleasure (1967) brings out. For a discussion of Sidgwick's ethics along the lines presented in this paragraph, see Darwall 1974.

sort of normativity it has.[16] It is enough for our purposes that, whatever normativity it might have, the proposition that an act would bring about the most valuable outcomes is neither identical with nor entails the proposition that the agent should perform the act (all things considered). Whether or not any form of consequentialism is true as a normative thesis, it is certainly not a conceptual truth.[17]

Moore says in *Principia* that, if something has intrinsic value, it "ought to exist for its own sake." It is hard to see how to take such "ought to exist" or "ought to be" claims literally, since it would seem that only what can be normatively guided can be subject to oughts, and neither mere existence nor being are capable of that. The most natural way of interpreting such claims is to understand them as asserting that certain valuing attitudes, namely, the one we have toward possible states of affairs, are warranted, say, that something is desirable or worth bringing about. If we interpret them in this way (and assume that, as a conceptual matter, being desirable or worth bringing about makes a normative claim on action), then it will follow from the fact that an outcome is valuable that there is some reason for the agent to realize it. It is the entailment in the other direction—between there being a reason for the agent to do something and there being an intrinsically valuable outcome that the action would realize—that is not conceptually guaranteed. Hence, it cannot follow from the fact that an action would realize the most valuable outcomes that it is what the agent should do, all things considered. So far as the concept of reason for acting, or of what an agent should do, goes, there might be reasons for acting other than those provided by the value of outcomes.

But just for this reason, again, the aim of bringing about outcomes can be regarded as substantive with respect to action. Although it cannot be action's formal aim, it might nonetheless be action's substantive aim. And, again, this is the way things seem from the naïve practical standpoint. What action seems to be for is the bringing about of valuable states.

16. Neither need we concern ourselves with whether such value can be agent-neutral (as Moore himself certainly supposed) or whether it is agent-relative. What matters, for present purposes, is the relation between the value of outcomes and reasons to act.

17. That no interesting claim about the good could be a conceptual truth was, of course, one of Moore's main points in *Principia*. That is why it is so ironic (or so revelatory of the depth of his error) that he could have failed to see that the same thing must be true about the right (or the rational) to do.

Free Agency and the Second-Person Standpoint

What Fichte's arguments demonstrate, however, is that the perspective we get on our own agency in the second-person standpoint shows us that this cannot be right. When we are summoned to the second-person perspective, we deliberate under the assumptions that we are agents and that as agents we can act on reasons that are not outcome-based. In taking up a second-personal summons, I relate to another who is relating to me as an agent and perforce presuppose this common agency in my deliberations. My deliberative stance requires me to assume that we both have a kind of freedom that has no analogue in theoretical reasoning, just as Fichte says, and, consequently, that bringing about valuable outcomes could not possibly be action's substantive aim. Because believing only what is true is belief's substantive aim, it is psychologically impossible to believe something on grounds unrelated to that, say, because it would be more desirable to believe it. If you are considering whether to believe p and reason that believing p would be desirable, you cannot then conclude your reasoning in a belief that p (as you could if you thought that p was more likely to be true than not). Considerations other than those appropriately related to truth are reasons of the wrong kind for belief. If action's substantive aim were to bring about valuable states, it would likewise be psychologically impossible to decide, intend, or do something on any other grounds. Considerations of other kinds would be reasons of the wrong kind for action. But we see from the second-person standpoint that this is not the case; someone can decide not to step on your foot just by acknowledging your authority to demand that he not do so.

Moreover, in deliberating second-personally, I assume not just that my co-deliberator and I are both free agents, but also that we therefore have a common second-personal authority that grounds second-personal reasons. And here again I confront a fundamental difference with theoretical reasoning. Second-personal practical authority has no clear analogue in theoretical reasoning about what to believe. There can be no fundamentally second-personal reasons for belief, and hence there is no theoretical standing that is fundamentally second-personal. I can, of course, believe something because you say so, but if I do, the second-personal standing I give you in my reasoning is defeasible by your epistemic authority, that is, by your relation to facts of the world as.[18] When we take up the second-

18. I emphasize that the second-personal theoretical authority is defeasible by epistemic

person deliberative stance, however, we recognize a kind of reason for acting, a second-personal reason, that neither derives from nor is reducible to any value of states or outcomes. And in so doing, we recognize a practical standing that is fundamentally second-personal, which neither depends upon nor can be defeated by the other's relation to any independent order of value, that is, by whatever facts there may be about how the world should be.

To see this more vividly, suppose, first, that you are considering what to believe about the economy's future direction, say, whether it will recover in the next quarter. You examine evidence of various kinds and form the belief that it will not. You then talk to me, who is convinced that the economy will bounce back. You and I engage in what Pettit and Smith (1996) call a serious "conversation of the intellectual kind." In the course of listening to my reasons, you become persuaded that what I am taking as evidence is misleading in various respects and that, even if it weren't, it would nonetheless be overridden by better reasons for thinking the economy won't recover for at least another two quarters. But I persist. "Trust me," I say, "things have to get better soon." Is it possible for you to believe that the economy will soon improve just because I have told you it will?[19] That is, can you believe that it will get better simply for the reason that I have told you (or, at least tried to tell you) that it will? You could certainly believe this if you suspected that, despite the weakness of my stated reasons, my beliefs might be responding to other evidence that I cannot perhaps articulate. You could even believe it if you thought for some other reason that my beliefs on this matter might be likelier than yours to be true (say, because God had caused this). But without your supposing some such connection between my beliefs and facts about the world as they are anyway, it would simply be impossible for you to believe that the economy will recover presently just for the reason that I say it will (though I could of course cause you to believe it). To give me authority in reasoning about what to believe, you must take me to have

---

authority. I take what I am saying to be consistent with various kinds of default second-personal theoretical authority that might be ordinarily presupposed in interpersonal theoretical reasoning (Burge 1993; Coady 1992; Foley 1994; Hinchman 2000; Moran 2005; Pettit and Smith 1996).

19. As opposed, say, to being simply *caused* in some nonrational way to believe it by my saying so without taking either anything I say or my saying it as a reason to believe that the economy will improve.

some (epistemic) authority on the questions of fact my beliefs concern. My claim on your beliefs and your freedom of belief are both constrained by belief's substantive aim: accurate representation of the world as it is anyway.

Now, as we have noted before, there is a kind of practical case, that of advice, that is structurally identical to the theoretical case. In fact, we might regard it as a special instance of theoretical reasoning, one in which the beliefs in question concern the practical question of what one should do. If you ask me for advice on where to invest your retirement funds during the next quarter, and you trust me, then any authority you accord me will similarly depend on what authority you take me to have on an independent question of fact, namely, what would be a sensible investment in the current economic circumstances.[20] If you take me to have no epistemic authority on this question, then it will simply be impossible for you to treat my advice as reason-giving in the normal way, that is, to give you any reason to think you should do something when I say you should. An advisor's claim on your reasoning, as well as your freedom to treat it as advice, are both constrained by belief's substantive aim: accurate representation, in this case, of (non-second-personal) reasons for acting, whose status as reasons has nothing to do with one person's authority to give them to another.

When, however, someone addresses second-personal reasons, a radically different kind of authority and freedom are in play.[21] Suppose, to vary our familiar example, that it is you who has your foot on top of mine. If you recognize my claim to your removing your foot and my authority to make it, you give me second-person standing in your practical reasoning. You recognize that you should move your foot because I have the authority to demand this as, indeed, does anyone on my behalf. The authority you thus accord me in regulating your conduct by my claim is fundamentally different from that of an advisor. It is on the side of "law" and "command" rather than "counsel," according to Hobbes's famous distinction (1983: XIV.1). Unlike advice, it neither depends upon nor can be defeated by the addresser's epistemic relation to any facts that are themselves independent of the addresser's second-personal authority. Authority of the kind I claim in asking (or implicitly demanding) that

20. I use 'fact' here in a sense that is not metaethically loaded, in which even noncognitivists can accept that there are facts about what one should do.

21. On this point, see, again, Wolff 1970: 7.

you move your foot is fundamentally second-personal. I presume upon your and my (presupposed) equal standing as free and rational persons, and if you recognize my demand, you and I both presuppose that you can move your foot simply by recognizing and acting on the second-personal reason I address to you (or that we both understand the moral community to have been addressing to you before I even opened my mouth).[22]

The crucial point here is that, since second-personal reasons neither reduce to nor derive from the independent value of any outcome, in assuming that you can act for this reason, you and I presuppose that you can act on a reason the recognition of which is independent of your (object-guided) valuation of outcomes, including as these might apparently be given in object-dependent desires. And because we take ourselves to be responsible for acting as these reasons direct, we must also assume that we have a source of motivation to do so that comes just from what makes us subject to these reasons in the first place. As I have argued, therefore, we presuppose the autonomy of our respective wills (as second-personally competent).

It follows that we must assume autonomy of the will from the same perspective through which we get a deliberative purchase on our own agency. In getting an agent's grasp of our own agency, we see that what seemed to be true from a naïve practical standpoint, that action has the substantive aim of bringing about valuable outcomes, is an illusion. If action had bringing about valuable outcomes as its substantive aim, then it would simply be impossible freely and self-consciously to act against this aim, just as it is to believe in the face of what one regards to be conclusive evidence to the contrary.[23] When, however, we summon one another as agents second-personally, we jointly presuppose autonomy of the will and assume we can freely govern ourselves by second-personal reasons, any object-dependent desires to the contrary notwithstanding.

22. Again, moral obligations involve implicit demands that are "in force," as I noted in Chapter 1, even when actual individuals have not explicitly made them. As Strawson points out, "the making of the demand *is* the [moral community's] proneness to [reactive] attitudes" (1968: 92–93). This, again, is like Hart's interpretation of Bentham's account of law (1990: 93–94) involving "quasi-commands." See the discussion of this point in note 17 of Chapter 1.

23. Note: "freely and self-consciously." Although we seem to be able to believe contrary to what we *believe* is better evidence, it is by no means clear that we can believe contrary to what we are then *seeing* as better evidence. And something comparable would be true of action if it had the substantive aim of bringing about intrinsically valuable outcomes.

We should note that the assumed freedom this line of thought supports is no liberty of indifference; action and the will still have a formal aim. Nothing counts as an action in the distinctive sense in which philosophers are interested, that is, as an exercise of genuine agency, unless the agent has some reason for acting, something she herself regards as a normative reason to perform the act and on which she acts, thereby making it her reason. What second-personal deliberation enables us to see is just that action cannot have the substantive aim of bringing about valuable outcomes.

The Metaethics of Practical Reason: Recognitional versus Constructivist Theories

Of course, we can then step back from the second-person standpoint and ask whether we should accept the presuppositions to which we are committed when we take it up. But when we do, we can no longer simply take the appearances of the naïve practical standpoint for granted. We have gained a sophistication about the nature of our agency that dispels our earlier naïveté. By the same token, however, although we can't help but assume autonomy and equal dignity when we deliberate second-personally, nothing compels us to continue to accept these when we step back and ask the most fundamental questions of practical reason.

Still, to deliberate at all, we must assume that there are some normative reasons for acting.[24] So to vindicate the presuppositions of the second-person standpoint, all we need to show is that we have no less reason to accept second-personal reasons than we do to accept reasons for acting of other kinds, for example, those relating to prudence, benevolence, or whatever. The fact is that we can step back from putative reasons of any kind and coherently question whether, or doubt that, what we take to be a reason for acting is a reason in fact. People often take it for granted, for example, that considerations of self-interest or the agent's own welfare give her reasons for acting. But that this is so is a substantive normative thesis and not a conceptual truth. Someone might have full command of the concept of reason for acting but nonetheless be so depressed that he doubts (without incoherence or conceptual confusion) that the fact that something would be for his good is any reason whatsoever for him to

24. For a particularly good discussion of the metaethical consequences of this familiar point, see Enoch forthcoming.

seek it.[25] And similar points can be made for any substantive reason for acting. It is enough, therefore, if we have no less reason to accept second-personal reasons than we do to accept putative reasons for acting of other kinds.

More ambitiously, we can seek to show that on the best philosophical explanations of there being normative reasons for acting at all, there is support also for autonomy and the second-personal reasons that are grounded in the second-person standpoint. Obviously, I cannot even begin to attempt a comprehensive theory of practical reason here.[26] What I can do, however, is to indicate briefly how, on either of two broadly popular strategies that seem to exhaust the field, there may be good philosophical reasons that vindicate the presuppositions of the second-personal standpoint.

An intuitive way of dividing the main alternatives is to consider the relation between normative reasons for acting, on the one hand, and the rationality of deliberation or agency, on the other.[27] Korsgaard formulates the "internalism requirement" by saying that "practical-reason claims, if they are really to present us with reasons for action, must be capable of motivating rational persons" (1986: 11; see also Darwall 1983: 80–81; Smith 1994: 61). But which is the independent variable: reasons or rationality of the person (or deliberative process, or whatever)? Is a person or deliberative process rational by virtue of the fact that she is motivated by or that the process identifies genuinely normative reasons, independently specified? Or is a consideration a normative reason by virtue of the fact that it would be taken as such and motivate a rational person or as the result of a rational deliberative procedure, independently specified?

Cullity and Gaut mark this difference with a useful distinction between *recognitional* and *constructivist* theories (1997: 4). (I take this to be roughly the same distinction as Korsgaard's between *substantive realism* and *procedural realism* [1996e: 36–37].) On a recognitional theory, there exist independent normative reason facts, and whether a person or deliberative procedure is rational depends upon whether she or it adequately registers or recognizes these. *Constructivism,* by contrast, holds, in this context, that what makes something a normative reason for acting is that it would

25. I argue for this at greater length in chapter 1 of Darwall 2002b.
26. I have, however, tried to take steps toward doing so in various places over the years: Darwall 1983, 1985, 1986b, 1990, 1992, and 1997.
27. On this point, see Darwall 1986b.

be taken as such by, and be motivating for, a free and rational agent or as a result of rational deliberation.[28]

This is not the place to consider the merits of these respective meta-ethical approaches, which, as we have defined them here, would seem to exhaust the field. What I seek to do in the rest of the chapter is to say why there are good reasons on either approach to accept the proposition that, as I have already argued in Chapter 10, we must assume from the second-person standpoint, namely, that we have a dignity as free and rational persons that grounds genuine second-personal reasons.

Constructivism and the Second-Person Standpoint

Constructivism (procedural realism) about practical reason is clearly the metaethical position that is most in the spirit of the Fichtean contrast between practical and theoretical reason that I have been emphasizing. The terms in which we have so far drawn the distinction do not require a constructivist account. I have argued that the Fichtean contrast requires a doctrine of autonomy of the will, but it seems possible for dignity and autonomy to be maintained at the deepest normative level within a more recognitionally realist metaphysics. Still, it seems uncontroversial that these doctrines have a greater affinity with a constructivist approach, especially of a Kantian sort (Korsgaard 1996e; Rawls 1980).

What makes someone a constructivist in our current sense is simply that she holds that the existence of normative reasons depends upon what a rational agent, or what someone deliberating about what to do rationally, would take as reasons and be motivated by. The central claim is that it is the rationality of the agent or deliberative procedure that determines normative reasons, rather than vice versa. What is then at issue within constructivism is how to specify the requisite ideal of rational agency or rational deliberation. And there have been, of course, various proposed specifications other than Kantian versions.

But all forms of constructivism agree in rejecting the recognitional realism of the naïve practical standpoint. Even non-Kantian versions of constructivism are committed to this aspect of Kant's "Copernican rev-

28. This is also a kind of *existence internalism*, since it holds that being motivating (for a rational agent) is essential to being a normative reason for acting. For the distinction between *existence internalism* and *judgment internalism*, see Darwall 1983: 54–55. I discuss different varieties of internalism more comprehensively in Darwall 1997.

olution" in the practical sphere. Practical normative facts are not just "there" to be recognized or not. Rather their "way of being" is within the practical standpoint, as presuppositions and commitments of practical reasoning. Constructivism is by definition, then, a "sophisticated" position. (Indeed, to its critics, this is its problem. It is too sophisticated, they think, and out of touch with reality.)

Moreover, it can be argued that much as constructivism is the meta-ethical position that is most in the spirit of the Kantian/Fichtean ideas and arguments of the last two chapters, so also is a Kantian constructivism the version that is truest to constructivism's spirit. Unsurprisingly, the most popular versions of constructivism build a measure of self-reflection into their ideals of the rational agent or of rational deliberation.[29] On these models, rational deliberation involves stepping back from full immersion in the agent's actual motivations and intuitive normative reason judgments. But even if we identify an agent's normative reasons, not with her actual motives, but with, say, the motives she would have if fully informed, or would want if fully informed for her actual self, or something similar, it seems we will still be treating her underlying motivational dispositions as a kind of practical "given," as having default normative status. But why should we do that? After all, we can step back from any disposition to be moved, as from any motive, and question its normative credentials. If we can't take the normative status of our actual motives for granted, why should we do so with our underlying dispositions to be moved?

Thinking along these lines leads Kantians to distinguish between the matter and form of volition and between material and formal principles of action. We can step back from any motivational bent we actually have and ask whether the object of this bent is something that there is reason for us to, or that we should, care about, try to realize, and so on. And if we reject a recognitional account of how our object-dependent desires acquire normative relevance through their relation to independent normative facts, we seem to lose any reason to grant them the default relevance that what Kant calls "material practical principles," that is, "principles that presuppose an object (matter) of the faculty of desire as the determining ground of the will" would require (1996a: 21–22). But, then,

---

29. For example, full information theories; reflective endorsement tests; self-reflective, fully informed tests; and so on. See, for example, Brandt 1979; Korsgaard 1996e; Railton 1986; and Smith 1994.

as Kant says, "nothing is left but the conformity of actions as such with universal law, which is alone to serve the will as its principle" (1996b: 402). Kantian constructivists argue therefore that what leads us to reject recognitional theories should lead us also to accept autonomy of the will.[30]

Of course, Kantians can't simply assume autonomy. But several factors now seem to converge to recommend the doctrine. First, we inescapably presuppose it when we address or acknowledge any (putative) second-personal reason. Second, within a constructivist framework, the will's being a law to itself by virtue of its form seems to be, for the reasons mentioned in the last two paragraphs, what the philosophical impulse leading to constructivism tends to in general. And third, we can combine these two ideas and say further that the standpoint from which we gain a self-reflective deliberative awareness of the autonomous agency that seems most deeply to underlie constructivism is one from which we pre-suppose autonomy of the will in the Kantian sense.[31] If, consequently, the metaethical theory we accept when we step back from the second-person standpoint is constructivist, there seem to be good reasons for thinking that the assumptions of dignity and autonomy we inescapably make within that standpoint are ones that will at least survive at the metaethical level, if not find further support.

On a Kantian constructivist picture, the doctrine of autonomy ex-presses itself in the idea that substantive, reason-grounding norms must be constructible through a procedure that can itself be seen to be internal to the exercise of the will. This requires companion conceptions of au-tonomous will and constructivist procedure that must fit one another. Our conception of what it is to be an autonomous will must itself include the capacity to engage in the relevant procedure of construction, and our conception of the relevant procedure must be such that it can be realized, in principle, in autonomous wills.[32] This, of course, is what we find in

30. The lesson that Kantian constructivists draw from this is, in effect, that agency could not, by its very nature, have a substantive aim. The lesson seems to be that the aim of action is autonomy, understood, not in nonnormative terms, but as following formal norms we are committed to as free and rational wills. For a defense of the idea that the substantive aim of action is autonomy, understood, roughly as self-direction driven by a desire for self-understanding, see Velleman 2000.

31. That there is a deep connection between autonomy, conceived as the capacity to step back from and critically evaluate actual motives, and the open question argument is a theme that is discussed in Rosati 1995 and 2003 and in Darwall 1990 and 1992.

32. Cf. Rawls's discussion of "rational autonomy" (of the parties to the original position

Kant's companion ideas of autonomy of the will and the CI, at least as these are interpreted within constructivism. The CI-procedure, as it is sometimes called, is a constructive process that involves considering what can be rationally willed from a perspective of one among other free and rational persons, where what it is to be such a person includes having the capacity to take up this perspective.[33]

Now I have been arguing that this is precisely the perspective we do take up when we address one another second-personally and, correspondingly, that we are committed to the second-personal version of the CI when we do. (I develop this latter theme further in Chapter 12.) The second-person standpoint itself presupposes, as we saw in Chapter 10, the companion ideas of autonomy of the will and of a kind of normative reason for acting, second-personal reasons, that we must assume to be acceptable to addressees as free and equal persons. And it provides as well a conception of the role of specific substantive norms of moral obligation, namely, as mediating reciprocal respect between mutually accountable free and equal persons.[34] As I argued at the end of Chapter 9, this can be provided by an interpretation of the CI-procedure that grounds it in dignity conceived as equal second-personal authority.

In addition, a Kantian constructivism can lead to a contractualist normative theory of these more specific norms and normative reasons. A constructive procedure can be mobilized not just at the metaethical level to vindicate the normative pretensions of the moral law (the dignity of persons) in general, but also in the foundations of normative moral theory to provide an account of what specific mandatory norms we are

---

as agents of construction) and "full autonomy" (of citizens as persons who can both take up the constructive position of the parties and regulate themselves by the principles they would rationally choose or construct) (1980: 520–521).

33. As in Rawls's interpretation of Kant and those who follow him. See Rawls 2000.

34. I discuss this in Chapter 12. It can sometimes seem to be missing from some of Kant's formulations of the Categorical Imperative, such as the Formula of Universal Law: "Act only in accordance with that maxim through which you can at the same time will that it become a universal law [or universal law of nature]" (1996b: 421). However, once we appreciate how holding someone responsible or accountable just is, essentially, relating to her as a person, we can see how the Formula of Humanity, which requires us to treat humanity or rational nature always as an end in itself, and the Formulas of Autonomy and of the Realm of Ends, should be interpreted in such a way that moral legislation involves legislating principles as norms with which we are accountable for complying.

committed to complying with as mutually accountable free and rational persons.[35] In the next chapter, we turn to how the second-person standpoint can help provide a rationale for contractualist accounts of moral obligation, where mandatory norms are seen to result from a hypothetical choice or contract from the perspective of free and equal persons. Whether we conceive of such a procedure, as Rawls does, in terms of a choice behind a veil of ignorance, or as Scanlon does, in terms of what no one could reasonably reject, or as Thomas Hill has proposed, as specifying an ideal of equal respect, contractualism provides a way of thinking of the justification of mandatory norms within moral reasoning for which, I argue, the second-person standpoint can provide a more fundamental rationale (Hill 1989; Rawls 1971: 17, 111; Scanlon 1998).[36]

Recognitional Theories and the Second-Person Standpoint

So far, then, we have seen some reasons to think that the equal authority of free and rational agents to which we are committed in the second-person standpoint can survive, indeed that it can find further support, when we step back from that perspective and pursue metaethical reflection in a constructivist vein. But there is no reason to think that this phenomenon is restricted to constructivism.

According to recognitional theories, deliberation is a matter of registering considerations whose status as reasons is independent of any ideal of rational deliberation. As we ordinarily experience it, a desire for some outcome involves its seeming as if there is some reason to realize the outcome and as if one is somehow in rapport with this normative fact. Now if a recognitional theory were to credit only the ethical intuitions and judgments we are inclined to from a naïve practical standpoint, then it would require us to think that no second-personal reasons exist and that both the dignity of persons and autonomy of the will are chimerical ideas. But there is absolutely no reason for a recognitional theory to

35. That these two levels should be distinguished is illustrated by the example of Scanlon (1998), a normative contractualist who does not advance constructivism as a metaethical position.

36. Here I have in mind Rawls's idea of "rightness as fairness," rather than the more specifically political philosophical uses to which Rawls put the contractualist idea after *A Theory of Justice* (1971: 17, 111).

restrict itself in this way. Object-dependent desires or Moorean intuitions surely do not exhaust the range of our ethical experiences and intuitive judgments. Most importantly for our purposes, reactive attitudes also present themselves as responding to normative reasons for acting, and in this instance the reasons are second-personal.[37] What possible reason could we have for thinking that our object-dependent desires and intuitive judgments of intrinsic value or desirability are evidentiary or veridical that we would not also have for so regarding intuitive judgments of second-personal reasons and second-personal authority? From a recognitional perspective, there seems no more reason to think that our desires give us access to the existence of normative reasons for outcomes than for thinking that reactive attitudes are evidence for second-personal reasons grounded in second-personal authority.

Moreover, whether addressing second-personal reasons invariably presupposes autonomy and dignity, as I have argued, or not, there seems no doubt whatsoever that we experience feelings that present themselves as responses to reasons grounded in dignity, that is, as instances of Kantian *reverentia*.[38] When Omar Khatib feels remorse at having shot David Blumenfeld and expresses it, calling him, for the first time, "David," must we not interpret Omar as having a powerful feeling that there was reason for him not to have done what he did that derives from David's dignity?[39] Similarly, when someone is subjected arbitrarily to the will of another, this can give her a sense of her own dignity through her reactive response to the other's self-conceit. Surely, we can hear something like this in Sojourner Truth's famous speech to the Women's Convention in Akron, Ohio, in 1851: "And ain't I a woman?"

When we have such feelings of recognition respect for persons, whether for ourselves or others, we seem to be presented with valid reasons for acting no less vividly than we are when we ardently desire an outcome. Absent some further explanation, there is no reason to credit the latter experiences but not the former. So here again, when we step back and reflect metaethically, this time in a recognitional realist vein, the equal

37. On this point, see Chapter 4.

38. See Chapter 6.

39. Recall here Adam Smith's remark, discussed in Chapter 4, that what resentment is "chiefly intent upon, is not so much to make our enemy feel pain in his turn, as . . . to make him sensible that the person whom he injured did not deserve to be treated in that manner" (1982a: 95–96).

dignity of persons to which we were committed in the second-person standpoint at least survives and arguably finds additional support.

To deliberate at all, you and I must presuppose that there are normative reasons for acting. But what reasons for acting are there? In this chapter, I have argued both that we have no less reason to accept second-personal reasons grounded in equal dignity than we do reasons for acting of other kinds and that these second-personal reasons can plausibly be accounted for on the major metaethical theories of reasons for acting. If we must assume the existence of normative reasons to deliberate at all, and if our best theories of normative reasons validate equal second-personal authority, then we should conclude that, for practical purposes, at least, second-reasons grounded in our common dignity really do exist.

— 12 —

A Foundation
for Contractualism

In the early and middle chapters of this book, I attempted to draw out some of the ways in which the second-person standpoint and second-personal reasons are implicated in our understanding of moral obligation and the equal dignity of persons. In more recent chapters, I have argued that the demands we have standing to make of one another as persons generate valid normative reasons for acting.[1] But what, more specifically, do these reasons require? What do "we owe to each other" (Scanlon 1998) as equal moral persons?

This final chapter is obviously not the place to try to answer that question. I invoke Scanlon's famous phrase in part to suggest, however, that although they do not require it, the arguments I have been advancing in this book lead naturally to a contractualist approach to attempting to do so. The fundamental idea of the dignity of persons, to which I have claimed we are committed from the second-person standpoint, is mutual accountability as equals. And this commits us to regulating our conduct by principles that are acceptable, or not reasonably rejectable, to each as free and rational agents. When we attempt to hold anyone accountable by addressing second-personal reasons of any kind, we presuppose that the authority and principles we implicitly invoke are ones our addressee

---

1. Have I shown that such reasons are supremely authoritative? If the argument of Chapter 10 is sound, we cannot avoid presupposing the equal dignity of free and rational persons when we address second-personal reasons of any kind. Since attempting to hold one another accountable through second-personal address itself apparently involves an assumption of the supremacy of the accountability-seeking second-personal reasons (see Chapter 5), it is hard to see how to avoid presupposing the supremacy of reasons of equal dignity.

can be expected to accept, or not reasonably to reject, as a free and rational agent who is apt for second-personal address.

In this final chapter, I briefly develop the idea that the second-person standpoint can ground a contractualist normative moral theory. It is a hallmark of contractualist theories that they hold principles of right to have a distinctive *role*, namely, as mediating relations of mutual respect. According to the "contractualist ideal," Scanlon says, we realize "mutual recognition" or reciprocal respect as equals when we conform to principles of right, understood as contractualism understands them (1998: 162). This is so for two different but related reasons. First, the *content* of contractualist principles specifies our obligations to one another as equals. Complying with these principles can thus show respect for each other as persons who may not be treated in some ways and who must be treated in others.[2] Second, but no less importantly, contractualism also maintains that the *form* of principles of right is mutual accountability to one another as equal persons. When, consequently, Scanlon says that an act is wrong "if it would be disallowed by any principle that no one could reasonably reject," we should understand this to mean: an act is wrong if the act would be disallowed by a principle no one could reasonably reject our holding one another accountable for complying with. It is the right's connection to accountability, indeed, that makes a "no-reasonable-rejection" test appropriate in the first place. It is because a moral obligation presents a demand that it is staked on its addressee's not being able reasonably to reject the principle that underlies it (again: to reject it as a basis for demands through mutual accountability). An art critic need not withdraw a critical judgment just because the artist she is criticizing might reasonably reject its grounds. But this is not so when we make demands in holding one another accountable. As we saw in Chapter 5 (and again in our discussion of Kant's "fact of reason" in Chapter 10), in addressing moral demands, we imply that there are conclusive second-personal reasons that our addressee is (second-personally) competent to accept and freely determine himself by. And that commits us to denying the possibility of reasonably rejecting a principle that it would be wrong to violate.

So this is the second place where mutual recognition or respect enters

---

2. Complying with these principles is not, however, sufficient to manifest full respect for persons, as I argued in Chapter 6.

the contractualist picture: the form and role that principles of right have in contractualism. In holding ourselves mutually accountable for conforming to contractualist principles of right, we recognize one another's equal standing to demand respect.

We may well think, however, that moral obligations have a wider scope, that their content extends beyond duties we owe (in the first instance) simply to persons. Many of us believe that we have moral obligations to nonrational humans and other animals and, indeed, to the natural environment that can neither be derived from nor be reduced to any "we owe to each other."[3] If, however, we take moral responsibility to be part of what moral obligation involves in such cases, then we must hold that we are accountable to one another (as members of the moral community) in these cases as well (that is, by virtue of principles' form). I am inclined strongly to think that the content of moral obligations does have this wider scope. But I know of no promising way of vindicating these thoughts that does not build upon or extend from accountability in the central second-personal case.[4]

Contractualism, then, is concerned by its very nature with second-personal relations of mutual accountability and respect. Principles of right express normative relations between persons, and violations must be understood against this background. If I wrong someone, then, as Scanlon points out, "my relation with them is already altered by that fact, whatever they do."

> They may retaliate in some way, or they may forgive me. But forgiveness is merely a willingness to forgo reacting to a wrong in ways one would be justified in doing, such as by being angry or severing friendly relations. It does not alter the wrong that has been done. (272)

The fundamental contractualist moral relation is thus mutual respect. Wrongs violate that relation; they fail adequately to recognize the dignity of persons and so call it into question. They therefore warrant a reciprocally recognizing response that seeks to reestablish mutual respect, demanding it of the violator in a way that simultaneously bestows it on him.[5]

3. I briefly discuss the accountability of human beings who are not fully morally competent in Chapter 4.

4. For a very interesting set of reflections on giving responsibility to (other) animals, see Hearne 1986. I am indebted to Elizabeth Anderson for this reference.

5. Recall, again, Strawson's remark that to respond to another with a reactive attitude is "to view him as a member of the moral community; only as one who offended against

Versions of Contractualism

Common to all contractualist theories is the idea that the content of the moral obligations we owe to one another as equal moral persons is to be explained as the result of a (hypothetical) agreement, choice, or "contract" from some perspective that situates individuals equally as moral persons (and so expresses respect for persons as such). This general idea can be developed in different ways. Justice as fairness, as Rawls presents it in *A Theory of Justice*, is a contractualist theory of justice. And Rawls there suggests a theory of moral right, "rightness as fairness," which can be developed along similar lines. Principles of right apply to individual conduct rather than to the basic structure of society, but otherwise rightness as fairness attempts to explicate such principles in a manner similar to the more familiar "derivation" of principles of justice. There are the same elements: the "original position" with its "veil of ignorance," a mutually disinterested choice of principles from that perspective as instrumentally rational in advancing the parties' interests ("primary goods") as free and equal persons, and so on (Rawls 1971: 17, 111).[6] But whereas the parties in the original position choose principles of justice to inform the public criticism of their basic social structure, we should understand principles in "rightness as fairness" as informing the kind of criticism that is distinctive of moral obligation—mutual accountability.[7] The parties in the original position choose principles with which people are to be held accountable for complying.

Scanlon's version differs from "rightness as fairness" in three important

---

its demands" (1968: 93) and Adam Smith's claim that resentment aims to make another feel our dignity (1982: 95–96). See the discussion of both of these in Chapter 4. Cf. also Hegel's famous idea of the right to punishment (1991: §100).

6. Rawls specifies these interests further by stipulating that the parties have "highest-order interests" in exercising their moral personality (living on terms of mutual respect) and in rationally choosing and revising their own conceptions of the good) and a "higher-order interest" in "protecting and advancing their conception of the good" (1980: 525). For a discussion of the so-called "Kantian interpretation" of Rawls's theory of justice, including of his idea of primary goods, see Darwall 1980. After his 1980 Dewey Lectures, Rawls presented his ideas wholly within the framework of political liberalism, and so turned away from questions of normative moral theory and from deeper philosophical rationales or other "comprehensive doctrines" that might be controversial in a liberal society.

7. Rawls distinguishes between moral obligations and natural duties, reserving the term "obligation" for those that arise from some sort voluntary initiating act; however, this distinction does not matter for our purposes (1999: 93–101).

ways. It employs no informational constraint like the veil of ignorance. Its derivation depends on an avowedly moral idea of "reasonable" rather than (a suitably constrained) "rational" acceptance or rejection (where standards of rationality are independent of moral criteria). And its procedural standard or benchmark is that no one be able reasonably to reject a candidate principle, as opposed to the principle's being one that any person could or would rationally or reasonably choose or accept.

We need not here consider the relative merits of these or other forms of contractualism.[8] My aim in this last chapter is to argue that what is common to contractualist approaches, that we are mutually accountable for regulating ourselves by principles that are acceptable (in some suitable sense) to each as equal moral persons, can itself be grounded in, and is best appreciated from, the second-person standpoint. Or, to put the point the other way round: the most promising way to work out the content of moral principles we are committed to by the equal dignity we must presuppose in the second-person perspective is through some version of contractualism.

Contractualism and the Categorical Imperative

Since Kant is the philosopher whose ideas stand most clearly behind contractualism, it may help to begin by sketching briefly the relations in Kant's ethics between the dignity of persons, as it operates within the Formula of Humanity (FH) ("So act that you use humanity, whether in our own person or in the person of any other, always at the same time as an end, never merely as a means" [Kant 1996b: 429]) and other formulations of the CI. Persons by their nature, have a dignity that makes treating them (or humanity or rationality in them) as a mere means a violation. They are, as Kamm (1989, 1992) and Nagel (1995) have put it, "inviolable": beings who may not be treated as a mere means. But what is it to treat someone, or to treat humanity or rationality in that person, merely as a means?

It is widely acknowledged that there are ways of wronging others— forms of deception, manipulation, and coercion, for example—that treat

8. Another example is Hill 1989. By contrast, "contractarianism" is the view that moral principles of right derive from a mutually advantageous contract, as in Harman 1977, Gauthier 1986, and, arguably, in Hobbes 1994. For a discussion of the differences between contractualism and contractarianism, see the introduction to Darwall 2002a.

a person's rationality merely instrumentally (Korsgaard 1996b; Wood 1999: 124–132). But when is utilizing someone's rationality or humanity using it merely as a means? Recall the contrast, which played a central role in the argument of Chapter 10, between coercing by threats and holding someone accountable through notice of a warranted sanction There is a sense in which threats are addressed to a person's rationality, or to a person as rational. After all, threats do their work through the threatened person's practical reasoning. But this just means that their target is the person's reason. A threat does not, however, address a person in the sense with which we have been concerned in this book; indeed, a threat need not address a person in any obvious sense. It could suffice for the threatened person simply to learn about a likely consequence of some act in a way that involves no communication at all, say, by seeing a gun trained on him in a mirror. When, however, someone addresses a second-personal demand, he purports to address (and, I have argued, to respect) the other as a free and rational agent.

Any valid second-personal reason must be addressable to free and rational persons as such not just in the way a threat is "addressed" to a person's rationality but to someone as having a normative standing as rational. It is a presupposition of this address that the (second-personal) reason and the authority relations in which it is grounded must be acceptable to the other as a free and rational person. If, consequently, it makes a demand on the other as an equal person, then it must be the case that the other would rationally endorse or not reasonably reject it as a demand with which persons are to be held accountable for complying. Second-personal reasoning is essentially justification to one another, just as Scanlon understands reasoning about our moral obligations.

Suppose, again, that a sergeant in a citizen militia of a free and democratic republic issues an order to a private to do ten pushups and that she informs the private that he will be confined to quarters if he fails to comply.[9] Such an address differs from a mere threat in a fundamental way.[10] If the sergeant had lacked her authority and simply threatened the same evil, then that would have been coercion pure and simple, using the person or his rationality as a mere means. Moreover, as we saw in Chapter 10, in holding the private accountable for complying, the ser-

9. Assume, again, that such sanction is fully within normal practice, that it is subject to democratic citizen review, that it is applied with due process, and so on.

10. This, again, is Pufendorf's Point.

geant must herself presuppose this distinction. And as we also saw, she can intelligibly assume this only if she can presuppose as well that the private can be expected to accept her authority, and the principles that give her orders normative force, as a free and rational agent. This is what ties accountability to a rational-acceptance, or to a no-reasonable-rejection, test. In attempting to hold another accountable, second-personally, one purports to address him as free and rational. And to make a demand of someone as free and rational, one must presuppose that the person can freely determine himself by that same demand, that the demand is one he can accept, or not reasonably reject, as free and rational, and therefore make of himself. Respecting the dignity of persons is thus tied to holding oneself accountable for complying with demand-authorizing-principles that free and rational persons would accept, or could not reasonably reject, as such.

In my view, this is what links FH to the formulations of the CI more usually associated with contractualism: the Formula of the Realm of Ends (FRE) and, when properly understood, the Formulation of Universal Law (FUL). The idea of a realm or "kingdom of ends," Kant says, is that of "a systematic union of rational beings through common laws."

> For all rational beings stand under the *law* that each of them is to treat himself and all others *never merely as a means* but always *at the same time as ends in themselves*. But from this there arises a systematic union of rational beings through common objective laws. (1996b: 433)

And this implies FRE: "Every rational being must act as if he were by his maxims at all times a lawgiving member of the universal kingdom of ends" (Kant 1996c: 438).

Contractualism is an interpretation of this fundamental Kantian doctrine. When we add in the Kantian claim by which we were guided in Chapter 10, namely, that dignity is a second-personal authority "by which" a person "exacts respect for himself from all other rational beings," we get that a "realm of ends" is a community of equal, free, and rational agents who hold themselves mutually accountable for complying with demands they can accept or not reasonably reject and so make of one another as free and rational (1996d: 434–435). Persons can make some specific demand of each other, therefore, only if they can expect that each would sensibly accept the demand, or that no one could reasonably reject it, as free and rational. And this means that they can make the demand only if they can expect that each would accept, or could not reasonably reject, as free and rational, that people be held accountable for complying with the principle that specifies the demand.

As we noted first in Chapters 4 and 5, the idea of moral accountability inevitably brings in the companion idea of moral community, which is implicit also in the ideas of moral obligation and the dignity of persons. We make moral demands, and hold ourselves and one another accountable, from the perspective of equal members of the moral community. In making ourselves mutually accountable we function as equal law-executing or law-enforcing members of the moral community. But FRE brings in the idea of moral community in another fundamental way: each person is to conduct herself as though she were a "lawgiving member" of the realm of ends. We have an equal standing not just in executing or enforcing the moral law (whatever its content), but also in "determining" its content. As with contractualism, I believe the most promising way of interpreting Kant's idea is not in terms of any actual determination of the moral law by actual persons but, rather, in terms of the law's being determined by some hypothetical, idealized process of agreement that situates the parties as equal persons. Persons function as equal law-giving and law-executing members of the moral community, the realm of ends, then, when they hold themselves and one another responsible for complying with mandatory principles that would rationally be accepted by all free and rational persons as such, or reasonably rejected by none, that is, from a hypothetical perspective that situates the parties equally in these respects (for example, behind a veil of ignorance regarding individuating differences). For this reason, Kant calls the principles that specify demands we can make on each person as free and rational "common laws." They satisfy Rousseau's famous formula of mediating a form of association "by means of which each, uniting with all, nevertheless obeys only himself" (1997: 49–50).

Now FRE differs substantially from the letter of FUL: "Act only in accordance with that maxim through which you can at the same will that it become a universal law [or universal law of nature]" (Kant 1996b: 421). Read narrowly, FUL says that it is morally unacceptable to act on some maxim or principle if one could not oneself will (choose, accept) that it become universal law. So interpreted, it says nothing about what others must be able to accept or be unable to reject. By contrast, what Parfit (2004) calls "Kant's Contractualist Formula" requires that "we ought to act on the principles that *everyone* could rationally choose," which clearly seems more in the spirit of FRE.

Now I argued in Chapters 9 and 10 that we should take the most fundamental idea in the Kantian framework to be the dignity of persons, conceived as an equal basic second-personal authority. As I see it, contractualist formulae are a way of developing or further specifying this idea.[11] We can think along the same lines in Kant's framework if we take FH as fundamental, interpret FH in terms of FRE, and then interpret FUL in its light. This gives us a way of unifying all formulations of the CI, as Kant clearly and explicitly intends (1996b: 436). The underlying idea is that we treat rational nature, whether in ourselves or in others, as an end in itself by holding ourselves and each other responsible for complying with principles that we and they could will (or not reasonably reject) as universal law. The relevant willing must be of a certain kind and from a certain perspective, however. If, for example, the reason I (or anyone) could not will that some principle universally govern conduct is because of some idiosyncratic interest that is neither rooted in nor supported by any interest I have as a free and equal rational person, then it is hard to see how Kant could hold it to be morally relevant. Alternatively, if the interest meets this test but I object to a principle's being universally governing because of the way it affects my interests as an equal member, though I wouldn't if it were someone else, then this is also an objection of the wrong kind to a candidate moral principle.[12] Similarly, the Formula of Autonomy (FA) holds that we are to constrain our conduct by "the idea of the will of every rational being as a *will giving universal law*"

11. Wood (1999) also thinks that the dignity of persons is Kant's fundamental idea, but unlike Wood, I believe neither that we can simply interpret FH directly, in its own terms, nor that the various universalization procedures, including FUL, should be ignored as empty or morally problematic. Furthermore, in my view, what is fundamental is not dignity as a freestanding value, but second-personal authority.

12. This may seem to be incompatible with a Rawlsian version of contractualism, because the parties in the original position choose principles in a mutually disinterested way, as instrumentally rational in furthering their own (highest-order) interests as rational persons. But that would misunderstand the way in which the motivations of the parties works in combination with the veil of ignorance constraint. It would work equally well to suppose that the parties are trustees for an individual citizen and her interests (about whom the veil of ignorance prohibits further knowledge) and gave no weight to their own interests. The arguments from the original position would be exactly the same in both cases. On this point, see Darwall 1980: 340–343. Rawls notes this point himself (2001: 84–85).

(1996b: 432, see also 434, 438, 440). Here again, it seems clear that we should take FA to be governed by FRE. In general, then, FRE, which is the most clearly contractualist version of the CI, also seems to be its most fundamental "procedural" version. And this procedural idea, in turn, is grounded in the most fundamental idea to which we are committed from the second-person standpoint: FH and the equal dignity of free and rational persons.

The Basis for Rational Acceptance or Reasonable Rejection in Contractualism

An ideal of moral community as mutually accountable free and rational persons can also provide a basis from which to argue within contractualist procedures, namely, through interests individuals have as such members. This is perhaps clearest in Thomas E. Hill Jr.'s version of "Kantian Constructivism" (1989), which includes a less restrictive veil of ignorance than Rawls's and considers what principles ideal legislators could accept when they attempt to specify more precisely the equal dignity of persons. And even though Rawls's standard of "rational" choice in the original position is instrumentalist and morally neutral, it is harnessed to a conception of the "fundamental aims" of the parties that privileges "highest-order interests" they have as mutually accountable free and rational persons in exercising their "two moral powers," namely, their capacity for a sense of justice (or, in "rightness as fairness," to hold themselves and one another morally accountable) and their capacity to "form, revise, and rationally to pursue a conception of the good" (Rawls 1980: 525).

Scanlon is less concerned to provide a unified account of the grounds for reasonable acceptance or rejection, but he does say that the "range of reasons which are taken to be relevant" comes from the parties' aim of "finding principles that others who share this aim could not reasonably reject" (1998: 192; see also Kumar 2003). The shared aim, fully spelled out, is to find principles that, now to use my vocabulary, free and rational persons concerned to live mutually accountably on terms of equal respect could not reasonably reject. It is hard to see what could be relevant to this other than interests that free and rational persons can be presumed to have in living self-directed lives on terms of mutual respect with others, that is, something like the highest-order interests in exercising their "moral powers" to which Rawls refers.[13] In whichever of these ways the contractualist approach is specifically developed, therefore, the idea of mutually accountable free and rational persons (to which we are committed from the second-person standpoint) can be appealed to within it to help assess whether candidate principles of moral obligation can be rationally accepted or reasonably rejected. A natural example is the interest in freedom from arbitrary direction by others to which we appealed in the argument of Chapter 10. This is evident in Fichte's principle of right ("I must in all cases recognize the free being outside me as a free being, i.e., I must limit my freedom through the concept of the possibility of his freedom" [2000: 49]) and in Kant's "universal principle of right" ("Any action is *right* if it can coexist with everyone's freedom in accordance with a universal law, or if on its maxim the freedom of choice of each can coexist with everyone's freedom in accordance with a universal law" [1996c: 230].

Contractualism and Rule-Consequentialism

We can help consolidate these points by considering Parfit's recent claim (2004) that "Kantian Contractualism" (KC) implies rule-consequentialism, the view that we should comply with whatever principles the general acceptance of which would have the best consequences. KC holds, again, that "we ought to act on the principles that everyone could rationally choose." KC rules out act-consequentialism for familiar consequentialist reasons. The consequences that matter from the standpoint of contractualist choice are those of a principle's universal acceptance—both in practical reasoning and through mutual accountability. And consequentialists widely accept that things most likely go better overall when everyone accepts and regulates themselves interpersonally by principles other than act-consequentialism.[14] That, after all, is what lies behind Mill's rule-utilitarian theory of justice.

Actually Parfit does not claim that rationality requires a choice of

13. Kumar 2003 can be interpreted somewhat along these lines.

14. This is a point about the "acceptance-utility" or "acceptance-consequences" of candidate principles, as opposed to their "conformance-utility" or "conformance-consequences." See, for example, Lyons 1965. In Parfit's terms, act-consequentialism is "indirectly collectively self-defeating," and possibly also "self-effacing" (1984: 27–43). See also Hare 1981.

principles whose acceptance would make things go best overall (that is, effectively, a choice of rule-consequentialism). What he argues, very roughly, is that rationality always permits choosing whatever leads to the best outcomes, impartially considered, and that in this instance rationality permits everyone to choose principles whose acceptance would be optimific, that is, principles with which compliance is mandated by rule-consequentialism.

We need not worry about the details of Parfit's argument, since what we have already enables us to formulate a contractualist response. The argument's major problem is that it ignores the form that principles of right have on a contractualist theory, namely, their role in mediating mutual respect through mutual accountability. The contractualist can acknowledge the existence of impartial outcome-given reasons in general, and she can also agree *arguendo*, without threatening anything she is committed to, that it can be rational for an individual to sacrifice self-interest in order to further impartially better outcomes. But, consistently with this, she can nonetheless deny that such a ranking of outcomes itself provides a reason of the right sort for principles of moral obligation or right. Principles of right are not simply standards for individual choice; they lay out what we have standing to demand from one another by holding each other accountable. To be a reason of the right kind to warrant a principle of right, therefore, a consideration must relate to interests we are entitled to presuppose from within a second-person standpoint, as members of a community of independent, mutually accountable, free, and rational persons.

This, of course, is Strawson's Point transposed to the issue between rule-consequentialism and contractualism. The desirability of outcomes, taken by itself, is a reason of the wrong kind to ground claims of moral responsibility, and, consequently, claims of moral obligation. The basis of choice that Parfit mentions is not this crude, however. It does not propose to substitute direct consequentialist reasoning for the principles we employ in practices of accountability. Rather, like Mill in chapter 5 of *Utilitarianism*, it proposes to treat the desirability of outcomes as a test of principles' suitability for employment in these practices.[15] But, as we have noted before, this seems simply to postpone the problem: how can the authority of someone to demand something derive simply from the de-

15. See also Rawls 1955.

sirability of his being able to do so? This seems, again, to be a reason of the wrong kind for second-personal accountability not just in individual cases, but also for establishing the relevant practices themselves. The most that it can ground is a desire to be able to demand something, not any demand, or practice of accountability, itself. The problem with rule-consequentialism, then, is that it attempts to derive principles of right from reasons of the wrong kind.

That said, contractualism might be represented as a kind of rule-consequentialism in a purely formal sense. Suppose we consider a Rawlsian version of contractualism with a choice of principles from behind a veil of ignorance. And suppose we accept the argument of Harsanyi (1978) and many of Rawls's critics that it is rational for the parties to assume that it is equally probable that they could be anyone (once the veil is lifted).[16] Now it would be a mistake to conclude from this that the parties should choose principles that would maximize their "actual," "extra-veil" utilities, as defined by whatever preferences they will come to have, for reasons we have just discussed. Rawls's idea is rather that we impute to the parties certain preferences and interests, their "highest-order interests" in living self-directed lives on terms of mutual accountability and respect, and that the parties are to be understood as making a rational choice of principles from the standpoint of furthering these imputed preferences, subject to the constraints of a veil of ignorance.

But if we allow the parties the assumption that it is equally likely they could be anyone, then why wouldn't it be rational for them to choose principles the acceptance of which would maximize the average satisfaction of these imputed preferences, that is, principles that would maximize average utility when the relevant utility measure is defined not on actual preferences but on the imputed preferences that parties have as members of the realm of ends (as mutually accountable free and rational persons)? Such a choice would seem to maximize the expected utility of the parties and thus be the instrumentally rational choice from their standpoint.[17] I

16. Rawls denies this, arguing that the decision problem must be considered as one under uncertainty rather than under risk, in the technical decision-theoretic sense, and that the appropriate decision principle is maximin (1971: 154–157).

17. Again, Rawls gives various reasons for rejecting the equi-probability assumption and treats the problem of choice as one of uncertainty rather than risk. We need take no stand on how cogent these reasons are. My point is that even if they aren't, and even if Kantian contractualism is a form of rule-consequentialism in a purely formal sense, nothing of

see no deep reason for a contractualist to resist this proposal. Just as once we have the distinction between object-dependent and principle-dependent desires, we can accommodate autonomous, mutually accountable conduct within belief/desire psychology without conceding anything a Kantian moral psychologist need care about, so also it seems that a Kantian contractualist might concede that her view is a version of rule-consequentialism in this purely formal sense without compromising anything of fundamental theoretical importance.[18] Since the relevant interests themselves cannot be defined independently of the idea of second-personal accountability, and so long as the contractualist framework rests ultimately on equal second-personal authority, any consequentialism of this purely formal sort does not risk getting authority simply from desirability of outcomes, that is, being based on reasons of the wrong kind.[19]

What matters most for the contractualist is what we are committed to from the second-person standpoint, namely the equal dignity and mutual accountability of free and rational persons. This both provides the foundation for a contractualist account of principles of right in general and shapes the specific interpretations of rational choice or reasonable rejection that are employed within different contractualist accounts.

The Role of Publicity and Principles

The right's connection to mutual accountability also explains why it essentially involves publicly articulable principles in a way that other ethical standards, such as ideals of virtue, need not.[20] Standards of right and

theoretical importance hangs on this point. For example, it is consistent with this that the parties should also choose the Difference Principle (that is, that the Difference Principle would satisfy a rule-consequentialism of this formal kind).

18. I am indebted to Allan Gibbard for discussion of these points.

19. Cf. Scanlon: "The fact that it would be a good thing if people were discouraged from [certain] actions by threat of legal punishment and social disapproval, or by an ingrained tendency to feel disapproval toward themselves, could provide a reason to acquire such a tendency, but that does not amount to a reason not to so act. What we need to do, then, is to explain more clearly how the idea that an act is wrong flows from the idea that there is an objection of a certain kind to people's being allowed to perform such actions, and we need to do this in a way that makes clear how an act's being wrong in the sense described can provide a reason not to do it" (1998: 153).

20. For a defense of "particularism" in ethics, see Dancy 1993, 2001, and 2004. John McDowell (1979) is another influential source of the idea that ethical ideas, especially those relating to the virtues, are uncodifiable.

wrong are, in their nature, bases for public expectations, for what we justifiably expect of one another. So they must be able to be publicly articulated and accessible.[21] It would be unreasonable to hold people accountable to standards whose application required some special sensibility ordinary moral agents could not be assumed to have or that could not be formulated in ways that ordinary agents can understand. In this way, standards of moral right are a moral "law," modeled on law as we generally understand it.

It is notable that this idea also plays an important role even in the utilitarian tradition, although it is often in conflict with other strains. It is, again, a strength of contractualism that its rule- or principle-regarding character complements its deepest (non-outcome-based) justification of principles. Mill's thesis that right and wrong essentially involves moral responsibility has been a recurrent theme in this book. Much less well-appreciated or even known is that a major argument of Bentham's for the principle of utility also derives from the role he thinks moral principles of right play in public directive criticism.[22] Bentham (1962) argues that to play that role, any principle must be able to be publicly advanced on some "extrinsic ground" or "external standard," by which he means some reason that supports the principle that one can be expected to accept without already accepting the principle (or sharing the sensibility that it codifies). The argument occurs in the midst of his critique of what he regards as the many ethical philosophies that reject this constraint, whether they champion moral sense, rational intuition, common sense, or whatever.

> The various systems that have been formed concerning the standard of right and wrong all of them [consist] in so many contrivances for avoiding the obligation of appealing to any external standard. (Bentham 1962: 8)

Any such theory, Bentham argues, is guilty of simply "prevailing upon the reader to accept of the author's sentiment or opinion as a reason for

21. This I take it, is the correct response to the criticism that Rawls's constraint that the parties to the original position choose candidate principles as public principles of justice begs the question against utilitarianism. Although this condition may seem ad hoc when considered in relation to ethics more generally, it is utterly central to any adequate theory of moral right to which we are appropriately held publicly accountable.

22. For a more extended discussion, see Darwall 1994, which I draw on here. For relevant discussion concerning the broader context of liberal democratic moral debate, Railton 1992.

itself" (1962: 9). Bentham's concern is not with some merely intellectual fault, like begging the question.

> The mischief common to all these ways of thinking and arguing (which, in truth, as we have seen, are but one and the same method, couched in different forms of words) is their serving as a cloke, and pretence, and aliment, to despotism; if not a despotism in practice, a despotism however in disposition: which is but too apt, when pretence and power offer, to show itself in practice. (1962: 9n)[23]

Bentham's worry is rather that putting forward a principle of right without an external standard amounts to coercion. It is to make demands of others that they cannot reasonably be expected to accept. And Bentham's case for the principle of utility is that it can be applied uncontroversially, since it turns on empirically ascertainable facts, and that it can be expected to motivate since it concerns the "two sovereign masters" of human motivation, pleasure and pain.[24]

This line may be somewhat unexpected in Bentham since it grounds the principle of utility in constraints on public directive ("demanding") discourse and practice on distinctly liberal grounds, rather than vice versa. But Bentham makes it clear that he intends precisely this (in this strain of argument, at least). Whether a "moral sentiment" might "be originally conceived" or "upon examination and reflection . . . be actually persisted in and justified on another ground" than "a view of utility" is, he says, something about which he neither knows nor cares. "It matters not, comparatively speaking, how they are decided." But whether in "point of right [a principle of right] can properly be justified on any other ground, by a person addressing himself to a community," is a "question of practice," the answer to which "is of as much importance as that of any can be" (1962: 9n).

Vindicating the Reasonable

As Rawls and Scanlon employ it, 'reasonable' expresses a different concept than does 'rational' or 'normative reason'; it refers to the putative nor-

---

23. Also, concerning someone who would put forward "his own *unfounded* sentiments" (i.e., unfounded in an extrinsic ground), Bentham says, "let him ask himself whether his principle is not despotical" (1962: 3).

24. This is the deep connection between positive social science and liberal moral and political theory.

mative reasons that are distinctively associated with the claims we have the (second-personal) standing to make on one another as equal free and rational persons. Recall the Rawlsian dictum: persons are "self-originating sources of valid claims" (Rawls 1980: 546). (It follows, I believe, that 'reasonable' expresses a second-personal concept.) So in arguing that presuppositions of the second-person standpoint vindicate the equal dignity of persons, I have also been arguing that these vindicate the normativity of the reasonable.

Now, as I mentioned briefly in Chapter 1, Scanlon understands the problem of vindicating morality's authority to be that of explaining "the *priority* of right and wrong over other values," or of explaining their special "importance" (Scanlon 1998: 146, 147). In his original paper, Scanlon (1982) took the view that the "motivational basis" of contractualist morality is a desire to act in a way that can be justified to others. In *What We Owe to Each Other,* however, Scanlon takes a different approach, largely because of his skepticism there that desire can ground reasons for acting of any kind.[25] Far from its being the case that reasons for acting are grounded in desires, he there argues, it is closer to the truth to say that desires typically respond to apparent reasons. In "the directed-attention sense," a desire involves having one's attention "directed insistently toward considerations that present themselves as counting in favor of" what one desires (and, hence, of a desire for it) (Scanlon 1998: 39–41).

Scanlon's more recent argument for the priority of right has complexities we cannot fully pursue here.[26] Its basis, however, is what Scanlon calls the "value" and "appeal" of standing to others in the relation of mutual recognition, both in itself and as an ineliminable aspect of valuable relations like friendship (1998: 158–168). It is because this value gives us (better, in "buck-passing" fashion, consists in) "reason[s] we have to live with others on terms that they could not reasonably reject insofar as they also are motivated by this ideal" that "we have reason to attend to the question of which actions are right and wrong" (154).[27] Scanlon likens this to Mill's position in *Utilitarianism* that although the criterion or standard of right is provided by the greatest happiness of all, the moral

25. For other arguments along similar lines, see Bond 1983; Dancy 2000; Darwall 1983; Hampton 1998; Pettit and Smith 1990; Quinn 1991.

26. See especially Scanlon's description of the "three-part strategy" (1998: 166–168).

27. For the "buck-passing" analysis of value, see Scanlon 1998: 11, 95–100.

"sanction" (Mill's term for what makes considerations of right reason-giving for us) is "the desire to be in social unity with our fellow creatures" (Mill 1998: ch. 3; Scanlon 1998: 154). Roughly, for Mill, it is because of the desirability of living in unity with others that considerations of right (which are themselves based indirectly on the general happiness) give us reasons to act. Similarly, for Scanlon, it is because of the value or appeal that we take living with others on terms of mutual recognition and respect to have that considerations of right (and, relatedly, of what is reasonable) are reason-giving and, indeed, have priority for us.

There is, however, a problem with Mill's position that will infect any contractualist position that is modeled too closely upon it. Considerations of desirability, as we have seen throughout this book, are simply reasons of the wrong kind to ground (second-personal) reasons of moral obligation and right. If, consequently, the reasons we have to stand in relations of mutual recognition with others are only that it is desirable that we do so (either impartially or from our own point of view), then, no matter how weighty these reasons may be, they cannot ground the distinctive (second-personal) reasons of moral right. The most they can ground, again, is the desire to be such as to recognize the validity of moral claims; they can give us no reason to accept or recognize moral claims in their own terms.

There are actually two problems here, each connected respectively, to different aspects of moral obligation that, I have argued, are interrelated: moral obligation's (purported) supremacy or superiority, on the one hand, and its tie to mutual accountability, on the other.[28] The first problem is that it is hard to see how, from the fact it would be desirable for us to treat considerations of right as having priority over other values (including the desirable), it can possibly follow that such considerations actually have this priority. The second problem, yet another reflection of Strawson's Point, is that it is hard to see how its being desirable that we relate to one another on terms of mutual accountability can possibly ground the distinctively second-personal claim that we are mutually accountable.

For the value of relating to one another on terms of mutual respect to be connected in the right way to the reasons we appeal to within such

28. The relation, again, is that it is because of moral obligation's essential tie to mutual accountability that its reasons must purport to be supreme. For this argument, see Chapter 5.

relations, we must see this respect as itself called for by the equal dignity of free and rational persons. It is this, I have argued, that most deeply underlies the rationale for a contractualist procedure and that we are committed to from the second-person standpoint. The reason we have for relating to others with respect is not just that this is desirable in some way or other, whether for us individually, or impartially, or whatever, but, the dignity of persons pure and simple, their having equal second-personal standing, which we are committed to accepting when we address them second-personally at all.[29] In presupposing this, I have argued, we must presuppose that we have the standing to lay claims on one another as free and rational, where this means both that we cannot treat one another as mere means and that we are accountable to one another for not doing so.

It is the reciprocal recognition that is always already implicit in second-personal address that gets us into the space of the reasonable and justification to one another. Consider two naïve agents, A and B, reasoning first-personally on the basis of their respective evaluations of the desirability of outcomes as these are given in their desires and other practical experience. Suppose, for example, that A and B both desire the same apple and both see their desire for the apple as evidence that it would really be good for them to have it, respectively. At this point, neither A nor B will see the other's desire, will, or agency as a source of reasons for him, but neither will each see his own will and agency in this way either. From this naïve perspective, their agency and will are deliberatively "backgrounded" (Pettit and Smith 1990). What is foregrounded for both is the desirability of the objects of their respective desires, as it seems to them under their desires' influence. For A: my (A's) having the apple would be good (desirable). For B: my (B's) having the apple would be good (desirable).

Suppose that at this point, A attempts to give B a reason to let him, A, have the apple by expressing his desire, saying that his (A's) having the apple would be a valuable outcome, a state that should be brought about (noting that, so far as he can tell, B's having it is not). This will probably not succeed, since from B's perspective, there may be, so far as she can see, nothing to be said for A's having the apple and everything

---

29. With the usual caveats about children and other nonstandard cases, impure address, and so on.

to be said for her (*B*'s) having it. *B* may have no reason to trust *A*'s judgment, since, from *B*'s perspective *A*'s judgment may simply seem illusory, a mere expression of *A*'s desire. Any such attempt of *A*'s to give *B* a reason would be structurally analogous to theoretical reason-giving. It could succeed only if *B* has some reason to think there exists some evidentiary relation between *A*'s judgment and the normative world it purports to represent.

At the same time, however, *A*'s expression of desire might give *B* pause in the credit she accords her own desire's appearance. From a first-person perspective, corrected only by further appearances that come with better informed desires and unchallenged by another's desires and will, *B* could comfortably credit the epistemic access she apparently got to reasons through her own desires. But now she sees that *A*'s desires appear to him to provide access to reasons no less than do *B*'s for her.

To be sure, there are ways that *A* and *B*'s conversation could progress within the space of (apparently) outcome-based reasons. *A* or *B* could come to care about the other through sympathetic concern and see the other's welfare (and, consequently, the other's having the apple) as a good thing. Or they might come to regard the practical experiences and desires of the other as no less evidentiary of desirable outcomes than their own. Any of these reasons, however, can only show why it would be a good thing for *A* or *B* or both to have the apple in whole or in part. It could not show why either might have a reasonable claim to the apple, whole or part, or show, consequently, why any particular disposition of the apple might be reasonable.[30] In particular, abstracting from phenomena like diminishing marginal utility, nothing would recommend dividing the apple between them. And certainly there would be no place for the idea that either has any moral obligation, even *pro tanto*, to give any weight to the other's interest (or, indeed, to his own).

Suppose now that *A* lays a claim of any kind to the apple (or some part of it or chance for it) and addresses it second-personally to *B*. No matter what the basis of *A*'s claim is, *A* thereby presupposes a second-personal relation to *B*. *A* presupposes the standing to address the specific claim he makes, on whatever basis, and, therefore, a second-personal authority to make claims on another person at all. And if *B* takes up the claim, if only by giving it consideration publicly between them, then *B*

---

30. I am indebted here to conversation with Mark van Roojen.

implicitly acknowledges A's second-personal authority, even if she rejects, on reflection, A's specific claim. But likewise, in addressing his claim to B, A must simultaneously presuppose B's second-personal authority. Finally, in acknowledging a claim or second-personal summons from A, B must also acknowledge, and presuppose in her practical reasoning, her own second-personal authority as a free and rational agent.

In the reciprocal recognition of the second-person standpoint, addresser and addressee are committed alike to their mutual accountability as equal free and rational persons, and this commits them to the demand for justification to one another, at least within the scope of their mutual accountability. Their reciprocal address commits them both also to a constraint of reasonableness of any demands they address; they must be able to expect their addressees to accept, or not reasonably to reject, their demands as free and rational persons, in light of their interest as independent, mutually accountable (second-personally competent) agents. It commits them both to imposing no demands on others that they would not also be prepared to impose upon themselves from a common standpoint they share as free and rational.

The second-person standpoint thus vindicates the reasonable and so grounds contractualist moral theory. By presupposing the equal dignity of persons, it commits us to contractualism's deepest idea: a community of mutually accountable free and rational persons.[31] And in so doing, it gives us a reason of the right kind to comply with principles that mediate respect between mutually accountable equals.

31. Elizabeth Anderson (1999) proposes what she calls a "relational theory of equality" along these lines. I am much indebted to her work.

Works Cited

Index

Works Cited

Adams, Robert. 1999. *Finite and Infinite Goods.* New York: Oxford University Press.

Alexander, Richard D. 1987. *The Biology of Moral Systems.* New York: Aldine de Gruyter.

Allen, Karen, Jim Blascovich, and Wendy B. Mendes. 2001. "Cardiovascular Reactivity and the Presence of Pets, Friends, and Spouses: The Truth about Cats and Dogs." *Psychosomatic Medicine* 63: 727–739.

Allison, Henry. 1986. "Morality and Freedom: Kant's Reciprocity Thesis." *Philosophical Review* 95: 393–425.

Anderson, Elizabeth. 1999. "What Is the Point of Equality?" *Ethics* 109: 287–337.

———. 2000. "Beyond Homo Economicus: New Developments in Theories of Social Norms." *Philosophy & Public Affairs* 29: 170–200.

Anscombe, G. E. M. 1957. *Intention.* Oxford: Basil Blackwell.

———. 1958. "Modern Moral Philosophy." *Philosophy* 33: 1–19.

Aristotle. 1980. *The Nicomachean Ethics,* ed. David Ross. New York: Oxford University Press.

Arpaly, Nomy. 2003. *Unprincipled Virtue.* Oxford: Oxford University Press.

Austin, J. L. 1975. *How to Do Things with Words.* Cambridge, MA: Harvard University Press.

Axelrod, Robert. 1984. *The Evolution of Cooperation.* New York: Basic Books.

Bagnoli, Carla. 2003. "Respect and Loving Attention." *Canadian Journal of Philosophy* 33: 483–516.

Baier, Annette. 1991. *A Progress of the Sentiments.* Cambridge, MA: Harvard University Press.

———. 1993. "Moralism and Cruelty: Reflections on Hume and Kant." *Ethics* 103: 436–457.

Baier, Kurt. 1966. "Moral Obligation." *American Philosophical Quarterly* 3: 210–226.

Baron-Cohen, Simon, A. Leslie, and U. Frith. 1985. "Does the Autistic Child Have a 'Theory of Mind?'" *Cognition* 21: 37–46.

Barry, Brian, and Russell Hardin, eds. 1982. *Rational Man and Irrational Society*. Beverly Hills, CA: Sage Publications.

Ben-Ner, Avner, and Louis Putterman, eds. 1998. *Economics, Values, and Organization*. Cambridge: Cambridge University Press.

Bennett, Jonathan. 1980. "Accountability," in *Philosophical Subjects*, ed. Zak Van Stratten. Oxford: Clarendon Press.

Bentham, Jeremy. 1962. *Introduction to the Principles of Morals and Legislation*, in *The Works of Jeremy Bentham*, ed. J. Bowring. New York: Russell & Russell.

Blackburn, Simon. 1995. "Practical Tortoise Raising." *Mind* 104: 695–711.

Blumenfeld, Laura. 2000. *Revenge: A Story of Hope*. New York: Simon & Schuster.

Bohman, James. 2000. "The Importance of the Second Person: Interpretation, Practical Knowledge, and Normative Attitudes," in *Empathy and Agency*, ed. Hans Herbert Kögler and Karsten R. Stueber. Boulder, CO: Westview Press.

Bond, E. J. 1983. *Reason and Value*. Cambridge: Cambridge University Press.

Brand-Ballard, Jeffrey. 2004. "Contractualism and Deontic Restrictions." *Ethics* 114: 269–300.

Brandt, Richard. 1965. "Towards a Credible Form of Utilitarianism," in *Morality and the Language of Conduct*, ed. Hector-Neri Castañeda and George Nakhnikian. Detroit, MI: Wayne State University Press.

———. 1979. *A Theory of the Good and the Right*. Oxford: Oxford University Press.

Bratman, Michael. 1992. "Shared Cooperative Activity." *Philosophical Review* 101: 327–341.

———. 1993. "Shared Intention." *Ethics* 104: 97–113.

Bricke, John. 1996. *Mind and Morality: An Examination of Hume's Moral Psychology*. Oxford: Clarendon Press.

Brink, David O. 1997. "Kantian Rationalism: Inescapability, Authority, and Supremacy," in *Ethics and Practical Reason*, ed. Garrett Cullity and Berys Gaut. Oxford: Clarendon Press.

Broome, John. 1999. "Normative Requirements." *Ratio* 12: 398–419.

Brosnan, Sarah F., and Frans B. M. de Waal. 2003. "Monkeys Reject Unequal Pay." *Nature* 425 (2003): 297–299.

Buber, Martin. 1965. *The Knowledge of Man: Selected Essays*, ed. Maurice Friedman. New York: Harper & Row.

———. 1970. *I and Thou*, trans. Walter Kaufman. New York: Touchstone, Simon and Schuster.

Burge, Tyler. 1993. "Content Preservation." *Philosophical Review* 102: 457–488.

Buss, Sarah. 1999a. "Appearing Respectful: The Moral Significance of Manners." *Ethics* 109: 795–826.

————. 1999b. "Respect for Persons." *Canadian Journal of Philosophy* 29: 517–550.

Butler, Bishop Joseph. 1900. *The Works of Joseph Butler,* ed. J. H. Bernard. 2 vols. London: Macmillan.

————. 1983. *Five Sermons,* ed. Stephen Darwall. Indianapolis: Hackett Publishing Co.

Carroll, Lewis. 1895. "What the Tortoise Said to Achilles." *Mind* 4: 278–280.

Chafe, William. 1980. *Civilities and Civil Rights.* New York: Oxford University Press.

Coady, C. A. J. 1992. *Testimony: A Philosophical Study.* Oxford: Oxford University Press.

Cohon, Rachel. 1997. "Hume's Difficulty with the Virtue of Honesty." *Hume Studies* 23: 91–112.

Corwin, Miles. 1982. "Icy Killer's Life Steeped in Violence." *Los Angeles Times,* May 16.

Cranor, Carl. 1975. "Toward a Theory of Respect for Persons." *American Philosophical Quarterly* 12: 309–319.

Cudworth, Ralph. ~1670. Manuscripts on freedom of the will. British Library, Additional Manuscripts, nos. 4978–4982.

————. 1996. *A Treatise Concerning Eternal and Immutable Morality,* ed. Sarah Hutton. Cambridge: Cambridge University Press.

Cullity, Garrett, and Berys Gaut. 1977. Introduction to *Ethics and Practical Reason,* ed. Gailett Cullity and Berys Gaut. Oxford: Oxford University Press.

Dancy, Jonathan. 1993. *Moral Reasons.* Oxford: Blackwell.

————. 2000. *Practical Reality.* Oxford: Oxford University Press.

————. 2001. "Moral Particularism." *Stanford Encyclopedia of Philosophy* (http://plato.stanford.edu/).

————. 2004. *Ethics without Principles.* Oxford: Oxford University Press.

D'Arms, Justin, and Daniel Jacobson. 2000a. "The Moralistic Fallacy: On the 'Appropriateness' of Emotions." *Philosophy and Phenomenological Research* 61: 65–90.

————. 2000b. "Sentiment and Value." *Ethics* 110: 722–748.

Darwall, Stephen. 1974. "Pleasure as Ultimate Good in Sidgwick's Ethics." *Monist* 58: 475–489.

————. 1977. "Two Kinds of Respect." *Ethics* 88: 36–49.

————. 1980. "Is There a Kantian Foundation for Rawlsian Justice?" in *John Rawls' Theory of Social Justice,* ed. H. G. Blocker and E. Smith. Athens: Ohio University Press.

————. 1983. *Impartial Reason.* Ithaca, NY: Cornell University Press.

————. 1985. "Kantian Practical Reason Defended." *Ethics* 96: 89–99.

————. 1986a. "Agent-Centered Restrictions from the Inside Out." *Philosophical Studies* 50: 291–319.

————. 1986b. "Rational Agent, Rational Act." *Philosophical Topics* 14: 33–57.

————. 1987. "Abolishing Morality." *Synthese* 72 (1987): 71–89.

————. 1990. "Autonomist Internalism and the Justification of Morals." *Nous* 24: 257–268.

————. 1992. "Internalism and Agency." *Philosophical Perspectives* 6: 155–174.

————. 1994. "Hume and the Invention of Utilitarianism," in *Hume and Hume's Connexions,* ed. M. A. Stewart and J. Wright. Edinburgh: Edinburgh University Press.

————. 1995a. *The British Moralists and the Internal "Ought": 1640–1740.* Cambridge: Cambridge University Press.

————. 1995b. "Human Morality's Authority." *Philosophy and Phenomenological Research* 55: 941–948.

————. 1997. "Reasons, Motives, and the Demands of Morality: An Introduction," in *Moral Discourse and Practice,* ed. Stephen Darwall, Allan Gibbard, and Peter Railton. New York: Oxford University Press.

————. 1998. "Empathy, Sympathy, Care." *Philosophical Studies* 89: 261–282.

————. 1999a. "The Inventions of Autonomy." *European Journal of Philosophy* 7: 339–350.

————. 1999b. "Sympathetic Liberalism." *Philosophy & Public Affairs* 28: 139–164.

————. 2001. "Because I Want It." *Social Philosophy & Policy* 18: 129–153.

————. 2002a. *Contractarianism/Contractualism.* Oxford: Blackwell.

————. 2002b. *Welfare and Rational Care.* Princeton, NJ: Princeton University Press.

————. 2003a. "Autonomy in Modern Natural Law," in *New Essays on the History of Autonomy,* ed. Larry Krasnoff and Natalie Brender. Cambridge: Cambridge University Press.

————. 2003b. "Moore, Normativity, and Intrinsic Value." *Ethics* 113: 468–489.

————. 2004a. "Equal Dignity in Adam Smith." *Adam Smith Review* 1: 129–134.

————. 2004b. "Respect and the Second-Person Standpoint." *Proceedings and Addresses of the American Philosophical Association* 78: 43–59.

————. 2005. "Fichte and the Second-Person Standpoint." *International Yearbook of German Idealism* 3: 91–113.

————. 2006. "Contractualism, Root and Branch: A Review Essay." *Philosophy & Public Affairs* 34 (2006): 193–214.

————. Unpublished. "How Is Moorean Value Related to Reasons for Attitudes?"

Darwall, Stephen, Allan Gibbard, and Peter Railton. 1997. "Toward *Fin de Siècle* Ethics: Some Trends," in *Moral Discourse and Practice,* ed. Stephen Darwall, Allan Gibbard, and Peter Railton. New York: Oxford University Press.

Davidson, Donald. 1980. "Actions, Reasons, and Causes," in *Essays on Actions and Events.* Oxford: Clarendon Press.

———. 2001. "The Second Person," in *Subjective, Intersubjective, Objective.* Oxford: Clarendon Press.

Davies, Martin, and Tony Stone. 1995. *Psychology: The Theory of Mind Debate.* Oxford: Blackwell.

Deigh, John. 1983. "Shame and Self-Esteem: A Critique." *Ethics* 93: 225–245.

———. 1995. "Empathy and Universalizability." *Ethics* 105: 743–763.

Dewey, John. 1998a. "The Moral Self," in *The Essential Dewey,* vol. 2, *Ethics Logic, Psychology,* ed. Larry A. Hickman and Thomas M. Alexander. Bloomington: Indiana University Press.

———. 1998b. "Three Independent Factors in Morals," in *The Essential Dewey,* vol. 2, *Ethics Logic, Psychology,* ed. Larry A. Hickman and Thomas M. Alexander. Bloomington: Indiana University Press.

Dillon, Robin S., ed. 1995. *Dignity, Character, and Self-Respect.* New York: Routledge.

———. 1997. "Self-Respect: Moral, Emotional, Political." *Ethics* 107: 226–249.

———. 2004. "Kant on Arrogance and Self-Respect," in *Setting the Moral Compass: Essays by Women Philosophers,* ed. Cheshire Calhoun. New York: Oxford University Press.

Downie, R. S., and Elizabeth Telfer. 1970. *Respect for Persons.* New York: Schocken.

Dummett, Michael. 1990. "The Source of the Concept of Truth" in *Meaning and Method: Essays in Honour of Hilary Putnam,* ed., George Boolos. Cambridge: Cambridge University Press.

Dworkin, Gerald. 1988. *The Theory and Practice of Autonomy.* Cambridge: Cambridge University Press.

Dylan, Bob. 2004. *Lyrics: 1962–2001.* New York: Simon & Schuster.

Ekman, Paul, Maureen O'Sullivan, and Mark G. Frank. 1999. "A Few Can Catch a Liar." *Psychological Science* 10: 263–266.

Emmons, Robert A., and Michael E. McCullough. 2003. "Counting Blessings versus Burdens: An Experimental Investigation of Gratitude and Subjective Well-Being in Daily Life." *Journal of Personality and Social Psychology* 84: 377–389.

Enoch, David. Forthcoming. "An Outline of an Argument for Robust Metanormative Realism," in *Oxford Studies in Metaethics,* vol. 2, ed. Russ Shafer-Landau. Oxford: Oxford University Press.

Ewing, A. C. 1939. "A Suggested Non-Naturalistic Analysis of Good." *Mind* 48: 1–22.

Falk, W. D. 1953. "Goading and Guiding." *Mind* 62: 145–171.

———. 1986. "Fact, Value, and Nonnatural Predication," in *Ought, Reasons, and Morality*. Ithaca, NY: Cornell University Press.

Fehr, Ernst, and Simon Gächter. 2002. "Altruistic Punishment in Humans." *Nature* 415: 137–140.

Fehr, Ernst, and Bettina Rockenbach. 2003. "Detrimental Effects of Sanctions on Human Altruism." *Nature* 422: 137–140.

Fehr, Ernest, and Klaus M. Schmidt. 1999. "A Theory of Fairness, Competition, and Cooperation." *Quarterly Journal of Economics* 114: 817–868.

Feinberg, Joel. 1980. "The Nature and Value of Rights," in *Rights, Justice, and the Bounds of Liberty*. Princeton, NJ: Princeton University Press.

Fichte, Johann Gottlieb. 2000. *Foundations of Natural Right,* ed. Frederick Neuhouser, trans. Michael Bauer. Cambridge: Cambridge University Press.

Fleischacker, Samuel. 2004a. *On Adam Smith's Wealth of Nations: A Philosophical Companion*. Princeton, NJ: Princeton University Press.

———. 2004b. *A Short History of Distributive Justice*. Cambridge, MA: Harvard University Press.

Foley, Richard. 1994. "Egoism in Epistemology," in *Socializing Epistemology: The Social Dimensions of Knowledge,* ed. Frederick F. Schmitt. Lanham, MD: Rowman & Littlefield.

Foot, Philippa. 1972. "Morality as a System of Hypothetical Imperatives." *Philosophical Review* 81: 305–316.

Frank, Robert. 1988. *Passions Within Reason: The Strategic Role of the Emotions*. New York: W. W. Norton.

Frankena, William. 1992. "Sidgwick and the History of Ethical Dualism," in *Essays on Henry Sidgwick,* ed. Bart Schultz. Cambridge: Cambridge University Press.

Freeman, Samuel. 1991. "Contractualism, Moral Motivation, and Practical Reason." *Journal of Philosophy* 88: 281–303.

Gauthier, David. 1979. "David Hume, Contractarian." *Philosophical Review* 88: 3–38.

———. 1986. *Morals by Agreement*. Oxford: Clarendon Press.

———. 1992. "Artificial Virtues and the Sensible Knave." *Hume Studies* 18: 401–428.

Gewirth, Alan. 1978. *Reason and Morality*. Chicago: University of Chicago Press.

Gibbard, Allan. 1990. *Wise Choices, Apt Feelings*. Cambridge, MA: Harvard University Press.

Gilbert, Margaret. 1990. "Walking Together: A Paradigmatic Social Phenomenon." *Midwest Studies in Philosophy* 15: 1–14.

————. 1996a. "Is an Agreement an Exchange of Promises?" in *Living Together: Rationality, Sociality, and Obligation.* Lanham, MD: Rowman & Littlefield.

————. 1996b. *Living Together: Rationality, Sociality, and Obligation.* Lanham, MD: Rowman & Littlefield.

Goffman, Erving. 1961. *Asylums: Essays on the Social Situation of Mental Patients and Other Inmates.* Chicago: Aldine.

Goldman, Alvin I. 1989. "Interpretation Psychologized." *Mind and Language* 4: 161–185.

————. 1992. "In Defense of the Simulation Theory." *Mind and Language* 7: 104–119.

Goldsmith, Oliver. 1901. *The Vicar of Wakefield.* Chicago: Scott, Foresman and Co.

Good, Erica. 1999. "To Tell the Truth, It's Awfully Hard To Spot a Liar." *New York Times,* May 11.

Gordon, Robert M. 1986. "Folk Psychology as Simulation." *Mind and Language* 1: 158–171.

————. 1992. "The Simulation Theory: Objections and Misconceptions." *Mind and Language* 7: 11–34.

Greenspan, P. S. 1975. "Conditional Oughts and Hypothetical Imperatives," *Journal of Philosophy* 72: 259–276.

————. 1992. "Subjective Guilt and Responsibility." *Mind* 101: 287–303.

Grotius, Hugo. 1925. *The Law of War and Peace,* trans. Francis W. Kelsey. New York: Carnegie Endowment for International Peace.

Haakonssen, Knud. 1981. *The Science of a Legislator.* Cambridge: Cambridge University Press.

Habermas, Jürgen. 1990. *Moral Consciousness and Communicative Action,* trans. Christian Lenhardt and Shierry Weber Nicholsen, intro. Thomas McCarthy. Cambridge, MA: MIT Press.

Hampton, Jean. 1998. *The Authority of Reason.* Cambridge: Cambridge University Press.

Hare, R. M. 1971. "Wanting: Some Pitfalls," in *Agent, Action, and Reason,* ed. Robert Binkley, Richard Bronaugh, and Ausonio Marras. Toronto: University of Toronto Press.

————. 1981. *Moral Thinking: Its Level, Methods, and Point.* Oxford: Oxford University Press.

————. 1993. "Could Kant Have Been a Utilitarian?" in *Kant and Critique: New Essays in Honor of W. H. Werkmeister.* Dordrecht: Kluwer Academic Publishers.

Hare, Robert D. 1993. *Without Conscience: The Disturbing World of the Psychopaths among Us.* New York: The Guilford Press.

Harman, Gilbert. 1977. *The Nature of Morality: An Introduction to Ethics.* New York: Oxford University Press.

Harsanyi, John C. 1978. "Bayesian Decision Theory and Utilitarian Ethics." *The American Economic Review* 68: 223–228.

Hart, H. L. A. 1961. *The Concept of Law.* Oxford: Clarendon Press.

———. 1965. "Are There Any Natural Rights?" *Philosophical Review* 64: 175–191.

———. 1990. "Commands and Authoritative Legal Reasons," in *Authority,* ed. Joseph Raz. New York: New York University Press.

Hartley, Christie. 2005. "Justice for All: Constructing an Inclusive Contractualism." Ph.D. diss., University of Michigan–Ann Arbor.

Hearne, Vicki. 1986. *Adam's Task: Calling Animals by Name.* New York: Knopf, distributed by Random House.

Hegel, Georg Wilhelm Friedrich. 1977. *Phenomenology of Spirit,* trans. A. V. Miller. Oxford: Oxford University Press.

———. 1991. *Elements of the Philosophy of Right,* ed. Allen W. Wood and Hugh B. Nisbett. Cambridge: Cambridge University Press.

Henrich, Joseph. 2000. "Does Culture Matter in Economic Behavior? Ultimate Game Bargaining among the Machiguenga of the Peruvian Amazon." *American Economics Review* 90: 973–979.

———. 2001. "In Search of Homo Economicus: Behavioral Experiments in Fifteen Small-Scale Societies." *American Economics Review* 91: 73–78.

Herman, Barbara. 1996. *The Practice of Moral Judgment.* Cambridge, MA: Harvard University Press.

Hill, Thomas E., Jr. 1980. "Humanity as an End in Itself." *Ethics* 91: 84–99.

———. 1985. "Kant's Argument for the Rationality of Moral Conduct." *Pacific Philosophical Quarterly* 66: 3–23.

———. 1989. "Kantian Constructivism in Ethical Theory." *Ethics* 99: 752–770.

———. 1997. "Respect for Humanity," in *The Tanner Lectures on Human Values,* vol. 18, ed. Grethe B. Peterson. Salt Lake City: University of Utah Press.

———. 1998. "Respect for Persons," in *Routledge Encyclopedia for Philosophy,* vol. 8, ed. Edward Craig. London: Routledge, p. 284.

Hinchman, Edward S. 2000. "Trust and Reason." Ph.D. diss., University of Michigan.

———. 2005. "Telling as Inviting to Trust." *Philosophy and Phenomenological Research* 70: 562–587.

Hobbes, Thomas. 1983. *De Cive: The English Version, Entitled in the First Edition, Philosophical Rudiments Concerning Government and Society,* ed. and trans. Howard Warrender. Oxford: Clarendon Press.

———. 1994. *Leviathan,* ed. Edwin Curley. Indianapolis: Hackett Publishing Co.

Hoffman, Martin L. 2000. *Empathy and Moral Development.* Cambridge: Cambridge University Press.

Hohfeld, Wesley Newcomb. 1923. *Fundamental Legal Conceptions,* ed. Walter Wheeler Cook. New Haven, CT: Yale University Press.

Honneth, Axel. 1995. *The Struggle for Recognition.* Cambridge, MA: Polity Press.

Hooker, Brad. 2000. *Ideal Code, Real World: A Rule-Consequentialist Theory of Morality.* Oxford: Oxford University Press.

Horney, Karen. 1970. *Neurosis and Human Growth: The Struggle Toward Self-Realization.* New York: W. W. Norton.

Hudson, Stephen D. 1980. "The Nature of Respect." *Social Theory and Practice* 6: 69–90.

Hume, David. 1978. *A Treatise of Human Nature,* ed L. A. Selby-Bigge, 2nd ed., rev. P. H. Nidditch. Oxford. Oxford University Press.

———. 1985a. *An Enquiry Concerning Human Understanding,* in *Enquiries Concerning Human Understanding and Concerning the Principles of Morals,* ed. L. A. Selby-Bigge, 3rd ed., rev. P. H. Nidditch. Oxford: Clarendon Press.

———. 1985b. *An Enquiry Concerning the Principles of Morals,* in *Enquiries Concerning Human Understanding and Concerning the Principles of Morals.*

Imam, Ayesha. 2002. Interview with Terry Gross, "Fresh Air," December 5, 2002 (http://freshair.npr.org/day_fa.jhtml?display=day&todayDate=12/05/2002).

Jefferson, Thomas. 1984. *Writings.* New York: Library of America.

Johnson, Conrad D. 1985. "The Authority of the Moral Agent." *Journal of Philosophy* 82: 391–413.

———. 1991. *Moral Legislation: A Legal-Political Model for Indirect Consequentialist Reasoning.* Cambridge: Cambridge University Press.

Kahneman, Daniel, and Amos Tversky. 1982. "The Simulation Heuristic," in *Judgment under Uncertainty,* ed. D. Kahneman, P. Slovic, and A. Tversky. Cambridge: Cambridge University Press.

Kamm, Frances. 1989. "Harming Some to Save Others." *Philosophical Studies* 57: 227–260.

———. 1992. "Non-Consequentialism, the Person as an End-in-Itself, and the Significance of Status." *Philosophy & Public Affairs* 21: 381–389.

Kant, Immanuel. 1900– . *Kant's gesammelte Schriften.* Berlin: Georg Reimer, later Walter de Gruyter.

———. 1996a. *Critique of Practical Reason,* in *Practical Philosophy,* trans. and ed. Mary J. Gregor. Cambridge: Cambridge University Press. Page references are to page numbers of the Preussische Akademie edition.

———. 1996b. *Groundwork of the Metaphysics of Morals,* in *Practical Philosophy.* References are to page numbers of the Preussische Akademie edition.

———. 1996c. *Metaphysical First Principles of the Doctrine of Right,* in *The Metaphysics of Morals,* in *Practical Philosophy.* References are to page numbers of the Preussische Akademie edition.

———. 1996d. *Metaphysical First Principles of the Doctrine of Virtue,* in *The Metaphysics of Morals,* in *Practical Philosophy.* References are to page numbers of the Preussische Akademie edition.

———. 1996e. *The Metaphysics of Morals,* in *Practical Philosophy.* References are to page numbers of the Preussische Akademie edition.

———. 1996f. *Practical Philosophy,* trans. and ed. Mary J. Gregor. Cambridge: Cambridge University Press. References are to page numbers of the Preussische Akademie edition.

———. 1998. *The Critique of Pure Reason,* trans. and ed. Paul Guyer and Allen W. Wood. Cambridge: Cambridge University Press. References are to page numbers of the Preussische Akademie edition.

———. 1999. *Religion Within the Boundaries of Mere Reason,* ed. Allen W. Wood and George Di Giovanni, foreword Robert Merrihew Adams. Cambridge: Cambridge University Press.

———. 2002. *Groundwork for the Metaphysics of Morals,* ed. Allen Wood. New Haven, CT: Yale University Press. Page references are to page numbers of the Preussische Akademie edition.

Kavka, Gregory. 1995. "The Rationality of Rule-Following: Hobbes' Dispute with the Foole." *Law and Philosophy* 14: 5–34.

Kennett, Jeanette. 2002. "Autism, Empathy, and Moral Agency." *The Philosophical Quarterly* 52: 340–357.

Kerstein, Samuel. 2001. "Korsgaard's Kantian Arguments for the Value of Humanity." *Canadian Journal of Philosophy* 31: 23–52.

Kögler, Herbert and Karsten R. Stueber. 2000. *Empathy and Agency: The Problem of Understanding in the Human Sciences.* Boulder, CO: Westview Press.

Kohlberg, Lawrence. 1981. *Essays on Moral Development.* San Francisco: Harper & Row.

Korsgaard, Christine. 1986. "Skepticism about Practical Reason." *Journal of Philosophy* 83: 5–25.

———. 1996a. "Creating the Kingdom of Ends," in *Creating the Kingdom of Ends.* Cambridge: Cambridge University Press.

———. 1996b. "Kant's Formula of Humanity," in *Creating the Kingdom of Ends.*

———. 1996c. "Morality and Freedom," in *Creating the Kingdom of Ends.*

———. 1996d. "The Reasons We Can Share: An Attack on the Distinction between Agent-Relative and Agent-Neutral Values," in *Creating the Kingdom of Ends.*

———. 1996e. *The Sources of Normativity.* Cambridge: Cambridge University Press.

———. 1996f. "Two Distinctions in Goodness," in *Creating the Kingdom of Ends.*

————. 1997. "The Normativity of Instrumental Reason," in *Ethics and Practical Reason,* ed. Garrett Cullity and Berys Gaut. Oxford: Oxford University Press.

————. 2003. "Realism and Constructivism in Twentieth-Century Moral Philosophy." *Journal of Philosophical Research* 28: 99–122.

Kumar, Rahul. 1999. "Defending the Moral Moderate: Contractualism and Common Sense." *Philosophy & Public Affairs* 28: 275–309.

————. 2003. "Reasonable Reasons in Contractualist Moral Argument." *Ethics* 114: 6–37.

Laurence, Michael. 1997. "Death Be Not Proud," *Bates Magazine.*

Leibniz, Gottfried Wilhelm. 1989. *Political Writings,* ed. Patrick Riley, 2nd ed. Cambridge: Cambridge University Press.

Leimar, Olof, and Peter Hammerstein. 2001: "Evolution of Cooperation through Indirect Reciprocity." *Proceedings of the Royal Society of London* 268: 745–753.

Leiter, Brian. 1995. "Morality in the Pejorative Sense: On the Logic of Nietzsche's Critique of Morality." *British Journal for the History of Philosophy* 3: 113–145.

————. 1997. "Nietzsche and the Morality Critics." *Ethics* 107: 250–285.

Lévinas, Emmanuel. 1969. *Totality and Infinity: An Essay on Exteriority,* trans. Alphonso Lingis. Pittsburgh: Duquesne University Press.

Lincoln, Abraham. 1989. *Speeches and Writings, 1832–1858,* ed. Don E. Fehrenbacher. New York: Library of America.

Lloyd, Sharon. Forthcoming. *Cases in the Law of Nature: The Moral Philosophy of Thomas Hobbes.*

Locke, John. 1975. *An Essay Concerning Human Understanding,* ed. Peter H. Nidditch. Oxford: Oxford University Press.

————. 1988. *Second Treatise of Government,* in *Two Treatises of Government,* ed. Peter Laslett. Cambridge: Cambridge University Press.

Lotem, Arnon, M. A. Fishman, and L. Stone. 1999. "Evolution of Cooperation between Individuals." *Nature* 400: 226–227.

Lyons, David. 1965. *The Forms and Limits of Utilitarianism.* Oxford: Clarendon Press.

Mack, Eric. 1976. "Hart on Natural and Contractual Rights." *Philosophical Studies* 29: 283–285.

Malanowski, Jamie. 2002. "Human, Yes, but No Less a Monster." *New York Times,* December 22, sec. 2, pp. 1, 36.

Mansbridge, Jane J., ed. 1990. *Beyond Self-Interest.* Chicago: University of Chicago Press.

Margalit, Avishai. 1996. *The Decent Society.* Cambridge, MA: Harvard University Press.

Mason, Michelle. 2003. "Contempt as a Moral Attitude." *Ethics* 113: 234–272.

————. Unpublished. "Shamelessness."

McDowell, John. 1979. "Virtue and Reason." *Monist* 62: 331–350.

McNaughton, David, and Piers Rawlings. 1991. "Agent-Relativity and the Doing-Happening Distinction." *Philosophical Studies* 63: 167–185.

———. 1993. "Deontology and Agency." *Monist* 76: 81–100.

———. 1995. "Value and Agent-Relative Reasons." *Utilitas* 7: 31–47.

Melnick, Arthur. 2002. "Kant's Formulations of the Categorical Imperative." *Kant-Studien* 93: 291–308.

Milgram, Stanley. 1974. *Obedience to Authority.* New York: Harper & Row.

Mill, John Stuart. 1988. *The Subjection of Women,* ed. Susan Moller Okin. Indianapolis: Hackett Publishing Co.

———. 1998. *Utilitarianism,* ed. Roger Crisp. Oxford: Oxford University Press.

Miller, William I. 1997. *The Anatomy of Disgust.* Cambridge, MA: Harvard University Press.

Moore, G. E. 1966. *Ethics.* London: Oxford University Press.

———. 1993. *Principia Ethica,* rev. ed. with the preface to the (projected) 2nd ed. and other papers, ed. with an intro. Thomas Baldwin. Cambridge: Cambridge University Press.

Moran, Richard. 2005. "Getting Told, Being Believed." *Philosophers' Imprint* 5:5 (http://www.philosophersimprint.org/005005/).

Morissette, Alanis. 1995. "You Oughta Know." Milwaukee, WI: MCA Music Publishers, H. Leonard Corp.

Morris, Herbert. 1976. "Guilt and Shame," in *Guilt and Innocence.* Berkeley: University of California Press.

Mulgan, Timothy. 2001. *The Demands of Consequentialism.* Oxford: Oxford University Press.

Murdoch, Iris. 1999. "The Sublime and the Good," in *Existentialists and Mystics,* ed. Peter Conrad. New York: Penguin Books.

Murphy, Jeffrie G., and Jean Hampton. 1988. *Forgiveness and Mercy.* Cambridge: Cambridge University Press.

Myejes, Meno. 2002. *Max.* Natural Nylon II; Pathé.

Nagel, Thomas. 1970. *The Possibility of Altruism.* Oxford: Clarendon Press.

———. 1986. *The View from Nowhere.* New York: Oxford University Press.

———. 1995. "Personal Rights and Public Space." *Philosophy & Public Affairs* 24: 83–107.

Neiman, Susan. 2002. *Evil in Modern Thought: An Alternative History of Philosophy.* Princeton, NJ: Princeton University Press.

Neufeld, Ephraim, trans. 1951. *The Hittite Laws.* London: Luzac.

Neuhouser, Fredrick. 1994. "Fichte and the Relationship between Right and Morality," in *Fichte: Historical Contexts/Contemporary Controversies,* ed. Daniel Breazeale and Tom Rockmore. Atlantic Highlands, NJ: Humanities Press, pp. 158–180.

Nietzsche, Friedrich. 1994. *On the Genealogy of Morals,* ed. Keith Ansell-Pearson and Carol Diethe. Cambridge: Cambridge University Press.

Nowak, Martin A., and Karl Sigmund. 1998a. "The Dynamics of Indirect Reciprocity." *Journal of Theoretical Biology* 194: 561–574.

———. 1998b. "Evolution of Indirect Reciprocity by Image Scoring." *Nature* 393: 573–577.

Nowell-Smith, P. H. 1948. "Freewill and Moral Responsibility." *Mind* 57: 45–61.

Nozick, Robert. 1969. "Coercion," in *Philosophy, Science, and Method,* ed. Sidney Morgenbesser, Patrick Suppes, and Morton White. New York: St. Martin's Press.

Oakes, James. 1990. *Slavery and Freedom.* New York: W. W. Norton.

Olson, Jonas. 2004. "Buck-Passing and the Wrong Kind of Reasons." *The Philosophical Quarterly* 54: 295–300.

Orbell, John M., Robyn M. Dawes, and Alphons van de Kragt. 1988. "Explaining Discussion-Induced Cooperation." *Journal of Personality and Social Psychology* 54: 811–819.

———. 1990. "Cooperation for the Benefit of Us—Not Me, or My Conscience," in *Beyond Self-Interest,* ed. Jane J. Mansbridge. Chicago: University of Chicago Press.

Parfit, Derek. 1984. *Reasons and Persons.* Oxford: Clarendon Press.

———. 1997. "Reasons and Motivation." *Aristotelian Society,* supp. vol., 71: 99–130.

———. 2001. "Rationality and Reasons," in *Exploring Practical Philosophy: From Action to Values,* ed. Dan Egonsson, Bjön Petersson, Jonas Josefsson, and Toni Ronnøw-Rasmussen. Aldershot: Ashgate Press.

———. 2004. "Contractualism," in *Tanner Lectures on Human Values 2004,* ed. Grethe Peterson. Salt Lake City: Utah University Press.

Parisoli, Luca. 2001. "Hume and Reid on Promises," *Thèmes,* Année 2001 (http://www.philosophiedudroit.org/parisoli,%20hume.htm).

Pettit, Philip, and Michael Smith. 1990. "Backgrounding Desire." *Philosophical Review* 99: 565–592.

———. 1996. "Freedom in Belief and Desire." *Journal of Philosophy* 93: 429–449.

Plato. 1969. *The Collected Dialogues of Plato, Including the Letters,* ed. Edith Hamilton and Huntington Cairns. Princeton, NJ: Princeton University Press.

Platts, Mark. 1979. *Ways of Meaning.* London: Routledge & Kegan Paul.

Postema, Gerald. 1995. "Morality in the First Person Plural." *Law and Philosophy* 14: 35–64.

Pound, Roscoe. 1922. *An Introduction to the Philosophy of Law.* New Haven, CT: Yale University Press.

Price, Richard. 1974 [1758]. *A Review of the Principal Questions in Morals,* ed. D. D. Raphael. Oxford: Clarendon Press.

Prichard, H. A. 2002. "Does Moral Philosophy Rest on a Mistake?" in *Moral Writings,* ed. Jim McAdam. Oxford: Oxford University Press.

Pufendorf, Samuel. 1934. *On the Law of Nature and Nations,* trans. C. H. Oldfather and W. A. Oldfather. Oxford: Clarendon Press.

Putnam, Hilary. 2002. "Levinas and Judaism," in *The Cambridge Companion to Levinas,* ed. Simon Critchley and Robert Bernasconi. Cambridge: Cambridge University Press.

Quinn, Warren. 1991. "Putting Rationality in Its Place," in *Morality and Action.* Cambridge: Cambridge University Press.

Rabinowicz, Wlodek, and Toni Ronnøw-Rasmussen. 2004. "The Strike of the Demon: On Fitting Pro-Attitudes and Value." *Ethics* 114: 391–423.

Radzinsky, Edvard. 1997. *Stalin.* New York: Anchor Books.

Railton, Peter. 1986. "Moral Realism." *Philosophical Review* 95: 163–207.

———. 1989. "Naturalism and Prescriptivity." *Social Philosophy & Policy* 7: 151–174.

———. 1992. "Pluralism, Determinism, and Dilemma." *Ethics* 102: 720–742.

———. 1997. "On the Hypothetical and Non-Hypothetical in Reasoning about Belief and Action," in *Ethics and Practical Reason,* ed. Garrett Cullity and Berys Gaut. Oxford: Oxford University Press.

Rawls, John. 1955. "Two Concepts of Rules." *Philosophical Review* 64: 3–32.

———. 1971. *A Theory of Justice.* Cambridge: MA: Harvard University Press.

———. 1980. "Kantian Constructivism in Moral Theory." *Journal of Philosophy* 77: 515–572.

———. 1993. *Political Liberalism.* New York: Columbia University Press.

———. 1999. *A Theory of Justice,* rev. ed. Cambridge, MA: Harvard University Press.

———. 2000. *Lectures on the History of Philosophy,* ed. Barbara Herman. Cambridge, MA: Harvard University Press.

———. 2001. *Justice as Fairness: A Restatement,* ed. Erin Kelly. Cambridge, MA: Harvard University Press.

Raz, Joseph. 1972. "Voluntary Obligations and Normative Powers." *Proceedings of the Aristotelian Society* 46: 79–101.

———. 1975. *Practical Reason and Norms.* London: Hutchinson.

———. 1986. *The Morality of Freedom.* Oxford: Clarendon Press.

Regan, Donald H. 2003a. "How to Be a Moorean." *Ethics* 113: 651–677.

———. 2003b. "The Value of Rational Nature." *Ethics* 112: 267–291.

Reginster, Bernard. 2003. "The Moral Distinctions of Self-Conceit." Presented at the Kantian Ethics Conference, University of San Diego.

Reid, Thomas. 1969. *Essays on the Active Powers of the Human Mind.* Cambridge, MA: MIT Press.

Rochefoucauld, François (duc de) la. 1976. *Reflexions, ou sentences et maximes morales suivi des reflexions diverses*, ed. Jean Lafond. Paris: Gallimard.

Rosati, Connie S. 1995. "Naturalism, Normativity, and the Open Question Argument." *Noûs* 29: 46–70.

———. 2003. "Agency and the Open Question Argument." *Ethics* 113: 490–527.

Rosenkoetter, Timothy. 2003. "A Semantic Approach to Kant's Practical Philosophy." Presented at the APA Central Division Meetings, Cleveland, OH.

Ross, W. D. 1930. *The Right and the Good*. Oxford: Clarendon Press.

Rothschild, Emma. 2001. *Economic Sentiments: Adam Smith, Condorcet, and the Enlightenment*. Cambridge, MA: Harvard University Press.

Rousseau, Jean-Jacques. 1997. *The Social Contract and Other Later Political Writings*, ed. and trans. Victor Gourevitch. Cambridge: Cambridge University Press.

Rumfitt, Ian. 1998. "Presupposition," in *Routledge Encyclopedia of Philosophy*, vol. 7, ed. Edward Craig. London: Routledge.

———. Forthcoming. "An Anti-Realist of Classical Consequence," in *The Library of Living Philosophers: Michael Dummett*.

Sabini, John, and Maury Silver. 1982. *Moralities of Everyday Life*. New York: Oxford University Press.

Sartre, Jean-Paul. 1957. *Being and Nothingness: A Phenomenological Essay on Ontology*, trans. Hazel Barnes. New York: Washington Square Press.

Scanlon, T. M. 1982. "Contractualism and Utilitarianism," in *Utilitarianism and Beyond*, ed. Bernard Williams and Amartya Sen. Cambridge: Cambridge University Press.

———. 1990. "Promises and Practices." *Philosophy & Public Affairs* 19: 199–226.

———. 1995. "The Significance of Choice," in *Equal Freedom*, ed. Stephen Darwall. Ann Arbor: University of Michigan Press.

———. 1998. *What We Owe to Each Other*. Cambridge, MA: Harvard University Press.

Schapiro, Tamar. 1999. "What Is a Child?" *Ethics* 109: 715–738.

———. 2001. "Three Conceptions of Action in Moral Theory." *Noûs* 35: 93–117.

———. 2003a. "Childhood and Personhood." *Arizona Law Review* 45: 575–594.

———. 2003b. "Compliance, Complicity, and the Nature of Nonideal Conditions." *Journal of Philosophy* 100: 329–355.

Scheffler, Samuel. 1982. *The Rejection of Consequentialism*. Oxford: Clarendon Press.

———. 1992. *Human Morality*. New York: Oxford University Press.

———. 2004. "Doing and Allowing." *Ethics* 114: 215–239.

Schlick, Moritz. 1939. *Problems of Ethics.* New York: Prentice-Hall.

Schneewind, J. B. 1990. *Moral Philosophy from Montaigne to Kant.* Cambridge: Cambridge University Press.

———. 1998. *The Invention of Autonomy.* Cambridge: Cambridge University Press.

Searle, John. 1964. "How to Derive an 'Ought' from an 'Is'." *Philosophical Review* 73: 43–58.

Sellars, Wilfrid. 1997. *Empiricism and the Philosophy of Mind.* Cambridge, MA: Harvard University Press.

Seuss, Dr. [Theodor Geisel]. 1971. *The Lorax.* New York: Random House.

Shafer-Landau. 2003. *Moral Realism: A Defense.* New York: Oxford University Press.

Shah, Nishi. 2003. "How Truth Governs Belief." *Philosophical Review* 112: 447–482.

Shah, Nishi, and J. David Velleman. Forthcoming. "Doxastic Deliberation." *Philosophical Review.*

Sherman, Nancy. Unpublished. "Manners and Morals."

Shiffrin, Seana Valentine. 2000. "Paternalism, Unconscionability Doctrine, and Accommodation." *Philosophy & Public Affairs* 29: 205–250.

Sidgwick, Henry. 1964. *Outlines of the History of Ethics for English Readers,* 6th ed. Boston: Beacon Press.

———. 1967. *The Methods of Ethics,* 7th ed. London: Macmillan.

Skorupski, John. 1999. *Ethical Explorations.* Oxford: Oxford University Press.

Slote, Michael. 1992. *From Morality to Virtue.* New York: Oxford University Press.

Smart, J. J. C., and Bernard Williams. 1973. *Utilitarianism: For and Against.* Cambridge: Cambridge University Press.

Smith, Adam. 1976. *An Inquiry into the Nature and Causes of the Wealth of Nations,* ed. R. H. Campbell and A. S. Skinner. Oxford: Clarendon Press.

———. 1982a. *Lectures on Jurisprudence,* ed. R. L. Meek, D. D. Raphael, and P. G. Stein. Indianapolis: Liberty Classics.

———. 1982b. *The Theory of Moral Sentiments,* ed. D. D. Raphael and A. L. Macfie. Indianapolis: Liberty Classics.

———. 1995. *Essays on Philosophical Subjects,* ed. W. D. Wightman and J. C. Bryce. Indianapolis: Liberty Classics.

Smith, Michael. 1987. "The Humean Theory of Motivation." *Mind* 96: 36–61.

———. 1994. *The Moral Problem.* Oxford: Blackwell.

Sripada, Chandra. 2005. "Punishment and the Strategic Structure of Moral Systems." *Biology & Philosophy* 20: 767–789.

Stalnaker, Robert. 1974. "Pragmatic Presuppositions," in *Semantics and Philosophy,* ed. Milton K. Munitz and Peter K. Unger. New York: New York University Press.

Stampe, Dennis. 1987. "The Authority of Desire." *Philosophical Review* 96: 335–381.

Stern, Lawrence. 1974. "Freedom, Blame, and Moral Community." *Journal of Philosophy* 71: 72–84.

Stocker, Michael. Forthcoming. "Shame, Guilt, and Pathological Guilt: A Discussion of Bernard Williams."

Strawson, P. F. 1968. "Freedom and Resentment," in *Studies in the Philosophy of Thought and Action*. London: Oxford University Press.

Stroud, Ronald S. 1979. *The Axones and Kyrbeis of Drakon and Solon*. Berkeley: University of California Press.

Suarez, Francisco. 1944. *A Treatise on Laws and God the Lawgiver*, trans. Gwladys L. Williams, Ammi Brown, and John Waldron, rev. Henry Davis, S.J., intro. James Brown Scott, in *Selections from Three Works of Francisco Suarez, S.J.*, vol. 2. Oxford: Clarendon Press.

Sussman, David. 2003. "The Authority of Humanity." *Ethics* 113: 350–366.

Swanton, Christine. 2003. *Virtue Ethics: A Pluralistic View*. Oxford: Oxford University Press.

Thibaut, John, and Laurens Walker. 1975. *Procedural Justice: A Psychological Analysis*. Hillsdale, NJ: Lawrence Erlbaum Associates.

Thompson, Michael. 2004. "What Is It to Wrong Someone? A Puzzle about Justice," in *Reason and Value: Themes from the Philosophy of Joseph Raz*, ed. R. Jay Wallace, Philip Pettit, Samuel Scheffler, and Michael Smith. Oxford: Oxford University Press.

Thomson, Judith Jarvis. 1971. "A Defense of Abortion." *Philosophy & Public Affairs* 1: 47–66.

———. 1990. *The Realm of Rights*. Cambridge, MA: Harvard University Press.

Trivers, R. L. 1971. "The Evolution of Reciprocal Altruism." *Quarterly Review of Biology* 46: 35–57.

Tugendhat, Ernst. 2004. "Universalistically Approved Intersubjective Attitudes: Adam Smith." *Adam Smith Review* 1: 88–104.

Velleman, J. David. 2000. "The Possibility of Practical Reason," in *The Possibility of Practical Reason*. Oxford: Oxford University Press.

———. 2001. "The Genesis of Shame." *Philosophy & Public Affairs* 30: 27–52.

———. 2005. "The Voice of Conscience," in *Self to Self*. Cambridge: Cambridge University Press.

Vranas, Peter. 2001. "Respect for Persons: An Epistemic and Pragmatic Investigation." Ph.D. diss., University of Michigan–Ann Arbor.

———. Forthcoming. "I Ought, Therefore I Can." *Philosophical Studies*.

Wallace, R. Jay. 1994. *Responsibility and the Moral Sentiments*. Cambridge, MA: Harvard University Press.

Watson, Gary. 1987. "Responsibility and the Limits of Evil: Variations on a Strawsonian Theme," in *Responsibility, Character, and the Emotions: New*

Essays in Moral Psychology, ed. F. D. Schoeman. Cambridge: Cambridge University Press.

———. 1996. "Two Faces of Responsibility." *Philosophical Topics* 24: 227–248.

———. Unpublished. "Promising, Assurance, and Expectation."

Wedekind, Claus, and Manfred Milinski. 2000. "Cooperation through Image Scoring in Humans." *Science* 288: 850–852.

Westlund, Andrea. 2003. "Selflessness and Responsibility for Self: Is Deference Compatible with Autonomy?" *Philosophical Review* 112: 483–523.

Williams, Bernard. 1973. *Problems of the Self.* Cambridge: Cambridge University Press.

———. 1981a. "Internal and External Reasons," in *Moral Luck.* Cambridge: Cambridge University Press.

———. 1981b. *Moral Luck.* Cambridge: Cambridge University Press.

———. 1985. *Ethics and the Limits of Philosophy.* Cambridge, MA: Harvard University Press.

———. 1993. *Shame and Necessity.* Berkeley: University of California Press.

———. 1995. "Internal Reasons and the Obscurity of Blame," in *Making Sense of Humanity.* Cambridge: Cambridge University Press.

Wolff, Robert Paul. 1970. *In Defense of Anarchism.* New York: Harper & Row.

Wollheim, Richard. 1984. *The Thread of Life.* New Haven, CT: Yale University Press.

Wood, Allen. 1999. *Kant's Ethical Thought.* Cambridge: Cambridge University Press.

Woodward, Bob. 2004. *Plan of Attack.* New York: Simon & Schuster.

Zimbardo, Philip G., Ebbe B. Ebbesen, and Christina Maslach. 1977. *Influencing Attitude and Changing Behavior: An Introduction to Method, Theory, and Applications of Social Control and Personal Power.* Reading, MA: Addison-Wesley Publishing Co.

Index